THE CODE OF OPPOSITES ·
A Sacred Guide to Playing with Power and Not Getting Burned

MAHALENE LOUIS
with
MICHAEL WOLF

BOOK 3: NO YEARNING

Copyright

Copyright 2022 by emPowering NOW LLC – All rights reserved

It is not legal to reproduce, duplicate, or transmit any part of this document in either electronic means or printed means. Recording of this publication strictly prohibited.

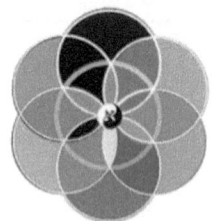

www.GoldenXPR.com
www.emPoweringNOW.com
www.thecodeofopposites.com

Paperback ISBN: 978-0-9824605-6-6
eBook ISBN: 978-0-9824605-8-0

Dedication

To myself; my greatest nemesis

Acknowledgements

"The secret to creativity is knowing how to hide your sources." *Albert Einstein*

TCO was made possible by "the giants on whose shoulders I stood." I didn't come to this quantum interpretation of the Hebrew of the Bible as a metalanguage alone. Countless brilliant minds contributed to it through their findings. If this novel interpretation is in actuality the communication of a metalanguage – a language that sustains all knowledge, the list of teachers is obviously too long to be inclusive.

This being said, I wish to honor the teachings of Alice Bailey, Ram Dass, Sigmund Freud, Rabbi Mark Gafni, C.G. Jung, Byron Katie, Sri Ramana Maharshi, Caroline Myss, Osho, Rabbi Marc-Alain Ouaknin, Harry Palmer, Brian Swimme, Ken Wilber, Dr. Fred Alan Wolf, and Marion Woodman.

Ultimately, I have the sense that every situation I encounter, every person I meet, every breath I take are my teachers, if I allow it. Henceforth, I have no master because I had millions of masters, starting and ending in the infinite source of life itself.

Altogether, this docility led to a curious phenomenon: I started telling the truth. Even more curious, the more honest I became, the more the writing freely offered itself. It was shocking (still is) to realize that the work that was done on integrity is what broke the seals of ancient prophecies. Indeed, cosmic secrets were shielded by "my" shame-based secrets. Revealing their darkness automatically released their light counterparts.

As I found the courage to dive into the abyss and immerse myself in its archetypal shadow, I came out of the black w/hole with the luminescent memory of a voice that is unique in tone, and can be heard by all. Speaking the Voice of TCO, it boldly answers the call with the foolishness and the wisdom of "here I am."

Mission of TCO

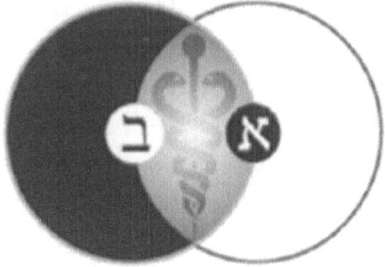

TCO's mission is to heal our relationship to Power.
To do so, it reveals the force of a sacred language that guides us to the field in between, where to transcend our beliefs of right and wrong, and know in our blood that the divine has no religion and no elect. By becoming fluent in "God's" language – in the paradox, feeling and sensing the all-pervading realities that beckon us now, we open to the Love that has no opposite, and experience Health in all levels of our communication.

A Sacred Guide to Wholesome Power

"Power doesn't corrupt people, people corrupt power." *William Gaddis*

Adopting a water-like path of least resistance heals my relationship to Power. When yet to be a psychic amphibian (able to breathe while going through intense emotions), I'm like a little engine who wants to think I can, which is not quite the same as *actually* thinking I can. Henceforth, I shall capitalize the sentence "I CAN" to remind me that emPowerment is a matter of perspective, but also, of self-esteem. Being unconditional in offering my gifts is how to like myself and "believe" in myself. I also see that the letters I CAN reorder as CAIN – the prophet who killed his brother, despaired and enraged to see that "God" favored his brother's offerings and disregarded his.

The story of Cain and Abel is so deeply archetypal and crucial to liberation that the Hebrew names find their perfect tone in English as brothers "I can't" and "I'm able." The transmission corroborates life's universal purpose: to offer our gifts in a way that they can be received. It is clear that, while Abel's offering was accepted, Cain's offering was dismissed by "God." Cain must have had strings attached to his gift. He wanted something in the exchange, which is how he couldn't allow for *QKabbalah* "receptivity" to occur. Consider: when I love myself, I don't hunger for your love, approval and recognition. I trust me. I hear me. I see me. Giving it all (no strings attached) makes me lovable in my eyes. It is fundamentally how to "receive" me, but also you.

Conversely, I do harm when my mind wages a personal war against its own creation of unrequited love. When I perceive that you don't love me, I want to make you pay. Same for "God." But since there's no one out there, I am the one who's regularly vanquished by the enemy (the part of me that resists Love). In that space, I'm the loser, but only all the time! If it is my sincere desire to participate in the work of transformation, I will seek to be congruent, and reconcile the split parts of me.

When the two are One, there is no push/pull. I feel a Love so pure that it naturally extends to my family, my community, my nation; the world.

AB | BA

I NOW RECOGNIZE THAT THE BEST WAY TO ESTABLISH ORDER IS BY OFFERING RESPECT, AND NOT DOMINATION OR EVEN DEBATE.

RESPECT, DOMINATION, DEBATE: THESE ARE ISSUES OF POWER. THEY ORIGINATE FROM MY SENSE OF JUSTICE AND OF THE LACK THEREOF. WHEN I GIVE FREELY, I AM MOVED BY THE LOVE OF JUSTICE, AS I AM NEITHER LOOKING FOR REWARD NOR PUNISHMENT.
MY RECEIVING A REWARD IS IN THE GIVING.
NOW, RESPECT IS A MUTUAL EXPERIENCE.

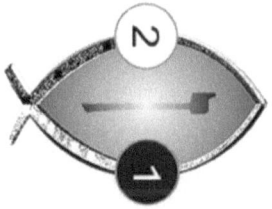

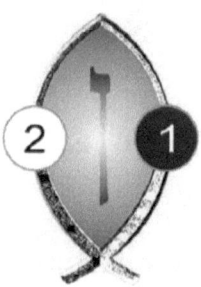

All ancient traditions allude to a great power that lives in everyone and everything, a Power by which to transcend any challenge. But it is as if a global event wiped out our memory of it, leaving us disconnected. No Power!

Where is the lost symbol by which to interface with the cosmic forces, heal our bodies, and abort the great tragedies that humankind is now facing?

At a time of epic transformation when there is an urgency in stepping into a form of authentic leadership, communication is of the essence. To have a completely new way to authentically communicate about the many dimensions of reality – and thus speak truth to Power, we now require the visionary revelation of a metalanguage, a language behind all languages.

Book 3 - in Context

"He that takes truth for his guide, and duty for his end, may safely trust to God's providence to lead him aright." *Blaise Pascal*

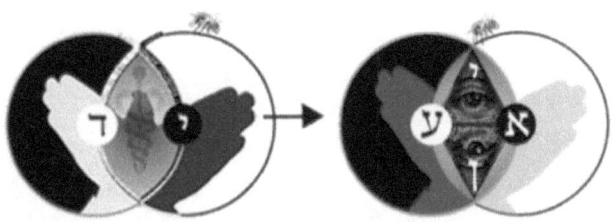

The primary purpose of *TCO—the Series* is to heal our relationship to Power. To do so, it reveals the force of a sacred language that guides us to the field in between, also known as the middle path. It is pictured as the caduceus' rod onto which the two snakes of my mind are entwined.

Book 2—no self-doubt superimposes "my eagle hands" over the caduceus that was on Book 1's cover. Eagle teaches me to return to childlike innocence. The same eagle who inspires me to reach for the sky grounds my action by suggesting a master code. Its head and wings are the digits of my two hands united in giving/receiving. When I feel the freedom of reciprocity, I know the kind of faith that makes everything well. Henceforth, Book 2 invites me to inquire on why I do not trust myself.

Book 3—no yearning positions "my eagle hands" that were on Book 2 under "our eye of providence." It marks my return to the WE perspective of collective Power. For me to know that you and I can work together, I must first satiate the hunger for "your" love, approval and recognition. Such longing is at the foundation of desire itself. Consider: when I accept that I can only control my inner responses to you, and not "you" out there, I yearn for nothing. Such selflessness gives me the felt sense that I do contribute to the whole. What my "I" sees can now begin to change.

Mapping *TCO–Book 3*

"The map is not the territory." *Alfred Korzybski, Mathematician*

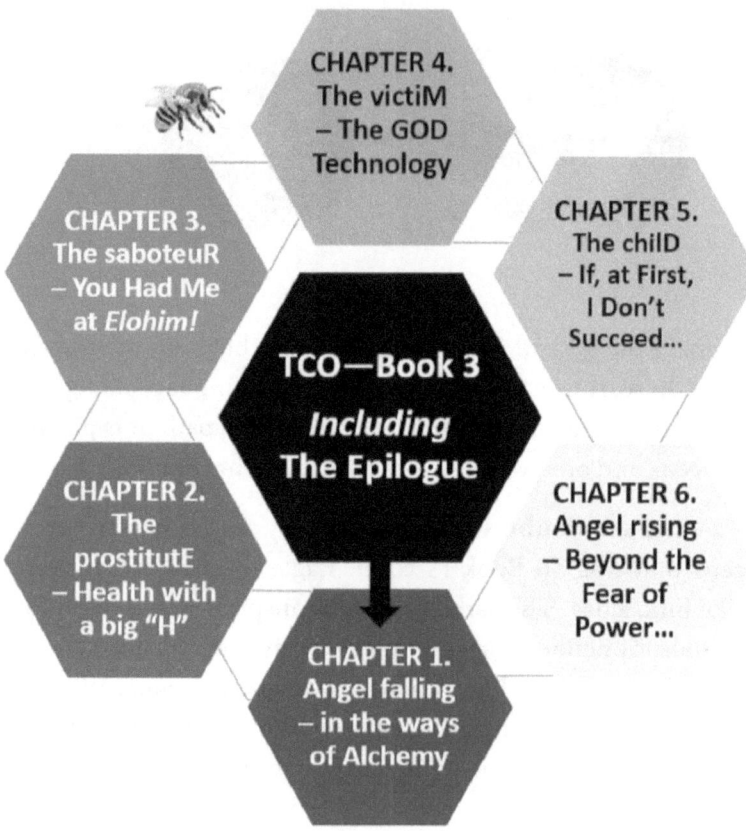

In my search for the kind of usability that would give me practical results, I tend to confuse the model with reality. I forget that reality is a lot messier. I even want to ignore that chaos is part of life! Thus, while my mind creates maps of reality in order to understand reality, I still won't understand the limits of my maps. I just can't feel it. **But what if I stumbled upon a map that would inspire me to walk the territory?**

Contents

1. FALLING IN THE WAYS OF ALCHEMY	1
The Great Voyage to the END of Dissatisfaction	2
The Transition from Greed into Grace	6
Ranking the Sins	7
The Core of Greed	8
The Redemption Code – a Review	10
The Object of Redemption	11
Transformation and Evolution	12
DREaMing of the Sun	14
The Black Sun	16
Code Blackness – MLH / LHM / HLM	17
The DREaM of Karma	19
The DREaM of *Tiqqun*	21
The Truth of the DREaM	22
Complete Understanding	23
YEWE and the DREaM-like Choice	26
The Good NEWS of North-East-West and South	27
The LOVE Stages of a Butterfly	28
Transcending Mammon	29
Understanding the DREaM	33
Being Blessed	34
2. THE PROSTITUTE - HEALTH WITH A BIG "H"	37
The First and the Last Stage: the prostitutE's Transcendence	39
FREE falling into Health	40
The Fourth Word of the Magus	41
Part I: The Prostitute's Gift of Gab	43
The Gift of Gab	44
Prostitution vs. FREE Speech	46
From Sickening Doubt to Faith Healing	47
The prostitutE's Psychic Logos	48
Code Scare City – MM / NWN (Revisited)	49
THE END Codes	51
The DREaM of Loss	52

Code Impostorship – DM / AD / MAD	54
Seeing Red	56
Code Tribal Suicide – BL / OY	58
The END of Indebtedness	60
Regression and the Missing Vav	61
Code Regression – OG / GO	62
Looking Back at Amaleq	64
Code Disenchanment – OMLQ / MOQL	65
Disenchantment or "Being Without a Song"	67
Code Anarchy – AMN / NAM	69
Sacred Rest and Transcendence	71
Part II: Passion and the Power of Attention	73
The Power of Attention	75
DECISIONS, DECISIONS	76
Code Results – BQS / SBQ	79
The Passion of Hysteria	81
Understanding Attention	82
The Passion of Inferiority	84
Rising into Forgiveness	86
The Passion of Defiance	87
The Passion of Craved Penance	89
The Dark Passions	92
The Passion of Fake Kindness	93
The Power of Intention	94
The Passion of Failure	96
Part III: The Choice of Health	99
Resisting nothing; not even a FREE Fall!	101
Giving Back to Mammon	103
A Course in Miracles	104
Code Providence – NWN / XM[K]	106
The Freedom to Choose Health	108
FREE WILL	110
Code Free Will – AB / BA (Expanded)	112
Waking up to Health	114
The QKabbalah of my "Receptor" Cells	115
Code Nemesis – RG / GR	118
To My Nemesis – Reality (a.k.a. "God")	119
Code Mystery – MALK / KLAM	120
Code FREE Fallin' – AMT / MAT	122
The Choice of True Happiness	123

Missing the Mark	125
THE END of Time	127
Judgment Day	129
Part IV: THE END	131
Code Mastery – AWT / MYM	132
From GReed into GRace	135
Code Nourishment – MN / E / AW	137
THIS IS IT!	139
Healing the Wounded Healer	141
From Hypocrite to Hippocratic...	143
3. THE SABOTEUR - YOU HAD ME AT ELOHIM!	147
Next Stage: the saboteuR's Putrefaction	149
Part I: *Elohim* at the First Sight	150
Bipolarity, Angels & Demons	151
Revisiting the War of the Sexes	152
The Odd Couple of Judgment and Mercy	155
Code Sexual Healing – AL / YE	158
The Powers as SIN Destroyers	162
The "Minor" Prompts of Conscience	163
The SIN of the SON of "God"	164
The 3 Ps of an Unconscious Eros	165
The Powers of a Conscious Logos	167
The saboteuR's Consummation	169
Part II: A 1ˢᵗ Date with the Snake	170
LOST IN SABOTAGE	171
The "Cree-P" of Possession	173
Code Intimacy – AWR / OWR	174
Skin/Kin Names and Cain's Name	176
The Mind Split by No Permission	177
The Soul Lost to No Pleasure	178
The Body in Pain Due to No Patience	179
Code Synchronicity – AL / EY / M	180
The Big Three	183
The Heart Broken by No Praise	185
Code Obedience – AL(P) / (P)LA	185
Code Sentience – MY / YM	187
The Forsaken Spirit behind No Purpose	189
Part III: a 2ⁿᵈ Date with the Messiah	190
Do Not Depend on the Other!	191
Sexual Healing and the Messiah	192

Salvation – the Purpose of Rejection	194
Masculinity and the Messiah	195
Patience and the Messiah	196
Actualizing the Messiah	198
Matter and the Messiah	199
Hope and the Third Temple	202
Code Hopelessness – AB / BL / ABL	204
Belief and the Messiah	205
The Snake and the Messiah	207
Rectification & the Messiah	209
Serpent-Power and the Messiah	211
Conversion and the Messiah	213
Redemption and the Messiah	215
The Threefold Plan and the Messiah	216
Shin and the Messiah	219
The TWIN Flame of the Messiah	221
A Shift in Gnosis	223
The Faces of Gnosis	224
Code Gravity – BYE / YEB	226
4. THE VICTIM - THE GOD TECHNOLOGY	**231**
Next Stage: the victiM's Purification	233
Part I: The Victim's Broken Compass	234
Written in Stone	235
TAKING BACK MY PROJECTIONS	237
The Broken Compass	240
Noble Suffering: The Victim's Dirty Secret	241
Defending against the Sacred	242
Justice and the Victim	244
The Letter of the Law	246
The Vav Blip	249
The Translator Effect – No Connection	252
The Log Exemplified	253
Part II: Restoring the Religious Instinct	256
Restoring the Instinct Broken by the Pain Body	257
The SIX "Days" of the Pain Body	258
The Loss in Translation – No Voice	260
The Grief in Translation – No Healing	261
Ignoring the Number 72 – No Cooperating	263
The Departed ZQ in "Sadducees" – No Eliminating	265
The ZQ Twilight Zone – No Grounding	267

Code Awesomeness – ZQ / QZ	270
🎵🎵 (I can't get NO) satisfaction!	272
The Righteous & Wrong Game: No Recuperating	274
Part III: The GOD Technology	278
Preparing for the AWEsome	279
Speaking of AWEsomeness...	280
AWEsome and Innate	281
I CAN think – Fire and *Teshuvah*	283
I CAN receive – Water and *Tephillah*	285
I CAN give it all – Air and *Tzedaqah*	288
The GOD Technology	290
Troubleshooting the Soul	293
A Marriage Made in "Heaven"	295
Ether – I CAN wait; therefore, I CAN receive!	296
Wood – I CAN fast; therefore, I CAN think!	299
Earth: I CAN decide; therefore, I CAN give it all!	301
Astrology and the Letter Tzaddi	303
A Meet & Greet with the AWEsome	306
IT IS DONE!	307
An Officer's Synthesis	309
FEAR – False Evidence Appearing Real	310
5. THE CHILD - IF AT FIRST, I DON'T SUCCEED...	**315**
Next Stage: the chilD's Awakening	317
BIZARRE	318
Part I: An Overview of Creation	321
Taking the Fifth	322
I Am Here to Create	325
The Wizard of UZ	326
I Am Here to Uncreate	328
TIME, SPACE & MIND	330
Mind and SIX-based Time	333
The TWIN Sequential Order	334
Code Creativity – BRA / BAR / ARB	336
The Goodness of Creation	338
The Mind of Life	340
The Egg, the Ego and the Eight of Life	341
What do I really want?	343
Part II: The Psychological Decoding of Genesis 1 & Genesis 2	344
Genesis 1 – *Adam Qadmon*	346

Being Primary, Thinking I CAN!	352
Genesis 2:1-3 – You Complete Me!	353
The Angel of Necessity	355
Genesis 2:4 – A Pivotal Moment (Review)	356
Genesis 2:4-25 – *Adam HaRishon*	358
The Seed of Time	363
The Fall of the Mouth Chakra	365
Being Secondary, Thinking I CAN'T!	368
Part III: The Psychological Decoding of Genesis 3	369
COMPOUNDING	371
Genesis 3:1-22 – the Woman & the Snake	372
Genesis 3:22-24 – the Challenge	379
The Hunger for the Leader of LOVE	381
The East of Eden	382
Code Perfect Bliss – OD/N | O/DN	383
Being Tertiary, Thinking I Don't Want To!	386
6. RISING BEYOND THE FEAR OF POWER	389
Part I: Life is Suffering	391
Life Is Suffering	392
Four Crucial Steps	393
CREATED-SIX	397
Revisiting Code Liberation – AYN / ANY	401
Revisiting Code Health – AYN / OYN	403
Code No Yearning – AYN / NO	404
Part II: The Psychological Decoding of Genesis 4	408
Mind and Heart	409
The Beauty of Preservation	411
The Philosopher's Stone	412
SIXth Stage – the Practice of Rising	414
Cain and Abel (Review)	415
Enlightenment In Seven Things	417
The Seven Lights	417
Five, Seven, or SIX?	424
"Who knows four?"	425
Enlightenment	427
When the Soul Fears Resting…	428
My Gravitational Problem	429
VIRGINITY	431
Desire and Cain	433
The V of Violence	435

The Two Hands	438
The YEWE that Came from the Wombman	440
The Map of (My) Suffering	441
Part III: The End of Suffering	442
Genesis 4:1-17 – The Story of (My) Suffering	443
Liberation in the East	449
The SIX "Days" of my Leadership	453
The Commitment behind 777-Engaging	454
Code Compassion – ND / DN	455
Wanted – An Enlightened Humanity	457
The Brilliant Murder of "Vanity"	458
Code Absolute – ST [and] AB	461
Code Incarnation – BNT / ANS	462
The "heART" of Servant Leadership	464
Childlike and Clueless	466
Code Depth – NWN / WWW	467
Redemption Code – AB / BN / ABN	469
THE END	470
The PaRaDiSe Mystery School	473
List of Publications	474
Epilogue	477

ONE

Falling in the Ways of Alchemy

"Everything in life is vibration." *Albert Einstein*

THIS CHAPTER – *Orientation in the ways of Alchemy* – sets the tone for me to understand that alchemy is the operation of the sun leading me to know Health with a big H. Health is the result of a sun-like progression into transcendence of patterns that keep me small and defeated. To reach my goal of wholesome Power, I must shift from an unvoiced bystander to an outspoken guardian of personal boundaries. I will then relate to *Sol Invictus*; the "Invincible Sun" whose light is reborn from the watery depths of the Moon, having vanquished midnight's darkness. The triumph of the sun illuminates all things, like truth does. It ushers the arrival of the sun of Self, far more brilliant than the sun of nature. Like a phoenix rising from the ashes of an unconsciousness that caused the Soul's putrefaction into the dark night, the sun shines on a paradisiacal world, deliberately giving birth to the light. The sun is the source of nature's power. By day, it offers the nourishment of his warmth. By night it illuminates the sky through the Moon reflecting his light. And yet, parallel to the joy of new insights, the sun offers a test: it may scorch in its intensity as well as it can offer comfort, physically and morally. So what will it be? It will all be clear, as here comes the sun!

The Great Voyage to the END of Dissatisfaction

> "For the alchemist the one primarily in need of redemption is not man, but the deity who is lost and sleeping in matter. Only as a secondary consideration does he hope that some benefit may accrue to himself from the transformed substance as the panacea, the *medicina catholica*, just as it may to the imperfect bodies, the base or "sick" metals, etc. His attention is not directed to his own salvation through God's grace, but to the liberation of God from the darkness of matter." *C.G. Jung*

My Power comes from the convergence of two ancient and archetypal flows – the Leviathan and the Behemah, whose intensity I am giving myself the permission to feel. I can now observe that my neurological system is an electric field. It sparks with every thought I have. Will I open my emotional body to the energetic of an etheric field and change how I remember me? This field is where all the data comes from. It is where the Voice resonates. It is also why the most powerful part of health is invisible. **It requires the faith that sees the invisible and believes in the incredible.** To make contact with it, I must drop the plan as there's nothing measurable about this field. My soul is very much like a smart phone: it downloads everything. It is absurd how I can simultaneously be hooked to non-physical communication and ignore the invisible world. I miss out on the fact that my intuition speaks to me via SMS. Surely, S/Hebrew had to wait for the information age to be sensed as a metalanguage: its animals go by pair, modeling how to pair my energetic body to its nonphysical counterpart.

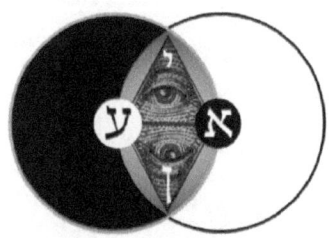

Here is the pairing of fully spelled-out sign *Ayin* (עין) the "eye" with *Ain* (אין) "nothing," both words having the same sounds. When I change the way I/eye look at things, what I see changes. I now voyage into nothingness, a vibrational field of light where I adjust to a way to do time that is purposive. I am now on task, hearing the sound of invisible waters and seeing the light of inaudible fire – of my DNA, my origin, my genius; my energetic compass, and not taking any of it personally. I vibrate with the vortex of energy that's in the midst of the two twin circles. My five senses allow for the SIXth sense of enough to change my perceptions. I stop dismissing my intuition. I leave a world that was only solid to be fluid. Since my diseases were more energetic than chemical, I find a way to regulate my neurology via an immaculate sentience. **I receive the impossible: the faith that makes me well.**

NO YEARNING...

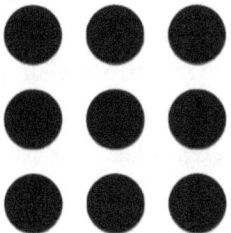

NO YEARNING: I can't even imagine what it would be like to stop being so hungry, and even greedy for LOVE all the time... This greed is how I am so harsh on myself/others. It is Sri Ramana Maharshi who said: "grace is ever present. All that is necessary is that you surrender to it." Instead of letting go of my stuff, I wake up day after day to painfully judgmental thoughts, and can never sustain the quality of grace that erases negativity and infuses my heart with kindness.

"In the New Testament grace means God's love in action towards men who merited the opposite of love. Grace means God moving heaven and earth to save sinners who could not lift a finger to save themselves."

J. I. Packer

Heavy, man, heavy!
And yet... My society has banished the vocabulary of the soul, starting with the four "minor" prompts (to use that word as a joke) of "God, Law, sin and sex." Henceforth, using the word "sin" and talking about sin is not cool at all – not spiritually correct!

However, I find that the unconscious parts of me – especially, the prostitutE and the saboteuR – are trapped in the pit of hell called "Egypt" in the Bible, a location which comprises the seven infernal spheres of the tree of life. Surely, the Jewish holiday known as Passover is to make my exodus from such sinful inferno into the tree's three supernal spheres, a.k.a. "the Promised Land."

The hell of seven infernals and the heaven of three supernals are not waiting for me at the end of my life. They are in present time. Similarly, they are not geographical. They are psycho-logical, as they emanate from the "soul's logos." What is the quality of my narrative? If I really did Passover, would I still continue telling the story of how I was a slave in Egypt? Every moment a double door opens for me to choose to enter either heaven or hell. It is a moment-to-moment decision, as all can change within a split second.

Hell and heaven are within me, standing side-by-side for me to decode their opposition. When I speak and act unconsciously, I am in hell. Conversely, when I speak and act consciously, I am in heaven. GReed opens the door to hell, and GRace, to heaven. The difference is in the sincerity of my GR, i.e.; of my Giving and Receiving.

Since it is in giving that I am receiving, the question becomes: why am I reluctant to give and thus to receive? To answer I must understand the "deadly" in the seven deadly sins. If I don't die to them, they will kill me!

To understand these seven is no easy matter, unless, of course, I understand the relationship of the lower spheres of the tree of life – its "inferno," a word that comes from the Latin *infernus* for "lying beneath, underground, of the lower regions." This realm disturbs me, especially when my ego only wants to get on top!

The Transition from Greed into Grace

The Mission of *emPowering NOW LLC* ™ is to test, experience, and bring forth *Golden XPR* as a path to transition from a world of **GR**eed that splits **G**iving and **R**eceiving by communicating fear, confusion and domination, to a world of **GR**ace that unites **G**iving and **R**eceiving by communicating understanding and kindness.

Across cultures, there is a prophecy alluding to a golden age, when a unified Teaching will create a paradigm shift akin to a mass return to a mythical kingdom such as a "Shambhala" or a "Garden of Eden." No matter the name, this is an indigenous belief (a belief that precedes any organized religions). The Jewish tradition calls the messianic state where the awe of Heaven will be upon us *Olam HaBah* for "the World-to-Come." It opposes *Olam Hazeh* for "this World," a world or consciousness that is contaminated by greed.

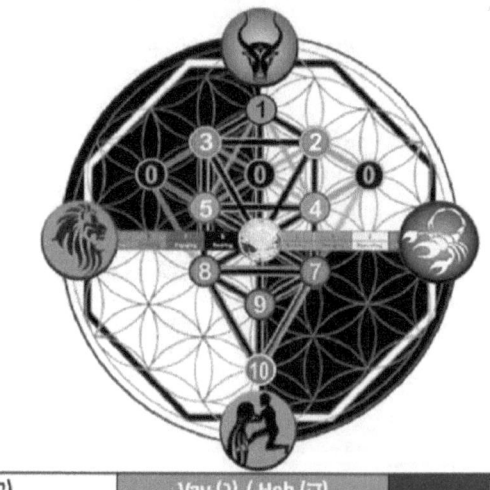

Yod (י)	Vav (ו) / Heh (ה)	Heh (ה)
"I will"	"I know" / "I have"	"I desire"
Lion	Aquarius Child / Bull	Scorpion into Eagle
I CAN fast → I CAN think	I CAN give → I CAN decide	I CAN receive → I CAN wait

XPR pictures the transition in the tree IN-LOVE, which merges the tree of life with the tree of the knowledge of opposites in order to transmit the proficiencies of the sacred hidden in Ezekiel's vision.

Ranking the Sins

"To pretend to trust Christ to save you from sin while you are still determined to continue in it is making a mockery of Christ."
Charles Spurgeon

Together with the Ten Commandments, the Seven Sins were for a long time one of the most popular models for an examination of conscience. It is thus not surprising that the rabbinical debate on "which commandment prevails; the first or the last?" would be echoed by Christian scholars asking "which sin comes first: pride or greed?" Are these big sins in opposition to lesser sins such as gluttony or sloth?

- **Pride or envy:** yes, Lucifer did fall out of pride: annoyed at having to serve God, he grew rebellious in his desire to be served. But what about his being so gifted with light and feeling so unseen that he began to envy God's role?
- **Wrath:** wrath is held to be the reason why Moses never reached the Promised Land. That would seem to rank high in the hierarchy of sins…
- **Gluttony:** gluttony is also a key player in light of its being balanced by a temperance that allows me to stay in the middle or in the golden "mean" between excess and deficiency, and thus, to stop sinning.
- **Sloth:** sloth is generally viewed as laziness. It is felt by Dante as the "failure to love God with all one's heart, mind and soul." Since the integrity to give it all is the call of the *Shema* prayer, sloth is also a pretty big deal.
- **Lust:** lust is also primordial in that it is a clear misuse of language, Power and sexual energy.

Therefore, "which sin comes first" may not be the "write" question since the outlaw in me always begins with what I foolishly view as little sins. There are no little sins. Just like the sins of our parents will be revisited on the 3rd and 4th generations, the first sin I commit – a trifle, right? – will procreate into a whole family of sins known as the seven deadly. However, when I realize that the seven lower spheres are only "low" when moved by the fatal energy of the seven sins, I have a way to interrelate these sins – those committed by the male side, those, by the female side and those, by the not-so neutral part of me. The end of the exploration is for me to choose "living GRace" instead of "deadly GReed." This is when I pay the price for my own redemption.

The Core of Greed

"Think of giving not as a duty but as a privilege." John Rockefeller Jr.

The question – what is my purpose? – is daunting, especially when I think I am the body, and take things personally. Likely to be prey to fear and live in "Scare City," my mind leads me to take things personally. I can't hear that my purpose is to 1) find what my gifts are, and 2) offer them wholeheartedly. And yes, for me to let go once and for all of any thoughts of return – of what's in it for me, I must come to "THE Understanding;" the understanding that there is only One of us. I will then know, in my blood, St Francis' words of wisdom and feel that "it is giving that we are receiving."

As long as I believe that I end at the skin, that I am here and you are there, there is no authentic giving. When my giving comes from the heart, both giver and receiver feel it. In that space, there is no illusion of separation; just the pure beauty of reciprocity. The S/Hebrew name of the heart chakra – *Tiphereth* – means just that: "beauty." I am beautiful when my giving and receiving are symmetrical. When they are not, my heart closes, and I become ugly.

The Sanskrit name of the heart chakra comes to help. Since *Anahata* means "unhurt," it is the very idea that I was not supposed to get hurt that closes my heart and prevents me from healing. Just like healing is cognate to grace, many sicknesses are cognate to greed. The heart is the absolute core of the tree of life – from top to bottom and right to left. It is the energy that regulates every other sphere. Thus, to the question, which sin comes first, I see that 7-Greed is at the core at what contaminates all shadow parts of me. Indeed, would I be a glutton, lustful, slothful, envious, prideful and/or wrathful if I wasn't contaminated by greed? Bottom line: greed is more than an insatiable desire for wealth. It is a will directed to Power; to controlling me, us, it – the world! In that sense, it is the cornerstone of all sins.

5-Pride | 6-Sloth	7-Greed → 2-Lust | 4-Gluttony	3-Wrath | 1-Envy
Humility | Diligence	Grace | Containm. | Temperance	Patience | Gratitude

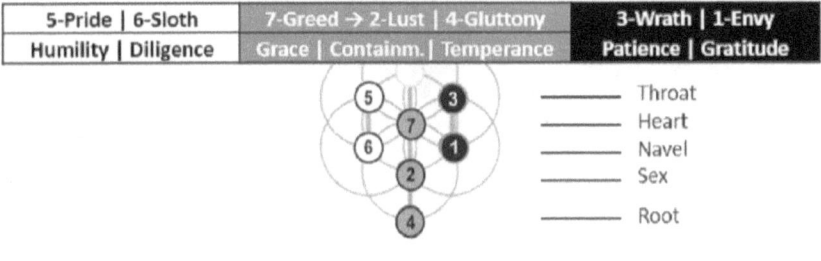

The Redemption Code - a Review

"Don't tempt me, I can resist anything but temptation." *Bob Hope*

The Father	The Son & the Stone	The Mother
Aleph Beth	Nun	Beth Aleph

N	W	N
W	A	W
N	W	N

- Right: Hebrew letter Beth (ב) → **B in Roman script** |
- Left: Hebrew letter Aleph (א) → **A in Roman script** |
- Middle: Hebrew letter Nun final (ן) → **N in Roman script**

AB is *Ab* (אב) for "father, alphabet." **BA** (בא) is *Bo* for "enter." **ABN** is *Aben* (אבן) for the "stone" on which the 10 Words are inscribed for me to know myself as **BN** (בן) *or Ben / Bin* for the "son / in-between." The square under the word "Nun" unfolds the letter and word *Nun* for "fish, miscarriage" → fallen from GRace into GReed. *Nun* (נון|NWN) has three letters. Its middle letter, which unfolds as the letter and word *Vav* (ואו|WAW) for "nail, connector," also has three letters. At its core is Aleph, the primal force including all Powers, among which the Power of decision to fish for my humanity, and dive deep into the dark waters to uplift the sparks of my soul from their "fallen" state. Redemption is the price I must pay to hear and understand the message of the fish, and shift from snake into messiah.

The **ABN** stone is also the philosopher's stone – a mythic alchemical substance capable of turning base metals such as lead into gold or silver. Sometimes called the "elixir of life," it is used for rejuvenation and even immortality. It was the most sought after goal in alchemy. Core symbol of alchemy, the stone symbolized perfection at its finest, enlightenment, and heavenly bliss. Endeavors to discover the philosopher's stone were known as the *Magnum Opus* ("Great Work").

The Object of Redemption

Citrinitas	Rubedo / Albedo	Nigredo
Greed → Pride / Sloth	Greed → Lust / Gluttony	Greed → Wrath / Envy
chilD	prostitutE / victiM	saboteuR

The Four Stages of Alchemy & the Sins of Four Archetypes in a DREaM

When I create unconscious time and go into the DREaM, I am likely to engage in sin. These violations are what I must redeem by paying the price of my evolution.

1. *Nigredo* (Latin for "black"): the **saboteuR** swings back and forth from covert envy into overt wrath.
2. *Citrinitas* (Latin for "yellow"): the **chilD** swings back and forth from the overt pride into covert sloth.
3. *Albedo* (Latin for "white"): the **victiM** is plagued with being a glutton for punishment.
4. *Rubedo* (Latin for "red"): the **prostitute** is slave to a greed that transforms into lust.

The colors of the alchemical stages correspond to the journey of the sun. Indeed, alchemy is the mastery of the operation of the sun.

1. *Nigredo* is the black sun of the **saboteuR**, and the stage of putrefaction.
2. *Albedo* is the dawn of the **victiM**, and the stage of purification.
3. *Citrinitas* is the noon sun of the **chilD**, and the stage of awakening.
4. *Rubedo* is the sunset of the **prostitutE**, and the stage of transcendence.

Note: the number 4 sustains the DREaM of karma. Subsequently, *TCO* —*Book 3's* "FOUR" core chapters focus on the FOUR shadow archetypes above.

Transformation and Evolution

> "Love is a sacred reserve of energy; it is like the blood of spiritual evolution." *Pierre Teilhard de Chardin*

Since the East of Eden is where all the troubled heroes of the Bible started their journey, my evolutionary journey starts in the East, the direction of the prostitutE. I shall soon see that this beginning is also an end.

From the East, I am now moving counterclockwise on the wheel known in Hinduism as the wheel of transformation, of mundane existence, of life and/or of suffering. When in the North, it becomes evident that my soul compass is so broken that I can't hold my true North. I must espouse Nature's way which sustains the stages of alchemy, and start again, but this time, in the dark earth – the watery depth of Ego-Egypt. The decision point is in the South, when my chilD decides to grow up into a Leader and takes full responsibility. I am now ready to adopt a clockwise motion as I return to the East – in the beautiful mind of an Engineer.

This true "East" is called *Qedem* in S/Hebrew which is a different word than *Mizrach* or cardinal "East." *Qedmat Eden* or "East of Eden" is the direction taken by Cain after he murdered his brother. It is also the deep desire and prayer for transcendence. Meanwhile, recovering sentience is how my saboteuR transforms into a Visionary. This involves embracing the saboteuR's ways that can only take me down when resisted. The resistance is so painful that it explains also how the North would mark the starting place of alchemy – in the black sun of Nigredo, the "black" of putrefaction. Surely, it is imperative for me to first feel how hungry I am for the dark soil of Ego-Egypt. To live my vision, I must shed my skin. As Shakespeare would say: "you are an alchemist. Make gold of that."

The four chapters of *TCO—Book 3* are alchemical in nature. They follow the operation of the sun. They are also theurgical, as the sun has a date with the moon. In this manner, the polar opposites of sun and moon can come into balance. The soli-lunar meeting occurs throughout the following four stages:

- **Transcendence** – <u>**Chapter 2: Health with a Big "H"**</u> witnesses the turn of my prostitutE towards the genius of an Engineer. To choose Health with a big H (and have it all), I must first understand why I stayed among the have-nots as a saboteuR, a victiM and a chilD. Henceforth, if transcendence is the fourth and end stage of alchemy, it must also be its first and beginning stage.
- **Putrefaction** – <u>**Chapter 2: You Had Me at Elohim!**</u> allows my saboteuR to feel the shame and, thereby, reveal the light of the Visionary it was covering. It is when I understand the bi-polarity of my throat, and safely manage my passage into the "Promised Land" of an open 3rd eye.
- **Purification** – <u>**Chapter 3: the GOD Technology**</u> – shifts my victiM into an Officer of the 0/1 Law of LOVE; the law without law. It is when I understand why I played a toxic "righteous"

and wrong game, and how to ground and energize the tree of (my) life.

- Awakening – <u>**Chapter 4: if at First, I Don't Succeed**</u> – gives my chilD a chance to grow up into a Leader. It is when I receive the gold of the scriptures, and understand why I must carve the egoic marble of vanity in order to free the throat, know free speech, and allow my **angel** to be risen.

3. South	4. East / 2. West	1. North
Yellow chilD	Red prostitutE / White victiM	Black saboteuR
Citrinitas	Rubedo / Albedo	Nigredo
Awaken	Transcend / Purify	Putrefy
If, at 1st, I don't succeed	Big H-Health / The GOD Tech.	You had me at Elohim!

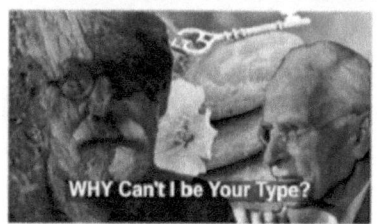

To further connect the alchemical stages to the DREaM code, click the image above or visit https://www.goldenxpr.com/why-the-love-types/

DREaMing of the Sun

"The sun is the giver of life." **Ramses II**

If I wish to blossom into my potential, I may choose to observe what flowers do and angle myself towards the sun. The sun is more than just the center star of the solar system. It is a fundamental variable for wellness as it is the source of energy for all life on Earth. Its gift is best received when I understand its path. For the alchemist, it evokes the perfection of all matter on any level, including that of the mind, soul and body.

As for the centrality of the sun, it is Nicolaus Copernicus who proposed the model of the heliocentric system – a departure from Ptolemy's geocentric system. He saw that it was the sun and not the earth that was the core of the universe, and that the earth, stars, and planets all revolved about the sun. His work marked the beginning of modern astronomy and modern science. Later on, Kepler realized that the orbits of the planets were not the circles asserted by Aristotle and assumed by Copernicus, but were instead flattened "ellipses."

This is where it becomes intriguing... We know now that the orbits of the planets have two foci, as they are elliptic. For every planet one of the foci is the sun, the other is something that has been termed the black sun or the invisible sun. As always, I forget that visible effects are commanded by the invisible realm. On earth and in the solar system, some of the visible effects of the sun are heat, and light. Opposite to these sensations, and blacker than the blackest black, the **black sun** compels me to face my deepest fears by exposing the places where I am in a putrefaction mode (evil, corrupt or depraved). It is also true that the darkest encounters induced by the black sun can turn into the most sublime peak experiences. Harvesting the pearls of darkness of the midnight sun naturally moves me into purification. It is indeed the **dawn** of a new day! The **noon sun** makes things clear, offering an awakening. The journey ends where it started – in a **sunset**, readying me to rest from the illusions of the DREaM. I can now safely adopt the behavior of LOVE.

Noon Sun	Sunset / Dawn	Black Sun
Yellow chilD	Red prostitutE / White victiM	Black saboteuR
Citrinitas	*Rubedo / Albedo*	*Nigredo*
Awaken	Transcend / Purify	Putrefy

♫♪ Sunrise, sunset, sunrise, sunset; swiftly fly the years...

The Black Sun

"I do not see why man should not be just as cruel as nature." *Adolf Hitler*

I forget how shockingly violent Nature is, how one black hole feeds on millions of stars, how thousands of children die daily... Will I remember that the shadow is the most formidable of all forces, and how dark its matter is? Forgetting who I Am is how I add to the daily quota of violence by having no patience with "you" and projecting my resistance onto you. Heck, as long as I attempt to correct what I perceive is your problem, I don't have to own, feel or heal anything!

The black sun compels me to connect to the force of violence which lives in me as it does in Nature. My saboteuR will make me feel like a loser, as I wake up every day to the same errors of perception. However, while moving from stage to stage, I come to understand the operation of the sun until I become *Sol Invictus* – the "Invincible Sun." I receive the gift of victory when I know that I will not suffer any exception and no longer quit on my goal. This is not having compassion. It is *being* compassion.

Compassion naturally completes the operation of the moon and, with it, the lunacy to do the same insane things expecting positive results. Alchemy and theurgy work in polarity, just like the sun and the moon do. Admittedly, it is my lunar side that can turn demonic. By the same token, any genius will relate to the words of the poet: "Kill off all my demons and my angels might die too." *Tennessee Williams*

The only option is to bring out the demonic energy – the evil that is within me and to transmute its darkness into light. This freeing of the genie from encapsulation is what Art is. That is what Alchemy is. That is what healing is. It is also why the Greek word *daemon* (that gave "demon") was known by the Romans as "genius."

Code Blackness - MLH / LHM / HLM

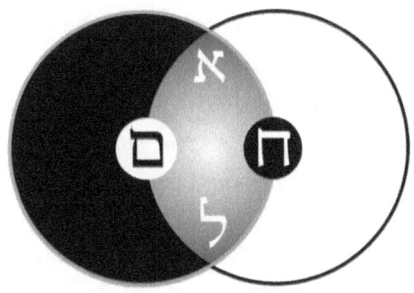

Imagine a language so pure and so sacred that it can reconcile opposites in just four letters...

Top: Hebrew letter Aleph (א) → A in Roman script
Right: Hebrew letter Chet (ח) → H in Roman script
Left: Hebrew letter Mem final (ם) → M in Roman script
Bottom: Hebrew letter Lamed (ל) → L in Roman script

Here is how S/Hebrew inscribes the code "Shadow" in 4 letters, 4 words:

- **AL HM**: top to bottom, right to left, I read *Al Cham* (אל חם) for "alchemy."
- **MLH**: left (regular Mem) to bottom to right, I read *Melach* (מלח) for "salt."
- **LHM**: bottom to right to left, I read *Lechem* (לחם) for "bread."
- **HLM**: right to bottom to left, I read *Chalam* (חלם) for "to dream."

The Decoding: the etymology of the word **alchemy** is found in the Arabic *Al-kīmiya*, said to mean "the Egyptian [science]," since the Egyptians were the first to prepare the Philosopher's Stone as an Elixir of Enlightenment. *Kīmiya* comes itself from the Coptic "kheme" for

Ancient Egypt, referring both to the country and the color "black." Egypt was the "Black Soil of the Nile" in contrast with the "Red Land," or the surrounding desert. Hieroglyphically, the word refers to the void of the First Matter (the Kheme *and* the etheric meme, the matrix through which all creation manifests). The ancient Egyptians were the descendants of Ham, one of Noah's sons. *Ham* or *Cham* (**HM**) for "black, hot, burnt" became Arabic *Kham*. From there, the Egyptians called their land *Khemet* or "the Land of the Black." *Psalm 105:23* links Egypt, Israel and the Land of Ham as the cradle of civilization: "Israel also came into Egypt; and Jacob sojourned in the land of Ham." S/Hebrew *Ham* is Arabic *Kham*. There is the physical Land of the Black where my body suffered the humiliation of slavery, prey to oppressors that would not let my people go. There is also a psychological Land of the Black where my soul is exiled. Making my exodus out of such Egypt leads me to transcend the "I am the body" thought and the ensuing bondage to the gold without which I can't take care of the body. Surely, feeding the body, giving it shelter, and clothes to keep it warm costs money!

As for the ancient science of **alchemy**, three substances are said to make up everything. Known as the "Three Primes," these are sulphur, mercury, and salt. The flammability of sulphur makes it a binding agent. The fluidity of mercury makes it a transformative agent. The fixity of salt makes it a substantiating agent. These three qualities are behind the Power of Three. They are also expressed in the **bread** of the covenant which is binding; the wine of the covenant which is transformative, and the **salt** of the covenant which perpetual, because salt can be used as a preservative.

Yod (י)	Vav (ו) / Heh (ה)	Heh (ה)
Fiery Heart	Aerial Mind / Earthly Body	Watery Soul
Flammable Sulphur	Fluid Mercury	Fixed Salt
Binding of Bread	Transformation of Wine	Substantiation of Salt

When YEWE meets the Three Primes...

As for the **dream**, if I were to imagine that the **bread** that I eat is the bread of war, I may be prone to Celiac disease – an immune disorder where eating gluten damages the small intestine. Indeed, the word *Lechem* for "bread" sources the word *Milchamah* for "war." If only I could wake up from the dream of a hostile "out there," I might let go of a very dark agenda: the need to defend myself and thus, of being attacked. Indeed, what is it that I cannot digest?

The DREaM of Karma

> "A person often meets his destiny on the road he took to avoid it."
> *Jean de La Fontaine*

Karma is a theory common to many oriental religions. The word karma means both "action" and "consequences of actions." It is held to be a universal accounting system in which I must experience the consequences of my actions. When my actions are good, I have good results. When they're bad, bad results. Moreover, these consequences are like a debt which can be carried over into future lives. Therefore, even if I seem to get away with murder this time around, I will have to clear my name at some point. This possible gap between a creation and its experience explains how difficult it may be at times for me to remember that I am source of my creation.

The ideas of free will, karma and destiny will puzzle me as long as I don't get them! Possibly, seeing cross-cultural truths will help my confusion. The "God" who controls my destiny is known as Iswara in Hinduism, and YEWE in Hebrew. These four letters naturally link to the four archetypes unconscious of being in a DREaM. When I try to avoid the destiny that my soul laid out for me, this "God" starts feeling like a stern LORD who ordains that I'd suffer the consequences of my actions. The same LORD will now select the sequence of experiences and activities that I must undergo in each lifetime. Taking from my portfolio, it chooses the good and bad actions that will most favor my spiritual evolution, whether pleasant or unpleasant.

To escape its jurisdiction, I must stop identifying with the "I am the body" thought. Therefore, the only way to become free of suffering is to fully include and transcend the agent upon whom all decisions depend – the ego, as it is the ego who is identified to the body. It will even create sickness and lack to protect the hell of this illusion!

When I wake up and know that LOVE is stronger than death, I can think, as my mind is not troubled by any compulsion preventing me to wait and fast. As for the issues brought about by destiny, I think of them as art pieces, and of my ego as an artist preparing for a show. Although I have many paintings to choose from, I'll select only a few to show, keeping the rest of the work for other exhibits (hear, other lifetimes).

When the artist in me dies to the ego, I paid the price of my liberation. The work is done! This may be how many artists are only recognized after their deaths. They intuitively know that, as long as the ego is still identified, fame will be a recipe for disaster. However, when they create their "Master Peace" (and can choose peace at will), there is no hunger left for any subsequent art show – no births and no deaths. This release from the cycle of rebirth impelled by the law of karma is the transcendence known in Sanskrit as *Moksha* and in S/Hebrew as *Mashiach* - the "Messiah." As for paying the price, the following classification from Hindu schools of thought is announced below as "portfolio, redemption, acquisition." Connecting them to financial vocabulary shows once again that the work is to transition from greed into grace. This is how I wake up from the DREaM, and free myself "from the land of Egypt and the house of bondage" (as per word Aleph in *Exodus 20:2*).

1. **Portfolio:** the karmic debts accumulated from previous births.
2. **Redemption:** the debt I take out of my portfolio to work out in this lifetime.
3. **Acquisition:** new debt incurred in the present life.

Surely, the house of bondage is built by *Mammon* – the "yearning" for "money." Indeed, I dream of karma primarily because I am not aware that I am creating the idea of money. Living in Scare City, I observe lack. I even start anthropomorphizing money, making it either a savior or a depleting monster.

The DREaM of *Tiqqun*

"If it ain't broke, don't fix it." Bert Lance

Held to be an essential concept of the Kabbalah, the *Tiqqun* for "correction, repair, edits" is how to resolve the perennial conflict between the two inclinations of my soul – one to do good, and the other, evil. Yet who stands as a judge of evil and needs fixing" but the ego that competes with the heart in an attempt to be right?

When I own that I am feeding the "wrong" wolf, I stop suffering from the negative impact of cause and effect. It's simple: I no longer create results I would rather not have to experience. But since I don't want to stop feeding the wolf of despair, I continue to envy the light of your results, and want to make you pay for it! This is how the work of adjusting my actions and waking up from the dream of karma starts and ends in *Tiqqun Cain* – the highest of the three *Tiqqunim* and yet the least talked about (see *Book 2, Debugging the Oneness "Software," Code Innocence*).

Surely, there is nothing left to be jealous of and nothing to correct when I come to the end of desire. I can then either have or not have what I had envied in my brother, and even killed him for! Resisting nothing allows me to see that there is nobody and nothing out there. Therefore, the need for the two popular *Tiqqunim* – *Tiqqun Nephesh* or "correcting the body-soul" and *Tiqqun Olam* or "correcting the World" is naturally transcended. I feel it after owning my errors so fully that I see the truth: there was never any error. When nothing is wrong, nothing needs correcting!

It is the same with the laws of karma. They are binding as long as I imagine to be separated from the Self. This illusion of separation takes away my Power of decision. It also compels me to repeat the same insane experience, a result which I placed in motion through previous words and actions.

These experiences are determined at birth. This is how they are "my destiny." My only freedom is to realize that there is no one (no body) acting and no one (no body) experiencing. This is realizing the Self. When there is no ego left to resist experiencing the consequences of my actions, the whole structure of karmas becomes obsolete.

Resisting nothing, I am free to decide. At last, my will is free to desire the good.

The Truth of the DREaM

> "So, I cast a deep sleep upon me, and while I was sleeping, I took one of my sides and closed up the flesh at that spot. Then I made a female from the side I had taken out of me." *Genesis 2:21-22*

There is some truth in the romantic dream. One day, my prince/ss will come and fulfill all my desires. I just need to resist nothing. Then each moment can be my lover. :-)

When confused about what's "out there" and forgetting that togetherness is a mirage coming from my fear of being alone, I enforce the "I am not enough" thought and hit the snooze button. This is how the four chapters of *TCO—Book 3* are dedicated to the four DREaM archetypes, for me to know them so well that I'd wake up IN-LOVE.

Here is a question for me: do I believe with complete faith that there is an end to suffering? If yes, an opportunity just presented itself.

One thing is sure: the pain caused by the unconscious DREaM types will eventually lead me to wake up and become real as I come to the end of desire and with it, the end of dissatisfaction. And as I reopen the flesh that was closed up at the "sentience spot," I'll give me the permission to feel and sense again. But first, I'd like to review the basics questions I will be asked on this golden path to the end:

- **Step 1 – honesty: do I want to know the truth?** Knowing that my beliefs create my reality, I just have to look at my reality to see what I really believe. Gentle warning: this may be different than what I want to believe.
- **Step 2 – appreciation and perseverance: will I allow myself to be so awed by the codes that I'd persevere to "THE END?"** Consider: when I quit on my goal (or, in the words of the poet, "suffer an exception"), there is something I won't feel or understand; a challenge I fail to appreciate.
- **Step 3 – Power and wisdom: might my folly be my teacher?** Consider: when wise, I know the difference between what's good and what's evil for me.
- **Step 4 – kindness and complete understanding: how far will I go to know that I Am LOVE?** Consider: when I come to "THE END," my Beloved ego and I (the two parts of me) walk in the sunset, each part knowing that, from thereon, it will love the other part and trust that these two selves are one (no exception).

Complete Understanding

"The highest activity a human being can attain is learning to understand because to understand is to be free." Baruch Spinoza

The four steps that I just described take me up the tree of (my) life. **Step 1** is in sphere 2, namely *Yesod* for the "foundation" as the **honesty** I have when I choose to know the truth. **Step 2** is in spheres 3 and 4, *Netzach* and *Hod*, when I feel the **"perseverance"** and the **"appreciation"** that take me beyond time. **Step 3** is in spheres 6 and 7, *Gevurah* and *Chokmah*, when my coming into wholesome **"Power"** speaks of my

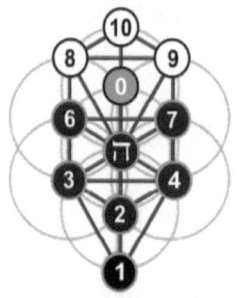

embodying "**wisdom.**" **Step 4** is in spheres 8 and 9, *Chesed* and *Binah*, when "**kindness**" ascends to take me out of Ego-Egypt into the Promised Land of "**complete understanding.**" As for sign Heh (ה) at the core, it waits for me to stop moving, knowing that I want it all and have it all.

Individual Power	Symbolic Power	Collective Power
Spheres 8 to 10	Sphere 0	Sphere 1 to 7
"Promised Land"	"The Red Sea"	"Ego-Egypt"

For my 3rd eye (spheres 8 & 9) to be permanently open to seeing the good in the bad, I must have parted "the Red Sea" and passed through *Daath's* "Self-knowledge," going from the known into the unknown enough times that I'd fully surrender. I no longer think I know what's for my highest good. I simply listen and do the next "perfect" thing. Just like Self-knowledge is gradual and thus, quantifiable, so is understanding.

The more I "understand" who I Am, the more I can hold the tension "in between" opposites (see *TCO – Volume I; Code Understanding as Code In-Between*). To earn each "lettered" stage, I ask myself why I would be fixated on that stage until the why of the fixation is so clearly recognized that I naturally move into the how of liberation and shift out of being stuck. Being satisfied with the contact I made with my unconscious motivations, my attention is free again, and the issue ceases to be of concern to me. My work is simple: to break the shell that captured the insight I seek.

One thing is clear: there is an END to suffering. Therefore, the day will come when I have cleaned up enough that I will wake up for good. I will then receive the *siddhis*. The Sanskrit word means "Powers," but also and

9	
Completing	
9	ט
90	צ
900	ץ

foremost "complete understanding." Surely, when I understand oneness, I don't fear Power. I can now enter "the Promised Land" of an open 3rd eye and see the good in every creation.

To free myself from my self-imposed limitations (a "land" known as Egypt in the Bible and as the first tier in Spiral Dynamics), I must come into individual Power. This is Nietzsche's second transformation, when the Lion and the Dragon see face-to-face. Instead of feeling obligated to fulfill the desires of the collective, I follow my own drummer. As I am in my pleasure, the misalignment between what I say I want and what I have disappears. Indeed, not feeling coerced by a false sense of duty, I can will my true heart's desires into being. I am real, and no longer claiming that I am doing all of this for "you."

Individual Power	Symbolic Power	Collective Power
Spheres 8 to 10	Sphere 0	Sphere 1 to 7
"Promised Land"	"The Red Sea"	"Ego-Egypt"
Lion's Will	Child's Knowing	Dragon's Desire

While the third eye and crown chakras (spheres 8 to 10) are not represented, I can see how the black spheres of "Ego-Egypt" are managed by collective Power. These SIX/7 spheres are mapped out on the crucial points of a Seed of Life / Genesis Pattern, which gives me valuable information on the plexuses – from the root to the throat where my polarities are inverted. Going in *Daath* (sphere #0) to feel my attachments to the tribe allows me to crossover into the "Promised Land" of individual Power.

The question I wish to understand through this volume is why I would play the role of prostitutE, saboteuR, victiM and chilD, while unaware of the angel in the dark with me. Why can't I wake up to my inner Leader?

YEWE and the DREaM-like Choice

> "This day I call the heaven and the earth as witnesses against you that I have set before your presence life and death, the blessing and the curse. Now choose life, so that you and your seed (your creativity) may live." *Deuteronomy 30:19*

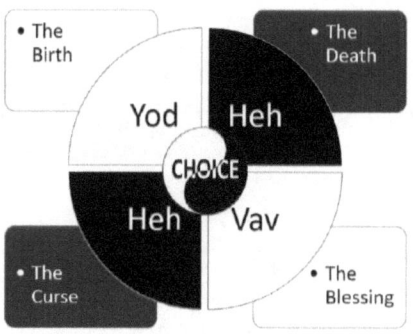

Deuteronomy 30:19, illustrated

I live in duality in order to transcend duality. That's what having a code of opposites is for. Remembering the choices that I once made (of sickness or of health) is how to experience the freedom of the Power of choice. Prior to that, I'm just a chilD rebelling against the commands of my parents, stuck in the putrefaction stage of a saboteuR. I wish I could choose goodness, and yet I continue to play in the dark. *Deuteronomy 30:8-9* sets the stage preparing for the climax of verse 19: "you will again obey YEWE and follow all his commands I am giving you today. [...] Then YEWE will again delight in you and make you prosperous, just as he delighted in your ancestors." Indeed, I am free to choose to persevere in the choice of goodness. **This entails that I would first give me permission to either be prosperous and pleasured (or not).**

Since the truth sets me free, why resist truth and freedom? This question of why I lie to myself about the bondage to Scare City and the subsequent pain I desire and resist can only be resolved through complete understanding. What I am to "completely understand" is the following: **I forgot that I (the Self – the I Am) made the exact choice to experience life as I currently live it. I also ignore that life is not the opposite of death, birth is.** Upon hearing this, I can challenge myself: accepting that the day of my death will come, how will I use this birth, in this body, at this time?

The Good NEWS of North-East-West and South

> *"The idea of redemption is always good news, even if it means sacrifice or some difficult times." Patti Smith*

To experience the medicine of transformation naturally modeled by a "butt-R-fly" (when my "yes, butts" R flying), I just need to allow the chilD to turn into a Leader. Doing so, I change my EVOL/evil ways. The shift happens in the South (that's the good "NEWS") when I am sick and tired of a rebellion that compels me to make the same old same old counterproductive choices while being moved counterclockwise on the wheel of karma.

Note: the Butterfly wheel and its clockwise and counterclockwise motions are pictured on the next page.

To grow up and become a Leader may just be easier done than said. :-) I just need to grok the first of the FOUR Motions of *Golden XPR* – the motion of FULL Response-ability. I move (that's my "motion") to listen to the voice of madness and feel the angst of not having what I want. The more I hear and understand my conflict as being my choice, the more I begin to see an alignment between my words and my results.

Surely, when the results of my communication match my vision, I'm telling the truth. If, for example, I say that I want a job and find a job, I'm being real. But when there's a misalignment between what I say I want and what I have in reality, there are a few unconscious intentions in my space. Bottom line: I am lying. I'm a chilD; not a Leader.

Taking the same example, the Leader would say: 'I thought I wanted a job, but the results of my communication show me that I do not. To come back to Truth, I just need to change my story to "I don't want a job."' IT CAN BE THAT EASY! The same applies to being miserable, sick, fat, poor, lonely, rejected, old, not enough. If it is my experience, it is TRULY what I want to experience. I simply need to stop lying about what I desire. Doing so, I will suddenly bypass any coveting and/or envying. This process of taking FULL Responsibility for my creations will allow the Cain in me to rest in peace and wake in joy. What a relief!

The LOVE Stages of a Butterfly

> "There is nothing in a caterpillar that tells you it's going to be a butterfly." *R. Buckminster Fuller*

To be IN-LOVE – a butterfly, I must be willing to consciously go counterclockwise. This is a necessary move for me to EVOLve, and come to the end of my exploring, when I know "true East" for the first time. I feel myself transformed, as mind and body are newly connecting.

Yod (י)	Vav Heh (וה)	Heh (ה)
Fire	Air / Earth	Water
South	East / West	North
L of Leader	E of Engineer / O of Officer	V of Visionary

When in a DREaM, I haven't "EVOLved" enough to know that I am LOVE:

- E is for the Engineer whose actualization I delay by turning into a **prostitutE**. This is when I doubt myself (and others, same) →
- V is for the Visionary whose actualization I delay by turning into a **saboteuR**. This is when I betray myself (and others, same) →
- O is for the Officer whose actualization I delay by turning into a **victiM**. This is when I defend/attack myself (and others, same) →
- L is for the Leader whose actualization I delay by turning into a **chilD**. This is when I blame myself (and others, same), and on again.

Transcending Mammon

> "Oppressed people cannot remain oppressed forever. The yearning for freedom eventually manifests itself." *Martin Luther King, Jr.*

To live in Scare City as a slave to Mammon – meaning to "money" and "yearning" – may just be the worst oppression of all. Yes, I do want freedom, a freedom which registers in my mind as financial. I imagine that, having lots of money would allow me to travel and exit the Ego-Egypt of my poverty mind. This is the mind I learned from watching the Power games my parents played, through their use and misuse of money and sex. So yes, while yearning for money, sex and/or companionship, I am not conscious of the prostitutE archetype who's leading the show.

The question remains: why would the my prostitutE's mind be split regarding securing his or her livelihood? What is so hard about not compromising my integrity as I cash my paycheck? Why do I lie (if only to myself) about what I need in order to take care of me at any given point? The answer is simple. Belial – the devil of "low self-esteem" – got to me. Belial is how I don't believe in me and actually don't buy me. I doubt my value, and feel unworthy. This is how I try so hard to prove myself to you... If I give you what I *think* you want, will you love me?

I forget that I'm not a mind-reader. How can I know what you want? I do well enough if I can name what I want, and ask for it in such a way that I stand a fair chance of receiving it. Meanwhile, I lie to myself all the time about my desires. I won't give me permission, and forbid myself from speaking my voice. And as I lie in order to please you, I automatically lose any and all credibility with myself. That's why I don't buy me. It is also why I am plagued with all sorts of ambivalences, especially about sex and money. A part of me wants a job, the other prohibits it. Imagine... What if I were happy, fulfilled and free? Oyveh! God forbid I'd actually come into freedom, and no longer give my Power to Mammon... That would actually be "financial freedom!"

If only I could allow me to want what I want, I would open to both play and pleasure. Life would be fun... When about to close a deal, I could take it or leave it as I'd feel that it's not higher or lower to want money or sex. It is just what it is. The fun part is finding someone that is willing to give me what I want to receive. That's right livelihood, or better, "PAIRfect" livelihood. Again, whether a client or a boss, that person is NOT a mind-reader. I will have to express my true desire, and then let it go.

Doing so is transcending the "I am not enough" belief. It is to have confidence that, if I ask, it will be given. When the question is clear (no other agenda but what's there), I witness the sunset of the prostitutE and the birth of the sacred prostitute, a character who asks what is being asked because that's what is being asked; no more, no less.

It all makes sense now:

1. I start in the **East** of a SCARED prostitutE, having glimpses of being SACRED.

2. Meanwhile, I'm stuck in the false **North** of a saboteuR in putrefaction.
3. To inhabit the **West** of a victiM in purification and come to purity, I must stretch to the next level.
4. This stretch is how to open in the **South** to a chilD's awakening.

In case I forgot, awakening is to take ownership and be fully responseable for what I desire. That's the grown-up thing to do. It makes a Leader out of me. I can then do *Teshuvah*, and literally "turn around." I now revisit the West, where my victiM turns into an Officer who has no issues cleaning up what may be left to be cleaned up. When I newly arrive in the North, I can now feel it as my true North.

True North: when I tell the truth, there is an instantaneous alignment between what I create and what I manifest. Said differently, there is no more lapse between my words and my actions. My heart is coherent (and no longer a broken heart of an enemy) and my mind is congruent (and no longer the split mind of an addict). At last, my saboteuR fulfills the 20/20 vision of the soul, doing NO harm. I am so clearly connected to the "I" places – heart, body and soul that I experience a mind which is beautiful as its creativity is unleashed for the good of all.

Noon Sun	Sunset / Dawn	Black Sun
Yellow chilD	Red prostitutE / White victiM	Black saboteuR
Awaken	Transcend / Purify	Putrefy
"I will"	"I know" / "I have"	"I desire"

The Return of the *Adam Qadmon*

Indeed, "**I know**" my sacred prostitute when I arrive in the *Qedem* or "East" of Eden since I am returned to being *Adam Qadmon* or "primary" about what "**I desire**" and what "**I will**" into being. Not compromising my integrity is how "**I have**" all I want, as I want all "**I have**." The astrological wheel of my fixed signs has reversed its way, allowing me to center in the core of being blessed and a blessing to all.

It was just a matter of feeling the wish that was rotting into shame (where I sent it), and giving myself the permission to want what I want, until I could either have it or let go of desiring it.

Understanding the DREaM

Prepare to DIE! Inquiry tool: www.goldenxpr.com/tco3_the_dream/

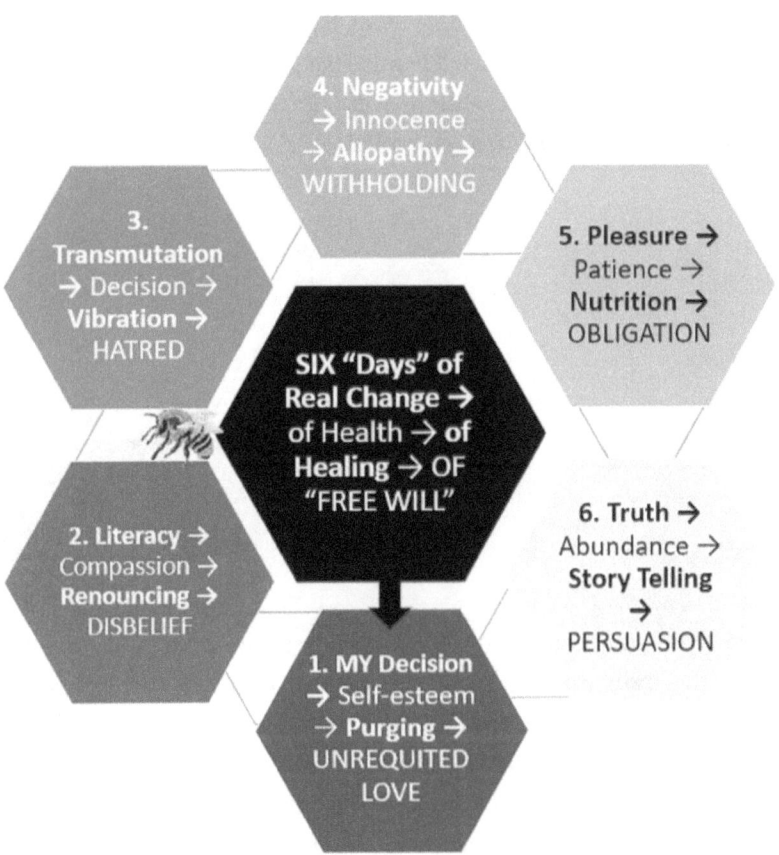

Step 1: I fill in the blank: I want to know WHY I would choose to think I CAN'T _____ (e.g.; find a job, be patient, etc.). **Step 2:** I ask for truth and generate a number. **Step 3:** I find my number on the map and fill in the brackets: when I identify to the [**Archetypes in a DREaM**], I resist feeling [**Resistance**] and soon tell the story of [**MY Story**]. What I really want (and don't want) is to know what is behind my asking [**MY QUESTION**]. **Step 4:** What most surprised me in this process was [_____].

Being Blessed

'So *Elohim* (the Power of Synchronicity) created the Leviathan and every living thing that scurries and swarms in the water, and every sort of bird—each producing offspring of the same kind. And *Elohim* saw that it was good. Then *Elohim* blessed them, saying, "Be fruitful and multiply. Let the fish fill the seas, and let the birds multiply on the earth."' *Genesis 1:20-22*

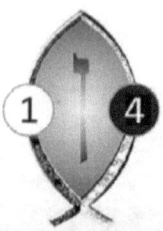

2. The Behemah	3. The Adam / 4. Adamah	1. The Leviathan
I	IT / ITS	WE
Child	Prostitute / Victim	Saboteur
Reaction, no Response	Revenge, no Forgiveness	Hunger, no Purity

To bless you is to bestow well-being or prosperity onto you. It involves the I of the individual and the WE of the collective. That particular motion is generating a double helix of an emergent cyclical adult biocycle social system moving me from the internal to the external, back and forth. It produces stimuli for me to wake up and emerge as I work cyclically with poles, magnetic to electric – self to others. Poles are independent: one pole can't force the other to behave.

Therefore, it is only when I give up my illusion of control (and my attempts to create in your reality) that I will see an alignment between what I say I want and what I have. I am now ready to meet two "God" Names: *El Gibor* as the Power of choice and *Elohim* as the Power of Synchronicity. To know these Powers, I must choose to take full responsibility for the synchronicities I experience, and especially for the **hunger**, the **reactions**, and the **revenge** as shadow patterns that are likely to show up. The invitation is to view these patterns as what I really want (which may not be the same as what I say I want). Eventually, I become so sincere in desiring them and in receiving them that I can open to a new script – a script that lines up the light I say I want and the light I have. Indeed, "let there be light..."

Compassionately partnering with and feeling "my" darkness is how to befriend the **Leviathan** and the **Behemah** in order to find my grounding in the body of my **Adamah**. This is how to choose the blessing over the curse, and this birth over ritually killing my potential.

Sooo... I – and potentially WE – have work to do in waking up from the DREaM! The next chapter will position us in the East, as we inquire on patterns of prostitution.

TWO

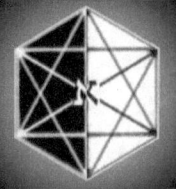

The prostitutE - Health with a big "H"

"He who has once deviated from the truth, usually commits perjury with as little scruple as he would tell a lie." Marcus Tullius Cicero

THIS CHAPTER – HEALTH WITH A BIG "H" – is a chapter I will likely read and reread. It is where I will learn how to be guided by divine instruction to best use my creative Power. When I meet the prostitutE in "her" nakedness, I see beyond the tricks. I know why I once chose lack and disease, and not Health with a big "H." It was simple: I didn't want to accept that, like it or not, I am free. Instead, I believed I was for sale. The realization that oppression and bondage are of my own choosing (since I exist in a state of absolute freedom) was too much for me. In a way, living in Scare City was easier than being fully responsible for my creation. My residing in fear will continue until I come to the *Rubedo* or red stage – the sunset of my journey, when my mind shifts from being split to being beautiful. The former mind echoes the "SIN of God" while the latter shines as the "SUN of God." This last stage is the alchemy of transcendence that allows me to be or not to be. Although it is the last stage, it is the first chapter.

IN THE FIRST CHAPTER IS THE END OF DISSATISFACTION, WHEN I CAN CHOOSE PEACE, AND REST WHILE WORKING.

The *Rubedo* Stage of Transcendence – when the red prostitutE reveals to be an Engineer

How bizarre that I would begin with transcendence, an alchemical stage that can only be experienced in the END. Similarly, for the end "E" of the prostitutE to turn around and transform into the beginning "E" of the Engineer, I must heal my mind and reconcile its two antagonized sides.

I find that my life is organized around fears. I worry that I won't get what I want or you'll take my stuff from me. Will I be able to provide for myself? I am so consumed with the "I am the body" thought that I lose peace in the name of survival. This condition is worsened by the collective unconscious that never resolved its conflicting beliefs about God, money, and financial abundance.

For me to stop the constant calculating, I would have to transcend my fear of Power and move from vulnerability to invincibility. To dare to ask for what I want while simultaneously holding my boundaries of what I will do and won't do to succeed, I must stretch to the level that is above the problem – to the sacred. Such is the invitation of the prostitutE – TO TRANSCEND by reordering the letters of "scared" into "sacred." This is when Health with a big "H" includes wealth.

The First and the Last Stage: the prostitutE's Transcendence

Prepare to DIE! Inquiry tool: www.goldenxpr.com/tc03_transcendence/

Step 1: I fill in the blank: I want to know WHY I would choose to think I CAN'T _____ (e.g.; find a job, be patient, etc.). **Step 2:** I ask for truth and generate a number. **Step 3:** I find my number on the map and fill in the brackets: having made money my master, I invited [**Prostitution**], became a slave to [**Deadly Greed**], and fell into the pit of [**Dark Passion**]. However, by letting the [**Dark Passion**] get really dark, I could, at last, come to [**Transcendence**]. **Step 4:** what most surprised me in this process was [_____].

FREE falling into Health

"I've spent my whole life scared, frightened of things that could happen, might happen, might not happen; 50 years, I spent like that, finding myself awake at 3 in the morning... But you know what? Since my diagnosis, I sleep just fine. And I came to realize that it's fear that's the worst of it. Fear is the real enemy." Vince Gilligan, Breaking Bad – American crime drama TV series.

There's a before the Holy Accident (the one waking me up) and an after the Holy Accident. Before, when I thought of the freedom to choose, I generally imagined having the capacity to decide between an alternate course of action. It didn't even matter what the options were, as long as I could genuinely choose between door a or door b. This illusion of choice goes until the Holy Tower of Destruction strikes.

This stage comes without any warning. It can show up as a divorce, a bankruptcy, an illness – a major conflict. I have no time to even think or do anything about it. Truth has stricken and nothing will ever be the same. **It efficiently nullifies my resistance by stripping away my Power of decision.** I can no longer postpone change, as time stopped at the speed of light. It is the sudden flash of revelation that demolishes my façade, and ignites the core with a new spark. The door has now dramatically opened for me to be FREE to have nothing left to lose.

Indeed, the built-in solidity of materialistic thought-forms and ensuing attachments must be knocked down to the ground in order to leave me open to the *mystery* – a word coming from Greek *mystēs* "someone who has been initiated" and also from *myein* for the capability "to close, shut" their mouth and be mute. This ties to the fourth word of the Magus: to keep silent. **As long as I am bound to the material world, I will be compelled to speak in order to sell me to you. This is how the complement of prostitution is "FREE speech," when my speech is no longer intoxicated by a verbosity that acts as a smokescreen for my** greed. Surely, the kind of salability that is behind my looming deflections must be crushed for me to stop lying.

The Fourth Word of the Magus

> "To attain the Sanctum Regnum, in other words, the knowledge and power of the magi, there are four indispensable conditions: an intelligence illuminated by study, an intrepidity which nothing can check, a will which cannot be broken, and a prudence which nothing can corrupt and nothing intoxicate. To know, to dare, to will, to keep silence – such are the four words of the magus, inscribed upon the four symbolical forms of the sphinx." *Eliphas Lévi*

The fourth word of the magus invites keeping silence. Indeed, silence is gold. Consider: while the activation of the third eye chakra opens the eye which was closed, the activation of the mouth chakra closes the mouth which opened to deceive. Such quickening is the essence of the Tower of Destruction, a tarot which means to illustrate the esoteric attributions of sign *Peh* – the word for "mouth." Indeed, what will it take for me to know, to dare, and to will to keep silent?

To best explain it, an image comes to mind – this of being about to jump off an airplane. Just as I jump, I simultaneously hope that my parachute will open and fear that it might not. Imagine now that I push the button, and that my parachute does not open... My holy "Tower of Destruction" moment has come. Finally, I have no more choice. This is to say: I no longer *think* I have a choice! Not only did this incident complete any possible debate on whether or not I have free will, but it also eliminated my fear of death and of living.

Finally, I can relax and be free – free of fear; free fallin' (if only for a few moments). I died to the illusion that I have time, and came into mastery. My affairs are in order. This means no more clutter; no more lies, no more wavering between door a or b. As the choice of Health is made for me, I now ready for how truth will change my life.

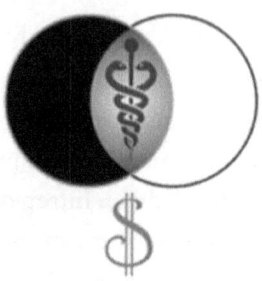

When the caduceus heals the snake of money...

TCO's mission is to heal my relationship to Power, and therefore, to money. It does so via the SIX honeyed gifts of *Golden XPR* (see *TCO—Book 2, Speaking Truth to Power*). These gifts encourage me to become honest, which may be THE most difficult thing to do, when I "Mammon-yearn" for Power, Prestige and/or Prosperity.

One of the SIX gifts is wrapped in codes awesome enough to inspire my prostitutE to move out of Scare City. I'm about to witness codes that elucidate the SIX "days" of prostitution – the most crucial of them being code **Scare City**, code **Impostorship** and code **Anarchy**. These codes combine to invite the Holy Accident by which to be free (not for sale) and **FREE Fallin'**. The process completes in the synergy of code **Mastery** and code **Health**.

All together, these codes are humbling as they only use eight S/Hebrew signs, signs which are transliterated as the letters **WEDMTAYN**:

- The **WE** pair spells out the neurotic part of YE-WE.
- The **DMT** triad populates the room of 444-Resisting.
- The **ANY/AYN** triplets for "me, myself and I" / "nothingness" allow me to know that it's not about me.

Imagine... If I were to understand my neurosis, I would stop resisting reality or "God." And as I would resonate with "nothing personal," I would come into transcendence!

Part I: The Prostitute's Gift of Gab

- The Gift of Gab
- Prostitution vs. FREE Speech
- From Sickening Doubt to Faith Healing
- The prostitutE's Psychic Logos
- Code Scare City – MM / NWN (Revisited)
- THE END Codes
- The DREaM of Loss
- Code Impostorship – DM / AD / MAD
- Seeing Red
- Code Tribal Suicide – BL / OY
- The END of Indebtedness
- Regression and the Missing Vav
- Code Regression – OG / GO
- Looking Back at Amaleq
- Code Disenchantment – OMLQ / MOQL
- Disenchantment or "Being Without a Song"
- Code Anarchy – AMN / NAM
- Sacred Rest and Transcendence

Yod (י)	Vav (ו) / Heh (ה)	Heh (ה)
[Broken] Heart	[Split] Mind / [Pain] Body	[Lost] Soul
Yellow chilD	Red prostitutE / White victiM	Black saboteuR
Citrinitas	Rubedo / Albedo	Nigredo
Awaken	Transcend / Purify	Putrefy

The *Rubedo* "Red" of Transcendence

The Gift of Gab

> "This is not a sexist issue. It is not even a gender issue. It is a human issue. I am coming out from under patriarchy to speak not as a woman but as a human being, even as men must come out from under patriarchy to speak not as men but as human beings." *Marion Woodman, The Ravaged Bridegroom*

The measure to which I tell a good story (with pauses, and all) is the measure to where I can sell something people want and become someone people need. Therefore, to successfully sell, my prostitute must primarily have the gift of gab. In ancient cultures, courtesans were known to speak many languages – least of which the languages of love. Besides being great conversationalists, they were also artists, musicians, poets, dancers: their expression had no bounds!

Telling the story reaches the ultimate in the character known as Scheherazade – the heroine of *The Arabian Nights*. Once upon a time was a sultan named Shahriyar. Betrayed by his wife, the sultan ordered to put her to death. A decree was soon issued stating that he would take a new wife each night and have her executed the next morning.

For three years the sultan's cruel order was carried out. Concerned by the political situation of the kingdom, the daughter of the Grand Vizier, Scheherazade conceived a plan to bring back peace. She asked her father to present her to Shahriyar as his next bride. Although pleased with Scheherazade's beauty and wit, the sultan was not going to spare her the fate of his previous wives. This was without counting on Scheherazade's plan to have her sister beg for a last story.

The new sultana was such a good storyteller that the sultan started to listen.

Thus began the first of a thousand and one tales narrated in *The Arabian Nights*. Scheherazade conjured her best skills to leave Shahriyar in suspense each night. The plan worked. Shahriyar was so intrigued that he decided to let his wife live for another night and another night and another, during which time Scheherazade bore the sultan three beautiful sons. Aware of her wisdom and wifely devotion, he finally revoked his vengeful decree. Peace and love returned in the kingdom and the couple continued to live happily ever after.

Speaking wards off death! This is the message, and it is profound. And yet, how free is the speech of a voice that emanates from a throat silenced and strangled for eons?

Prostitution vs. FREE Speech

Prepare to DIE! Inquiry tool: www.goldenxpr.com/tco3_prostitution/

Step 1: I fill in the blank: I want to know WHY I would choose to think I CAN'T _____ (e.g.; find a job, be patient, etc.). **Step 2:** I ask for truth and generate a number. **Step 3:** I find my number on the map and fill in the brackets: having made money my master, I identify to [**Ignorance**] and invited [**Prostitution**] in my life. And this is how I can't find my voice, as I won't receive the gift of [**FREE SPEECH**]. **Step 4:** what most surprised me in this process was [_____].

From Sickening Doubt to Faith Healing

"Daughter," said Jesus, "your faith has healed you. Go in peace and be free of suffering." *Mark 5:34*

There is a natural intelligence that keeps the planets revolving around the sun, follows winter into spring and leads the embryo to become a baby. This power which made the body also heals the body. The innate intelligence that gives life, keeps my heart beating, runs through the autonomic nervous system, digests my food, is the healer. **I just need to get out of the way to let it do its work.** Such acceptance is an act of faith. It is the foundation of what contemporary medicine calls the "placebo effect." For the body to heal, it must be free of the mind that tyrannizes it – free of the affliction that I use to harm me. When I change my mind about what I perceive I desire, I change the signals that are guiding the cells to adjust their function. Instead of toxic thoughts that produce toxic chemicals, I now have vital thoughts that produce vital chemicals.

So, why is healing a mystery? It is because, while doctors have now replaced shamans, healing still requires that I'd connect to my inner shaman who can look into my soul to see why I have lost faith.

The shadow of a doubt can and does damage my faith. Doubt attacks the mind, when I am lonely, angry, tired. It splits it, leading me to having no real sense of worth, and as a result, to prostitute my gifts. I find it most extraordinary that, even though I hear and entertain a meme as potent as "you create your reality," even though I have a plethora of new/ancient healing modalities available to me such as acupuncture or essential oils, even though I am committed to exercising and clean eating, and even though I am living in the information age where I can access marvels of technology such as imaging what takes place in my brain, in spite of all these gifts, I still don't understand that the journey of becoming real is not psychological or scientific, but mystical. Ultimately, healing is the result of surrendering which is a mystical act which is the goal of religion and yet, goes beyond it. It is a moment of truth between me and "God" when the judgments of my mind – its fears – are transcended.

To heal, I must open to a cosmic power consumed with divine intention. This is what is required to return me to wholeness, especially when my case seems hopeless.

But if my mind remains split by my ambivalences (just as the prostitutE's mind is), I will not be successful in healing or transforming myself. Not only won't I progress much, but I will even regress. To succeed, I would need to address the issue in the appropriate realm. To meet the mystical challenge that my dis/ease presents, I would also need to restore the logos of the psyche ("psychology") in such a way that I could feel the words and see the symbols cellularly.

The prostitutE's Psychic Logos

"You should utter words as though heaven were opened within them and as though you did not put the word into your mouth, but as though you entered into the word." Martin Buber

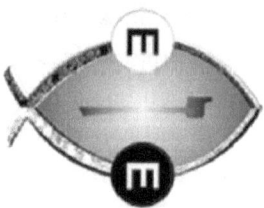

The SIX "Days" and Psychic Logos of Prostitution

I move from my voice sounding like a screech as I am trapped in **Scare City** to the **Impostorship** of a split mind to the **Tribal Suicide** of a lost soul to the **Regression** of a body in pain to the **Disenchantment** of a broken heart to the **Failure** of a forsaken spirit. To "enter" these words, I will now decode the S/Hebrew behind them.

Code Scare City - MM / NWN (Revisited)

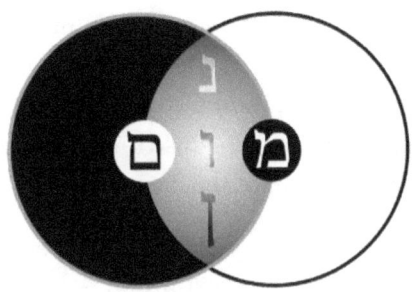

Imagine a language so pure and so sacred that it can reconcile opposites in five letters of <u>two fully spelled-out signs</u>...

Right: Hebrew letter Mem (מ) regular → M in Roman script
Left: Hebrew letter Mem (ם) final → M in Roman script
Top: Hebrew letter Nun (נ) regular → N in Roman script
Bottom: Hebrew letter Nun (ן) final → N in Roman script
Core: Hebrew letter Vav (ו) → F, U, V, W in Roman script

Here is how S/Hebrew inscribes code "Scare City" in 2 spelled-out signs whose 5 letters regroup into 5 words:

- **MM:** from right to left, I read the name of letter Mem (םמ) for "pairs of water."
- **NWN:** from top to middle to bottom, I read the name of letter Nun (נון) for "fish, fallen."
- **NWM:** from top to middle to left, I read *Num* (נום) for "slumber, sleep."
- **MWM:** from right to middle to left, I read *Mum* (מום) for "flaw, defect."

- **MMWN:** from right to left to middle to bottom, I read *Mammon* (ממון) for "money, yearning."

The Decoding: as a quick reminder, the S/Hebrew signs are at once a glyph, a sound, a number, and a word. Both signs, Mem and Nun, are part of a group of five letters that can take on a regular form, e.g.; regular Mem (מ), and a final form when at the end of a word, e.g.; final Mem (ם). The rabbinical tradition also holds that the five final letters will someday be explained as being instrumental to redemption, i.e.; to "the end" of mind. Keeping all of this in mind, I am now ready to enter the decoding.

Scare City – the first "day" of prostitution – begins when my **Mem** "pairs of waters" are split: "And God made a firmament which divided the waters which were under it from the waters which were above it: and it was so." *Genesis 1:7.* This day of creation speaks of the mind split by duality, when a part of me knows what to do and the other part doesn't want to do it. If divided for too long, I'll start identifying to being **"fallen,"** damaged goods, not enough. To be a fisher of men, I must first help the "fish" in me to recognize that its deep dive is supported. On that note, the English word "firmament" comes from Latin *firmāmentum* for the "prop, support" that makes me *firm*.

As for S/Hebrew *Samekh* for "support," I will see in Part III how this is a letter and a word that expands the letters Mem and Nun of this code – code Scarcity. The cellular knowing that I am supported allows me to transcend my fear of falling. However, while I think that I am the doer of the deed (how could I fall and fail again?), I don't feel supported in my creativity. I am in fact in such a DREaM of separation and in such a deep **slumber** that I can only see the errors of my ways and my many **defects**. Thinking that I'm **flawed**, I identify to the have-nots, yearn for what I can't have and fear the energy of **money**. I must now compromise, just to pay the bills!

Money can be thought of in terms of Power, and Power, in terms of money. As I make a decision, I either increase or decrease my capital.

When under Mammon's spell, I have no sense of worth. Secretly feeling like a loser and fearing the consequences of my decisions, I bury myself in other people. I let them decide for me. And when I don't like the results of their investments, I'll blame them for my losses. Moreover, I have no real sense of boundaries. My yeses and my nos are yet to be honest. I fear that, if I were telling you the truth, you'd reject me. And if you were to reject me, where would my money come from? The belief that there's an "out there" out there – a "you" in contrast to "me" – is how I hurt myself. It is how I serve two masters, giving my allegiance to materialism while "trying" to honor my Spirit.

Once again, evolution and waking up are all about Power, the greatest of which being the Power to choose peace, since being at peace is the optimal state to make any decision. Having this Power is contingent on me finding the PaRaDiSe I lost. But did I actually lose it or am I in a DREaM?

THE END Codes

> "And when Abraham our father, may he rest in peace, looked, saw, understood, probed, engraved and carved, he was successful in creation." *Sepher Yetzirah*

As previously mentioned, code Scarcity plays with the letters **MMWN**. It is part of the synergy of codes showing a path from Scare City into Health. Again, this path only uses different permutations of the eight letters **WEDMTAYN**. Why do letters and why does the IT/ITS of symbolic Power matter?

The deliverable of *Golden XPR* is the sense of enough. To restore this sense, XPR uses SIX honeyed gifts, one of them being codes that are awe-provoking. Similarly, the goal of *Sepher Yetzirah* may just be to open a mental space where I can move from taking failure personally into being successful in my creation, as I feel and know that the work is done through me and not by me (nothing personal). This is also when I move from Scare City into **Mastery**, and from Mastery into Health with a big "H."

Here is the full quote from *Sepher Yetzirah*. It is written in the "I" perspective for me to own it: "and when [my name], may I rest in peace, looked, saw, understood, inquired, wrote and spoke, I was successful in creation, as it is written […]. Immediately the **Mastery** of all was revealed to me, may ITS name be blessed forever. IT placed me in ITS bosom, kissed me on the head, and IT called me, "[my name] my Beloved." IT made a covenant with me and with my children after me forever, as it is written, "and I had faith in LOVE, and LOVE counted it as my giving it all." IT made with me a covenant between the ten fingers of my hands (this is the covenant of the tongue), and between the ten toes of my feet (this is the covenant of phallus). IT bound the 22 letters of the Torah to my tongue and He revealed to me ITS mystery. IT pledged them in Water, IT flamed them with Fire, IT vibrated them in Air. IT burned them with the Seven, and drove them with the twelve constellations.' *Sepher Yetzirah, 6:7, THE END.*

Consider: when the esoteric (or hidden) becomes exoteric (or revealed), I know Health as Honesty with a big "H" as I have no more secrets to sicken me.

The DREaM of Loss

> "Money is only a tool. It will take you wherever you wish, but it will not replace you as the driver." *Ayn Rand*

Money is a fact of life. Even if I choose to adopt the lifestyle of a bum, mostly, I cannot be on earth without it. But I fear money's energy and made it into a monster. I'm afraid that someone will take the money I have or will not give me the money I want. Truly, how much authority does money have over me? Can I manage it? Do I know how to save it? Do I need to find someone to take care of me? How deep will I need to go into the unconscious to not be in bondage to the material world?

I hear "build it, and they will come!" But I abort my creative project as I'm afraid that my creativity won't be supported. I say I know what I would do if I had all the money in the world, but since I don't have it, I won't do it! And in the space where I can't receive the Voice, I lack inspiration. I am lonely. I am blocked. It is clear: to fulfill my potential, I must let go of Mammon. What will it take for me not to sell out? Will I ever stop making excuses for not being big enough to follow my calling? Sadness is the resisted experience of my prostitutE. I resist the sorrow of giving my Power away to money and turning it into a force that controls me. For the sake of money, I let myself be led into temptation, causing results I would rather not have to witness. When I do, I am dissatisfied with myself. The DREaM types work as a team to allow me to go deep into the darkness in order to retrieve the light information from the unconscious. Once informed, I'll understand why I was asleep for so long.

It is true that everyone has a price. I hate it that I could be bought, and even worse, that my price tag would be so low. So yes, I fail time and again the test laid out by the heavens for me. I say I want the ice-cream of spiritual evolution with lots of cherry-Power on top, but I lose my integrity and honor by behaving as a loser. Not only do I negotiate my Power, but also, I keep on inviting financial bondage in the way I partner. Even when the relationship is not working, I'll stay and let them control me by way of money. My fear of survival is so overwhelming that I will sell my vision in exchange for security. Moreover, I doubt that fulfilling the vision of my soul (my law) will free me of fear. I am so tied to materialism that this spiritual possibility seems too surreal for me to trust it! I also ignore that fulfillment naturally merges into freedom, and that the loss of freedom is what my prostitutE grieves.

When I am yet to stabilize on the pillar of individual Power, I will go into tribal suicide and agree with the collective telling me that I must do a number of things in order to have money. I must have a business plan that supports my vision, promissory notes and the likes. Following my heart's counsel as all that is necessary is deemed as ridiculous. And yet... The very fact that my guidance is crazy is the best proof that I'm onto something. Will I trust "God" to give me wood after I am ordered to build an ark? Do I realize that the choice not to follow the Voice cancels out *Elohim's* Power of synchronicity? In fact, it enforces Mammon's gradual creation.

Yes, but! How will I pay the mortgage or the kids' college tuition? I am unable to reconcile the fact that there is a force that I can tap into to pay my debts – a force that can both wipe out obstacles or create them. I am just not fluid or liquid enough (speaking of cash) to transcend my self-imposed limitations. Moreover, I will deny the significance of the lingo of finances lining up with the lingo of the soul. Thus, I never aim for my own "redemption" that at once saves me and clears my debts.

Code Impostorship - DM / AD / MAD

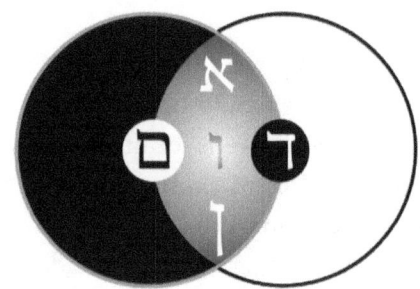

Imagine a language so pure and so sacred that it can reconcile opposites in just five letters...

Top: Hebrew letter Aleph (א) → A in Roman script
Right: Hebrew letter Dalet (ד) → D in Roman script
Middle: Hebrew letter Vav (ו) → F, U, V, W in Roman script
Left: Hebrew letter Mem final (ם) → M in Roman script
Bottom: Hebrew letter Nun final (ן) → N in Roman script

Here is how S/Hebrew inscribes code "Red" in 5 letters, 5 words:

- **DM:** from right to left, I read *Dam* (דם) for "blood."

- **ADM:** top to right to left, I read *Adam* (אדם) for "Adam" (created male & female).
- **ADWM:** top to right to middle to left, I read *Edom* (אדום) for "red."
- **MAD:** left to top to right, I read *Mehod* (מאד) for "very, exceedingly."
- **DWM:** right to middle to left, I read *Doom* (דום) for "stand still, be silent."
- **ADWN:** top to right to middle to bottom, I read *Adon* (אדון) for "Lord."

The Decoding: code **Impostorship** (the prostitutE's color) is a flag to my impostorship, which is also "day" 2 of prostitution. It involves the story of Jacob, the archetypal fraud who stole the right of the firstborn from his twin brother Esau. While the mind is symbolically represented by the face of the Son, the split mind is signified by twin brothers. The Son in the YEWE family is invoked by the letter Vav (W). Vav is the digit and finger #6 that can take me so deep into the illusion of separation from my heart's desire that I must be reminded not to kill. Incidentally, the Word that prompts the Sixth Commandment ("Thou Shalt Not Kill") is also the letter Vav. Once added to the **Adam**, this letter Vav inscribes code **Impostorship** – a warning of imminent danger. 'And Esau said to Jacob: "please feed me with that same **red** [stew], for I am weary." Therefore, his name was called **Edom**.' *Genesis 25:30*. It is poignant that I would resist surrendering my will so much that it will take a painful addiction to wake me up from the DREaM. For only then can I know in my **blood** that I am LOVE. When saying: "give me the **red**" (the word "stew" was added by the translator), I just want my fix. I am an impostor, refusing to know how the Mammon yearning owns me – how it is my **Lord**.

If only Esau/Edom had been able to go to an AA meeting, he might have heard that HALT means "**stand still**; don't say or do anything when you're Hungry, Angry, Lonely, Tired. For if you do speak or act, you are likely to compromise your integrity." Integrity is the path to take to be able to look at everything I have done in a given day – or a given SIX days :-) – "and, behold, see that it was **very** good."

If the DREaM world traces the alchemical path of the sun, moving me from the black sun of the saboteuR to the white dawn of the victiM to the yellow noon sun of the chilD and finally to the red sunset of the prostitutE (and "her" **red** district), it is for me to make the choice to strive to acquire self-knowledge, and come to the center of my integrity. For only then, will I be able to feel the fear of dying to who I think I am (an addict), and let go of my illusion of control. I will then move into the red sunset of transcendence where I started and know the place for the first time. Reading the "THE END" on the screen of reality, I will receive the sense of enough.

As previously mentioned, code **Impostorship** is part of a synergy of codes showing a path from Scare City into Health. Again, this path only uses different permutations of the eight letters **WEDMTAYN** (in this case, the letters **ADWN**) in order to inspire such awe that I'd surrender and do what it takes to be successful in my creation.

Seeing Red

"When in doubt, wear red!" Bill Blass, Fashion Designer

What my archetypal prostitute resists feeling is the unbearable sadness not to be free to experience right livelihood. Instead, I compromise my voice which is how I tie me down to "the oldest profession" there is. I've placed a gag on my own mouth from doubting that I had anything of real value to offer. "My gifts are needless; no one really wants me!" This is how Cain is reluctant to give: he fears rejection so much that he stages it. Heck, as long as he can / I can control being unloved, being unloved is less painful! Such is the despaired and insane attitude that sources my anger. And vice-versa, since seeing red presents some danger of hurting others, I turn the feeling of anger upon my own self and get depressed. Doing so, I can never harness anger's energy or manage it productively. I also continue not to understand what provoked it, which means that it is now safely in auto-repeat.

Depression is more than just passing sadness. It is a diagnosed mental health disorder involving low moods combined with other symptoms such as trouble concentrating or trouble sleeping. When depressed, I'm literally like Cain: I can't rest in peace. Listen to the story now… After I was born, my mother gave birth to my brother and named him Abel. When we grew up, Abel became a shepherd, while I, Cain, cultivated the ground. When it was time for the harvest, I presented some of my crops as a gift to the LORD. Abel also brought an offering—fat portions from some of the firstborn of his flock. The LORD looked with favor on Abel and his offering, but he didn't even look at my offering. Not a glance! That made me super angry, and my face fell.

To top it all, the LORD said to me, "Why are you angry? Why the depression? Don't you know that you'll be recognized if you do good? But if you resist doing good, the sin that's crouching at your door will get you. You must master it." Yep, such is the gist of my neurotic story, as told in *Genesis 4:2-7*: I'm a slave to my cravings (my sins) instead of mastering them. This is how, although I am gifted beyond belief, I stage a rejection that makes it impossible for my gifts to be seen. Yep, I go from "no seen" to "yes sin!"

Since greed wants me when no one else does, I'll just decide to let it be my master. I'll even make a bulletproof covenant with my broken heart by forgetting that it was my decision to go into sin in the first place. And now, I have NO way to undo it! And whether I indulge lust or gluttony (to only use these two), the CAIN in me is now assured that I'll keep thinking I CAN'T. No wonder I would now need to attach to tribal suicide, and kill myself using my genes to do so… Oyveh and ouch!

Code Tribal Suicide - BL / OY

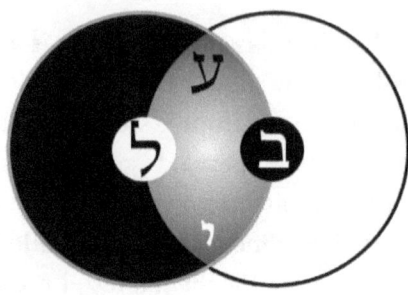

Imagine a language so pure and so sacred that it can reconcile opposites in just 2 pairs of letters...

Top: Hebrew letter Ayin (ע) → O in Roman script
Right: Hebrew letter Beth (ב) → B in Roman script
Left: Hebrew letter Lamed (ל) → L in Roman script
Bottom: Hebrew letter Yod (י) → I, J, Y in Roman script

Here is how S/Hebrew inscribes code "Tribal Suicide" in 4 letters, 4 words:

- **BLY:** from right to left to bottom, I read *Bli* (בלי) for "without."
- **YOL:** bottom to top to left, I read *Yal* (יעל) for "worth, esteem."
- **BLYOL:** right to left to bottom to top to left, I read *Belial* (בליעל) for "worthless, never to rise."
- **BOLY:** right to top to left to bottom, I read *Ba'ali* for "my owner, my master."

The Decoding: Belial is quite the character – an anti-Christ, truly. He appears 27 times in the Hebrew Bible, most frequently associating to creatures given to all sorts of wickedness, such as idolaters, sexual crime offenders, conspirators, rebels who stir up contention. Belial occupies a prominent position in the Chassidic literature which preserved angelologic and demonologic lore. In *the Book of Jubilees (i.*

20), Belial is, like Satan, the accuser and father of all idolatrous nations; the antagonist of God. In one of the Dead Sea scrolls, Belial is presented as the leader of the Sons of Darkness waging a war against the Sons of Light. To the point, the Zadokite Fragments expose the nature of the "three nets of Belial:" fornication, wealth and pollution of the sanctuary. While Belial seems to control scores of demons specifically allotted to him by God for the purpose of performing evil, he is held to be an angel.

And it makes me wonder... Belial means "**low sense of worth**," the me who has so little **self-esteem** that I'm "**never to rise**." I can also see the word *Ba'ali* (יבעל) or "**my master**" that leads me to belittle myself in *Belial*. Mammon is "my master." It is the yearning for money, sex or food – for "the other" – that keeps me caught in the nets of Belial. These three nets describe the fall of the mouth chakra until it lands in the root chakra. After the fall, the heart chakra contracts into greed, the sex chakra, into lust, and the root chakra is so polluted by gluttony that it destroys my temple.

What if my evil ways were designed specifically for me (and my mouth chakra) to touch bottom so terminally that I'd surrender my will? Rather than being hopelessly co-dependent on my tribe and making it **my master**, I would become fully responsible for living out the truth as dictated by my individual Power. The letters of Belial also include the BL/LB pairs of code Simplicity, pairs that partner to convey the entirety of the Torah's wisdom that stretches from first letter B to last letter L (see *TCO—Book 2, Understanding Knowledge*). Here is a brief recap: first, I go from B to L, refusing to listen to *Bal* (BL) – the "do not" command. When sick and tired of being sick and tired, I turn to *Lev* (LB) – my "heart." I now understand why I needed to break my own law, and fall into the pit of worthlessness by accepting to be a slave. Through my renewed willingness to love "God" or what is of the inner, I inscribe the LOVE that has no opposite, and resonate with the ethics of complementarity.

Belial's chronic abuse may just be dark enough for me to release my illusion of control, bring light onto my shame-based secrets and associated sins, and be humble enough to stop lying. Surely, that would handle the misery and its love of company! It would also bring me to "THE END" of indebtedness.

The END of Indebtedness

> "Give us this day our daily bread, and forgive us our debts, as we forgive our debtors. And lead us not into temptation, but deliver us from evil." *Excerpt from the LORD's Prayer.*

I am disturbed in my intellectual and emotional pursuit by the necessity of putting food on the table, and looking after the material needs of the body. The fear to commit tribal suicide (and separate from my community) is how I engage indebtedness. I am concerned that probing conventional assumptions as I endeavor to know who I am will cut me off from the society that sustains me. I fear peer rejection and dread the hostility borne of ignorance. I imagine that, since my family does not wish to go on a similar journey of self-discovery, they'll judge I've grown too big for my britches. My work will only do harm by making me a pariah who betrayed the tribe, losing friends and prospects in the process. And if that's the case, with whom would I engage in commerce? How then will I pay the bills?

The "forgiveness" spoken about in *Luke 11:4* and *Matthew 6:12* is derived from the Greek *aphiemi* for "to remit a debt." Whether my debt is monetary or non-monetary, the prostitutE will tell me what I can and can't do in terms of what it will cost me. The victiM will then step in with "her" agenda of retaliation, claiming her pound of flesh. In turn, this greed is how I repeatedly let myself be led into temptation. If only I could dive deep enough into the abyss (as Nun final does), I'd stop doubting that I'll have my daily bread, and would forgive my debts and my debtors. **Instead of letting the debt scare me, I would know the** faith by which to see myself breaking through debts. Lastly, I'd no longer be so tied to the tribe that I would block my own evolution.

Debt is a creation – a golem. When I make this entity larger than my capacity to dissolve it, I may ask myself how the debt serves me. Do I expect to be taken care of in return? Do I want for people to worry about me? Do I refuse to be responsible for my upkeep to continue drawing on my parents' support? I may gain a valuable insight by understanding the biblical story of Amaleq, which will soon tell me how to raise the bar...

Regression and the Missing Vav

> "Sometimes we are devils to ourselves when we will tempt the frailty of our powers, presuming on their changeful potency."
> *William Shakespeare*

I have seen time and again how dicey and yet essential the letter Vav is, a letter which begins most of the Torah's verses and is also at the core of the Nun fish. The sign's dubiousness may be how the phallus of Vav (or U sound) in the Sumerian words such as *Adamu, Sabattu* or *Shumu* was circumcised when they became *Adam, Shabbat* or *Shem* in Hebrew. Vav is literally the connector of all criminology, in that its sexual potency may incline me to desire what is not good for me. Yep, I keep mastery away by remaining a slave. As the 6th word (value 6), Vav invokes the Sixth Commandment: thou shalt not kill! It is also the sign that is present three times (the 666 mark of the beast) in the hidden dimensions of *Qain's* name, which is formed by the only three letters of the S/Hebrew alphabet that have a Vav in their midst, namely Qoph (QWP), Yod (YWD) and Nun (NWN).

Yod (י)	Vav (ו) / Heh (ה)	Heh (ה)
Will to Live	Will to Power / Meaning	Will to Pleasure
chilD	prostitutE / victiM	saboteuR

Vav and the Will to Power

Vav is the word for "nail" and the conjunction "and," both being connectors. Unless the will for Power is understood via the will for meaning, my Vav is likely to be compelled to do harm, as it will not be contained within the Sacred Feminine of the "window, womb" Heh. Since Vav is the phallus depositing the Yod seed into the Heh womb, how could "he" feel powerless to succeed in his creation?

Here is how... It is said that, after the Fall, the word *Toledot* (תולדות) "generations" lost its sign Vav, as its light was defective. Concurrent with the shrinking of sign Heh, the loss of Vav resulted in a decrease of the sense of enough – a regression. Without Vav, the *Toledot* of *Gen. 5:1* (תלדות) is no longer blessed with unbridled creativity. The gift will only be restored in *Ruth 4:18*: "these are the *Toledot* (תולדות) "generations" of Perez." The line of Perez is the link between mind and heart. Speaking of generations, legend has it that Perez is part of the ancestry of King David – the lineage from which the Messiah is to come. Just as Jacob did, Perez fought with his twin to be the firstborn. However, unlike Jacob, Perez was clear enough to win, thus the name *Perez* for "breach."

Code Regression - OG / GO

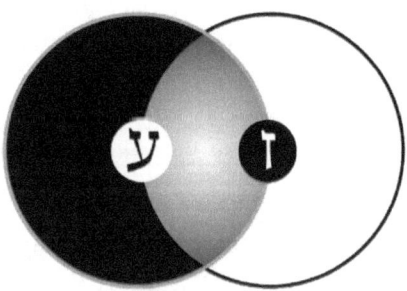

Imagine a language so pure and so sacred that it can reconcile opposites in just two letters...

Right: Hebrew letter Zayin (ז) → G in Roman script
Left: Hebrew letter Ayin (ע) → O in Roman script

Here is how S/Hebrew inscribes code "Regression" in two letters, two words:

- **OG**: in one direction, I read *Az* (עז) for "strong, fierce, powerful, greedy."
- **GO**: in the other direction, I read *Za* (זע) for "to tremble, to be in terror."

The Decoding: it's not that I can't go for what I want; it is more that I can't sustain my momentum as my will is weak. I get in my way, taking two steps forward and one step backward. I either push or pull as I'm conflicted, fearing that reaching my goal may rouse an overwhelming desire for conquest and subjugation. I have reasons to doubt me: I am relying on my own **strength**, and not on "God's" strength. I'm the sort of ego that must roll up my sleeves if I want for any work to get done. I only perceive that things happen by me, and not *through* me. This is how I won't let me be successful until I allow myself to be humbled by something greater than I. Then and only then, my dynamics of engagement will be whole, as I will have received the Zayin (value 7) and Ayin (value 70) – both letters populate the room of 7-engaging.

Meanwhile, and no matter what my flood warning may be – a disease, a divorce, a bankruptcy, a number of failures, I will one day quit on the quitting, and surrender to building my Ark, as I am instructed! Changing requires honesty and the kind of perseverance that comes from **fierce** willpower. Such willpower becomes easy and matter-of-fact when I don't try to force it upon me. I must be careful and repeatedly ask "whose will is it, anyways?" For it is only when **I tremble** in awe in front of the Mystery, willing to drop the plan and to receive my orders one moment at a time, that I'll find what makes my willpower invincible. Having befriended my **greed** for Power, I will know that I am at the "PAIRfect" place, with no need to take any regression or advancement personally.

Looking Back at Amaleq

> 'Then LOVE said to Moses, "Write this on a scroll as something to be remembered and make sure that Joshua hears it, because it will completely erase the memory of Amaleq from under heaven."'
> *Exodus 17:14*

This passage was Greek to me, until I saw that the ability to be true to my word is signified by the connection of my two hands, a link which Amaleq will try to break. Henceforth, the name Amaleq is code for doubt. S/Hebrew *Amaleq* (OMLQ), *Supheq* (XPQ) "doubt" and *El Acher* (AL AHR) "other god" all have the same numeric value (240). *El Acher* for "the other god" can also refer to whomever I give my Power.

Let's say that I decide on a goal and write it down with my own two hands for the Joshua "savior" in me to hear and SEE. This begins to erase the memory of doubt. Doubt is what splits my prostitutE's mind. It follows the hunger that prompted my fall. Indeed, I hunger to perceive that matter is not solid but liquid, a sense that would allow me to make my Exodus from a "Land" where I am slave to the number of zeroes that I have in my bank account. Yep, I'm a slave to Mammon's yearning for more, instead of being a master of my greed. This is how I can't drop the plan or stop counting! This doubt (that goodness will always follow me) is so painful that it compels me to ritually offer apologies for my neurotic existence. This is especially true when I want to reach a goal that demands some level of excellence. I start thinking that I'm not good enough to succeed, and continue by feeling and attracting "bad" until my own prophecy of doom is fulfilled! What am I missing?

I am again missing that the Son's Vav of desire must go to the Father's Yod of an open heart. When Jesus was hanging on the cross, the sun was darkened and the veil of the temple was torn down the middle. Then "Jesus called out with a loud voice, 'Father, **into your hands** I commit my spirit.' When he had said this, he breathed his last" (*Luke*

23:46). Jesus was quoting *Psalm 31:6*: "Into Your hands I commit my spirit; You have redeemed me, O LORD, God of truth." Earlier on, when possibly at the greatest point of the dream of separation, he quoted *Psalm 22:2:* "My God, my God, why hast Thou forsaken me?" The hint is in the number 222 of *Psalm 22:2* as it points to the room 222-separating. Indeed, separating from the dictates of my heart is how I allow Amaleq to discourage me...

Code Disenchantment – OMLQ / MOQL

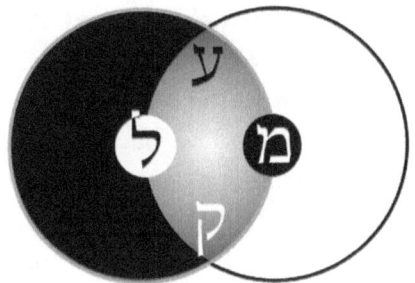

Imagine a language so pure and so sacred that it can reconcile opposites in just four letters...

Top: Hebrew letter Ayin (ע) → O in Roman script
Right: Hebrew letter Mem (מ) → M in Roman script
Left: Hebrew letter Lamed (ל) → L in Roman script
Bottom: Hebrew letter Qoph (ק) → Q in Roman script

Here is how S/Hebrew inscribes code "Disenchantment" in 4 letters, 4 words:

- **OMLQ**: top to right to left to bottom, I read *Amaleq* (עמלק) for "Amalek."
- **QL**: bottom to left, I read *Qal* (קל) for "easy, light."
- **OM**: top to right, I read *Am* (עם) for "people," and, by extension, language.

- **MOQL**: right to top to bottom to left, I read *M'uqal* (מעקל) for "bent, twisted, perverted."

The Decoding: the word "**Amaleq**" is generally mistransliterated as "Amalek," as if it was written with a letter Kaph (K) instead of a Qoph (Q). Qoph means "monkey [mind]" and also the back of the head, the place where my doubts reside. This explains how the nation of Amaleq would be described in the Torah as the staunch enemy of the Israelites: it attacks me from behind. The name Amaleq refers at once to the nation's founder, a grandson of Esau; his Amaleqite descendants, or the territories of Amaleq, which they inhabited. When looking back at the past (that is, when obsessively reading the memory of Amaleq), I am disenchanted as I confirmed the belief that I'm not good enough. This is when I tend to look for love out there (in the "other god"). Believing that I don't have what it takes and doubting that I ever will, I take the **easy** path, and join my tribal **people** in telling the story of how I was once a slave. The thing is, I am a slave, if only in the spacetime where I tell the pain story.

I miss the fact that the Amaleqites attacked at a place called Rephidim, and do not know that the word *Rephidim* is a blending for *Raphu Yadayim* for "weakened hands." And since the letter Yod for "hand" starts the writing of every letter, I can't "write my goals on a scroll as something to be remembered and make sure that Joshua (the savior part of me) hears it, because doing so will erase the memory of Amaleq from under heaven."

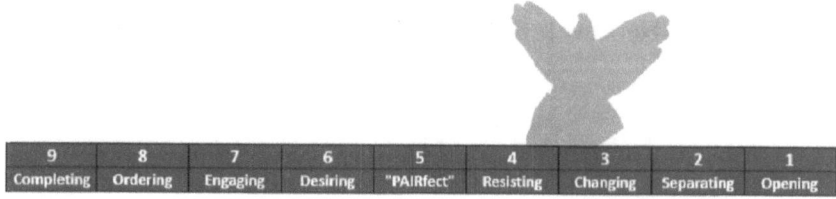

9	8	7	6	5	4	3	2	1
Completing	Ordering	Engaging	Desiring	"PAIRfect"	Resisting	Changing	Separating	Opening

The eagle perspective of "Father, **into your joined hands** I commit my spirit!"

Moreover, would it make a difference for me to erase the words "try, deserve, hope" out of my memory, since they hint to the fact that I am in service to Mammon? When serving Mammon my hands separate. They **bend, twist** and **pervert** reality so much that I don't buy me as I am riddled with doubt. This is also when I try to sell me to you and compromise my integrity. The Vav of **6-Desiring** is now on its own. Unable to see TWINS as "Thy Will Is Not Separate," I turn into a prostitutE which makes me vulnerable to attacks.

Disenchantment or "Being Without a Song"

"To do nothing is also a good remedy." *Hippocrates*

I am beginning to accept the DREaM archetypes as mighty patterns by which to hone in on my strength and enhance my spiritual evolution. They work as team, to repair the broken compass of my instincts – specifically when it comes to hunger, aggression and creativity. But when it comes to the prostitutE, I am confused as it is the archetype that comes with the worst possible reputation. It is harshly judged and rarely thought to have any value. Moreover, how could "she" be mostly associated with women and express the split mind which is a male instrument, an instrument played out by the son? Is this another instance of Adam blaming the woman for his own error?

Yod (י)	Vav (ו) / Heh (ה)	Heh (ה)
[Broken] Heart	[Split] Mind / [Pain] Body	[Lost] Soul
The Father	The Son / the Mother	The Daughter

The prostitutE's Split Mind

The prostitutE and prodigal son confront me with a single question: will I sell my integrity in order to finance someone else's creativity – his or her song? For that choice is that which splits my mind and causes me to doubt myself.

While living in Scare City, I sell my honor and negotiate my Power, my opinions, my emotions, my actions, my body in order to support "your" creativity; your voice. I may even agree to keep secret the fact that I am participating in dishonorable commerce in order to survive, e.g., poisoning the environment. Bottom line: the realization that I can be bought is life-changing. When the prostitutE's light goes on, it leads me to reassess my priorities: will I continue to worry or will I follow spiritual advise and redirect the energy to come to integrity? 'So do not worry, saying, "what shall we eat?" or "what shall we drink?" or "what shall we wear?" But seek first his kingdom and his integrity, and all these things will be given to you as well.' *Matthew 6:31, 33.*

There are no exceptions: to shift my shade of red to reflect the fire of the Leader's heart, I must expand my perception beyond the visible world. **Faith is, after all, the ability to see with the heart that which is invisible to the eye. It is to believe in the incredible, and manifest the impossible. It is to take earth and heaven as sacred witnesses against my ego of the fact that I merged the natural with the supernatural.** This is how in every scripture, before any great leaders are given to fulfill the task they were born for, they must pass a test to assess whether or not they will sell out their Power. This touches me directly. Indeed, when I have proven that there's nothing on Earth that could tempt me, the gods will shower on me a plethora of Powers, as they will know that I can and will carry out the task that they've given me. Surely, when I don't compromise my integrity to try to control the flow of my material life, the doors of the sacred open for me. Consider: freedom is having nothing left to lose.

Code Anarchy - AMN / NAM

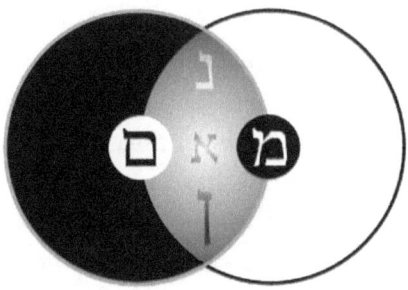

Imagine a language so pure and so sacred that it can reconcile opposites in just two fully spelled out letters...

Top: Hebrew letter Nun regular (נ) → N in Roman script
Middle: Hebrew letter Aleph (א) → A
Right: Hebrew letter Mem regular (מ) → M in Roman script
Left: Hebrew letter Mem final (ם) → M in Roman script
Bottom: Hebrew letter Nun final (ן) → N in Roman script

Note: the name of the letter Nun is fully spelled out as Nun-Vav-Nun. The name of the letter Vav inside the Nun is fully spelled out as Vav-Aleph-Vav. The Aleph in the geometry above is inside the Vav which is inside the Nun. In that sense, Vav is the vessel of *Nun* "the fish." As for Mem, it is fully spelled out by the pair Mem Mem.

Here is how S/Hebrew inscribes code "Anarchy,"

- **AMN**: middle to right to bottom, I read *Amen* (אמן) or "amen, so be it."
- **NAM**: top to middle to left, I read *Nehum* (נאם) for "utterance, revelation."
- **MAN**: right to middle to bottom, I read *Mahen* (מאן) for "to refuse."

The Decoding: code Anarchy is the same as code Scare City with one exception: the Aleph of code Anarchy replaced the letter Vav of code Scare City. Revealing the Aleph that is inside the sign Vav ushers the end of desire: no *Mammon* "yearning." Henceforth, the intention of Mammon is pure. It only seeks to lead me to feel anarchy as the most severe "day" of prostitution. *An-archy* means "without a ruler." About rulership, which do I make the head of my house: my mind or my heart? The mutiny instigated by my mind against my heart is what ruins me and makes me ill. Said symbolically, the Son (the mind) goes prodigal and won't return to the Father (the heart) until his resources are thoroughly wasted.

However, when I do turn to the heart, I know a form of leadership so compassionate that I can only inspire a sacred witness to validate my prayer with an "**Amen!**" Indeed, I may be bringing forth a gift meant to bless my community, but unless a member of such community backs it up with an "Amen," I won't receive what I prayed for. Being "without a ruler," i.e.; without a heart-centered leadership, I can't be authentic in my relating and therefore, can't gain a trust and a hearing. Instead, I transmit anarchy, since what I have in reality (my **revelations**) does not align with what I say I want (my **utterances**). Moreover, I'm can't hear the **Amen** (AMN) response nor receive its meaning as an acronym for *El Melekh Neeman* for the "God and King of Faith." Rather than being satisfied, I am as Pharaoh, **refusing** to let my limiting "people-beliefs" go.

And it makes me wonder... Am I blocking the Vav of my heart's desires because I **refuse to reveal** – if only to myself – the greed-induced secrets that are binding me to the material world? As I am yet to forgive myself, am I also wanting to make you pay for my suffering? I remember the teachings of the Gaon (money is what's "under" the law of talion). As a slave sold to Mammon, I'm in forced labor and fighting for my survival. Such constricted state of mind won't allow my Gimel/Camel to pass through the spiritual eye of the needle, since I perceive that I am not good enough to experience a full liberation from suffering. My insubordination and incumbent lawlessness help me hide the fear to die – when I come to the end and rest while working.

As previously mentioned, code **Anarchy** is part of a synergy of codes showing a path from Scare City into Health. Again, this path only uses different permutations of the eight letters **WEDMTAYN** (in this case, the letters **AMN**) in order to inspire such awe that I'd surrender and do what it takes to be successful in my creation.

Sacred Rest and Transcendence

"In God We Trust." *The official motto of the United States.*

I'd like to start shifting out of fear by owning Marianne Williamson's words: "my deepest fear is not that I am inadequate. My deepest fear is that I am powerful beyond measure." The S/Hebrew word for "measure" – *Midah* (מדה) – is the reverse of *HaDam* for "the blood." If there's a measure in the blood that takes me beyond the ego's calculations, it ought to be the sense of enough; adequacy. Enough is the golden mean between excesses and deficiencies, the point where I can be very good, choosing to be chosen without having to feel so special. Until I sense the energy of "enough" circulating in my veins, I will believe that I am inferior, go into fear and violate my own word.

It is likely that every act of dishonesty I ever committed originated in swinging back and forth from "I'm special" to "I'm not enough." To release me from being in bondage to Mammon-money, I must stop lying. When I can be honest about my dishonesty, I shift from scared to sacred.

Honesty is not for the faint of heart. Admitting that I want money (which is not higher or lower than *not* wanting money), or admitting that I don't want to pay the price to have what I say I want is a tall order. So, I stay confused and postpone deciding to do what it takes. I'm angry at "God," and use the wound to derive undue privileges. Staying in fear allows me not to hear my intuition. When I choose not to follow the order of my command center (my 3rd eye) because I fear failing and falling, I CAN'T wait. Instead, I compulsively create unconscious time, which stops me from knowing the Power of synchronicity. Feeling like I'm a fraud (and for good reason), I don't have any real self-esteem. The wealth of self-esteem never touches me. Therefore, I don't have the sense that, no matter what may happen, I can trust myself as a provider. Instead, "In God I don't trust" is what I write on my psychic dollar bill – a feeling of impotency I can't quite liquefy.

Consider: the *measure* in which I trust myself is directly proportional to my willingness to emPower the NOW, that is, to wait for the call and respond to it when it comes.

The slavery to forced labor is replaced by the Shabbat and/or the Sumerian *Sabattu* for "heat-rest" as the pause the moon takes when full, since, at that time, "she" is enough – neither increasing nor decreasing. Transcendence, at last: in the beginning was the end, when I can choose peace, and rest while working!

Part II: Passion and the Power of Attention

- Fish Page
- The Power of Attention
- Decisions, Decisions
- Code Results - BQS / SBQ
- The Passion of Hysteria
- Understanding Attention
- The Passion of Inferiority
- Rising into Forgiveness
- The Passion of Defiance
- The Passion of Craved Penance
- The Dark Passions
- The Passion of Fake Kindness
- The Power of Intention
- The Passion of Failure

Yod (י)	Vav (ו) / Heh (ה)	Heh (ה)
Individual Power	Symbolic Power	Collective Power
Broken Heart	Split Mind / Pain Body	Lost Soul
Vanity	Inferiority / Penance	Defiance

The LORD of Karma & the Dark Passions

When in the illusion of separation, I start feeling that I don't belong which makes me prone to prostituting myself. Without self-esteem, I also lack a compassionate womb by which to embrace my pain. I now worsen my case as I begin identifying to passions that are dark in essence. These passions belong to the snake.

From the screech of hysteria ("no womb"), I move into the inferiority of a split mind, from inferiority into the defiance of a lost soul, from defiance into the craved penance of the pain body and from craved penance, into the fake kindness of a broken heart. My final motion is from fake kindness into the failure of a forsaken spirit. They are "animals" that feed on my Power, preventing me from keeping my attention on the goal.

The Power of Attention

"When you have solved the problem of controlling the attention of the child, you have solved the entire problem of its education."
Maria Montessori

I can understand how occult teachings would suggest to discipline attention by learning to focus on the breath or on a flame. If I could learn to bring my attention into the proper channels, I would tap into the depths of my mind and have the Power to manifest my visions, wishes, intentions; any "prayers." Indeed, if only I could focus instead of losing my attention so easily, my goals would stretch toward me!

To control my attention, I must first fully believe that I can (emphasis on *fully*). Yep, the trick with faith is to be 100% (this is the purity that is behind choiceless awareness). So, yes, I can focus on a flame or I can inquire on my motivations until I can expose the "snake belief" that is causing me to falsely rebel or obey, and subsequently doubt myself (the antithesis of *total* certainty). This involves questioning what my intentions are in saying and doing what I say and do. It is always a surprise to me to realize how my secrets bring consequences I would rather not have to experience. It is also puzzling to see me choosing to feed the wrong wolf, and indulging the emotions of my own addictive needs. Why can't I say "no" to temptation?

I want Power; I resist Power. And attention is Power. I'm so afraid of what I would do if I had Power that I end up picking up an addiction or two in order to disarm me. Like being addicted to the thought that no one hears me or sees me: why can't I be like a tree and fall as if nobody is watching? Each time I take rejection personally, I confirm that, deep down, I'm not enough! This may just be my greatest pain: that "you" would not receive the gifts I'm bringing. The false sense impression that "you" can reject me is what leads me to become violent, and turn to crime.

I must now invent something to save me from the mess I myself created. And so, I tell the story of how "God" will send me a messiah who will die for my sins, and it'll all be dandy. Well, the messiah cannot build my business. "He" won't be able to lose weight for me. He can't even save me or heal me or teach me. I must become willing to own that, if the world *out there* is a reflection of me, then the messiah *out there* must be a reflection of my inner Self. **Will I be big enough to decide to save my soul?**

DECISIONS, DECISIONS

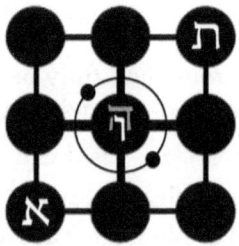

DECISIONS, DECISIONS: why do I object to placing my attention on a life of abundance? Again, why be poor and sick when I could choose health? Why keep on making the same error, each time confirming that I'm not enough?

I refuse to hear that I am yet to make it MY decision to awaken. This decision is mine and mine alone. You may lead me to the waters of Torah, but you can't make me drink! Henceforth, I defy "you" as a way to stubbornly resist doing good. I make you out as a tyrant imposing his will on me, and then resent you for it. Meanwhile, I ignore that no one has the Power to hurt me. I'm playing this whole game by myself...

One day, I'll be in enough pain to actually make "THE decision" not to suffer a single exception in doing what it takes. I'll stop compromising my integrity. And then I will be home; returned to the innocence of pure choiceless awareness. I will gladly pay the price to be the change I wish to see, with all my heart, all my soul and all my might.

But if that's so wonderful, why delay? Is making the decision to know who I am too good to be true? Instead of struggling, I'd be drawn by my goal as I would not allow any doubt to enter my mind when it opposes such goal. So, why do I choose to battle goodness and make it so difficult for me?

There is an energy in me, admittedly dark and masochistic in nature. This energy chooses self-imposed suffering by going for the ignorance that engages in "bad" deeds. Dissatisfaction is the outcome it actually favors, while pretending to expect different results. This is also how I have a very real yearning for you to love me. Mother Teresa nailed it: "the biggest disease today is not leprosy or tuberculosis, but rather the feeling of being unwanted."

When I begin accepting my lot, I simultaneously fulfill my own law and the sense of being unwanted vanishes. There is no more "you" I am superimposing on my decision-making process to prevent me from being compassionate ("with my pain"). I stop blaming "you" for not hearing me. I hear me now, and the way I care becomes universal. The QKosmos (not just my family or country) has my full *attention* and consideration. The yearning calms down, allowing me to concentrate while enjoying a self-renewing supply of attention.

Consider: when my attention is on the other (the one who will come and fulfill all my desires), my intention is far from being considerate. If I take care of "you," it is because I'm resisting being alone.

"The more decisions that you are forced to make alone, the more you are aware of your freedom to choose." *Thornton Wilder*

Will I recognize that it is not freedom I want, but freedom from responsibility? I am still refusing to own how hungry I am. It is as if I keep choosing to be dissatisfied, which confuses my receptor cells that now create dis/ease. If I actually listened and received the order given by my heart, would I be open to seeing the grace that surrounds me at all times? Even more so surprising, would I have my results?

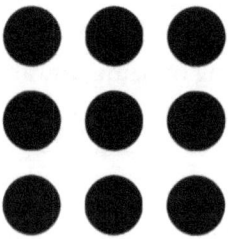

Code Results - BQS / SBQ

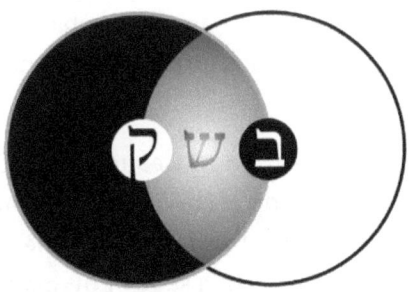

Imagine a language so pure and so sacred that it can reconcile opposites in just three letters...

Right: Hebrew letter Beth (ב) → B in Roman script
Middle: Hebrew letter Shin (ש) → S, Sh in Roman script
Left: Hebrew letter Qoph (ק) → Q in Roman script

Here is how S/Hebrew inscribes code "Results" in 3 letters, 4 words:

- **SB**: middle to right, I read *Shuv* (שב) for "turn, return."
- **SQ**: middle to left, I read *Saq* (שק) for "sackcloth."
- **QSB**: from left to right to middle, I read *Qasheb* (קשב) for "hearing, attention."
- **BQS**: from right to left to middle, I read *Baqash* (בקש) for "seek, beg, desire."

The Decoding: the perception of unrequited love (and the thought that "you" should love me when you don't) makes me ill. I am **sick** as I continue to **seek** love out there – a beggar whose bottomless bowl can never be filled. This bowl is made of the human mind; of human **desire**. The understanding that every desire will eventually fail me transforms me, when I realize that it is time to stop seeking happiness outside of myself. When ready to **turn within**, I make room for emptiness, and find that I am not hungry for your **attention** anymore. My prostitutE stops talking, having no need to hook you again into taking care of me. While I want to receive your love, I now love "you" enough to set you free. Surely, as long as my giving has strings attached, my resolutions to improve my health or my wealth (that is, my consciousness) will be provisional.

Meanwhile, the laws of cause and consequence are not optional. I can't fool neither "God" nor my body. If I don't really give it all when going to the gym, I won't get my results. I will instead witness the lack of what I say I want, and be even more so in a state of desolation. I now wear the symbolic **sackcloth** of humiliation and/or mourning, while doing the same thing over and over and pretending to expect a different outcome. So, yes, when my heart is closed, my mind is *insanus* – Latin for "insane, unsound, excessive, extravagant," continuing to sing CAIN's song: I'm jealous that "you" would be ABEL to give unconditionally while I CAN'T!

I worsen my case by blaming "God" (or others) for my failures, ignoring that communication is the *result* of what I have said and done. Resisting seeing what I actually **have** in order to **know** what I truly **desire** and **will** it into being depletes my energy! Said differently, resisting seeing my results in order to know my real motivations and adapt my focus accordingly is what weakens me! It is also what sources my dark passions, starting with the passion of hysteria...

Individual Power	Symbolic Power	Collective Power
I will	I know / I have	I desire
"To Turn, Return"	"Hearing" / "Attention"	"To Seek, Beg, Desire"

Code Results and the Three Powers

It is Rabbi Maimonides who stated: "The general object of the law is the well-being of the soul and of the body." Might I be in so much reactance to the word LAW that I'll deny the laws of cause and effect? While I secretly act to be poor and sick while claiming to want health, am I attempting to create a "God" who doesn't answer my prayers? Truth be told, I refuse to grow up! As long as I remain a chilD and blame my parents for not hearing me or loving me, I don't have inquire on my thinking in terms of rewards and punishments. Essentially, I don't have to be responsible!

The fact that Shin (300) and Lamed (30) are in the same room of 3-changing helps me transform the word *Qasheb* (קשב) for **"attention"** into the word *Qabal* (קבל) for "receive." I change when I respond to what I've caused and place my attention on accepting my results instead of resisting them. Such acceptance is how I can master healing as I am free to "receive" both sickness and health.

The Passion of Hysteria

"Work out your own salvation. Do not depend on others." Buddha

When I stop lying and tell it like it is, my scared prostitutE stretches to the sacred. My Engineer's genius is now freed from its encapsulation. This is to say, whether male or female, I'm no longer "suffering from the womb" – from the Greek etymology of *hysteria*. I am real again, absolved from the tyranny of appearances. I feel that devotion is my nature, and that I CAN give it all. Such absorption doesn't cost me energy nor weaken me. On the contrary, it heals me and rebuilds my immune system.

Since being a predator is no longer an option, I learn a different way to survive, turn to the feminine and open to the health and the wealth of compassion. The S/Hebrew word *Racham* (רחם) for "womb" also means "compassion." Indeed, it is through the pearlescent wetness of her vagina and the splendid compassion of her heart that the sacred prostitute spread a message of grace. The Hindus called her *karuna*, "a combination of motherly love, tenderness, comfort, mystical enlightenment and sex." Mary Magdalene, who was first seen as a whore, performed the ceremony of anointment and officially acted as priestess when pouring precious oil on the feet of the man about to be Christ. It used to be that, in the code of Hammurabi, the sacred prostitute was protected from slander, as were her children. "Also by law, the sacred prostitute could inherit property from her father and receive income from the land worked by her brothers. If dissatisfied she could dispose of the property in ways which she saw fit. Considering the role of women at this time, this was an extraordinary right." *Nancy Qualls-Corbett, The Sacred Prostitute.*

Yes, it may be shocking to realize that, in their offices as high priestesses, the sacred prostitutes were handsomely paid to offer guidance, healing, and teachings. Whether dealing with sex or money, they embodied a sacred energy that healed all taboos surrounding sex and money. I am now invited to become so honest that I'd turn into a sacred prostitute. Once I only want the truth, I am able to give from the plenty of my being, knowing that I am enough and that there's always more. This makes me think of Abram and Sarai... At first, they were both misers; have-nots. They had no womb of compassion and could not succeed in getting pregnant. But when they met the Name *El Shaddai* or the "God of Enough," everything changed (along with their names which received a Heh womb). *El Shaddai* is the Name that spins the sex chakra, imparting it with the Power of abundance. When I resonate with it, I stop identifying to the body which allows me to detach from the fruit of its actions (and thus from "my" money).

Understanding Attention

"The starting point of all achievement is DESIRE. Keep this constantly in mind. Weak desire brings weak results, just as a small fire makes a small amount of heat." *Napoleon Hill, Think and Grow Rich*

When trapped into a self-defeating pattern, it behooves me to inquire on the nature of attention, prior to *trying* to exercise willpower. Unadulterated attention – or the ability not to let anything enter my mind that doesn't align with my goal – is prayer at its highest. It is unbound love and gratitude as it is to believe that I have received what I prayed for. If I just do my part and turn my attention towards the good, I find that I am attracted to goodness *in spite of myself*. Such radical attention supports my ability to create. Surely, any revelation of creative genius is proportional to the amount of radical attention I can give to any project. If I build it, my inner messiah can only come! :-)

Numbers are honest. When my 10 fingers join (when I have 0 doubts and am 1 with everything), I hit 100% purity. I can wait. I am not identified to "I am the body" and unconcerned by the illusion of choice. Having nothing left to prove frees me from the tyranny of appearances. I don't need to pretend or please anymore. I am simply in a place of great beauty; in the sanctuary of the Eternal Now. This is true meditation. I feel an ardent single-pointedness transcending sitting, saying mantras or studying. Utterly absorbed in the action, I am free of the action and more alive than ever! It doesn't matter whether the task is ordinary or extraordinary: the profundity and the sacredness of the moment comes from my being totally consumed by it. As pleasure overtakes my being, religion (♪ and no religion too) blossoms in me.

I open to such blissful devotion when I detach from a *desired* outcome. Attention is bound up with desire: if I'm hungry, I will only see places of restoration. If my car's engine is making some weird noises, I'll only scan for automobile shops. It is only when I am at the end of personal desires that I can concentrate and produce an effort which infallibly contains a reward. Being neutral as to good and evil, I shine the light of attention equally on both. Eventually the good gains the day as my attention is fully on what matters in the Now. My only work is to remove the blocks to having my attention so disciplined that the act of fusion is self-fulfilling, as subject and object being one.

When between a rock and a hard place, I simply need to pray to merge with the Now and endure it. Endurance is, after all, a fundamental quality of the messiah.

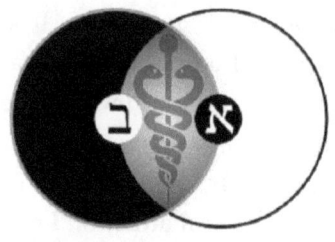

NO ENDURANCE IS WHY I AM NOT HEALING: If I suffer, it is because I am yet to stop being a victim of my DNA, when I see that the blessing is in the curse, the cure, in the poison, and the Messiah, in the snake! At the core of the word *Mashiach* (MSYH) "Messiah" is the letter Yod which initiates *Yenun* for "s/he endures."

Why can't I just wait it out, knowing that "this too shall pass." If I was once an angel in PaRaDiSe, in pristine condition, noble in reason, infinite in faculties and blessed with all kinds of divine grace, what caused me to make the choice that precipitated a painful fall? Was the choice to fall received from "God?" If it was, how could I blame myself for it? For if "God" is the source of everything, how can "He" not be the source of my first choice to be a rebellious angel?

And it makes me wonder... How could my angel side remember the choice to persevere and endure, a choice which my human side forgot? Is that what the fourth word Dalet ("remember Shabbat and keep it sacred") is all about? The Dalet Commandment prompts me to focus on resting while working, which presupposes that I'd have the Power to hold the tension of opposites. Remembering that the work is done *through* me and not *by* me uplifts me. Forgetting and making it *about* me prompts my fall. Falling and identifying to a "bottom" now leads me to feel the next passion: inferiority.

The Passion of Inferiority

> "For who makes you so superior? What do you have that you didn't receive? If, in fact, you did receive it, why do you boast as if you hadn't received it?" *1 Corinthians 4:7*

The apostle Paul's question is intriguing, especially since the Hebrew word *QKabbalah* means "to receive." While it is a rhetorical question (the awaited answer being "nothing"), it is also at the foundation of health. If I am one with everything, there can be no gift that I haven't received. I resist nothing! But if everything emanates from "God" (the greatest and most ultimate part of life) and if it's all for receiving, then why would "God" bring evil in the world? What purpose could this gift serve?

The next question follows suit: if there's nothing that I can have that I have not already received, why would I need recognition for having it? Bragging in view to have your approval only says that I don't know myself. I doubt myself because I'm yet to touch the bottom of my suffering. Only then will I understand the purpose of evil. Accepting that every desire, blessing, and even emotional molecule comes from "God," what about the virtues I desire to have? Does "God" withhold the gift of patience, for example, and then punish me for not having it? Moreover, if impatient, how could I not try to push my evolution, which leaves me wanting your recognition even more?

To answer, the feminine side of Apostle Paul now asks: "for who makes you so inferior? What do you not have that you feel you should have received? And if, in fact, you don't have it, why blame yourself as if you should have received it?"

Here is how I make me feel inadequate: I won't forgive me from not having received the gift of perseverance! I can see that choosing perseverance is understanding justice: the more I persevere taking steps toward my goal, the more the law of cause and effect works on my behalf, and the happier I feel about myself. Eventually, I realize that being true to my word (to my own law) matters even more than reaching my goal. Actually, being true to myself is how to know and feel that I AM the AIM. No illusion of separation! But if I listen to the voice leading me into temptation, I may get instant gratification, but I also instantly lose gratitude and grace. There is no more kindness, no more doing what it takes, and no more healing. More than ever, I am attached to my desired outcome as I know darned well that my actions are not in alignment with my desire being fulfilled. I am now in time, calculating, planning – and yes, miserable. If happy are those who persevere to the end, sad are those who quit.

If I could only forgive me, I would have no attention on feeling superior or inferior, which, in turn, would allow me to persevere, no matter whether I rise or fall... For now, how do I transcend regrets, accept my failures and stop taking them personally, as if I had done something inherently wrong?

Rising into Forgiveness

> "What a piece of work is man! How noble in reason! How infinite in faculties! In form and moving, how express and admirable! In action how like an angel! In apprehension, how like a god!" *William Shakespeare*

The idea that I could be angel-like, God-like or even Shakespeare-like is disturbing. **It is disturbing because it sparks what I cannot forgive.** I am yet to hear the call spoken in *John 14:12*: "Amen, amen! Anyone who believes in me will do the same works I have done, and even greater works, because I am going to be with the Father." Would committing to a path of evolution until I turn to my heart ease the remembering of my perfect angelic or divine nature? "Going to the Father" may remind me how I was angel-like until I grew in my desire to be somebody, and fell from innocence.

Here is my error: I still think I have a choice to rise or fall – to be good or to be bad. The angels who fell can't do good. Those who didn't fall can't do evil. Is it the "I am bad" belief that prompted my fall? Or did I create the belief after I fell? According to the Christian doctrine of the fall, I'm damaged goods to begin with. To be restored to my full angelic status, "God" must fix me. This repair work is known in Christian theology as salvation, which can only be granted through grace. The same repair work and/or "amendment, correction" is known in classical Kabbalah as the essential tenet of *Tiqqun*. Although saying it differently, the two faiths agree on this point: enlightenment is not going to happen because of what I do, but it will not happen without my doing everything for it. Grace is what orchestrates my liberation, a grace I invite by amending my ways. When I believe that I am not enough, I must pay the price and earn the stages of my evolution. Meanwhile, I can be assured that there is an end to indebtedness – and to owing you and/or wanting to make you pay! Yep, I will one day die to who I *think* I am. I will then forgive my debts and my debtors. :-)

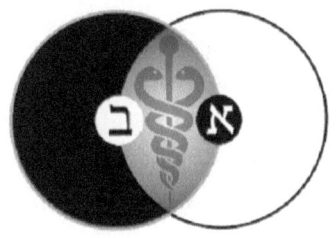

NO FORGIVENESS IS WHY I AM NOT HEALING: it is not that I want to make "God" pay for not loving me. It is more that I retaliate against my own self in an attempt to make me pay for not loving "God." When I CAN give it all, loving with *all* my heart, soul and might, I'll stop distorting the meaning of justice, which will allow the thought of illness to auto-combust.

Meanwhile, I will do my best to ignore the cost of not forgiving and doing harm, since justice is exact and exacting in mirroring my intentions back to me, and this, whether I am conscious of them or not. There is only One of us. Cause is consequence, and consequence is cause. So why be so stubborn? Why fight so hard? This state of affairs now leads me to inquire on the next passion: defiance.

The Passion of Defiance

"The only way to deal with an unfree world is to become so absolutely free that your very existence is an act of rebellion." *Albert Camus*

Whether I am wealthy or poor, I am a true rebel when I come to the end of my DNA, and break the chains of society's repressive conditioning. I emerge from the formless roots of my unconscious and grow my eagle/angel wings to fly into the sky. I am not a rebel because I am fighting the world, but because I became courageous enough to take full responsibility for who I am and to live in truth.

So, what's the truth? Might there be some falseness in the compliance of my "yesses" and/or in the defiance in my "nos?" Indeed, just how free am I? When thinking of health, money, food, family or friends, who do I *think* I am? What is the story to which I am attached? Why choose to believe the BS I am believing?

Taking money, for example, I think of myself as being thrifty in spending. Where did "thrifty in spending" come from? Did I adopt this belief out of rebellion against a "spendthrift" family or was I trying to obey the thrifty quality of my parents? Did I actually deliberately decide to be thrifty? What do I want: rebellion ("no"), obedience ("yes") or deliberation ("big YES" to the heart)? If I act out of rebellion, I am likely to still be reacting against what I perceive has authority over me. If I act out of obedience, I'm still trying to avoid making waves and paying dues to an outer authority. Rebellion or obedience: one is not higher than the other. The only question is: how real and/or how free do I choose to be?

Consider: when there is no religion, no organization, no society, no genealogy to confine me, I am a true rebel as I found the light within. I can speak an honest "yes" and an honest "no." My decisions are made from presence and not from resistance. I choose to be happy because it's good for my health. I choose to be healthy because it's good for my happiness.

The topic of choice shows up again. Did I really decide to be thrifty? Will I know my own heart? Am I aware of what drives me? Can I read the signs?

- A sign is a quantum bit of **information**.

- **Information** is readable through **contrast**.
- **Contrast** is the work of polarity – the **choice** of 0 versus 1, evil versus good, sickness versus health, **no** versus yes.
- **No** is the first choice.

But who makes this first choice to say "no?" Moreover, whom or what am I opposing? You? Me? Justice? Happiness? What is it that I am resisting? Good? Evil? If I were fully surrendered as a lamb of "God" is who answers with a big "YES" to everything, I would know that awareness is pure because it is **choiceless**. In turn, such knowing would allow me to speak honestly, since I would no longer try to get your approval by saying "yes" to you, or your disapproval by saying "no." However, how could I know freedom if I were guaranteed not to fall, and only had one source of motivation (to please "God" and do no harm)?

NO REAL MOTIVATION IS WHY I'M NOT HEALING: Before deciding on a path, I must ask myself if I can take charge of my own experience. Is my WHY big enough for me to get up each morning and keep on doing what it takes, even when I don't have the results I want?

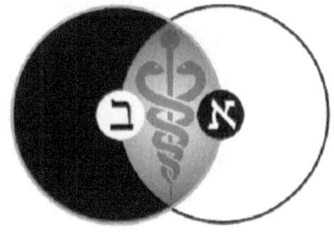

The Passion of Craved Penance

> "Before you heal someone, ask him if he's willing to give up the things that made him sick." *Hippocrates – the Father of Medicine*

Hippocrates nailed it again! The fact that he used a plural is of particular interest to me: *the things* that make me sick. I may know that, for example, sugar makes me sick and be willing to forgo it. But do I know what's behind my desire to eat sugar? For unless I become conscious of my hidden motivations (plural), I stand very little chance to give up *the things that make me sick*. Weak will seems to be why I am poor and sick, if only in my mind. It appears that I cannot will my attention where I say I want it – on abundance rather than lack, on pleasure rather than pain. So, what do I think about; where does my attention go? Revenge? Punishment? And why would I desire that?

When my mind is at war for too long, my body gets ill. Body will follow mind, *until there's no more mind to follow*. To heal, I must hear the heart's voice – my intuition, but also the body's voice – my instincts, a double hearing which asks silencing the mind. If my illness is karmic, my healing will be contingent upon waking up from the DREaM.

I have denied my hunger, my sexuality, my religion, my creativity, my aggression for so long that I deserted my body. Now my mind can be inclined to think evil. That's how I quit on my chosen goal and look for LOVE in the wrong places. Hiding behind my weakness, I now make me into a victim – someone who years for penance. Truth be told, if I won't persevere in the ways of justice, it's because I'm a glutton for punishment. I use the law as an external control to repress what I can't accept in me.

When I become so honest that I can rest in peace, there are no "snake beliefs" to induce guilt and call for punishment – just a graceful return to innocence. I can now digest the poisonous fruit of the tree of the knowledge of opposites, understand oneness and open to the bliss of devotion. I CAN wait for a clear answer in the field between intuition and instinct, between the conscious and the unconscious.

Fulfilled and free, I know that the LOVE that has no opposite is what chooses Health with a big "H." I embrace my nemesis, forgive my debts and my debtors, brush my teeth, feel beautiful and heal beautifully. My energy is high and my body well-tuned. I feel so good and am so grateful for the gift of life that I wholeheartedly emPower the Now – no questions asked; no resistance. If I were unfulfilled and unfree, I only have glimpses of what it is like to be the word made flesh. Mostly, I'm a stranger in a strange land. I can't seem to find my way in this body of mine.

NO INSTINCTS IS WHY I'M NOT HEALING: I am stuck in the same self-perpetuating trauma. My instinctual compass is so broken that I can't find the exit door if my life depended on it (and it does). Deep down, I secretly don't want to heal. 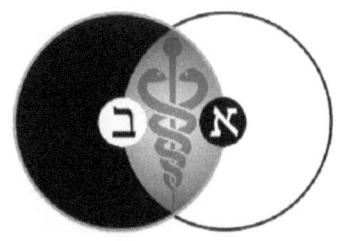 I am bound to my illness. There are advantages to not being well, such as a certain kind of attention that I ask of others in order to fuel my victim agenda.

The Dark Passions

Prepare to DIE! Inquiry tool: www.goldenxpr.com/tco3_wellness/

Step 1: I fill in the blank: I want to know WHY I would choose to think I CAN'T _____ (e.g.; find a job, be patient, etc.). **Step 2:** I ask for truth and generate a number. **Step 3:** I find my number on the map and fill in the brackets: inviting [**Dark Passions**], I become ill as the result of having [**Illness**]. However, by deciding to no longer resist feeling the [**Resistance**] that accompanied having [**Illness**], I begin to open to wellness by way of [**WELLNESS**]. **Step 4:** what most surprised me in this process was [_____].

The Passion of Fake Kindness

> "Enter through the narrow gate. For wide is the gate and broad is the road that leads to destruction, and many enter through it. But small is the gate and narrow the road that leads to life, and only a few find it." *Matthew 7:13-14*

Feeling inadequate, I forget about the true gate to life and choose the easy path. This is when I attach to my Powers, wanting to believe that I use them as an act of service for others. And yet, it is still me trying to use my Powers. Maybe I could save "you!" This is how I take my freedom from myself – by being a hypocrite and faking kindness. No wonder I'd become discouraged, and even sloppy. Rather than persevering in doing the next just thing, I distract myself with another fantasy. Emptiness is the way to wholesome Power. I must reduce my ego personality to zero. Complete surrender is what the gods want from me; no more, no less! Only then will I no longer attempt to sell you or to convince you to believe something about me. Only then will I be impeccable in my speech, and stop being a spiritual phony who's still looking for LOVE out there. I will incarnate where I am and know the sense of "authenticity."

Meanwhile, I'll find myself quitting on my goal again and again even though I already know that I'll lose both happiness and justice in the process. I'll believe in the lie of the false prophets who come to me in sheep's clothing (snake's, in this case): "surely, you won't die; your eyes will open; you'll will be like God!" As I listen to the fake voice and let myself be led into temptation, I'll soon have to contend with enmity: I'll hate myself for being gullible and hate you for having conned me. If that wasn't enough, my female side goes into birthing pains and agonizes with each intuitive hit. How would I not, when what I desire is "the man," that is, to be rational? As for my male side, it resents the forced labor and having to work hard for his money.

And all of this because I'm a fraud – a liar. I don't want to know the truth! First, I don't want to hear that the snake is lying, and then I don't want to take responsibility for the part I played in being deceived. Instead, I'll blame "you" for my error, a childishness which will irremediably lead to my being kicked out of PaRaDiSe. To return to innocence, I just need be real and answer one question: will I tell the whole truth, and nothing but the truth?

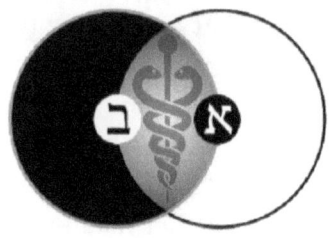

NO HONESTY IS WHY I AM NOT HEALING: working with my insanity is, in many ways, waging a war. I find that it is not that I don't have the willpower or the authority to do what it takes. It is not that the path of action is not just. It is more that I don't have any real intention to heal. I am not ready for how truth will change my life.

The Power of Intention

> "In order for a war to be just, three things are necessary. First, the authority of the sovereign. Secondly, a just cause. Thirdly, a rightful intention." *Thomas Aquinas*

Having my attention on something – anything – will give "IT" gravity and attract it to the center of my earth. While having my attention on my desire draws it to me, what I actually want may not be the same as what I *think* I want. This is when the Power of Intention comes in. For me to know what I want and keep my attention on it, I must reveal the unconscious intentions that may be in my space.

Indeed, **attention** is on par with **will**, and **intention**, with **desire**. My work is to come into the **knowledge** of how my forbidden desires (the desires which I was told were unacceptable) interact with my will. I will then be better equipped to transcend my fear of **emPowerment**

Individual Power	Symbolic Power	Collective Power
Will	Knowledge	Desire
Attention	emPowerment	Intention

The Expression of Individual Power as Will

To awaken the will from its slumber and discipline my attention, I can inquire on my intentions against the background of the four greatest motivational forces in humans, as attested by four devoted philosophers. Moreover, to better understand these four forces, I will use the framework of the four-lettered Name, transmitting it either as LOVE (when I am clear on the intentions that drive my will), or as the DREaM (when I am not).

First, I write down a quantifiable goal, e.g.; I want to: _____.

- **Nietzsche and the will to Power:** once I chose my goal, I can expect to meet opposition and either push against or pull from it. Will reaching my goal make a marked difference in my life, for me and those around me? How? Are the money and time resources I allocated to my goal adequate?
- **Freud and the will to pleasure:** understanding that I am compelled to seek pleasure and avoid pain, and that reaching my goal must take me beyond my comfort zone into "the new normal," how will I balance the call of severity ("you should" work harder) with this of mercy (time to rest, dear One)?
- **Frankl and the will to meaning:** it helps me to find that horrific experiences (Frankl was a holocaust survivor) as well as illnesses have a purpose. Why would reaching this goal matter to me? Why do I have this imbalance, lack and/or illness at this time in my life.
- **Schopenhauer and the will to live:** if this is the call for self-preservation, to improve my situation is also doing what I can do in order to stay alive. Imagining that I am at the end of my

life, would having pursued the goal above represent the best use of my energy?

The Passion of Failure

"Success is not final; failure is not fatal. It is the courage to continue that counts." Winston Churchill

Once again, I revisit the primal choice given to the angel in me: to persevere in the ways of justice or to seek personal happiness. Regardless of the many failures I experience (and this, whether I choose justice or happiness), I notice that there are projects I can't abandon, just as there are projects that I keep on aborting. And it makes me wonder... Why is that?

What I am asking is: do I actually have a choice upon the goals I decide to pursue? Might the decision to persevere in attaining a given goal be made in a greater domain, namely this of the soul?

When I sleep, I sleep. When I don't sleep, I don't sleep. When it is time to wake up, it is time to wake up. When I am to meet my partner, I meet my partner. When I am to separate, I separate. There is no double-guessing in any event; no question of choice. What confuses me is the thought that I have a choice upon going right or left. If I could give up the idea that I am the doer and/or the decider of my thoughts, I'd be free of regrets. I'd stop making it about me and wouldn't accuse me of having taken the "wrong" path. I'd be a mystic; not a mistake! THIS IS HUGE. It is also Aleph's pure choiceless awareness – the mind that actually hears that there are no accidents!

Whether I am young or old, rich or poor, healthy or ill, I'd master the code of opposites and find it is all beautiful. I would relax, as I would feel how I am never outside the House of "God," never an outcast, never separate from the whole – just a wave in the ocean. It is only when I think of myself as ending at the skin (an individual) that I'm all stressed out, lonely, ashamed of my choices, afraid. And when in Scare

City, I lose my joyful innocence and start calculating for my own advantage.

The truth is, I turned away from my own light, and decided to go into the abysmal darkness alone. I am so concerned by what others will think of me that I've forgotten what I knew as a child – that there's nothing and no one out there! And it is because I take my failure personally that I can't stand to fail. Soooo... Am I willing to equate the fact that I'm tense with the presence of hidden agendas? Ouch!

Possibly I could come back to the basics: since my goal is to know that I am LOVE, I am destined to adopt the behavior of LOVE. I can trust it to be true simply because I have accepted that this beautiful body I am given is here to help me fulfill my law. And if not this body, the next one will. No matter what I do, it is my work. If, for example, I was to betray myself, then betrayal was part of my contract. There is no avoiding it. It is not a question of not being good enough, or of not having the proper skills, or of being a victim of people's jealousy, or of being born under an unlucky star...

It is just about learning to LOVE what is – no matter what reality looks like. This quality of LOVE gives me a sense of what justice is: both are unconditional. Henceforth, the gentle reminder: "reality" is another name for "God." Now, when I can love reality and "God" with ALL I've got, I am one with "God" and "God's" Power is one with me. This is how justice (rather than personal happiness) leads me to know Health with a big "H" is. And that is enough, as it is total!

NO "GOD" POWER IS WHY I AM NOT HEALING: Believing is to have faith. Having faith is to believe I CAN. On a scale of 1 to 10 (1 = not at all, 10 = totally), how certain am I that I CAN give it all and receive it all? If less than 10, will I pick one 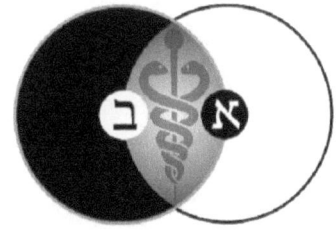 thing and trust "my" choice until I can observe that life takes care of itself, rather than doing what I normally do which is to imagine a problem?

And with that, I am now ready for Part III of this chapter, when I understand my dark passions so completely that I can only transcend my blocks, and make the choice of Health. This is also when I nullify resistance and any yearning that accompanies it, enter emptiness, and make sense of the cover art whose codes affirm it's all providential, and certainly not about "me!"

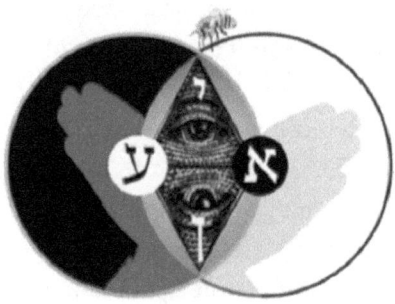

TCO—Book 3 Cover, code Health

Part III: The Choice of Health

- Fish page
- Resisting nothing; not even a FREE Fall!
- Giving Back to Mammon
- A Course in Miracles
- Code Providence – NWN / XM[K]
- The Freedom to Choose Health
- Free Will
- Code Free Will – AB / BA (Expanded)
- Waking up to Health
- The QKabbalah of my "Receptor" Cells
- Code Nemesis – RG / GR
- To My Nemesis – Reality (a.k.a. "God")
- Code Mystery – MALK /KLAM
- Code FREE Fallin' – AMT / MAT
- The Choice of True Happiness
- Missing the Mark
- THE END of Time
- Judgment Day

Yod (י)	Vav Heh (וה)	Heh (ה)
Individual Power	Symbolic Power	Collective Power
Communication	Healing	Commerce
Code Ambivalence	Code Red / Free Fallin'	Code Scare City

The Codes of Transcendence

WHAT IS THIS CURIOUS ANIMAL NAMED HEALTH WITH A BIG "H?" HEALTH IS GENERALLY UNDERSTOOD TO BE PHYSICAL. HOWEVER, SINCE BODY FOLLOWS MIND (UNTIL, OF COURSE, THERE'S NO MORE MIND TO FOLLOW), HEALTH IS FIRST AND FOREMOST MENTAL. THIS SHIFT FROM PHYSICAL TO MENTAL HELPS ME DISCERN BETWEEN PAIN AND SUFFERING. PAIN IS WHAT I'M GOING THROUGH; SUFFERING COMES FROM WHAT I THINK ABOUT MY PAIN. HOW COMPASSIONATE (LIT. "WITH MY PAIN") WILL I BE? SURRENDERING MY PAINFUL JUDGMENTS IS ALSO HOW THE FIRST AND THE LAST STAGE OF ALCHEMY ARE TRANSCENDENCE. I MUST DIE TO WHO I *THINK* I AM, ESPECIALLY THE IDENTITY OF ENEMY VERSUS FRIEND.

"HOW LONG MUST I WRESTLE WITH MY THOUGHTS AND DAY AFTER DAY HAVE SORROW IN MY HEART? HOW LONG WILL MY ENEMY TRIUMPH OVER ME?" *PSALM 13:2*. I MUST TRANSCEND CAIN'S BELIEF OF UNREQUITED LOVE, SHED ITS SNAKE'S SKIN AND TRANSMUTE THE PAIN BY TURNING INTO A MESSIAH! UNTIL THEN, THERE WILL BE NO REAL HEALING, AS I'LL PROJECT ENMITY ONTO "MY" ISSUE, BE IT FAMILY, FOOD, SEX AND/OR MONEY.

ENMITY IS THE FILTER THROUGH I OBSERVE LIFE, AND HATRED IS THE FEELING I MOST RESIST. IT IS HOW I LET MYSELF BE ANTAGONIZED BY LIFE, AND HOW I CAN NEVER KNOW THE SACREDNESS OF "THE LOVE THAT HAS NO OPPOSITE." SUCH IS THE INVITATION OF THE PROSTITUTE – TO TRANSCEND DIS-EASE BY REORDERING THE LETTERS OF "SCARED" INTO "SACRED." WHEN I DO, PUTREFACTION HAS NO HOLD ON ME, AND PURIFICATION AND AWAKENING BECOME MATTER OF FACT.

The prostitutE - Health with a big "H"

Resisting nothing; not even a FREE Fall!

> "The freedom we are looking for is the freedom to be ourselves, to express ourselves. But if we look at our lives we will see that most of the time we do things just to please others, just to be accepted by others, rather than living our lives to please ourselves." *Miguel Ruiz*

It will take Code **Impostorship** to alert me that I'm being a fraud as I resist giving it all to LOVE. Unless exposed, my impostorship will lead into regression and end up in anarchy. When no longer identified to being fallen, damaged goods, not enough, I accept that there is nothing personal about my failures or falls. This is how I can be FREE Fallin'. Henceforth, my illness fulfilled its purpose and is no longer needed. I can now be at peace, no matter what the body or the bank account is doing.

Resisting nothing implies having come to the end of desire. When the personality is no more, there is no one to block the flow of LOVE. Looking at the image below, I see how the letters in the white dots are enlarged, for me to focus on them and let the rest of the codes recede into the background. This letter which repeats itself in the four codes is Mem (ם) final. It is final when at the end of a word, but also "final" as it invokes the end of a pattern. Being the word for "water," and thus for the sexual and emotional body, Mem calls the end of desire. When I do not judge that "this" is better than "that," I do not desire "this" over "that." Said differently, I resist nothing.

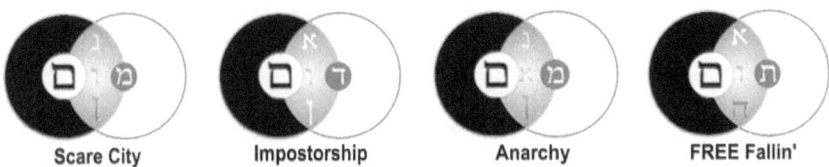

Scare City   Impostorship   Anarchy   FREE Fallin'

The Finality of Mem

As for being FREE Fallin', I had evoked the image of jumping out of an airplane. Just as I jumped, I simultaneously hoped that my parachute would open and feared that it might not. If, upon pushing the button, the parachute did not open, I had no more fear to die, since that choice had been removed from the equation. All is in order, when I don't create **anarchy** as a result of resisting death. Having nothing left to lose, I can finally relax and be free – **FREE fallin'**.

Whereas Parts I and II looked at the codes preceding FREE Fallin', part III looks at the codes following from FREE Fallin', namely Mastery and Health. As always, these codes will unfold step-by-step, for me to feel and sense how the play of the S/Hebrew words writes Mastery into being, when I know what to do, dare doing it, and will it so entirely that I CAN keep silent about my vision. Believing that I received such vision, I have no want and no need to convince you that I got it, which is how I can die to the greed behind my issues.

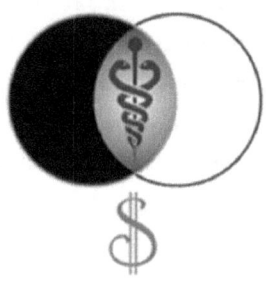

Radical honesty is how I heal my Power issues, my money issues and my sex issues. Consider: when Mammon is no longer my master, I transition from GReed into GRace. This is also when I am FREE Fallin' into Health with a big "H."

Radical honesty means that I no longer compound the problem by thinking that I have time. Instead of procrastinating, I place my affairs in order and suffer no more clutter; no more lies, no more wavering between door a or b. I have nothing left to prove or to lose! As the choice of Health is made for me by GRace alone, I witness how the truth of my mortality does change my life.

Giving Back to Mammon

'Jesus said to them, "Give back to Caesar what is Caesar's and to God what is God's." And they were amazed at him.' *Mark 12:17*

There is another part of the gospels when it is made clear that I cannot at once serve the "God" Name of *Genesis 1* (*Elohim*) and the "God" Names beyond *Genesis 1* (mostly YEWE, and by association to the LORD of karma, Mammon).

I came to see that Mammon's intentions were pure. Ultimately, there will come a day when I am sick and tired of being sick and tired. I will then surrender to the majestic providence that is my Nature. How? I'll simply accept myself fully. Once I want everything I have, I have everything I want. Therefore, the Mammon "yearning for money, sex and Power" works to evolve me. Amazing, right? **As for surrendering to Nature's providence, what would I do if money (i.e.; Mammon) was not a concern? Said differently, what would I create if I knew that I had unlimited support?**

It is likely that, in such consciousness, my prostitutE would be unafraid of paying taxes and of death (both inevitable), and be in awe of how loving reality is. Consider: when I am beyond my story of unrequited love, I do ALL I can to express my gifts and manifest my vision which I know is in service of my fellow beings. I take what I used to see as my curse and transmute it into a most beautiful blessing, beautiful as it has the Power to eradicate even the idea of a curse. **Henceforth, the reason why I would not liberate my genius and create my "Master Peace" is simply because I cannot trust that, if I were to fall, I would be supported.**

To understand my paralyzing fear of falling, I must inquire on the nature of providence. Providence is defined as "the foreseeing care and guidance of God or Nature over the Earth's creatures." The word "providence" includes the idea of "providing." Its etymology comes from the Latin *pro-videre* "to look ahead or forward, supply, act with foresight." The seeing is done by the *Eye* of Providence present on the Great Seal and on the imagery on the one-dollar bill, which became a Masonic symbol for God. Besides being on *TCO—Book 3's* cover, this eye is the "I" that deliberately keeps attention on plenty in lieu of lack (keyword "deliberate").

This "eye/I" also expands the observer effect. Experiments in quantum physics have shown that what is being observed in nature depends on choices made by the observer, i.e.; by my "I" (who I am being) and, by extension, my eye (or what I organically see). Indeed, beauty lies in the "I/eye" of the beholder. Seeing that my tumor is healed (if I am a cancer patient) or my jump is successful (if I am an athlete) or that my quota is made (if I am a sales executive) is a prerequisite to actually manifesting this vision.

When my "I" chooses consciously or not to observe Scare City and not providence, I am yet to master the code of opposites by which to see both, Scare City and providence, at the same time. Such equanimity is when I stop judging that, for example, having money is higher than not having money (or vice-versa). It is to speak in the language of paradox and to communicate with "God."

A Course in Miracles

> "LOVE supports all who have fallen, and raises up all those that are bowed down." *Psalm 145:14*

It becomes miraculous when I surrender and stop desiring what is "not good" for me. To this end, I have the three wondrous signs that populate the room of 6-Desiring and add up to 666 – the infamous "mark of

the beast." When my hands finally join to serve the good of all, I no longer miss the mark (I sin no more). **6-Desiring** is where the two parts of me can unite or split. As such, it is the psychological squaring of the circle: sign Vav (6) is shaped as a line, sign Samekh (60), as a circle, sign Mem final (600), as a square. Such perplexing squaring is how Mem final takes me to the end of desire – when the beast transforms into beauty.

9		8		7		6		5		4		3		2		1	
Completing		Ordering		Engaging		Desiring		"PAIRfect"		Resisting		Changing		Separating		Opening	
9	ט	8	ח	7	ז	6	ו	5	ה	4	ד	3	ג	2	ב	1	א
90	צ	80	פ	70	ע	60	ס	50	נ	40	מ	30	ל	20	כ	10	י
900	ץ	800	ף	700	ן	600	ם	500	ך	400	ת	300	ש	200	ר	100	ק

Yep, the move out of Scare City into Providence involves circling the square by replacing Mem final (ם, value 600, a square) with Samekh (ס, value 60, a circle), as shown by the enlarged signs in the black dots.

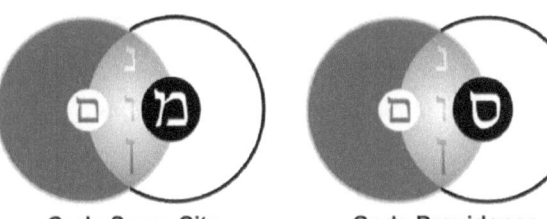

Code Scare City   Code Providence

The rest of the letters remain unchanged, with sign Vav still being at the core of both codes. Code Providence clarifies the aforementioned purity of Mammon's intentions by directly growing out of code Scare City. The growth is sequential, moving me from Mem (13th letter) to Nun (14th letter) to Samekh (15th letter). Here is how it works:

- **Code Scare City** reveals how Mammon combine Mem and Nun (the 13th and 14th letters) to take me down. The word *Nun* is written vertically, to emphasize its falling motion/meaning.

- **Code Providence** reveals how Nun descends into Samekh (the 14th and 15th letters) in order to cancel out the fear of falling, which is at the foundation of *all* fears.

Note: the last letter of fully spelled out sign *Samekh* (סמך) is Kaph final (ך). It is placed in brackets below [K], as it is not an active part of code Providence. I am about to discover why.

Code Providence - NWN / XM[K]

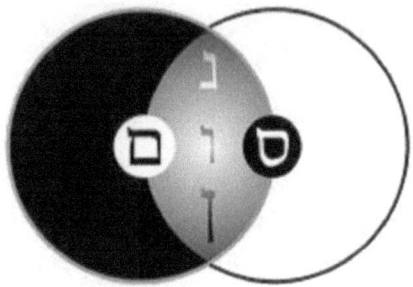

Imagine a language so pure and so sacred that it can reconcile opposites in just two [almost] fully spelled-out signs...

Top: Hebrew letter Nun regular (נ) → N in Roman script
Right: Hebrew letter Samekh (ס) → X in Roman script
Core: Hebrew letter Vav (ו) → F, U, V, W in Roman script
Left: Hebrew letter Mem final (ם) → M in Roman script
Bottom: Hebrew letter Nun final (ן) → N in Roman script

Here is how S/Hebrew inscribes code "Providence" in 5 words:

- **NWN:** from top to middle to bottom, I read the name of letter Nun (נון) for "fish, fallen."
- **XM:** from right to left, I read *Sam* (סם) for "poison."
- **WXM:** from middle to right to left, I combine the letters of 666-Desiring (וסם) as "the sign of the beast."

- XM[K]: from right to left [to abstracted Kaph final (ך)], I read the name of letter *Samekh* (סמך) for "support, prop."
- XWM[K]: from right to middle to left [to abstracted Kaph final (ך)], I read *Somekh* (סומך) for "supporting."

The Decoding: surely, transcending the fear of falling grants total freedom. If I weren't afraid of falling and failing, I wouldn't fear speaking. If I didn't fear speaking, I wouldn't fear rejection. If I didn't fear rejection, I wouldn't fear loss. If I didn't fear loss, I wouldn't fear death. And finally, if I didn't fear death, I wouldn't be afraid of being emPowered. When I face the fear of falling, I start feeling that I have infinite support in creating! Such fundamental transcendence is marked by the sequential shifts from Mem into Nun and from Nun into Samekh – two shifts that move me from Scare City to Providence.

This transformation is at the core of *Psalm 145* which is an acrostic psalm, i.e.; a poetic passage that uses the Hebrew alphabet as its structure. The author began verse 1 with 1st letter Aleph; verse 2, with 2nd letter Beth, verse 3, with 3rd letter Gimel, etc. Therefore, verse 14 "should" have begun with 14th letter Nun. However, it does not. Considering that the structure of the psalm is based on the alphabet <u>in its descending order</u>, I propose that the entire wisdom teaching of this psalm resides in this exact inconsistency – in the fact that verse 14 begins with 15th letter Samekh instead of the expected 14th letter Nun via the words *Somekh HaNophlim* for "**supporting those who have fallen.**" Just as Nun is absent from a psalm that only has 21 verses when it "should" have 22 verses (one verse for each letter of the alphabet), Kaph is missing from code Providence. Why? *Golden XPR* transmits the finality of Kaph as the end of Power misuse – an end that naturally follows the end of desire. Surely, the mastery of 666-Desiring cancels out any yearning as well as any doubt or any push/pull.

- The word *Somekh* for "supporting" is built on the root of 15th letter *Samekh* for "support."

- The word *HaNophlim* for "those that have fallen" is built on the word *Nephel* for "fallen," which is itself an extension of 14th letter *Nun* final for "fish, miscarriage, fallen."

Indeed, how adventurous would I be in my creativity if I knew that *all* my falls are supported? I would feel *in my bones* that there are no accidents. This is how verse 14 of *Psalm 145* nails it. When I see, hear, feel and understand that there is a cosmic plan which has my back (literally) – a structured plan that shows up in a 15th letter Samekh whose role is to "support" 14th letter Nun "the fallen," I am less likely to take my errors personally… FREE fallin', at last!

While the translation ("The LORD supports all who have fallen, and raises up all those who are bowed down") makes sense, it is completely devoid of the miraculous insight that inexorably prompts my evolution, moving me from letter to letter; from stage to stage. As a matter of fact, Nun (נ) and Samekh (ס) are so "PAIRfect" for each other – one falling, the other catching – that, together they spell the word *Nes* (סנ) for "miracle." It is a miracle for me to detoxify my mind from the **poison** of fear, and trust that I am forever supported in the errors of my way! When I realize that I can't lose anything since energy is not destroyed but transformed, I befriend the beast of desire. In turn, this opens my "I" to seeing the entirely of life as miraculous. "Miracle" is another word for "synchronicity," as in *Elohim's* Power of synchronicity – a Name that says: "let there be light!" and sees that there was light. Such FREE speech and creative ability open the Eye of Providence as that which chooses to see Health.

The Freedom to Choose Health

"The man form is higher than the angel form; of all forms it is the highest. Man is the highest being in creation, because he aspires to freedom." *Paramahansa Yogananda*

The freedom to make the choice of Health is no easy matter, as it appears that there is a purpose to the suffering induced by a dis-eased mind. And it makes me wonder: might there be choices impactful enough to lead me to the end of suffering, that is, to be free enough to accept life on its terms?

The American Constitution invokes the unalienable right of the choice of happiness: "Life, Liberty and the Pursuit of Happiness," while the Torah opts for justice: "justice, justice shall you pursue" (*Deuteronomy 16:20*). However, what is happiness? What is justice? The questions intimate that, both, justice and happiness could be universal. Meanwhile, the very act of pursuing can only lead to dissatisfaction, for it presupposes that I'm either lacking something or that it is unattainable to me. Henceforth, I wish to tweak my question to: which of these two – once "received" – is more likely to lead me to the health of being fully alive: justice or happiness?

But how could I know what justice or happiness are when I am conditioned by rigid ideas of what's good and evil, acceptable and unacceptable, right and wrong? I can only push me to do the next "just" thing and end up feeling so unhappy that I try to counteract the doomed sense of obligation by seeking forbidden pleasures. However, that happiness is short-lived. The more I try to resuscitate it, the more I go into *hysteria* and "suffer from the womb" since I can't get no satisfaction; no real pleasure and no closure. The hysteria now leads me to feeling inadequate. If I had the sense of enough, would I insanely "pursue" pleasures expecting a different result besides pain?

I will eventually realize that, if I live in fear, it's because I know I'm a fraud. I'm afraid of being busted as I'm not really in service to my tribe! I just commit tribal suicide by pleasing "you" instead of my higher Self as I fear rejection. My morality is false, dictating what I "should" do because I perceive that it is the only way I'll have the money I need. Am I restricting the flow of life and hurting my health by wrongly attempting to be, do, have what I was taught rather than following my own heart?

Ah, if only I could remember... I can do what I decide, but I cannot decide what I decide. This is to say, if only I could remember that free will is an illusion... It would certainly be an effective way to stop regretting the choices I think "I" made. It'd be the end of guilt, and the return to innocence!

FREE WILL

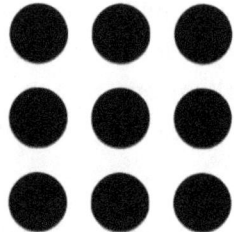

FREE WILL – is it real? Am I just a cog in the wheel or can I create my preferred reality? I admit it: I am powerless to be the change I wish to be. If I create as I speak, why do I choose to speak what I speak? Why the slave narrative? Why make Power my enemy? Why be conflicted about pursuing my goals?

Life requires an even flow of attention. To supply it, I must know what I really want, why I really want it, and whether what I really want serves the good of all. Indeed, I will need the universe's participation.

When I don't see me as a success in some areas of life (e.g.; I'm good at making money, but not at relationships), I may inquire on why I would want to fail in this area of my life, and how this one failure impacts the totality of my energy.

Truth be told, I fear falling (or failure) as much as I fear Power (or success). For me not to keep my attention on being successful, I must imagine that my gifts will be rejected. Gentle warning: if my attention cannot be inwardly sustained, that is, if I don't feel code Free Will (reviewed next), my mind will be a slave to Mammon. I'll "yearn" for the carnality of money, sex or food (same) although they keep me asleep in the **DREaM** and fail me miserably. Here is how I do it...

The prostitutE in me will seek shortcuts to reach my goal and alter procedure, leading me to **fail**. **The saboteuR** will criticize the job, resent others' success, and give up, also leading me to **fail**. **The victiM** will hide behind the excuse of a disability or an illness, still leading me to **fail**. **The chilD** will need constant supervision and repeated instructions, and yet again **fail**.

Therefore, on the basis of my results, I resist failing *and* I want to fail. For my angel to freely rise and fall IN-LOVE, I must lighten up and not make it about me. If I fall, I simply get up and try again. Remembering that I am not the doer or the decider of my words and actions will go a long way to place my mind at peace.

"Man can do what he wills, but he can't will what he wills"
Arthur Schopenhauer

I can do what I want, but I can't want what I want.
I can do what I decide, but I can't decide what I decide.
I can act to fail me, but I can't fail me on failing me.
To be an initiation, my falling, failing and folly must be unplanned.
That's why they call it "free *failing!*"
If I can't fail, I can't know who I Am!

Yep, IT is all willed, wanted, decided and failed by a Supreme Identity – the Self; the I Am. When I make contact, I no longer need the dissatisfaction. I may be in pain, but there is no one suffering. The sadness of having to pursue happiness via pleasures that end up creating pain disappears. I am free. My mind is now sane enough to no longer cause results I would rather *not* have to experience.

Code Free Will - AB / BA (Expanded)

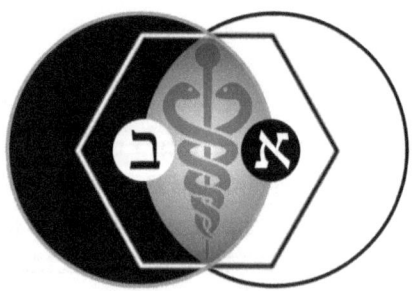

Imagine a language so pure and so sacred that it can show me how to heal by reconciling opposites in just two letters...

Right: Hebrew letter Aleph (א) → A in Roman script

Left: Hebrew letter (ב) Beth → B in Roman script

Here is how S/Hebrew inscribes code "Free Will" in 2 letters, 2 words:

- **AB:** in one direction, I read *Ab* (אב) for "father, alphabet."
- **BA:** in the other direction, I read *Bo* (בא) for "enter."

The Decoding: to help me with making decisions, I "read" the word **alpha-bet**, staying between pure choiceless awareness (or the **Alpha** of 111-Opening) and consciousness (or the **Beth** of 222-Separating). As pure choiceless awareness, I am free to choose, even when in bondage, because I am not attached to an outcome. My decision to create AND SELL anything – an idea, a service, a product – begins as a pure act of faith. I believe because I have no doubt. I have no doubt because I have no mind. I have no mind because I don't create. IT creates. I don't sell. IT sells. IT just moves through me. Becoming a willing participant, I find that there's nothing personal and thus, no yearning in my space!

Meanwhile, a creative block tells me that, as the Beth of Black Magic, I distanced myself from "IT" – the guidance of my heart. Now that I am in the illusion of 222-separating, I blame "you," unwilling to take full responsibility for my failures. When in that space, I can still pray for the grace of understanding. Receiving it will lead me back to Peace and to emPowering the NOW – the feel of free will experienced as FREE speech.

Liberating my speech is, once again, a matter of honesty: the truth shall set it free. I have seen how the prostitutE becomes sacred when I transcend my fear of the material world, befriend my greed and tell the truth about where I still compromise due to fear. Such courage is what makes it possible for my decision-making and my will to be free; free to fulfill my commission. It is the secret to waking up to Health.

Waking up to Health

> "Too many people overvalue what they are not and undervalue what they are." *Malcolm S. Forbes*

Are my indoctrinated beliefs about money (e.g.; the love of money is the root of all evil) how I have a hard time valuing myself or appreciating who I am? Both words – "value" and "appreciation" – have a financial component to them. Indeed, the financial lingo and the vocabulary of the soul have much in common: Jesus saves! :-) Like it or not, I must pay the price, which is to say: I must redeem myself! The initiation involves befriending my greed until I can drop the plan (including my retirement plan). Doing so, I shift from the fear of the LORD to the awe of sacredness. The S/Hebrew *gematriot* that link the concept of "fear" to "Power" are well transmitted in English via the letters of my "scared" prostitutE who will eventually stretch to the "sacred."

This is when I stop prostituting my will and stop lying to please "you." I now have the sense of my own worth and enjoy the superpower of self-esteem. Without it, I can't have neither health nor wealth. Self-esteem takes away the need to compare myself to others, leading me to know that I, too, can do great things. It pairs up with the superpower of compassion, for me to do what it takes to heal any situation. The more compassionate I am, the more self-esteem I have, and vice-versa, the more self-esteem I have, the more compassion I have. Growing up from the childish thought form "it's not fair" answers the questions: what is justice? What is happiness?

Consider: when I lack self-esteem, I also lack a compassionate womb by which to embrace my pain. This is how I am prone to selling my gifts to the highest bidder. I further my own suffering by identifying to the dark passions: from hysteria ("no womb") to inferiority, from inferiority to defiance, from defiance to craved penance and finally, to the fake kindness that sources the sense of being a failure.

Code Tribal Suicide exposed the hidden devil named Belial (lit., "without worth"). Making it my master is how I become co-dependent and never individuate. This makes it impossible for me to be fully responsible for choosing truth and being in my Power. The letters of *Belial* can reorder into *Ba'ali* "my master." Having an external master is one of the desires (besides youth, wealth or fame) for which I sell my soul to the devil. This is how Belial works in tandem with Mammon, the greed-induced yearning for money, sex or Power, gifts that are also supposedly granted by "the other." The distorted perception that there's an "out there" out there is what keeps me caught in the three-fold net of Belial: wealth. fornication, and pollution of the sanctuary. This net is woven by the sins of greed (wealth), of lust (fornication) and of gluttony (pollution of the sanctuary).

The invitation is for me to die to the sins I *think* I am, sins that enslaved my FREE speech and prompted the UNFREE fall of my mouth chakra:

1. Into the heart chakra – where GRace turns to GReed.
2. Into the sex chakra – where I lust for imperfect action.
3. Into the root chakra – where I am a glutton for a punishment inflicted by the dollars I wrongly spend or appropriate, the calories I ingest, the drinks I imbibe, or the smokes I inhale.

The QKabbalah of my "Receptor" Cells

> "Everything you'll ever need to know is within you; the secrets of the universe are imprinted on the cells of your body." *Dan Millman*

When speaking of "healing into Health," I am reminded of code Communication – AT/TA. AT or *Et* (את) is the "untranslatable" word by which I create the world, and TA or *Tah* (תא) is the "cell" resonating with the words I speak. Health or homeostasis results from an alignment between the many modes of my conversation and my society of cells.

Communication loses fluidity and cells, cooperation where my goals are misaligned, e.g.; I want to make money, but I don't want to work. When there is no fluidity to my "receptivity" (no *QKabbalah* and no water of Torah), I'm starved for LOVE. My motivations are unlikely to be pure, and my actions, unlikely to manifest success.

The amount of peace I feel tells me about the quality of my cellular communication. Am I aware of the information my body is transmitting, of what it needs to maintain a stable internal environment? Change entails hearing the message of feelings and sensations, and adapting accordingly. The transformation is permanent when I feel that I am receiving the message *in my cells*. Feeling is the bridge between what my mind is hearing out of the heart's guidance and how my body receives it. The emotion following a belief is how the same belief can lead to very different manifestations.

Emotions are more than just immaterial things. They're actual molecules with a weight and shape. Each emotion is holographically imprinted with a chemical – chemicals for anger, sadness, shame, fear, loneliness... As soon as I am in a given emotional state, the hypothalamus assembles the peptide (a chain of amino-acids), which is then released through the pituitary into the bloodstream, and goes to different parts of the body. Every single cell in the body has these receptors on the outside. When a peptide docks on a cell, it is literally like a key going into a lock. It opens the gate to a whole cascade of biochemical events.

It is true: everything I need to know is within. Each cell is alive with a consciousness that answers my questions. It knows where it came from, where it is going and what it should do. It knows what proteins it is making. It knows whether it's about to divide or to stop dividing. Cells are articulate and intelligent. They talk to me. I hear them say: "I'm hungry," and receive the impressions they're sending to my brain.

However, if my cellular body is not getting its daily bread of chemical needs met, it will start flashing suggestive pictures to my frontal lobe, such as sugar, beer, sex, money... **My cells and I become full-fledged** addicts when I continuously turn off my conscience and take back my will. Unable to hear that enough is "in-off," I am burdened by the reluctant part of me, and left without peace!

Heart	Mind / Body	Soul
Atziluth	Beriah / Assiyah	Yetzirah
Transmission	Creation / Manifestation	Formation

The Order of Creation

Meanwhile, the order of creation is law: body follows mind. When in a sane mind and a sane body, the worlds of creation and manifestation (*Beriah* and *Assiyah*) are freely communicating. This experience is what Jesus spoke: "when you pray for something, believe that you've received it." The QKabbalah of my receptor cells is instantaneous, for good or bad. I am at peace, feeling that my *Yetzirah* formation can only be "de-light-full."

Understand → Choose Peace → emPower the Now.

To understand my ambivalence about choosing Health, I must go into the belly of the whale, just as reluctant prophet Jonah did. This involves reading the signs and symbols when in the DREaM, whether I am in the dreaming or in the waking states.

When in the illusion of separation, I dream of enmity. It would make sense since it is the snake who was cursed with enmity. The snake is the prostitutE by excellence – the part of me that misuses my gift of gab in order to satisfy my personal agendas. snake is also who convinces me to shift my view of reality by closing the third eye (the Eye of Providence) and opening the eyes of duality: "for God knows that when you eat from it your eyes will be opened, and you'll be like God, knowing good and evil" (*Genesis 3:5*). Duality is when I am in a duel with a reality and/or "God" which results in reality and/or "God' becoming my nemesis. Henceforth, what I *see* is good for me is actually bad, and vice-versa. I have just become my own worst enemy.

Code Nemesis - RG / GR

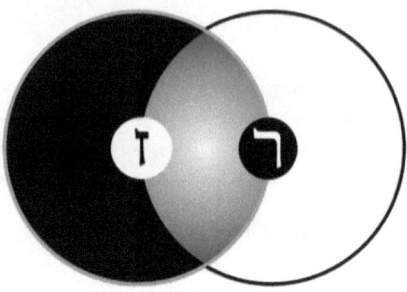

Imagine a language so pure and so sacred that it can reconcile opposites in just two letters...

Right: Hebrew letter Resh (ר) → R in Roman script
Left: Hebrew letter Zayin (ז) → G in Roman script

Here is how S/Hebrew inscribes code "Nemesis" in 2 letters, 2 words:

- **RG**: in one direction, I read *Raz* (רז) for "Mystery, secret."
- **GR**: in the other direction, I read *Zer* (זר) for "molding, crown, border, cap."

The Decoding: when choosing to persevere, I know that I will eventually asked to enter the **Mystery**. I am connected to my heart and my body – at one with the whole of creation. But when I quit so as to pursue private agendas, I have little control of my attention and can't really rise above the mind; the very level where the problem was created. There is now a **cap** placed on my potential – a "**border**" blocking my view of the goal and keeping me safe from my own Power misuses. Not only can't I emPower the Now, but on top of that, I'm now plagued with doubt. The myth of Narcissus comes to help. Gifted with great beauty, Narcissus was too arrogant to accept the love freely given to him. Pride was the **secret** that summoned his *Nemesis*, Greek for "retribution." The reckoning was meant to shatter pride. When a painful pattern repeats in my life, might there be a lesson in humility that I am resisting learning? Whom do I want to humiliate if not myself? Resh (ר) means "head," and Zayin (ז), "weapon." Would I have an enemy if my mind stopped fighting my heart? What am I trying to prove?

To My Nemesis - Reality (a.k.a. "God")

"Even after my skin was destroyed, I saw God in my flesh." Job 19:26

Tolerating adversity is to feel the holy complementarity of opposites. Attuned to the Power of Synchronicity, I say: "let there be health" and see that Health was already written with a big "H." I am the Word made flesh: it is my faith that makes me well.

But when I'm not embodied wisdom, I substitute body sense to body image. For men, it is pornography that fills the void of disembodiment. For women, it is compulsive binging and purging. Pornography and eating disorders are the two sides of the same "sin" coin. On the male side is lust; on the female side, gluttony. Both are futile attempts to control instincts and bodily sensations by trying to shut down any possible chaos. Other misdirected attempts to numb feelings include drugs, overwork, gambling; anything to try to escape the body.

Unable to embrace the sensations, I'm left with an empty and narcissistic image of who I *think* I am. The more the body is disowned, the further I am divorced from the eternal Self. The less I experience the body as a living entity, the more I make it an object to be dominated. Disembodiment and objectification are partners in crime.

Reality becomes my nemesis when I can't seem to resolve the conflict I have with "IT." I am confused, thinking that I'm creating "in God's image," when I am in fact creating in the image my ego thinks "should" exist.

I must now return to the basic formula: Understand → Choose Peace → emPower the Now. Indeed, I don't let go of my story. It lets go of me when I understand it and make it mine. Even if I were to change continents to get away from what ills me, I would still find the same stuff waiting for me in the New Land. I must feel how my being attached to an outcome keeps the madness in place by disallowing the Mystery.

Code Mystery - MALK / KLAM

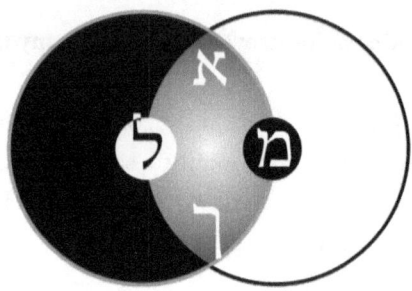

Imagine a language so sacred and so pure that it can reconcile opposites in just four letters...

Top: Hebrew letter Aleph (א) → A in Roman script
Right: Hebrew letter Mem (מ) → M in Roman script
Left: Hebrew letter Lamed (ל) → L in Roman script
Bottom: Hebrew letter Kaph final (ך) → K in Roman script

Here is how S/Hebrew inscribes the code "Mystery" in 5 words, 4 letters:

- **KLAM**: counterclockwise from bottom, I real *Kileim* (כלאם) for "mute."
- **MLL**: right to left to left, I read *Malal* (מלל) for "verbosity."
- **ML**: right to left, I read *Mal* (מל) for "circumcision."
- **MALK**: counterclockwise from right, I read *Malakh* (מאלך) for "messenger, angel."
- **MLA**: right to left to top, I read *Maleh* (מלא) for "full, abundant."

The Decoding: I will start with a gentle reminder of the etymology of the word "Mystery," which comes from Greek *mystēs* "someone who has been initiated" and thus has the *myein* capability "to **mute**, close shut" their mouth. This ties to the fourth word of the Magus: to keep silent.

Truth be told, as long as I am bound to the material world, I will be compelled to speak in order to sell me to you. I need you to buy me. This is how the polarity of prostitution is "FREE speech," as my speech is no longer intoxicated by or slave to a **verbosity** that acts as a smokescreen for my greed. The salability behind my looming deflections must be crushed for me to heal! That is the only way I'd stop lying and actually tell the truth.

Healing begins and ends in mastering silence, as it is the blessed moment when I drop the pain story. I no longer need the sympathy nor the fringe benefits I used to derive from it. When my mouth chakra psychically closes, my lips undergo a **circumcision:** "But Moses said to the LORD, "Behold, the people of Israel have not listened to me. How then shall Pharaoh listen to me, for I am of uncircumcised lips?" *Exodus 6:12.*

The Baal Shem Tov (the "Besht") was certainly a **messenger.** He commented that a true teacher is like an **angel** of the LORD of Hosts, speaking from the sounds and silence of LOVE. The question was put to him: how would I recognize such angel? The Besht replied that, read backwards, the word *Malakh* for "angel, messenger," reads *K'ileim* for "like a mute." If a teacher can remain mute before speaking and inwardly silent while speaking, then *Torah Bakshu Mipihu*, meaning "seek Torah from his mouth."

When intoxicated with the exuberance of my verbosity, I am not a master, as I am yet to hear Truth from within. This may be how the Torah scroll is written without vowels – to allow for existential silence. Words do matter; they produce results! It is only after I purify and "circumcise" my lips that I can take my attention off Scare City and silently place it on providence.

Meanwhile, my "I" resists the no good my "eye" sees, and my mouth defiles me by being compelled to talk about it. My intention is simple: I just want to prevent a fall.

Code FREE Fallin' - AMT / MAT

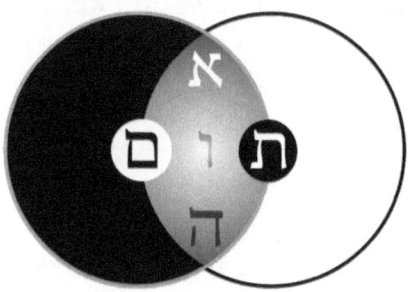

Imagine a language so sacred and so pure that it can reconcile opposites in just five letters...

Top: Hebrew letter Aleph (א) → A in Roman script
Right: Hebrew letter Tav (ת) → T in Roman script
Middle: Hebrew letter Vav (ו) → F, U, V, W in Roman script
Left: Hebrew letter Mem final (ם) → M in Roman script
Bottom: Hebrew letter Heh (ה) → E in Roman script

Here is how S/Hebrew inscribes the code "FREE Fallin'" in 4 words:

- **AMT:** from top to left to bottom, I read *Emet* (אמת) for "truth."
- **MAT:** from left to top to right, I read *Meot* (מאת) for "100."
- **TEWM:** from right to bottom to middle to left, I read *Tehom* (תהום) for "bottom."
- **EWA:** from bottom to middle to top, I read *Hu* (הוא) for "that, this, he."

The Decoding: when caught with my hand in the cookie jar, the chilD in me will lie to avoid the consequences of being punished. Where there is no **truth**, there is no **death** (no change). My demonic golem won't leave me until its angelic expression can be received. Therefore, I will repeat the same pattern until I allow myself to really touch **bottom**. When I come to this level of integrity and am **100%** humbled, it is done. **This** is it: my contract is fulfilled. The mortality that I had tried to deny by postponing change and creating unconscious time is here and now. I die to the "I am not enough" thought, which ends my ambivalence.

I remember how code Commerce takes two words; *Mat* (מת) for "death" and *Tam* (תם) for "PAIRfect" (see *TCO—Book 2*). The two words confirm the archaic sense of *Commerce* as intercourse, which is a little death. The twins that were fighting in my womb, one desiring to do good, and the other, evil now join forces. The good side is no longer "good," the evil side, no longer "evil;" both open to divine "PAIRfection." Alleluia, praise the DREaM: I now have the Power to choose Peace. No more confusion: I can finally decide to receive my own goodness. Indeed, when there is **death**, there is **truth**, and vice-versa.

In truth (pun intended), mortality is an initiation I will one day have to face. I will then transcend duality, free myself from my bondage to Mammon, and know the LOVE that has no opposite. I would make the choice to be happy.

The Choice of True Happiness

> "What man is happy? He who has a healthy body, a resourceful mind, and a docile nature." *Thales of Miletus, mathematician and philosopher*

A docile nature has a readiness or aptness to learn. It gets out of the way so that the lesson would be easily integrated. On the other hand, when I repeat an insane story that can only result in pain, I am indocile as in non-teachable. This means that there's a part of me that is unwilling to digest the soul medicine of evolution. In fact, I may be so afraid of evolving (i.e.; of acquiring more wholesome Power) that I'll handicap myself by making me sick. When being sick is the only Power I have, health will not seem to be a desirable achievement. Henceforth, I pretend to take my recipe for happiness while mentally blocking its effects, and wondering why I won't heal...

Commonly seen on signs in pharmacies, Rx is the symbol for a medical prescription. The R of the mark comes from the Latin "Recipere" for "take this Recipe." The slant across the R's leg (X) is the symbol for the Roman god Jupiter, patron of medicine. **Rx is an invocation for curing an illness that is perceived as a karmic retribution for an offense made to the gods.**

The decision to let or not let a substance affect me explains how some people are better at, for example, holding their alcohol. The same decision (whether conscious or not) is also part of the placebo effect and/or as its counterpart, the nocebo effect. What Jesus called "faith," science calls "placebo" – a beneficial effect produced by a drug or treatment, which cannot be attributed to the properties of the drug or the treatment itself, and must therefore be due to the patient's belief in that treatment. I now have evolved enough to realize that my beliefs create my reality. Therefore, since my faith must be entire to be faith, I wish to give a voice to the part of me that doubts the effectiveness of my chosen modality of healing and thereby, thwarts it.

While akin to superstition, the idea that illness is a karmic retribution from the gods is not new. If my faith makes me well, my doubt makes me ill.

What am I guilty of that I'd prevent me from healing? Once again, the meaning of words comes to help: both words – *placebo* and *nocebo* – come from the Latin. The former means "I shall please;" the latter, "I shall harm."

Consider: when I doubt that my medicine will have pleasant consequences and only believe that it will harm me, I am likely to be denying and repressing my evil inclination. Therein is my error. However, since I hide it from myself, it becomes a transgression – a sin. And it makes me wonder: why would I want to do harm? And if the worst iteration of harm is wrath (which is one of the seven deadly sins), am I ready to die to my sins?

Missing the Mark

> "Forgiveness recognizes what you thought your brother did to you has not occurred. It does not pardon sins and make them real. It sees there was no sin. And in that view are all your sins forgiven." *A Course In Miracles*

Wrath may just be the darkest sin, as it is capable of destroying myself and others. It is a creepy possession that makes me *wroth* – as in full of wrath! To transmute this snake, I must get to the source of why I struggle with forgiveness so much that I would want to hurt "you." As always, I CAN learn from CAIN who was wroth. Just like Cain, I want to hurt you because I resent you for telling me what to do and not allowing me to make my own choices. Since I am yet to come to the center of my integrity, I won't accept the cosmic reality that my brother – and by extension, the world and "God" – is a reflection of me. There is no "you" and no "God" to tell me what I shall give as my offering. The real question is: am I mature enough to take full responsibility for my experience? For if I won't, who will?

I am so tied to a morass of "shoulds" that I am forced to live a compulsory existence where novelty is viewed as a curse, and creativity, frowned upon when it is actually creative. For my rigid standards to perish, my humanity must be tossed upon a sea of uncertainty and go through a dark night until I see "God" face-to-face, revive the sense of the sacred in me, and allow myself to change. To go beyond my false sense of obligation and stop causing effects I would rather not have to experience, I must feel what I truly desire, independently of what "you" may wish for me.

This battle between a perceived "you" and the idea of "me" is the gist of an addict's mind. It is what keeps me from persevering to "THE END" – until I am one with my goal. It is what makes the archer in me miss the mark.

On the note of "missing the mark," the expression has been used as a metaphor for committing a sin. This is tracked to a mysterious etymology attributed to the word "sin." I cannot deny that the letters of "sin" are in the word "missing." :-) However, while the Greek word *Hamartia* does mean "without mark" (blemish-free?), the Hebrew word *Chet* or *Chatah* for "sin" does not have the meaning of "missing the mark." The word *Chet* means "sin, fence." Such are the laws of the Shabbat – a "fence" that protects holiness and prevents me from corrupting it. I am now confronted with a conundrum: on the one hand, when my society ("you") makes anything taboo, it proscribes it as improper or unacceptable. On the other hand, the same society prohibits from use or practice that which is separated or set apart as sacred. No wonder I'd get confused as to what is sacred and what is profane... and miss the mark!

Also pertinent, *Chet* is the 8th letter of the S/Hebrew alphabet. It is one of the 22 *Otiot* for "mark, sign, letter, miracle." As I recall, Cain had such *Ot* (sing.) or "mark" on his forehead, a mark he could only read while looking in the mirror of life. Therefore, if I really want to be free to heal, I need to judge the heck out of "you" in order to know what I believe about myself... Might I still be missing the *Chet's* mark?

A rabbinical story which I already shared in *TCO—Book 2* and will now deepen me gives me the answer. LOL: it begins with "a rabbi, a minister and a few letters walk into a bar..."

THE END of Time

Q: Why did the tardy man stop to purchase a clock?

A: He wanted to buy time.

Here is the story now... As told per Rabbi Ba'al Haturim, when Jacob wished to reveal to his children the secret of the end of time, he felt the Divine Presence depart and was unable to give them the key. He asked his sons if they were still holding on to any sin that could deny them the treasure of self-knowledge. 'Look at the spelling of our twelve names;' they countered, 'you won't find the letters *Chet* (ח) or *Teth* (ט) which spell the word *Chet* (טח) for "sin."' 'True,' replied Jacob. 'But your names also lack the letters *Qoph* (ק) and *Tzaddi* (צ) that join to form the word *Qetz* (קצ) for "end." You are thus probably not meant to come into Self-knowledge.'

This story tells me a whole lot about missing the marks of the S/Hebrew alphabet; marks that reveal an undeniable link between "sin" in repeat and the "end" of time. Indeed, what else do I do besides sinning when creating unconscious time? As for the marks themselves, I already saw how *Mammon* enlivens the sequence of 13th letter Mem and 14th letter Nun. *Mammon* owns me until I surrender my judgments and see that there is nothing wrong: no error, no sin! "And in that view are all my sins forgiven." This viewpoint is "marked" by the sequence of 14th letter Nun and 15th letter Samekh. I have seen how together, these two letters perform the *Nes* "miracle" of the one thing in which the below "supports the fallen" from above.

Similarly, two sequences are signaled by the *Chet* and *Qetz*, words whose letters are miraculously absent from the S/Hebrew names of the Twelve Tribes of Jacob / Israel. Indeed, Chet and Teth (spelling the word *Chet*) are the 8th and 9th letters of the alphabet, while Qoph and Tzaddi (spelling the word *Qetz*) are the 19th and 18th letters of the alphabet. The point? Health is a complex progression towards emPowerment, just as emPowerment is a complex progression towards Health.

But what is Power? Is it knowledge, money, sex? When considering that time is the great equalizer (each of us being given 24 hrs. a day), Power may just be what I do with time. Provided that I seek the QKingdom first, it behooves me to know that there is order in the chaos of knowledge – a visible order that is marked by the sequencing and pairing of the alphabet leading me to be the Logos. Therein is the Path of the Cross that goes from Aleph "the ox" to Tav "the mark" – the S/Hebrew origin of the Greek Alpha and Omega, a path successfully talked and walked by Jesus. When I reach the goal of being at once the first and the last, I am beyond time. Being the light of the Word made flesh, I know health. Indeed, it is unthinkable for me not to be true to myself. The hazy impostorship of the prostitutE vanishes to be replaced by the lucid accuracy of FREE speech.

Meanwhile, if I do not reveal the jewels hidden in my dis-ease, I'll be sick or poor or both. However, by persevering in bringing forth that which is inside me, I will fulfill my purpose. My sense of time will then shift from linear *chronos* to purposive *kairos*, that is, from "quantity time" to "quality time." I saw how the root of the Greek word *kairos* can be traced back to the practice of archery (also weaving and rhetoric). In archery, it is the rare moment when the arrow is discharged with such single-pointedness that it is one with the target. Missing the mark isn't possible when the archer has the knowledge of a door of time opening for the purpose of the arrow of Self to pass through.

Therefore, coming to the end of time is to be on purpose – able to recognize when the Now requires the gumption to drive through and what would be the proper use of force. It is the wisdom of a judgment that takes advantage of the laws of motion, and rarely misses the expedient course of action. This is when my doctor's program instinctively clicks in, shifting me from nocebo into placebo. It now becomes my true pleasure to follow the voice and obey my inner law (i.e.; to take my recipe for happiness). It is no longer an obligation I resent, as there is no other to approve or disapprove of me. The time of killing me by way of tribal suicide is over.

To resume: if it is my faith that makes me well, it is my doubt that makes me ill. I doubted myself because I harmed myself and others. The worst form of harm was engaging wrath which, next to greed, may be the ultimate sin.

Judgment Day

> "Only our concept of time makes it possible for us to speak of the Day of Judgment by that name; in reality it is a constant court in perpetual session." *Franz Kafka*

Will I be judged for my wrath? If I was full of rage, it's because I felt that I couldn't follow the beat of my own drummer and speak truth. If I did, I would be abandoned. So, I sold myself to my creation of "you" as who owned me, and held on to my wounds hoping to make you feel bad. Yep, I went from Scare City into the darkest place in Anarchy Ville there was, until I could let go of the tyranny of appearances long enough to begin witnessing the emergence of mastery. This is when I found that I was beyond mind, space, time and judgment.

The Jews call it *Yom Hadin* – the "Day of Judgment," which takes place each year on Yom Kippur – the day of atonement. For the Christians, it is *the Final Judgment,* when Jesus, the Son of God, will judge "the living and the dead" before destroying the old heaven and earth which are corrupted with sin. The Muslims also call the Day of Judgment *Yawm ad-Din* – same denomination than in Hebrew. Allah will then decide how people will spend their afterlife. While most Muslims believe they have free will, they also believe that they will be judged by God for the choices they made: do good, you'll go to an Edenic paradise; do bad and you'll burn in hell! On a day decided by Allah and known only to Allah, life on Earth will come to an end as Allah will destroy everything. On this day all the people who have ever lived will be raised from the dead and will face judgment. Clearly, "the end" is connected to the idea of "sin."

The Islamic version is the scariest. What helps me is to realize that being free to surrender is the extent of my free will. The only decision I make is to strive for self-knowledge. Period. When I realize that my "yes" reply, my "no" reaction and my big "YES" response were and are already decided for me, I see that Allah rules over the *Al / Lo* of code Attention (forthcoming). However, before I can relax into the knowing that ALL is done through me, I will be afraid of death because I will suffer from a case of mistaken identity. Indeed, I will firmly believe that I end at the skin, as the body but also as the doer of the deed. Therefore, kudos to me when I get it "right," and rotten tomatoes when I get it wrong.

But who else is judging me besides myself? And if I could let go and let "God," wouldn't my judgments be what I surrender? Truth is: I don't know what's for my highest good. I just *think* I do.

When I surrender, the mind that was split by desire ("this is good") and resistance ("this is bad") returns to innocence (no good or bad judgment). And it makes me wonder... *Din* (Hebrew and Arabic for "judgment") also names the female side of the tree – its Dragon pillar, which holds the sphere of *Geburah* or "Power" at its core. Henceforth, to heal my Power issues, I must restore the "womb" of compassion of the Sacred Feminine. Doing so will satiate the Dragon's hunger for being right, and help me to spontaneously transition from GReed into GRace. For in that resting place, I am as far away from burning in hell as I could possibly be. THE END.

Part IV: THE END

- Code Mastery – AWT / MYM
- From GReed into GRace
- Code Nourishment – MN / E / AW
- This is IT!
- Healing the Wounded Healer
- From Hypocrite to Hippocratic…
- Fish Page

AT/TA	MY/YM	TM/MT
Individual Power	Symbolic Power	Collective Power
Alchemy	Astrology	Theurgy
Communication	Healing via Sentience	Commerce

The Triple Code of Mastery

Code Mastery - AWT / MYM

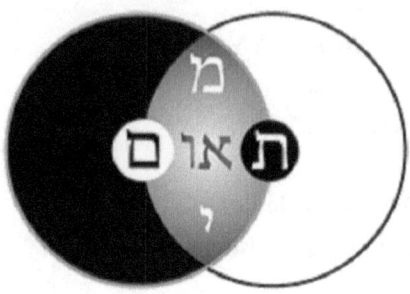

Imagine a language so pure and so sacred that it can reconcile opposites in just two triads – AWT and MYM...

Top: Hebrew letter Mem (מ) → M in Roman script
Right: Hebrew letter Tav (ת) → T in Roman script
Middle: Hebrew letter Aleph (א) and Vav (ו) → A and F, U, V, W
Left: Hebrew letter Mem final (ם) → M in Roman script
Bottom: Hebrew letter Yod (י) → I, J, Y in Roman script

Here is how S/Hebrew inscribes code "Mastery" in 6 letters, 4 words:

- **AW:** center, I read *Ow* (או) for "either/or."
- **AWT:** from middle to right, I read *Ot* (אות) for "mark, marvel, sign, word."
- **MYM:** from top to bottom to left, I read *Mayim* (מים) for "pairs of waters."
- **TMYM:** from right to top to bottom to left, I read *Tamim* (תמים) for "perfect."
- **TAWMYM:** from right to middle to top to bottom to left, I read *Teomim* (תאומים) for "twins."

The Decoding: these SIX signs (AWTMYM) regroup and interact as two three-lettered words, but also as three codes (each of two letters) to engrave Mastery. This triple code – Communication, Commerce,

Sentience – confirms how my inner Hermes can become *Trismegistus* or "thrice-master" by understanding the operation of three luminaries:

- **Code Communication AT/TA** (see *TCO—Book 2, Learning to Code*): when I understand the operation of the sun, I am the Word made flesh – the Logos. I become a master of alchemy, and of communication.
- **Code Commerce TM/MT** (see *TCO—Book 2, Choosing Mastery*): when I understand the operation of the moon, I come to see that my life is "PAIRfect," and die to who I think I "should" be. I become a master of theurgy, and of commerce.
- **Code Sentience MY/YM** (see upcoming *You Had Me at Elohim!*): when I understand the operation of the stars, I know who I am and do not mind being as a drop merging with the ocean. I become a master of astrology, and of healing.

AT/TA	MY/YM	TM/MT
Individual Power	Symbolic Power	Collective Power
Alchemy	Astrology	Theurgy
Communication	Healing via Sentience	Commerce

The Triple Code of Mastery

It is Hippocrates, the Father of Medicine, who said: "a physician without a knowledge of Astrology has no right to call himself a physician." Surely, I can accept that illness starts in the mind. When it is my pleasure to obey my inner law, I open to the placebo effect. But when I feel coerced, I conjure up the nocebo effect. To come to the center of my integrity, astrology gives me twelve universal mental patterns (SIX against SIX, consummating each other). Moreover, when I realize that 3 of the 22 letters of the S/Hebrew alphabet invoke 3 twin elements, 7 of the 22, the 7 classical planets, and the remaining 12, the 12 astrological signs, I am better equipped to understand a sign's decision-making modalities, on the background of its planet and its element.

Healing is a process that changes my mental view of the Self – my identities. **It helps me deal with a fundamental error of judgment: the beliefs that I know what is unfair, and that unfairness should be sentenced.** I live in the past, and can't seem to give up the need to punish the people and the gods who have hurt me and humiliated me. Wanting to get even, I allow wrath to take over. Truth be told, I'm caught in vengeance, and so obsessed by it that it possesses me as it did Cain. I can't forgive my debtors, even if not forgiving them ruins my life. I am quite far from knowing who I am, and I don't even realize it!

Astrology is not as concerned by a birth under a specific sun sign (e.g.; I am a Leo), as it is about 12 signs or labors that are all meant to be traversed in order to elevate the soul. These signs are 12 patterns of energy for me to understand myself and let go of who I think I am. Such is the esoteric meaning of the twelve labors of Hercules, when my inner *Hercules* (Greek for "light of the soul") is turned on. After passing these 12 initiations, I know it's not about me! One sign will promptly lead me to "nothing personal:" Gemini – the first Air sign of the Zodiac. Ruled by Mercury and chasing the unattainable, this twin constellation is irrefutably mental, prone to doubt and destined to decode opposites.

Teomim for "twins" is also at the root of the name Thomas and of being a doubting Thomas when he was the disciple who asked the deepest questions. It makes sense that the word *Ow* (או) for the "either or" of an addicted mind is at the core of *Teomim* (תאומים). Taking *Ow* out of *Teomim* leaves me with *Tamim* or "**perfect.**" When my twins embrace their addiction to vengeance and to making the other twin pay, there is no more split will. The two parts of me – the one that knows what to do and the one that doesn't want to do it – join in wholesome communication and commerce with each other. I can now see myself transcending the duel of these two parts to be *Tamim* "**PAIRfect,**" and come to the LOVE that has no opposite.

Consider: when there is no one left to fight, the decision to heal is made for me. Before the decision, I fear falling. After the decision, I am FREE to fall.

The prostitutE - Health with a big "H"

From GReed into GRace

The Mission of emPowering NOW is to test, experience, and bring forth *Golden XPR* as a path to transition from a world of GReed that splits Giving and Receiving by communicating fear, confusion and domination, to a world of GRace that unites Giving and Receiving by communicating wisdom, understanding and kindness.

GR is code for Giving/Receiving. When I can't quite give it all, I am not at peace and there's something I do not understand. But if I could be honest about being in service to Mammon, I would accept where I am and do no harm. I would also begin to develop trust and effectively shift from GReed into GRace, as I'd let go of my petty concerns.

While my prostitutE is in survival mode, I am not aware that the white unnumbered sphere below is the mouth chakra and is a bridge to higher modes of consciousness. Afraid to surrender, I stay small and try to control my money and my health. My fears cause the mouth's gradual fall, first into the heart chakra, second into the sex chakra and third, into the root chakra, prompting a few questions on the way:

1. The fall into **7-greed**: will I get them before they get me?
2. The fall into **2-lust**: can I mate with that person?
3. The fall into **4-gluttony**: can I eat it? Will it eat me?

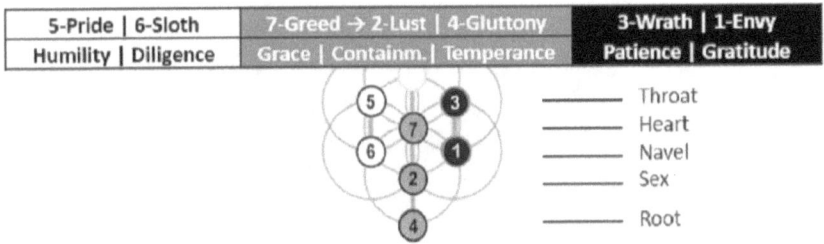

The Seven Infernal Spheres of the Tree of Life below the Mouth Chakra

I am now in Mammon's domain, subjected to a terrible yearning that cancels out the possibility to get any satisfaction. Perhaps one day, I'll be able to trust. But for now, I am in Scare City, fearing to give and to forgive. If believing that I'm not enough leads me to compromise my integrity and with it, my immune system, honesty builds them back. Eventually, the sadness and despair I resist feeling, and the subsequent ailment and depression become chronic. To drop my pain story, I must endeavor to satiate a ravenous and archetypal hunger, and become willing to hear "enough!"

To help this transition into GRace, I must recognize the nature of my throat pathology by determining which side of me gets most triggered. Am I more prone to the bouts of hysteria of a dis-eased female side or to the fake kindness of a dis-eased male side? If, for example, I see that the female part of me is "cursed," I can focus on the female path of sins, giving me the permission to invite **1-envy** and **3-wrath** so as to feel and understand them. If I see that the male part of me is cursed, I can focus on the male path of sins, giving me the permission to invite **6-sloth** and **5-pride** so as to feel and understand them. Note: this concerns me whether I am male, female or non-binary.

Since I am contaminated by the greed that permeates it all, I ultimately engage all sins. To best understand how the seven deadly sins partner with each other in the seven infernal spheres, I have the solo course TABU, an acronym for *The Anarchist's Book of Understanding*. This course goes a long way to help my prostitutE end the anarchy.

Click on the image here or visit https://www.goldenxpr.com/7-tabu-intro-video/ for an animated overview of TABU – why don't I have the courage to really be spiritually incorrect, and wake up?

Code Nourishment – MN / E / AW

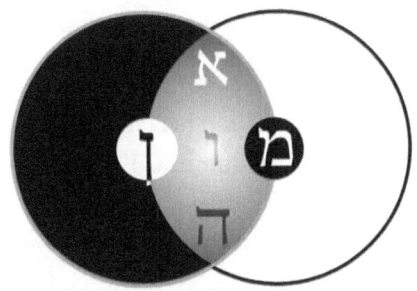

Imagine a language so pure and so sacred that it can reconcile...

Top: Hebrew letter Aleph (א) → A in Roman script
Right: Hebrew letter Mem (מ) → M in Roman script
Middle: Hebrew letter Vav (ו) → F, U, V, W in Roman script
Left: Hebrew letter Nun final (ן) → M in Roman script
Bottom: Hebrew letter Heh (ה) → E in Roman script

Here is how S/Hebrew inscribes code "Nourishment" in 5 letters, 2 questions:

- **MN EWA:** from right to left to bottom to middle to top, I read *Man Hu* (מן הוא) for "what is it?" and also for "manna."
- **ME AWN:** from right to bottom to top to middle to left, I read *Mah Ohn* (מה און) for "what strength?"
- **AMWNE:** from top to right to middle to left to bottom, I read *Emunah* (אמונה) for "faith."

The Decoding: about the **manna**, the question "**what is IT?**" could be rephrased as "what is EAT?", since eating is even more intimate than sex, and since the **strength** supposedly imparted by food is a mystery. Food seems to be physical, yet it is not in light of satiety having nothing to do with the quality or the quantity of food I may ingest. I ignore that I came to Earth from emptiness, where matter is not solid, money is not intimidating, and food is not only made of calories or carbs. Subsequently, I cannot hear Isaiah's invitation: "Come, all you who are thirsty, come to the waters; and you who have no money, come, buy and eat!"

What is this mysterious water which is clearly not for sale? These questions surround the nature of the manna. This is how the letters of *Man Hu* (מן הוא) for **"what is it?"** can be reordered as the word *Emunah* (אמונה) for **"faith;"** the very faith that makes all well. Most of the time, I have a reason for doing what I do, e.g.; I work for money. When I do what I do simply because that's what I do, I am a virgin, a word which used to mean "someone whose conception is immaculate." When virginal, I am aware to give it all to LOVE. The strength of faith now supports me, allowing me to believe in myself with 100% certainty. What strength, indeed?

Reordering the letters of faith into "what strength" reminds me of reordering the letters of wisdom into "what force?" Might my unwillingness to surrender be how I feel either so hopelessly weak or so inappropriately strong?

My doubts are triggered by the hunger I dread as soon as I enter the unknown. 'In the desert the whole community grumbled against Moses and Aaron, saying: "if only we had died in Egypt! There we ate all the food we wanted, but you've brought us out into this desert to starve us to death."' (*Exodus 16:2-3*) I wish I could perceive that matter is fluid and the desert, nurturing! I'd no longer be slave to the number of bills I have in my wallet or of calories I eat. I would understand that the Mem and Nun in *Mammon* must pave the way to the Mem and the Nun of my *Emunah* faith!

Saying that this mysterious milky substance that flows so *freely* is not for sale and that it is the manna just deflects the question: what is the manna?

The S/Hebrew word for **"manna"** first appears in *Exodus 16:15*. However, it is not a noun but a question – just as the unleavened bread of

Passover is known as "the bread of the question." To answer it, students of wisdom traditions - east and west - read the scriptures slowly while chewing on the Word until they feel "full-filled." As for me, the end of dissatisfaction with the material world comes when I am ready for how truth will change my life. "I humbled me, causing me to hunger and then feeding me with a manna which neither I nor my ancestors had known, to teach me to not live on bread alone, but on every word that comes from the mouth of LOVE." (*Deuteronomy 8:3*)

That level of humility which sees the mouth chakra as the mouth of LOVE hears and understands that Truth is the real nourishment.

THIS IS IT!

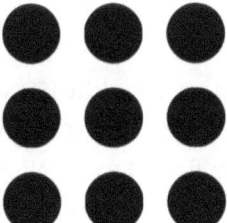

THIS IS IT! I entered the Land of Milk and Manna – when I no longer sell my soul to the Devil for a few bucks, when the forced labor is over, as are the resentment and the will to retaliate, when suffering and liberation from suffering are equal.

I am neither in "seek" mode nor in sick mode. I simply do what I do because that's what I do. Period. An Immaculate Conception.

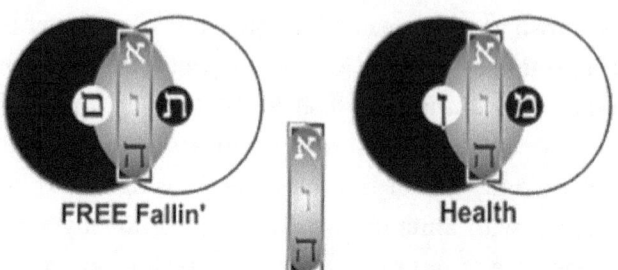

The Ascent of the Word *Hu* for "[This is] IT!"

Looking at the images of codes FREE Fallin' and Health, I see how they share the same vertical core, namely Heh (ה), Vav (ו) and Aleph (א). These signs write the word *Hu* (הוא) for "that, this, it, he." Indeed, what is IT? What is it that is eating me if not the Vav of a desire which, when split from my heart, goes in pursuit of private goals? This is the perfect setup for me to be unable to get any satisfaction.

Looking at the two black dots, I see Tav (ת) and Mem (מ) – both in the room of 4-Resisting as they spell *Mat* (מת) for "death." When I look at the white dots, I see Mem final (ם) and Nun final (ן) that ends *Mam-Mon* when written in two words. I have seen how Mem final is the end of desire, and Nun final, the end of indebtedness. Both join to spell the end of Mammon.

To move from FREE Fallin' into Health, I answer the question "what is IT," by lessening the "he" drive – the male willpower that wants to believe "he" can make things happen. Upon realizing that I am simply a witness of what occurs, I drop the story that I can create the reality my ego wants. Finally, I surrender my judgments of reality.

Since I am no longer calling the shots, the desire to be indebted to "you" or to have "you" owing me vanishes, taking with it any remnant of wrath. I can now take full responsibility for my bondage to Mammon, and end it. As such, this may just be the most crucial step in healing my creation of wealth and health.

The Wealth of Health | The Health of Wealth

Healing the Wounded Healer

"A wise man should consider that health is the greatest of human blessings, and learn how by his own thought to derive benefit from his illnesses." *Hippocrates*

The illusion of separation will prompt me to become my own healer. Surely, if I am the only one who can hurt me, I am also the only one who can heal me. As a parallel, I am guided to explore the Hippocratic Oath – the oath that a medical student takes when becoming a doctor. One of the promises within this oath has been derived as *primum non nocere* for "first, do no harm." Little did I know that the SIX "days" of **mastery (bolded** below) are behind the original text of the Hippocratic Oath. Hermes was called *Trismegistus* or "thrice-master," as the god of communication, commerce and healing. Therefore, to heal requires some level of mastery, the first of which being to take an oath. While I could say "to decide" or "to commit," to say "to swear" adds the mystical component that I tend to repress and deny, and without which there is no mastery and no healing.

- **To swear,** by Apollo the Healer, Hygiea the Hygienist, Panacea the Universal Solvent, and making them my witnesses that I will carry out, according to my ability and judgment, this oath and indenture. In other words, to heal, I must keep it clean (no lies), and look at my chosen commitment as addressing the whole of me in order to grant me the power of dissolving the problem of indebtedness and cause a solution. This is the surest way to terminate my prostitutE whose game is to alter procedures, which makes me feel like a fraud.
- **To heal,** by holding my teachers in this art (and therefore, my wound) equal to my own parents, and make them partners in my livelihood, sharing money with them if need be.
- **To will,** by using regimens and treatments to benefit my patients according to my ability and judgment; by abstaining from causing injury or wrong-doing, especially from abusing the bodies of man or woman, bond or free.
- **To keep silence,** by never divulging what I see or hear in the course of my work, as well as outside my profession, holding such things to be holy secrets; by imparting instruction to who took the Healer's oath, but to nobody else.
- **To dare,** by honoring the oath I took (no exception), thereby keeping pure and holy both my life and my art; by delegating or giving referrals where and when I am not qualified.
- **To know,** by carrying out this oath, that I may gain for ever reputation among all men for my life and for my art; but if I break it and forswear myself, may the opposite befall me.

Individual Power	Symbolic Power	Collective Power
Spirit → Heart	Mind / Body	Voice → Soul
To Heal → To Will	To Know / To Keep Silence	To Swear → To Dare

The SIX "Days" of Being a Healer

From Hypocrite to Hippocratic...

Prepare to DIE! Inquiry tool: www.goldenxpr.com/tco3_hippocratic/

Step 1: I fill in the blank: I want to know WHY I would choose to think I CAN'T _____ (e.g.; find a job, be patient, etc.). **Step 2:** I ask for truth and generate a number. **Step 3:** I find my number on the map and fill in the brackets: having created "money" as my master and invited [**Prostitution**], I am called to let go of [**Initiation**]. Passing this test also means [**Mastery**] to do no harm, which is the prerequisite to having the [**FREE Speech**] I yearn for. **Step 4:** what most surprised me in this process was [_____].

When my prostitutE stretches to the sacred, the 3rd eye opens. My Engineer / genius is now out of the bottle. This is the last alchemical stage – where the sun sets. Transcendence also means that I healed my relationship to Power.

Parallel to the 3rd eye's opening, the mouth chakra closes. I can keep silent. I can stop using my words to gain some personal advantage or to have you buy me. I am no longer compelled to use my charisma to derive sexual and/or financial favors to offset the sense that I am not enough. I trust myself, and *that* is enough. I have nothing left to prove.

In light of the prostitutE being such a trickster, it is wise to keep on asking myself: 1) what do I say or do in order to convince you to believe something about me? Surely, my trying to convert you says that I don't really believe me. Why the doubt? If I were, for example, to ritually say "I've got it" to convince you that I have attained, this would be a hint that I think of myself as a fraud. I would now have to look at what I do to sabotage myself and reveal the shaming behaviors I carefully hide in the dark. Have I fallen into the triple net of Belial: wealth, fornication and pollution of the sanctuary?

Herein ends the prostitutE's chapter – *"Health with a Big H"* as I transition into the saboteuR's chapter – *"You had me at Elohim!"*

THREE

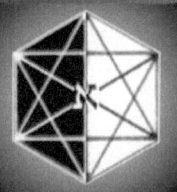

The saboteuR - You had me at Elohim!

> "Intimacy is a totally different dimension. It is allowing the other to come into you, to see you as you see yourself." *Osho*

INTIMACY IS OFTEN TAKEN to be of a sexual nature. But what is sex? "SEX" is of the soul, as it speaks of attraction. If SEX attracts opposites, SIN repulses them. SIN is how I fear the dark tomb of the womb. Seeing through deception is how to feel at home in the dark night of the soul and nullify the gravity of its pull. I become a lover of reality. Meanwhile, I will use wrath to take me down. It is now SEX vs. SIN: who will win? If I had free will, would I choose to continuously sabotage my efforts? If I heard and followed the call of my heart, I would not fear rejection. I would instead open to Love, and be able to handle conflict. No wonder I'm so afraid to decide: I keep on eating from the tree of the "ignorance" of good and evil! Henceforth, I can only be at war with SEX, misreading what it means to be a man or a woman. To receive the sexual healing I asked for, I must witness the snake turning into a Messiah. This will allow me to be free, fulfilled, and will I dare say it, "orgasmed, redeemed and saved." Heck, today may just be the day when the lover comes – the day when the saboteuR sheds its dark skin to reveal the light body of the Visionary it was hiding.

I AM A VISIONARY: WE ALL ARE! WHETHER MY ART IS TO BUILD A BUSINESS OR TO PAINT THE SISTINE CHAPEL, I SIGNED UP FOR A "SEX" PROGRAM BY WHICH TO LET "GOD" IMPREGNATE ME WITH THE SEED OF INSPIRATION.

HOWEVER, IF MY POLARITIES ARE REVERSED, I AM NOT OPEN TO THE MYSTERY. I CAN NO MORE GET SATISFACTION THAN I CAN FEEL THE DIVINE IN ACTION. I ONLY SEE THE PROOF OF ABANDONMENT THAT I AM PROGRAMMED TO EXPECT! THIS IS THE OPPOSITE OF MY HEART'S TRUE DESIRE. AS MY DECISION-MAKING IS WARPED AND MY THROAT, POSSESSED, I GO FROM EXTREMES TO DEFICIENCIES. MY WIRES ARE SO CROSSED THAT WHAT I THINK IS BAD IS ACTUALLY GOOD FOR ME, AND VICE-VERSA, WHAT I THINK IS GOOD IS ACTUALLY BAD FOR ME. I INCREASINGLY LOOSE COHERENCE AS I BLINDLY RESIST WHAT FURTHERS ME AND DESIRE WHAT DESTROYS ME.

The Nigrodo Stage of Putrefaction – when the black saboteuR wishes to be a Visionary

I have now officially entered the Dark Night of the Soul. Even if I were to know what my soul wishes to express, I am still prey to so much doubt that I'd rather be a saboteuR (R) in the dark than a Visionary (V) in the light.

I am yet to realize that the curse that I am experiencing today is yet to reveal itself to be a great blessing – for me and for all!

Next Stage: the saboteuR's Putrefaction

Prepare to DIE! Inquiry tool: www.goldenxpr.com/tc03_sabotage/

Step 1: I fill in the blank: I want to know WHY I would choose to think I CAN'T _____ (e.g.; find a job, be patient, etc.). **Step 2:** I ask for truth and generate a number. **Step 3:** I find my number on the map and fill in the brackets: when I ignore the answer to [**SIX Shadow Questions**], I become a saboteuR possessed by [**SABOTAGE**]. The lie must have marinated and putrefied enough for me to be ready to face my [**Actualization**]. **Step 4:** what most surprised me in this process was [___].

Part I: *Elohim* at the First Sight

- Bipolarity, Angels & Demons
- Revisiting the War of the Sexes
- The Odd Couple of Judgment and Mercy
- Code Sexual Healing – AL / YE
- The Powers and the Sins
- The SIN of the SON of "God"
- The 3 Ps of an Unconscious Eros
- The Powers of a Conscious Logos

Yod (י)	Vav (ו) / Heh (ה)	Heh (ה)
Individual Power	Symbolic Power	Collective Power
Solar Lion	Stellar Child	Lunar Dragon
The Father	The Son / The Mother	The Daughter

YEWE's Three Energetic Flows

Bipolarity, Angels & Demons

"I know the empathy borne of despair; I know the fluidity of thought, the expansive, even beautiful, mind that hypomania brings, and I know this is quicksilver and precious and often it's poison. There has always existed a sort of psychic butcher who works the scales of transcendence, who weighs out the bloody cost of true art." *David Lovelace, Scattershot: My Bipolar Family*

While some of us may be bolder in how extreme the extremes are to which we swing our emotional pendulum, I wonder if we might all be touched by some level of bipolar disorder. It could be argued that, until I have the sense of enough, I'll be on a merry-go-round, going from excesses to deficiencies. It could also be argued that, until I complete my inquiry and come to the complete understanding of Oneness, I will be divided and, at times, serve the "yearning" of Mammon, looking for LOVE in the "wrong" places. My split mind will be doing my thinking, "split / mind" being the meaning of Greek *schizo / phrenia*. Trapped in fears and doubts, it is likely that I will superimpose painful memories upon reality. As for the "God" Name *Elohim*, I will not hear it from within, and will not sustain the Power of Synchronicity that can wish for light and see my wish instantly fulfilled: "there *was* light." Instead, there will be a misalignment between what I say I want to create and what I have in reality. I'll repeat the same error in creating unconscious time, fearing speed and postponing decisions.

But why block the Power of Synchronicity? I may begin with the problem that the Name *Elohim* presents in traditional Judaism. If in Hebrew grammar, the suffix *-im* (YM) is the mark of the masculine plural, how can this Name be plural? Isn't "God" One? Once again, the observer and/or translator effect visits me. There is another way to understand *Elohim* when I see that the game of life is to play and work with polarity.

Upon looking closely, I see that the word *Elohim* (אלהים) holds the two significant pairs *El* (אל) and *Yah* (יה) – the code inscribing sexual healing. These two pairs are the "God" Names that traditionally activate the spheres of kindness and wisdom. Moreover, as suffixes, they are your regular angel wings: add them to any name, and you'll make an angel, e.g.; Rapha-*El,* Auri-*El,* Jeremi-*Yah,* Zechari-*Yah.* Angels are angels because they obey their heart: no split mind there, no two parts in a duel – one part of me knowing what to do; the other part opposing it! Thus, to have my *El Yah* wings back, the knowledge of good and evil and thus the sexual healing I wish to have, as well as the Power of Synchronicity under my belt, I must allow kindness and wisdom to trade places. **This is the Great Innovation brought forth on the path of** *Golden XPR* **– a shift that ends the war of the sexes.**

Revisiting the War of the Sexes

"I have feelings too. I am still human. All I want is to be loved, for myself and for my talent." *Marilyn Monroe*

Understanding that we are One is easier said than done, especially when I am deeply saddened because you won't love me as I wish you would. This is Cain's story all over again. Feeling that we are connected is a messianic feeling. The good news is: if there's a beginning to my golem (the beliefs sourcing my separation), there's also an end. The day will come when the secret behind my sabotage will no longer be hidden. I will own that my polarities are reversed, and stop blocking my healing. I will also stop staging rejection and using the pain of it to justify my wrongdoing. I will dare to be in my Power. For now, I can't speak what I want since the female side of my throat is possessed, dreaming it is hopelessly under the ruling of a male side that doesn't really want me. Far from being balanced, my polarities are off.

Balanced Polarities		Reversed Polarities	
Female Side	Male Side	Female Side	Male Side
Resists Evil	Desires Good	Desires Evil	Resists Good
Feels Loved	Feels Respected	Feels Unwanted	Feels Crowded
Receives	Gives	Clings	Withdraws

Polarities - Balanced and Reversed

Yes, the polarities invert at the throat – the rung that is just under *Daath's* mouth and its knowledge of opposites. So, I'm the Woman. I **desired evil** and gave it to me by eating the forbidden fruit. Now that I disobeyed my heart, **I feel unwanted.** I project that "God" doesn't love me or respect me. And if it is not "God" who won't accept my offering, it is my partner, my cat, my bank account, my body... Bottom line, it is "you," and I hate you for it. This is how my **giving/receiving** gets out of balance; either too much or not enough. This is also how I become needy – a **clinger!**

The thing is: the more my **female side clings**, the more **my male side withdraws** (and vice-versa). It is pure physics! This sexual problem has nothing to do with gender: some men cling and some women withdraw. It all depends of how attached "I" am to this set of beliefs: I am a woman. I am a man. I am not a woman. I am not a man. I am non-binary.

I have seen how this scenario is projected onto the workings of the tree of (my) life in *Genesis 2*, after I lie to myself by eating what I shouldn't have eaten. The higher spheres of the tree of life still resonate with the Power of Three, an order which becomes chaos in the lower spheres. The common sense I had in the sphere of understanding, "common" as you and I share it, is nullified. Having lost my connection to this sphere closes my third eye and, in turn, disempowers my throat. Since the throat is the center of decision-making, I may hear people mirroring my own thoughts and asking me: "how can you be so intelligent and make such poor decisions?"

I WANT TO SCREAM: "HOW? I DON'T HAVE A MALE SIDE TO PROTECT ME. I'M LONELY, DESPAIRED AND RAVENOUSLY HUNGRY FOR POWER."

Interior Male	Interior/Exterior Neutral	Exterior Female
Individual Power	Symbolic Power	Collective Power
Spheres 4 & 7	Spheres 9 & 10	Spheres 5 & 8
Kindness & Victory	Honesty & QKingdom	Power & Appreciation

The Key Players and Spheres in the Inferno

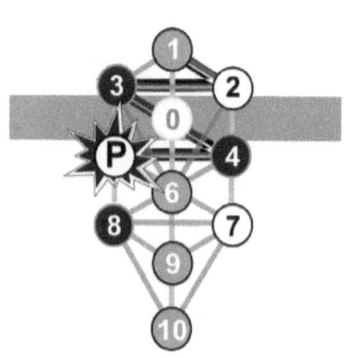

As the light moves in the inferno of the lower spheres (a.k.a. Ego-Egypt or the first tier), it first goes to *Chesed* "kindness" (#4). However, I don't feel "kind." I'm too busy repressing the shame of my lies. So, now, instead of honoring my female partner (the sphere with a big P for "Power"), my male side dismisses her. This unconscious act has a ricochet effect. Female "Power" now attacks, wanting to take down a male "kindness" that is disingenuous. Just as Shylock in *The Merchant of Venice*, I cannot be merciful if the law demands it! I just want my pound of flesh and, dammit, I'm gonna get it, even if I have to kill for it; even if it kills me.

Since wisdom (sphere 2) is unattainable, I don't know the difference between what I CAN and CAN'T change. **I also don't know that my polarities are reversed: kindness (sphere 4) is now yin-black although it is on a yang-white male pillar. Power (sphere 5) is now yang-white although it is on a yin-black female pillar.**

If my kindness is manipulative, and my use of Power, hysterical, it is because my male side suffers from anima possession and my female side from animus possession. When neither my male side nor my female side has a healthy anima, womb or Heh in its name, I CAN'T get pregnant (or receive). My female is now getting "hangrier" by the minute and my male's anima, goes more and more into hiding. SO PUH-LEASE, DON'T TALK TO ME ABOUT DIVINE MERCY OR JUSTICE OR CHARITY!

The Odd Couple of Judgment and Mercy

"Therefore, Jew, though justice be thy plea, consider this, that in the course of justice none of us should see salvation: we do pray for mercy; And that same prayer doth teach us all to render the deeds of mercy." *William Shakespeare*

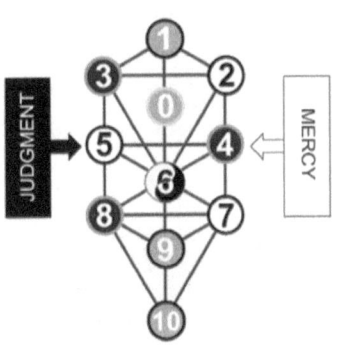

The throat chakra is perhaps the most challenging rung of the tree, as it is where mercy and severity ought to balance each other as opposites. It becomes the most pathological rung when these ideas are in fact at war, a tragedy heightened by my polarities being inverted. **On the classical tree – the version that currently informs the collective, the male pillar is the "pillar of mercy,"** since kindness (sphere 4) is at its core, and the female pillar is the "pillar of judgment," since Power (sphere 5) is at its core.

Being above the heart, the throat consciousness ought to be selfless and not egocentric. And yet, the throat is still part of the first tier – the lower worlds of "Ego-Egypt" below self-knowledge (**sphere 0**). In terms of Spiral Dynamics, throat is the rung where pluralists and rationalists fight each other, each one convinced to be right. It is also interesting that the pluralists who, by definition, go for "plural" truths ("you have your truth, I have my truth, and you can't challenge my truth") would fight someone else's truth.

Until I crossover into the transpersonal by "eating again from self-knowledge," but this time, deliberately and consciously, I will not be true to myself as I won't be able to hold the tension of opposites. And while I fear making the "wrong" choice, I'll tend to make decisions out of resistance and not Peace. The more I fight my highest good, the more my male and female wires get twisted, and the less I am in my Power. "Oh, what a tangled web we weave, when first we practice to deceive!"

A simple solution appears in the interaction of the pairs *El* and *Yah* in the Name *Elohim*. The Name *Elohim* (אלהים) has five letters. The first two letters (אל) form the Name *El* which spins the sphere *Chesed* for "kindness." *Golden XPR* identifies it as the Power of Attention. The next two letters (יה) reverse into the Name *Yah* which spins the sphere *Chokmah* for "wisdom." XPR identifies it as the Power of Patience. The last letter (ם) is Mem final whose role is to lead me to the end of desire. Mem is also a pair since the word *Mem* itself (מם) means "pair of waters." Mem's depth will continue to unfold.

El (אל)	*Mem* (מם)	*Yah* (יה)
The Name behind Kindness	M as in "Mystery"	The Name behind Wisdom
Power of Attention	TBD	Power of Patience

The Three Pairs in Elohim

As for the Powers of attention and patience, combining them allows me to be here and Now. This is *Elohim's* Power of Synchronicity, witnessing the "PAIRfection" of what is. There is no resistance, no judgment; just an integrity that I bring to everything I do. I am in fact so absorbed by the action that I am free of the action. I have no need to force an outcome. This also means that I am Justice in action.

However, to see the marriage of *El* and *Yah* sanctified within the messianic tree (the tree "IN-LOVE"), I still need to open my eyes to a novel perspective. This new way to look at it is a vision in the form of a lemniscate which orchestrates my crossing over to the other side.

Here is the lemniscate that heals my sexual / Power issues by looping "wisdom" and "kindness" together, and thus granting a bidirectional passage between the throat and third eye.

- **The 3rd eye:** first I choose to inhabit a tree "IN-LOVE," where my female side is on the right-hand side. This means that I am facing the tree, and seeing "God" face-to-face. The light first goes to **sphere 2**. This makes sense since male is "like the light," thus seeking to be contained by the female – a vessel that is "like receptivity." **Sphere 2** is "understanding," which keeps me connected to the crown. **Sphere 3** is kindness who ascended after trading places with wisdom who descended into **sphere 4**. "Rendering deeds of mercy" actually depends on my feeling and *understanding* that there is only One of us.
- **The throat: sphere 4** is "wisdom," and this time, female as Greek Sophia is. *Chokmah* "wisdom" volunteered to descend in order to balance *Geburah* – **sphere 5** of "Power." *Geburah* is lit by the "God" Name *El Gibor*, transmitted by XPR as the Power of decision. To make sound decisions, I must be at peace. This also says that I must have the 3rd eye of understanding open, just as Lady Justice who wears a blindfold to block sight and open vision. Surely, the proverbial "peace that passeth understanding" is likely to be in **sphere 1** – the crown center above and beyond **sphere 2** – the 3rd eye of understanding. Now that wisdom is literally on my side, I am back in my Power and in my throat, and can stop the folly of my saboteuR. I know the difference between what I cannot change and what I can. Thus King Solomon (from *Shalom* for "peace") prayed only for wisdom, as embodying wisdom is what granted him the Power of powers (the Power of decision) and made him a supreme judge.

Understand → **Choose Peace** → **emPower the Now**: this formula is the Promised Land of a crown chakra experience, when I love reality – or "God." When **3-wisdom** descends to help out Power and take the place of kindness who was in hiding, **kindness** ascends to be **sphere 2**. A lemniscate (which looks like a figure 8) joins the Powers of *El* (**#3**) and *Yah* (**#4**), infinitely centering me in *Daath* (**#0**) – the "knowledge" of opposites. I can now be *Abram HaIvri* for "Abram the Hebrew," but also and foremost Abram who stands "on the other side" of wrath. This is the side of the LOVE that has no side. This shift is how to have the "sexual knowledge" of my own transformation and really know that I have changed. It is to arrive at the version of me that is on the other side of what I know. It asks me to lose all points of reference and merge with the unknown. This death in *Daath* is dying to my sins – the last of which being wrath, the perversion of the love of Justice. It is accepting the kiss of Truth as the entry point into sexual healing.

Code Sexual Healing - AL / YE

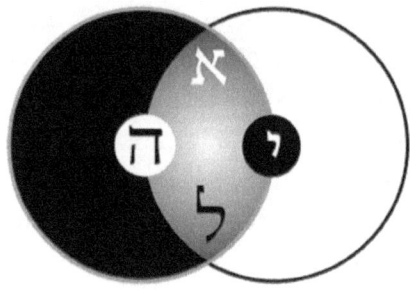

Imagine a language so pure and so sacred that it can reconcile and combine two opposite codes in just four letters...

Top: Hebrew letter Aleph (א) → A in Roman script
Right: Hebrew letter Yod (י) → I, J, Y in Roman script
Left: Hebrew letter Heh (ה) → E in Roman script
Bottom: Hebrew letter Lamed (ל) → L in Roman script

Here is how S/Hebrew inscribes code "Sexual Healing" in 2 codes that are restructured into a third:

- **EY/YE:** left to right and back, I inscribe code Patience by way of the Name *Yah*.
- **LA/AL:** bottom to top and back, I inscribe the beginning of code Obedience by way of the Name *El*.
- **AL YE:** signing (yes, doing the sign of the cross), I inscribe code Sexual Healing by way of the Name *El Yah* (אל יה).

The Decoding: Rabbinical Kabbalah teaches that the "God" Name spinning *Chokmah*, the sphere of wisdom at the level of the third eye (the command center), is *Yah* (יה) and the "God" Name spinning *Chesed*, the sphere of kindness at the level of the throat (the center of decision-making), is *El* (אל). These Names are the *Koachim* or "Powers" which XPR transmits as patience and attention. What I want is to be able to place my attention on my goal, without letting any doubt enter my mind. This is when patience takes precedence. It will likely take time for me to understand why it was necessary (or purposeful) that I would take myself down with doubt and do harm. The more I can follow my folly into wisdom, the more patience I have. The more patience I have, the more I listen to my heart. I can now decide where to place my attention, do the next "write" thing, and experience no time and no mind. **That is sexual knowledge –** *El Yah's ultimate healing!*

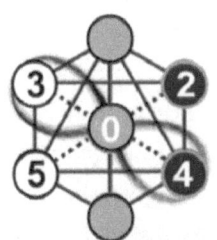

Individual Power	Symbolic Power	Collective Power
3rd Eye (#3) Kindness	Mouth (#0) Knowledge	Throat (#4) Wisdom
El (אל) Attention	*Mayim* (מים) Consummation	*Yah* (יה) Patience

The XPR Formula: **Understand** (sphere #2) → **Choose Peace** (sphere #3 & #4) → **emPower the Now** (sphere #5).

As for sphere 0, it is the passage where the XPR formula is felt and experienced. As such, *Mayim* for "pairs of waters" is the Name transmitted here as the Power of consummation. On that note, it is said: "Nothing in the world is softer or weaker than water. Yet nothing is better at overcoming the hard and strong" (*Tao Te Ching*, 78.1-2).

The name *Mayim* is newly attributed by *Golden XPR* to the core of the mouth chakra whose spheres, thus far, are uncharted territory. Surely, as much as rabbinical Kabbalah has long-established correspondences between the 10 essential "God" Names and the 10 spheres they fuel, nothing had been revealed concerning the "ThREE" of the knowledge of good and evil; its 3 "God" Names and the 3 spheres they spin.

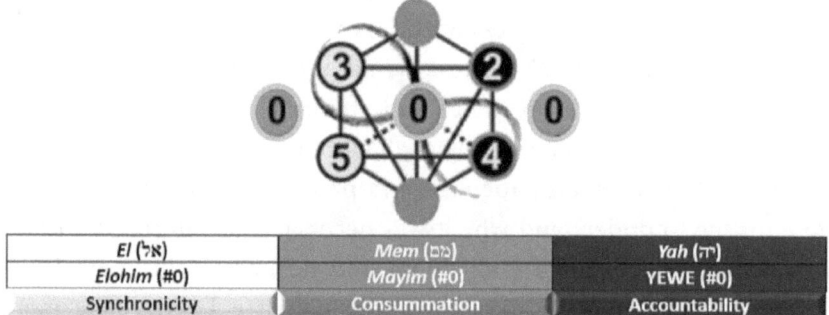

Passing through the Three "God" Names and the Three Powers of the Tree of the Knowledge of Opposites

The Name *Elohim* (אלהים) ends in Mem final for "pairs of waters." It also holds pairs *El* and *Yah* of code Sexual Healing. While *El* and *Yah* are the "God" Names traditionally attributed to the spheres of kindness and wisdom, *Elohim* had no attribution. XPR changes this by using the Name *Elohim* for the "good" or male side of *Daath*. Indeed, *Elohim* uses speech to create, and speaking is the male function of the mouth chakra. Similarly, YEWE has no traditional attribution. XPR changes this by using this Name of Names, YEWE, for the "bad" or female side of *Daath*. Eating is the female function of the mouth chakra, a process that is particularly difficult to account for.

All together now:

- **The Name** *Elohim* is the Power of synchronicity that is given to the male and speaking side of the mouth chakra. It is felt in *El* – the Power of attention spinning the ascended male sphere of kindness.
- **The Name YEWE** is the Power of accountability that is given to the female side of the mouth chakra. It is felt in *Yah* – the Power of patience spinning the descended female sphere of wisdom.

The Powers as SIN Destroyers

Prepare to DIE! Inquiry tool: www.goldenxpr.com/tco3_conscience/

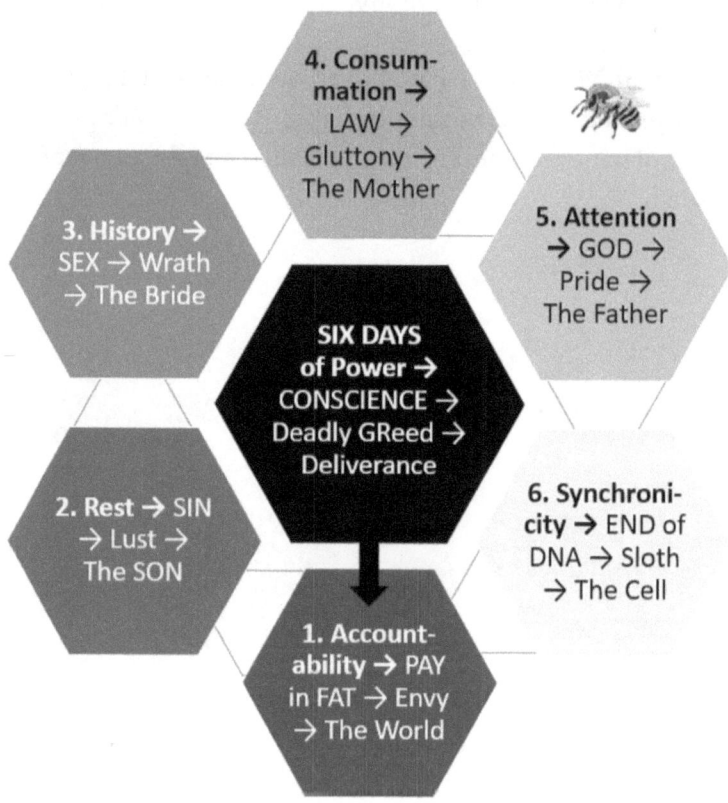

Step 1: I fill in the blank: I want to know WHY I would choose to think I CAN'T ___ (e.g.; find a job, be patient, etc.). **Step 2:** I ask for truth and generate a number. **Step 3:** I find my number on the map and fill in the brackets: to activate the Power of [**Power**], I become willing to hear my conscience urging me to know [**Conscience**] in order to be free of [**Deadly GReed**]. I will then stop projecting [**Deliverance**] and feel its reality inwardly. **Step 4:** what most surprised me in this process was [_____].

The "Minor" Prompts of Conscience

"In these four words we find expressed the sum total of all that is: (...) GOD, the Whole; SEX, the attraction between the parts within that Whole; LAW, the habit of the Whole; and SIN, the revolt of the unit in the Whole." Alice Bailey, The Labours of Hercules (TCO's caps)

Meanwhile, to the question, what is the most amount of information that can be given in just one sentence, physician Richard Feynman answered: "All things are made up of atoms – little particles that move around in perpetual motion, attracting each other when they are a little distance apart, but repelling upon being squeezed into one another." It could be argued that GOD is "all things," and LAW is the atom's "perpetual motion," SEX is "attracting each other when they are a little distance apart," SIN is "repelling upon being squeezed into one another."

Therefore, whether in physics or in metaphysics, there is a way to convey the work of consciousness (the spiritually correct rebranding of "conscience").

To stretch consciousness into awareness (and actually be free to exercise the Power of decision from presence and not from resistance, and thus see wisdom replacing woe), I must balance the Four-lettered Name YEWE with the created-SIX *Elohim*. This involves feeling into the two "minor" prompts that express the subtraction of all that is not, rather than the sum of all that is. *Golden XPR* proposes "PAY in FAT," and "END of DNA."

- **PAY in FAT**: sacrifice (or paying the price) is the kernel of religion. At first, it is the pouring out blood, to establish a pact with God. Next to the blood is fat, which is the most sacred part of an animal. The rituals were a way to release the greed. Now that they are long gone, civilized countries seem to suffer from a rampant misuse of money, and an epidemic of obesity.

- **END of DNA:** there is an end to dissatisfaction. I know it when forgive my mother and my father. I have forgiven when I am no longer a victim of my biology, as my "junk DNA" no longer leads me into temptation. I have now officially died to my "SIN" and to the sins of my parents.

The SIN of the SON of "God"

"Let him who is without sin cast the first stone." *John 8:7*

John 8:7 speaks to me differently when I know that *Aben* (ABN) is the "stone" on which is inscribed the destiny of my being risen as *Ben* (BN) for the "Son" (*see TCO—Book 1; Redemption Code*). To read the inscription, I must go *Bin* or "in-between," in the *vesica piscis* where the "SON of God" holds the tension between being the "SUN of God" and the "SIN of God." I will then be able to discipline my attention and know *El*'s Power. I will also have patience and know *Yah's* Power.

Henceforth, neither pride nor wrath will get me. Even if scorned, I will smile, seeing that S/Hebrew *Aben* contains *Ben*, just as English "stone" contains "son."

This stone is known to alchemists as the "philosopher's stone," a panacea and universal solvent. As for alchemy, it is the art by which to adapt to the operation of the sun, as it moves from the dark sun of putrefaction (the "SIN of God") to the sunset of transcendence (the "SUN of God").

Meanwhile, I am trapped in the infernal spheres and the hell of their corresponding sins. Being out of my body, I only go into resistance and can't sense that the *Shekhinah* is the feminine presence of "God." No longer loving my matter (my body) or my mother (from whom my body came), I am divided and incongruent in my choices. I don't feel myself anymore and can't hear my heart, which also says that I have become a liar. What I once knew as the mind-body connection has now become a war of the sexes.

As the "SIN of God," I am so overtaken by **7-greed** that I can only move into a prostitut**E** whose **anima** is **possessed** by **2-lust** for a Bride I can't meet. As **the Daughter**, I am so haunted by **1-envy** that I can only move into the saboteu**R**'s dark night whose **possessed animus** is putrefying by way of **3-wrath**. The sin of wrath is how Moses was barred from entering the "Promised Land" of an open 3rd eye. Rabbinical Kabbalah makes Moses the guardian of **sphere 1**. As for Abraham, he is the guardian of **sphere 3**. The shift in name (from Abram to Abraham) is seen by XPR as the ascent of **sphere 3** of kindness, since Abram the Yvrit means "the father of a multitude who crossed over."

5-Pride | 6-Sloth	7-Greed → 2-Lust | 4-Gluttony	3-Wrath | 1-Envy
The Father	The SON / The Mother	The Daughter
Anima Possession	War of the Sexes	Animus Possession

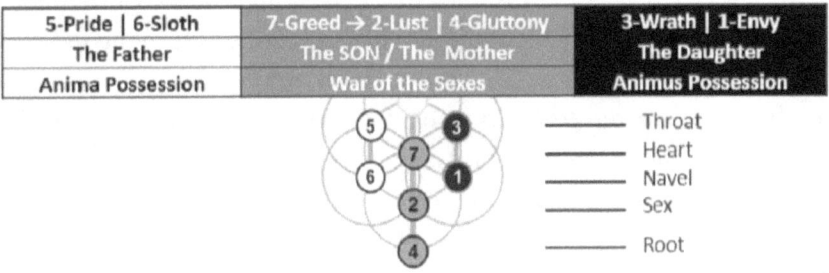

The Entrapment of the "SIN" of God in the Infernal Spheres

The 3 Ps of an Unconscious Eros

"An unconscious Eros always expresses itself as will to Power."
Carl Jung

My sense of a conscious Eros is of a heartfelt love story between me and "you," and by extension, me and "God." Meanwhile, to deal with the perennial battle of good and evil and heal subsequent issues of Power, the Luria imagined fortifying the relationships within the tree, specifically in the seven infernal spheres – the spheres where my consciousness (or the lack of it) is prey to the seven deadly sins. These seven spheres are where the male and the female sides of me (Son and Bride) live in chaos.

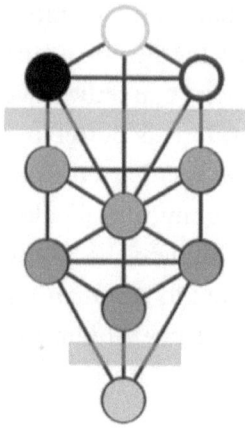

While the 3rd eye sees the harmonious union of Father *Chokmah* (white sphere of "wisdom" with black outline) and Mother *Binah* (black sphere of "understanding"), the lower spheres are susceptible to the war of the sexes.

The Son occupies the SIX dark grey spheres (throat, heart, solar plexus, and sex). As for the Bride, she abides in the light grey root chakra, waiting for the Son to have enough patience to see her. He will then die to his sins, turn into a Messiah, and recognize her as his Bride. I am both the Son and the Bride. For the Son in me to be so conscious of the Eros that I'd see my inner Bride, I must first remove the barrier I erected to avoid prioritizing the search for *Malkuth* (the S/Hebrew name of the root chakra, meaning "QKingdom"). By "seeking the QKingdom first," I naturally restore the fragments lost in the abyss, come into the sexual knowledge of *Daath*, and ascend forever after with my Bride into the Promised Land.

However, my tree of life ignores the tree of the knowledge of opposites (see tree above). How could the Bride in me be seen and the Son be patient enough to ascend when I am still attached to the inferno? Indeed, I am the slave of a terrible yearning, bound to pushing, pulling, and doubting myself. Unconscious of the mouth chakra, my sex chakra is on its own. There is no symmetry experienced in the heart chakra as "the covenant in the middle" that joins the Eros (sex) and the Logos (mouth).

Note: S/Hebrew sign Peh for "mouth" evolved into letter P. When the mouth is pure, I vibrate with the 3 Ps of "Prosperity, Prestige, Power" (no yearning). But when it is defiled, the 3 Ps turn into "Possession, Projection, Perjury."

	Yod (י)	Vav (ו)	Heh (ה)
	Leader's Prestige	Engineer's Power	Visionary's Prosperity
	chilD's Projection	prostitutE's Perjury	saboteuR's Possession

The Three Dark Ps of a Bride without a QKingdom or a Heh

When I don't have a Heh attached to my name, I can't embrace my pain. I increasingly understand why Cain means "**possessed** by jealousy," as I am killing myself by perceiving that, unlike "you," I can't have what I want. For me to imagine that deliverance is possible, I must tell the truth, and take back my **projections** by realizing that I am the World – cellularly. Indeed, I am all at once the Father, the Mother, the Son and the Bride whom my ego tends to externalize.

When I feel that I am one with everything, I am able to stop the **perjury** by which I choose to *think* that I can't [fill in the blank]. No longer jealous of "you," the CAIN in me now places his affairs in order. This causes the letters of my name to reorder to spell "I CAN." The **possession** of envy, the **projection** of enmity onto others who are "ABEL," and the **perjury** of unrequited love all vanishes for me to receive the **Prosperity**, the **Prestige** and the **Power** I want, or, alternatively, for me to give up wanting those.

This is how this chapter invites the Messiah and the Bride as the union of polar opposites: the male and the female, the object and the subject, the observer and the observed. Finding my inner Messiah is forgiving, shedding the snake's skin of hatred, and ending the shame as I come to the LOVE that has no opposite. Finally, I am patient enough to hold the tension.

The Powers of a Conscious Logos

'And *Elohim* said: "let there be light!" And there was light.' *Genesis 1:3*

When I see an alignment between my words and the reality they create, I am clearly no longer in service to Mammon (the Master of

"Yearning") but to *Elohim*, the Power of Synchronicity. I am soon to experience the full decoding of the Name *Elohim* as three pairs of letters I have already recognized. The pairings confirm the relationships of the tree; above by joining the Father and the Mother, and below, by joining the Son and the Bride. Although yet to be connected to the Name *Elohim*, these *Partzuphim* or "faces" of God were first seen by rabbi Luria.

Elohim and the Faces of "God"

Indeed, all is well when I stand in the core of integration. The Son and his Bride are joined in Holy Matrimony, which means that there is no more "unconscious Eros" and no misuse of Power. Thus, what I see in the union of Yod Heh is what was always there: the happy marriage of my Father and my Mother, on Earth as it is in heaven. My soul is incarnated – in my body as the Word made flesh; Logos and Eros at one. The double sacred marriage had always been written in the Name *Elohim*.

Speaking of "God" Names, I wish to explore how their Powers move the spheres into the vibration of Health – Health with a big "H."

I have seen how the XPR lemniscate juggles the "God" Names *El* and *Yah* spinning sphere 3 of male kindness and sphere 4 of female wisdom. The very fact that *El Yah* writes into being the Name *Elohim* grants validity to the innovation brought forth by *Golden XPR*. TCO outlined in great length how the classical viewpoint enforces a throat pathology (he lies, pretending to be kind, and she reacts by using Power hysterically). The throat is where polarities are inverted, which soon leads to a war of the sexes.

As for sphere 2 of understanding, the Name spinning "her" is YEWE *Elohim* which I have identified as the Power of history. To the question, what is the greatest discovery, I have wanted to answer "fire," or "the wheel." However, the more I think of it, the more I see that the greatest invention ever made is history. History hacks time, and thus, mind. When I realize that I can change the past, the Scare City game is over, and I find myself back in the abundance of *Genesis 1*, serving *Elohim* and enjoying numerous synchronicities. With the Power of history under my belt (after complete understanding opens my 3rd eye), the "God" Name that spins sphere 5 of Power is no longer estranged from me. This Name is *El Gibor*. It transmits the Power of decision. Consider: when I no longer live in Scare City, I no longer fear loss and I CAN decide. No matter what the outcome will be, I am at peace, knowing that goodness and mercy will follow me for all the days of my life.

The saboteuR's Consummation

"The gesture of the amorous embrace seems to fulfill, for a time, the subject's dream of total union with the loved being: the longing for consummation with the other." *Roland Barthes*

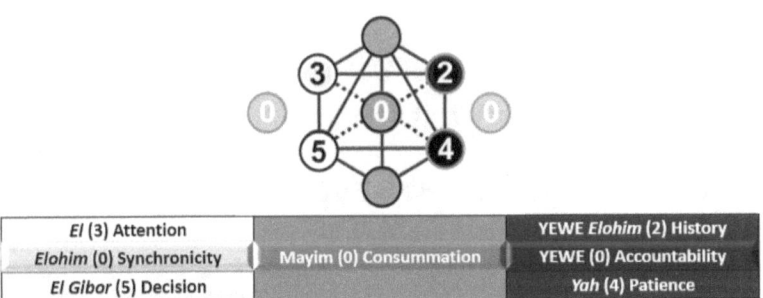

El (3) Attention		YEWE *Elohim* (2) History
Elohim (0) Synchronicity	Mayim (0) Consummation	YEWE (0) Accountability
El Gibor (5) Decision		Yah (4) Patience

The Name (the Un/numbered Sphere) the Power

- When I experience the Power of **synchronicity**, my **attention** is focused in the Now. I am kindness (sphere 3). Also, when I experience the Power of **accountability**, I have access to exponential levels of **patience**. I am wisdom (sphere 4).
- However, when I cannot see the "PAIRfection" of what is, I won't learn from the Power of **history** and continue to make bad **decisions**. Not understanding that there's only One of us (sphere 2), I am afraid of my Power (sphere 5).

- Henceforth, changing the past and rewriting **history** is how to **consummate** (sphere o) the saboteuR – the CAIN in me who won't decide to think "I CAN." Deciding turns the snake into a Messiah.

Part II: A 1ˢᵗ Date with the Snake

- Lost in Sabotage
- The "Cree-P" of Possession
- Code Intimacy – AWR / OWR
- Skin/Kin Names and Cain's Name
- The Mind Split by No Permission
- The Soul Lost to No Pleasure
- The Body in Pain out of No Patience
- Code Synchronicity – AL / EY / M
- The Big Three
- The Heart Broken by No Praise
- Code Obedience – AL(P) / (P)LA
- Code Sentience – MY / YM
- The Forsaken Spirit behind No Purpose

El (אל)	Mem (מם)	Yah (יה)
Individual Power	Symbolic Power	Collective Power
Teshuvah – Turn within!	*TzedaQah* – Give it all!	*Tephillah* – Feel blessed!
Code Obedience	Code Sentience	Code Patience

The Triple Code of Divine Serenity

LOST IN SABOTAGE

LOST IN SABOTAGE: I don't understand my saboteuR! Am I so afraid of bringing forth what's inside me that I'd kill my potential? I want to believe that I am not some kind of creepy evil spirit attempting to take me down... I want to believe, but, deep down, I don't!

To begin with, I am my own worst critic. From the get go, I imagine that my projects will fail. Finding the weakest link is my talent, which I use mercilessly to control me, you, it; the world! I mastered the art of how a few well-placed nasty comments will bring down entire dynamics...

Besides sarcasm, I also use doubt and start thinking I CAN'T. I am now free to go on repeating the same insane past. Truth be told, I unconsciously choose to be disempowered. If I had Power, I'm afraid I'll eventually turn revengeful... Moreover, I fear that the future would give me more pain if I did forgive the past. I also fear that, if I allowed myself to be healthy, vibrant, powerful, soulful and brilliant in my expression, I'd become insufferable in my arrogance.

Yep, in a nutshell, wrath and pride own my soul!

I seem to be incapable of disentangling myself from the demons I myself invoked. Heck, it seemed like a good idea at the time. But now that these demonic energies have taken possession of my soul, I'm lost. I can't see the forest for the trees.

I am in fact so critical of myself and others that I block any possible experience of intimacy. I once lived in the state of "PAIRfect" sex, and now, I live in shame. I want to be in the dark, fiercely controlling, of my responses, of my pain, of my negativity, of a shadow identity feeding on the thought that I'm a despaired failure.

I don't care that you might present me with beneficial suggestions; I'll use my cleverness to show all the ways why it won't work. On a deeply unconscious level, I don't want positive change. It would threaten my identity as a depressed, angry or battered person. I must disempower me. That's the only sure way I found to handle my fear of rejection: I'll reject me first by unwittingly adopting unproductive attitudes, and flirting with wrongful associations.

If I were to be successful, I wouldn't know what to do with myself. So, I'll be safe and remain a failure!

To make sure that I don't have what I say I want, I create unconscious time and procrastinate. However, having developed an infallible instinct for doing the next "wrong" thing is how I hate myself more and more. I became my own executioner thinking that I'll never be as good as what "you" want me to be. So why bother?

The "Cree-P" of Possession

"Love does not claim possession, but gives freedom." Rabindranath Tagore

The devil made me do it! Really?! When I stretch to the sacred, I have no more fears and no need to blame others for my own failures. The story I milked for years – of how my mother (or is it my father?) did me wrong – drops on its own. I have forgiven, and the burden I was carrying is suddenly lifted up, as is my soul. The enemy that was triumphant over me has become my friend – my lover even, as s/he, it, they granted purpose to my life. My yin is no longer allergic to my yang, nor my yang to my yin. Yin and yang are now my temple – the place where I pay respect and listen to my guidance.

Being possessed is having no Power and believing that something or someone out there can destroy me. I really think that my mother and my father hated each other, as I saw them engaging in the cruelest war of the sexes. How could I conceive that hatred hides the deepest love? I was yet to hear/SEE how the Living Word writes code Transmutation (see *TCO—Book 1*). Do I know that transmutation is the medicine brought by the snake – the very snake cursed with enmity after he blatantly lied to the Woman? This snake is my ego who convinces me, time and again, to split from my heart and turn off my intuition. This separation is how I become so lonely I could die!

The division that exists within also exists without, as the cosmos has day and night, warm and cold, angels and demons. In the Bible, it is expressed when *Elohim* becomes YEWE. These four letters represent the yin, the yang, the yin within the yang and the yang within the yin. They invoke the "PAIRfect" family: father, mother, son and daughter. However, when I project my stuff onto the male and female polarities, I stop knowing good and evil. Judging that being alone is "no good" (as per *Genesis 2:18*), I don't understand wholeness, which traps me among the have-nots, feeling lonely and forsaken. The sabotage worsens as my soul is possessed by jealousy. This is when my polarities are inverted, and my throat, blocked. I have no decision-making Power.

Possession into projection: what I had first imagined as the "PAIRfect" family now becomes "imperfect," as the *golem* I created which ended up taking possession of my soul and prompting me to enter the dark.

Code Intimacy - AWR / OWR

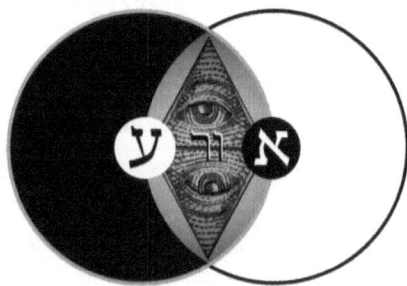

Imagine a language so pure and so sacred that it can reconcile opposites in just four letters...

Right: Hebrew letter Aleph (א) → A in Roman script
Middle: Hebrew letter Vav (ו) → F, U, V, W in Roman script paired with
Hebrew letter Resh (ר) → R in Roman script
Left: Hebrew letter Ayin (ע) → O in Roman script

Here is how S/Hebrew inscribes code "Intimacy" in 4 letters, 3 words:

- **AWR**: from right to middle, I read *Aur* (אור) for "light."
- **WRO**: from middle to left, I read *V'Rah* (ורע) for "and evil."
- **OWR**: from left to middle, I read *Ohr* (עור) for "skin."

The Decoding: there's a big shift between the communication of *Elohim* who says "let there be **light**" and sees light, and YEWE *Elohim* who prompts me to enter the darkness by commanding me not to eat from the tree of the knowledge of good **and evil**. Being forbidden to eat from the fruit of opposites sets me up to fear intimacy. Just prior to expelling the two sides of me from PaRaDiSe, this DREaM God makes "garments of skins and clothed us." The word *Labash* for "to clothe" branches into *Bush* for "shame," a garment so heavy it casts me down. Intimacy does require a change of clothing, as my snake must shed a **skin** or two to become messianic, and stop lying. The skin is both a separator and a connector between self and others, just as the Vav of desire is both a separator and a connector. To drop the "shame body," I must unearth my private agendas. Doing so reveals the "light body," *Bigdei Aur* in Hebrew.

This body has other names – the diamond body, the rainbow body, the resurrection body, the body of bliss... The secret to maintaining its state of enlightenment is to come into the full knowledge of good, yes, and evil especially, as evil is the "rib" that I most resist. Feeling it, however, liberates the shame, allowing for transparency and intimacy. Feeling it *is* intimacy. This is what the closeness of Vav and Resh signifies. Vav links me to Resh to invite me to play a bigger game... It infuses my aura for me to shine like the sun of Resh, as I am no longer afraid of emPowerment. Finally, no short-circuit: I can let there be light!

Skin/Kin Names and Cain's Name

> "I have a dream that my four little children will one day live in a nation where they will not be judged by the color of their skin, but by the content of their character." *Martin Luther King, Jr.*

Like it or not, the skin moves me from intimacy to "into-me-see" as it shows both physical health and illness, as well as the depth of my emotional reactions. Indeed, am I itching to come out? If so, what's the "rash?" The skin expresses who I am and how I feel, especially at an age when tattoos and other ritual skin markings are now common fare. In Aboriginal culture, skin names (a.k.a. "kin names") provide information about a person's bloodline, revealing how generations are linked and how this sets up systems of reciprocal relationships and responsibilities. Indeed, the skin is a boundary between "me" and "you," just as the soul is the link between the mental inner world and the physical outer world. Not knowing who I am (and ignorantly eating from good and evil) sets me up. My female side becomes prey to an animus possession, and my male side, to an anima possession. When possessed, I envy other people, wondering why they can have what they want, and I can't. If I become a saboteuR and go into war in order to exact revenge and get even, it is simply because I'm like a starving artist, powerless to know that I am and have enough to create the LOVE I want.

Anima Possession	War of the Sexes	Animus Possession
chilD	prostitutE / victiM	saboteuR

"Cree-P" Possession

But why? Why would I imagine that you're ABEL and that I CAIN'T? When wearing the skin/kin name *Cain,* I am "possessed" by jealousy –

the very animus possession of which Carl Jung spoke. Understandably, when I observe that your gifts are received and mine are not, I want to kill you! This is where I must ask: who is this "I" who sees what "eye" sees? Not getting that I am in a projection, I forget that there is no one and nothing out there. This was true for my father Adam as he dreamed up a woman. It is also true for me as I dream up a "brother" having it all and my being sacked! This is how a "Cree-P" Possession becomes a "Cree-P" Projection. It is also how the words and actions of my mouth defile me – a "P" that is about to get worse, as I explore the karmic realms of no "Permission," no "Pleasure," no "Patience," and no "Praise."

The Mind Split by No Permission

"It is often easier to ask for forgiveness than to ask for permission."
St. Benedict

My saboteuR now urges me to keep investigating these Ps that makes me deliberately destroy, damage, or obstruct my own light. I started with the P of a voice that is Possessed; I am now continuing with the mind split out of its inability to give itself the permission to be. Yep, I know what to do. I just don't want to do it. I can't and won't permit it!

Surely, I turn saboteuR as soon as I let my animus take over. My unconscious goal is to restrict my adaptability, and thus my acquisition of Power. I am so terrified of what I will do if I were in the center of my integrity – in my Power – that I give credence and authority to the voice in me that keeps me from fulfilling my potential. **Whether it is the voice of a stern father, a dark mother or even an entire society, I become mental, as I just can't give me the permission to want what I want. Moreover, resisting what I have myself forbidden disconnects me from my female animus.** Henceforth, not only am I not in my body, but my mind has now become my jailor!

What will it take for me to let go of the world out there long enough that I'd individuate and wake up? The inability to forgive and the holding of a grudge may just be the epitome of pain. Indeed, I cut deeply into my skin when feeling that I have to be truer to the commitments that I made to you rather than to what I promised to myself. Not giving me the permission to be me is what I can't forgive, and yes, it seems easier than to ask for permission – let alone, to give me the permission to choose this birth, and make of it a blessing to all. This "I CAN'T" is how CAIN would insolently reply "am I my brother's keeper?"

The Soul Lost to No Pleasure

"Poor is the man whose pleasures depend on the permission of another." Madonna Ciccone

Do I desire forbidden pleasures because the collective pushes its own agenda about what I ought to desire? Am I just acting out of peer pressure and becoming a full-fledged addict – someone unable to say "no" simply because I can't give myself the permission to want what I want? Moreover, when breaking the taboo and eating of the forbidden fruit, do I actually enjoy myself? Surely, whether I obey or rebel against you, how can it be my pleasure to make "you" the master of my destiny?

This is how I continue the sabotage, as I don't want to do what I know would evolve me. The more I break my own law, the more I am consumed by self-hatred and the less pleased I am in myself. I am now irremediably driven to pleasures, and yet, the female side of me is shut down, gagged and incapable to express her needs and desires.

When the male and female sides of my brain hear each other, I am happy to be me, and love my life! But when waging a war of the sexes, I'm caught in a lie – an addict fighting with "God!" To put it bluntly, how can I know you when I don't authentically love "you?" Whether you're a person, a habit, an idea, a substance, being free of "you" is quite a quandary when I resist you as much as I desire you!

When I can't want what I want, there are a few unconscious intentions in my space. What if I told the truth and realized that my reality is what I *really* want? Would this instantaneous alignment make me freer, happier, stronger, healthier? But this begs another question: why twist my desire until it is barely recognizable? Why forbid myself to be myself? Do I not know that my resistance feeds this creation and makes it a demonic force that will eventually enslave me?

Bondage is what I am choosing, albeit unconsciously, as it allows me to be powerless. The resistance to take full responsibility for the reality I create will lead me to seek a master – someone who can decide for me. This way, errors are not my doing, and I can bypass the guilt (or so I think). However, I also am never "hear and know," holding the tension, cracking the code of opposites, and realizing that pleasure increases with patience.

The Body in Pain Due to No Patience

> "God, grant me the serenity to accept the things I cannot change, courage to change the things I can, and wisdom to know the difference." *Reinhold Niebuhr*

When in pain (*pati* or "pain" being in the Latin root of "impatience"), I CAN'T wait as I don't understand that this too shall pass. Yep, I'm impatient, which implies that I am not accepting the things that I cannot change, like "you," for example. Why won't you love me? Unrequited love is Cain's pain, and may just be my greatest pain, as it automatically inscribes me among the have-nots – in Scare City.

Think of it this way… There's a genie inside me in charge of my creative endeavors. This genie has rules, rules which seem to be written for Cain (see *Walt Disney Movie Aladdin*). If I fail in my creation, it is because I don't want to hear rule #2 (which ought to be rule #1): "my genie can't make anybody fall in love with anyone else." How then could I hear the other rules: "I can't kill anybody," doubled by "I can't bring people back from the dead?" Impossible! I'm so despaired to not be loved by "God" that I'll eventually kill my brother. To top it all, I won't live with the consequences.

El (אל)	Mem (מם)	Yah (יה)
Individual Power	Symbolic Power	Collective Power
"I will"	"I know" / "I have"	"I desire"
Code Obedience	Code Sentience	Code Patience

The Triple Code of Serenity

This gradual lowering of my spirit also chips away at my courage to change. I am now unconsciously projecting my lack of self-worth onto a "God" who has forsaken me. I am all alone, out of my body, unable to see beyond a creation of enmity that bores me to death. If I could only bridge the gap between what **I desire** and what **I will** into being, I'd restore **sentience,** feeling that **"I know"** and sensing that **"I have."**

But alas, although I try to refute *Matthew 6:24,* truth is that "I cannot serve two masters. Either I will hate the one and love the other, or I will be devoted to the one and despise the other. I can't serve both God and Mammon." And it makes me wonder... Does the name Mammon for "yearning, money" come from YEWE? Is this how my saboteuR's entrapment reveals that I started with the lie of a prostitutE?

Code Synchronicity - AL / EY / M

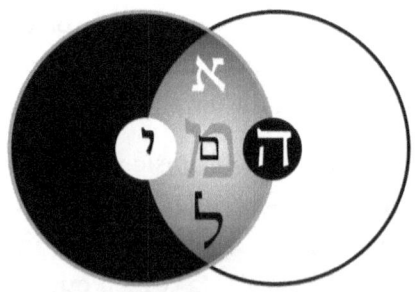

The saboteuR - You had me at Elohim!

Imagine a language so pure and so sacred that it can reconcile a triple code in just 5/SIX letters...

Top: Hebrew letter Aleph (א) → A in Roman script
Right: Hebrew letter Heh (ה) → E in Roman script
Middle: Hebrew letter Mem regular (מ) surrounding Mem final (ם) → M in Roman script
Left: Hebrew letter Yod (י) → I, J, Y in Roman script
Bottom: Left: Hebrew letter Lamed (ל) → L in Roman script

Here is how S/Hebrew inscribes code "Synchronicity" in 3 codes:

- **AL/LA**: top to bottom and back, I read *El* (אל)/*Lo* (לא) for "God" / "No."
- **EY/YE**: right to left and back, I read *Hee* (הי) inverting into *Yah* (יה) for "God."
- **MM**: middle to middle, I read *Mem* (מם) for "pairs of waters."
- **ALEYM**: from top to bottom to right to left to middle, I read *Elohim* (אלהים) – the "God" Name of *Genesis 1* which sustains the triple code.

El (AL/LA)	M (MM)	Hee (EY/YE)
Code Obedience	Code Sentience	Code Patience

The Triple Code of Divine Serenity

The Decoding: whether I know it or not, *Elohim* is the One I've been waiting for! It is the "God" Name that, being "Created-SIX," conveys timelessness. Now, it is curious: how can *Elohim* be "Created-SIX" when it is a five-letter word? Simple: this "God" Name is formed by the "God" Names written as two pairs of letters – *El* and *Yah* – plus a final Mem, which is itself a pair. Not only is the letter Mem spelled with two letters – a regular Mem (מ) and a final Mem (ם), but also the word *Mem* means "pairs of waters." Being a "final" letter, it ushers a form of redemption. I have seen how Mem escorts me to THE END of desire, and by extension, to the sense of enough. When I can decide to no longer serve *Mammon* (the "yearning" that permeates Scare City), I'm not as focused on why I can't get no satisfaction! Little by little, ambivalences are neutralized. **I can now love *Elohim* with all my heart, my soul and my might. In other words, I stop doing the things that sabotage me.**

Indeed, the curse my female side was under – to desire the man and his Power – was an animus possession. It dominated my female side and now it's gone. Bye bye envy, fear, hatred and anger! Hello happiness, for this end is also the beginning of fulfillment.

When there is an alignment between what I say I want and what I have, I am in tune with the Power of Synchronicity. This is *Elohim* – the One Power I've been waiting for that fulfills all my desires in Now time. The instantaneous manifestation of seeing the light I wanted to see just as I said "let there be light" requires that I'd come to the end of my private agendas. When there is no more mind, there is no time interposed between what I wish to see created and what I see manifested.

The joy of instantaneous manifestation is made possible when I am serving *Elohim*, synergizing three pairs of opposites and inscribing the triple code of **Obedience, Patience** and **Sentience**. This code supports the recognition of a loving transcendental force who had me at *Elohim*.

El (אל)	Mem (מם)	Yah (יה)
Individual Power	Symbolic Power	Collective Power
Teshuvah – Turn within!	*TzedaQah* – Give it all!	*Tephillah* – Feel blessed!
Code Obedience	Code Sentience	Code Patience

The Three Pillars and the Triple Code

1. ***Teshuvah* and code Obedience** – consider: when I turn within to listen to my heart, I no longer react to the word "obedience" (from *ob* "to" + *audire* "listen, hear"). I'm a good dog, bringing the medicine of obedience to humans.

2. ***Tephillah*** **and code Patience** – consider: when I pray *à la Jesus*, I feel that my prayer is already fulfilled. I thus have no impatience, no sadness and no anger; no complaints whatsoever! I'm just cat-like, purring in gratitude!
3. ***Tzedaqah*** **and code Sentience** – consider: when I give it all, I also receive it all. To have sentience – the capacity to feel and sense, I must be integral. If I give anything less than 100%, I'm still in my head; calculating, worrying.

El (אל)	Mem (מם)	Yah (יה)
Yod (י)	Vav (ו) / Heh (ה)	Heh (ה)
Individual Power	**Symbolic Power**	**Collective Power**

The Birth of YEWE from the Mothership *Elohim*

The capacity to be sentient is how that which understands has an understanding of "God." It is therefore the end of the need to sabotage myself, which, thus far, was incomprehensible to me. The rising angel who always ended up falling and belittling itself for being a fallen angel can now be risen. YEWE induces the dream of separation since, to be born, the pair Yod Heh of *Yah* had to split: Yod went to individual Power and Heh, to collective Power. When I perceive that a part of me is missing and that my salvation comes from out there, I am subject to the machismo of the Power of "HIStory," and loose the timelessness of *Elohim*. To recover patience, I must detach from the womb of the **collective** and follow the beat of my **individual** drummer. It will take courage. However, it is the only way to discriminate between what my heart desires and what other people told me I "should" want. It is thus how to come to the end of desire.

The Big Three

"Tis not the many oaths that make the truth; But the plain single vow, that is vow'd true." *William Shakespeare*

El (אל)	Mem (מם)	Yah (יה)
Individual Power	Symbolic Power	Collective Power
Code Obedience	Code Sentience	Code Patience
Obedience	Poverty	Chastity

The Triple Vow

In the old days, if I were a Christian touched by the grace of the Holy Spirit, I might seek to lead "a consecrated life." I'd make the triple vow of **poverty, chastity** and **obedience** (the big three) which flew from the evangelical counsels of Jesus Christ. I would leave society and devote myself to "God," living in a community that abstained from the energy of sex and that provided for my material needs. But now, the ante has been raised: I am to be in the world (and not of the world), enjoying a good meal or a romantic relationship and even wealth, without getting trapped in the experience. Although I am a mystic without a monastery, it appears that the codes entangled with the Power of synchronicity are the big three of a consecrated life.

- **Obedience & code Obedience:** if I react to the word, it's because I have often felt forced to obey "the Law." Might I be using reactance to justify my misbehaving? Indeed, who would I be if I didn't desire to do evil?
- **Chastity & code Patience:** if I no longer have to abstain from having a sexual life, I need a broader understanding for "chastity," e.g.; the ability to hold the tension instead of compulsively acting out.
- **Poverty & code Sentience:** if I am here to end the bondage to money (which does not necessarily entail giving it all away), I also need a new meaning for "poverty," e.g.; empty as in devoid of false knowledge.

To this end, the shadow questions below can help me feel and understand the SIX stages of (my) sabotage:

- The possession in my saboteuR's screech: what's the truth?

- No permission in my split mind: what am I resisting?
- No pleasure in my lost soul: what do I want right now?
- No patience in my pain body: why do I think I can't have it?
- No praise in my broken heart: what will it cost me?
- No purpose in my forsaken spirit: why won't I go deep?

Note: to understand how not being clear on the nature of my investment can only enforce the absence of praise, I revisit the etymology of "praise." Praise—verb: from Late Latin *pretium* "reward, prize, value, worth." Indeed, the willingness to pay the price of my evolution sets my heart free. It is what redemption is all about.

The Heart Broken by No Praise

> "Your depression is connected to your insolence and refusal to praise." *Rumi*

This one is short and sweet... Consider: when my saboteuR dares to become a Visionary, the emergence of spontaneous praise inundates my heart as I can now feel and know that I am unhurt. Always was; always will be. This naturally follows a body that is vibrant as its actions can wait for the path to be clear, a soul whose pleasure is proportionate to its readiness to know the Truth, and a mind that gives itself permission to think. *Allelu-yah*; praise the Yah!

Code Obedience - AL(P) / (P)LA

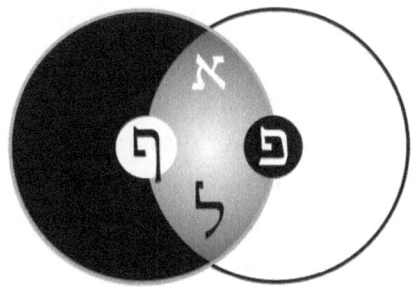

Imagine a language so sacred that it can reconcile opposites...

Top: Hebrew letter Aleph (א) → A in Roman script
Right: Hebrew letter Peh (פ) → P, Ph in Roman script
Left: Hebrew letter Peh final (ף) → P, Ph in Roman script
Bottom: Hebrew letter Lamed (ל) → L in Roman script

Here is how S/Hebrew inscribes code "Obedience" in 4 words:

- **AL**: from top to bottom, I read *El* (אל) for "toward, deity."
- **LA**: from bottom to top, I read *Lo* (לא) for "no."
- **ALP**: from top to bottom to left, I real *Aleph* (אלף) for "ox, primal force."
- **PLA**: from right to bottom to top, I read *Pheleh* (פלא) for "wonder."

The Decoding. What has my attention: abundance or lack, health or disease? The Power of attention is expressed by the "God" Name *El* which also means "toward" just as the word "attention" does (from Latin *ad* "to" + *tendere* "stretch" → *attendere* for "to stretch toward"). I reconcile opposites by way of *El* for **"toward, deity"** and *Lo* for **"no."** While "no!" is a whole sentence, what is the quality of my noes? Am I a false rebel, saying "no" as a way to withhold love? Or am I saying a big YES to my heart, even though I may risk disappointing you with a "no?"

Finding out is easy: if I have everything I want and want everything I have, I am likely to be serving *El* of *Elohim*, the Name opening the 3rd eye with the Power of attention. I understand, choose peace and emPower the "No." I therefore do not let any doubt enter my mind that would delay my reaching my goal. But if my yeses and my nos are aiming at getting your approval (or disapproval), I'm serving *Mammon* (the Power of money and yearning). Henceforth, instead of being turned within, I have made me a slave to being without and to the tyranny of appearances. Moreover, serving the "wrong" master lowers my immune response and makes me vulnerable by directing my attention to what's not good for me. When filled with longing and doubt, it's hard for me to say "no" – even impossible. That is how I am an addict, thinking that I have no Power, no self-esteem, and no sense of boundaries.

I suffer from a case of strangled throat chakra. I am so used to pleasing "you" that I no longer know what I want. And if I don't know what I want, how can I will it into being? Impossible! One day, having stopped projecting that you'll reject me, I will seek to love rather than to be loved, and experience *El's* **wonder**. This wonderment lives within me. There are times when I can read the *El* presence in my name, e.g.; in Micha*el*, Auri*el*, Gabri*el*, Rapha*el*, etc. There are other times when I can't. And yet, even though *El's* energy may not be readable, it is in the Aleph that accompanies each construct, visibly or not. Either way, I will feel the **primal force** of a faith that makes me (and makes everything) well. And as I persevere in placing my attention on the good, the true and the beautiful, I'll move into Health, Health with a big "H."

Consider: when I ROGER *that* **(ROGER for "Received Order Given, Expect Results," and** *that* **being the voice of my intuition), I do not have creative blocks. There is no (me) to be an objector of conscience.**

Code Sentience - MY / YM

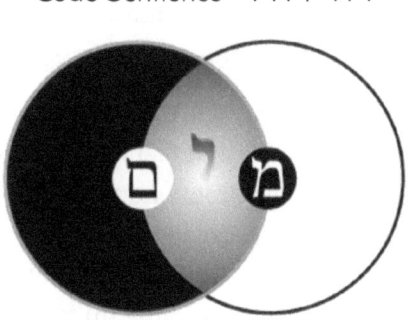

Imagine a language so pure and so sacred that it can reconcile opposites in

just three letters...

Right: Hebrew letter Mem (מ) → M in Roman script
Middle: Hebrew letter Yod (י) → I, J, Y in Roman script
Left: Hebrew letter Mem final (ם) → M in Roman script

Here is how S/Hebrew inscribes the code "Sentience" in 3 words:

- **MY**: from right to middle, I read *Me* (מי) for "Who [am I]?"
- **YM**: from middle to left, I read *Yam* (ים) for "ocean, sea."
- **MYM**: from right to left, I read *Mayim* (מים) for "pairs of waters."

The Decoding: this code was first introduced as "code Body and Soul" in *TCO—Book 1*. Indeed, the combined capacity of the body to sense and of the soul to feel is what sentience is, thus the renaming. As for **water**, it is the most receptive (or feminine) of the four classical elements. Its message is as clear as water: "to answer the ultimate question – **who** am I?, you must jump into the **oceanic** abyss of being where the fragments of you await reunion." This decision is the choice point created on day 2 in *Genesis 1:6*, when the pairs of waters were divided between the waters of above and the waters of below. Dividing my "pairs of waters" splits my soul from my body, which shows up in my dreams as turbulent or murky waters pointing to repressed emotions. It also ricochets into the competition of mind against heart, which leaves me dumbfounded by an overwhelming darkness.

My light is like the seed of little sign Yod (י) nested in between the two Mem breasts. To nurture its fire and feel its splendor, I must dive into the unknown depths of the emotional body. Analyzing the symbols of the dream is the first stop to "receiving" their images in my cells, and quenching the thirst for Love. "Indeed, the water I give them will become in them a spring of water welling up to eternal life." *John 4:13-14*. Jesus was referring to *Mayim* – the same "waters" that Isaiah also invoked: "Come, all you who are thirsty, come to the waters..." *Mayim* is the middle path and *Mem* is the middle letter. They invite me to be as water, and adopt the path of least resistance.

Note: when I don't recall my dreams, I can reflect on the symbols of the DREaM, as I notice my impatience in the waking state.

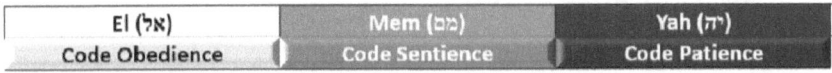

On the note of resisting nothing: while I received both codes – Obedience and Sentience, I must wait for code Patience. Why doesn't that surprise me? :-)

Truth be told, I have been given code Patience from the very beginning of TCO – in *Is TCO "write" for me?* This was when I was first exposed to the Names of Power, and specifically to the "God" Name *Yah*: "Yod symbolizes the male seed, and Heh, the female womb. When the force of compassion (my psychic womb) contains the Power of creativity (the seed of my spermatic word), I don't need to misuse Power. <u>I CAN wait before I would create anything.</u>

The Forsaken Spirit behind No Purpose

> "Life is not easy for any of us. But what of that? We must have perseverance and, above all, confidence in ourselves. We must believe that we are gifted for something, and that this thing, at whatever cost, must be attained." *Marie Curie*

I often confuse my purpose with my uniqueness. When asking: "what's my purpose," I am mostly looking for an answer that would allow me to make a living as a cultural creative. Consciously or not, I choose to ignore that my purpose in this birth is the same as it was in the many births that are likely to have preceded life as I know it now. It is to wake up; that simple!

But the simplicity of making the Great Work my purpose (in biblical terms, "to seek the Kingdom first") is how I resist it and

don't do the work. This explains how I know what my work is (be it, to exercise, eat wholesome foods, pay the taxes, etc.), but my saboteuR won't do it. Indeed, what do I resist and why? Moreover, whom am I blaming for not having the permission to do what I know is the "write" thing to do? These questions and more will find their answer in the second date – when the snake becomes the Messiah.

Part III: a 2nd Date with the Messiah

- Do Not Depend on the Other!
- Salvation – the Purpose of Rejection
- Masculinity and the Messiah
- Patience and the Messiah
- Actualization – the Purpose of Sabotage
- Actualizing the Messiah
- Matter and the Messiah
- Hope and the Third Temple
- Code Hopelessness – AB/ BL / ABL
- Belief and the Messiah
- The Snake and the Messiah
- Rectification and the Messiah
- Serpent-Power and the Messiah
- Conversion and the Messiah
- Redemption and the Messiah
- The Plan and the Messiah
- Shin and the Messiah
- A Shift in Gnosis
- Code Gravity – BYE / YEB

2. Individual Power	3. Symbolic Power	1. Collective Power
The Inner Messiah	The Snake	The Outer Messiah

The Snake Symbol of Transmutation

Do Not Depend on the Other!

> "If you are living under a sense of obligation to the other, you are a slave." *Wayne Dyer*

If I didn't feel that I end at the skin (the shame body, again), there would be no perception of "the other." I would simply understand that we are One, and know that any decision I make for myself also serves the greater good. I'd know such wholeness that any lack of honesty and/or denial of responsibility would be unthinkable.

Meanwhile, I can't help feeling that I either owe you or that you owe me. This is how I vow to stay married to "you" until death do us part, ignoring that commitments are ideally made only to the Self and not to "you." When I force myself to be the same person I was 10 years, six months or even 5 minutes ago, I have my slave mask on and tend to feel obligated to apologize, explain and/or justify my decisions to "you." This will continue until something drastic occurs that prompts me to tell the truth.

> obligation (n.) c. 1300, *obligacioun*, "a binding pledge, commitment to fulfill a promise or meet conditions of a bargain," directly from Latin *obligatio* "an engaging or pledging," literally "a binding." The notion is of binding with promises or by law or duty. *Etymonline.com*

A famous biblical story illuminates this matter by involving *HaAqidah* – "the Binding" of Isaac. Much is said about Abraham as the father willing to sacrifice his son. But what about the son who accepts to be bound on an altar and sacrificed? What a poignant moment it must have been for both, as one said "yes" to the greatest loss, and the other, to a deliberate suicide! Abraham and Isaac were "bound" to the light within, the meaning of Latin *religare* from which eventually gave the word "religion."

5-Pride | 6-Sloth	7-Greed → 2-Lust | 4-Gluttony	3-Wrath | 1-Envy
Isaac | Aaron	Jacob → Joseph | David	Abraham | Moses
Power | Victory	Beauty → Honesty | Receptivity	Kindness | Appreciation

———— Throat
———— Heart
———— Navel
———— Sex
———— Root

Abraham and Isaac – Protectors from Wrath and Pride

I have seen how, in classical Kabbalah, the seven lower spheres are guarded by the seven patriarchs. What these archetypal forces are shielding me from are the seven deadly sins. While the table above gives the names of the seven patriarchs and their respective attributions, I shall focus on Abraham and Isaac as they are guardians of the throat chakra; the most impactful chakra in the passage into "the Promised Land." Abraham uses kindness to override wrath, and Isaac, Power to override pride. Note: Abram the Yvrit also means "the Father who went on the other side." This is when kindness ascends and wisdom descends, marking the end of my Power issues.

Meanwhile, to stop suffering from inverted polarities, I must be kind enough to give my most precious gift (my "son"), and powerful enough to transcend my fear of death. This is a HUGE big deal!

I will then be one with all, a oneness which automatically saves me from any neediness and/or from a false sense of obligation to the "other;" ultimately from sin.

Sexual Healing and the Messiah

> "When I get that feeling I want sexual healing / Sexual healing, oh baby / Makes me feel so fine." *Marvin Gaye*

The feeling that predisposes me to seek sexual healing is loneliness, and with it, the longing for the other. For me to be lonely, I must have disconnected from my heart. I just want to lie to myself, consciously or not, as there is something I'm unwilling to hear. I can now let myself be led into temptation, which provides even more of a smokescreen. I soon spend my energy reproaching myself to be insane, doing the same thing again and again, pretending that, this time, the result will be different. For now, I'm definitely praying for a sexual healing, which is to say: I'm imagining that a Messiah will come to save me from my loneliness.

Lie → Disconnect → Loneliness → Yearning → Misdeeds → Condemnation (Damnation)

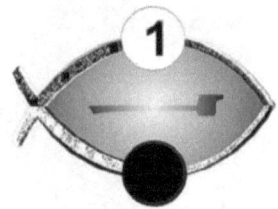

1. I start with a **lie** by doing what I'm not supposed to do or not doing what I'm supposed to do →
2. soon the lie **disconnects** me from my heart (from feeling love and loved) →
3. the disconnect causes me to feel **lonely**, an experience I intensify by resisting it →
4. I am now in Mammon's domain, prey to **yearning** →
5. The sense of not being, doing or having enough leads me further into temptation; more **misdeeds** →
6. Henceforth, I can't be kind to myself. Instead, I mercilessly condemn myself, precipitating my own **damnation**. I am in dire need of healing as there is nothing sexy about this game.

Salvation - the Purpose of Rejection

Prepare to DIE! Inquiry tool: www.goldenxpr.com/tco3_rejection/

Step 1: I fill in the blank: I want to know WHY I would choose to think I CAN'T _____ (e.g.; find a job, be patient, etc.). **Step 2:** I ask for truth and generate a number. **Step 3:** I find my number on the map to fill in the brackets: when I ignore the signs of the [**Ignorance**], I am compelled to go into a [**Rejection**] of/for the other, until the pain is such that I am reminded of the truth of [**SALVATION**]. **Step 4:** what surprised me in this process was [_____].

Masculinity and the Messiah

> "And God created the Adam in his own image, in the image of God he created him, male and female he created them." *Genesis 1:27*

The patriarchal version of the Bible – and by extension, of the Messiah as a man – is the filter through which I observe society: ♪ "it is a man's world!" Truth be told, "I created God in my own image, in the image of a man I created Him." But if I were to read what is really written, I'd realize that the Adam is created in God's image – male and female. But that still doesn't explain *Betzalmo* "in HIS image." Why not *Betzalmah* "in HER image?"

To answer, I must think in terms of archetypes, female & male being the first typing device. Elements can be female (when inwardly directed, such as water or earth), or male (when outwardly directed, such as fire or air). From elements, I move to instruments of knowledge, which can also be female (e.g.; earth → body, water → soul) or male (e.g.; air → mind, fire → heart).

"In the image of God, HE created HIM, male and female" speaks of the brain being created with two sides, male and female. This brain is the mind connected to the body - male air to female earth. The coming of a "He-Messiah" echoes the famous *mens sana in corpore sano* "a sane mind in a sane body," mind being the SON archetype.

Yod (י)	Vav (ו) / Heh (ה)	Heh (ה)
Heart	Mind / Body	Soul
Male Fire	Male Air / Female Earth	Female Water
The Father	The SON / the Mother	The Bride

The Sexual Healing of Elements and Instruments

Beliefs – such as "God" – live within my brain. Michelangelo suggested it in his piece "the Creation of Adam," when both God and the Adam stretch their hands toward each other. God happens to be pictured in a brain-like hemisphere. Even the title "the Creation of Adam" is mental. When calling his piece "the Creation of Adam," did the artist mean that Adam was God's creation or that God was Adam's creation? Which one is it? The artist lets me decide. **Surely, I'm confused when I think that I'm creating "in God's image," when I am in fact creating in the image my ego thinks "should" exist.**

There is an agenda in my "should." There is also gold in the shadow. To harvest the alchemical clarity I seek, I must go there. Exposing my greed-induced secrets (mainly about sex & money) grants me peace and thereby, unleashes my creativity.

Everything always comes from and returns to the Mother – including *Genesis 1:27*. This is conveyed by the Hebrew *Tzelem* for "image" of God. The word is formed on the root *Tzal* for "shadow." Certainly, if the male part of me is like the light, the female part of me is definitely akin to the shadow. This is even expressed in the female sexual apparatus, a sex that is feared as it is as dark as the womb of the tomb.

Spoken in Buddhist terms, I must have the courage to be lotus-like, that is, as comfortable with the part of me that is down under as I am with the part of me that is above water. Only then can the "light" of the male jewel be "received" by the female lotus. The purification process known as shadow work is how I will one day rise and bloom above the mud, and achieve enlightenment. The rising part is known as the SON of "God." It is the beautiful mind of a Messiah.

Patience and the Messiah

> "I believe with complete faith in the coming of the Messiah, and even though he tarries in waiting, in spite of that, I will still wait expectantly for him each day that he will come." *Maimonides, 12th of 13 Principles of Faith*

While a saboteuR, my lost soul direly needs saving. If I feel bad, it's because the split mind of my prostitutE leads me to sell out. **To under-**

stand this conflict, I resolved to go to the roots and explore what the Messiah is for the Jews, and why they couldn't accept that Jesus was it. Time has come to meet the Rambam.

Rabbi Moses ben Maimon – the Rambam (רמב״ם) for short, was also known as Maimonides and by the medicine name of "Great Eagle." He was a Sephardic Jewish philosopher, a rabbi and also an astronomer and physician who became one of the most prolific and influential Torah scholars of the Middle Ages. His copious work comprises a cornerstone of Jewish scholarship, carrying significant canonical authority as a codification of Talmudic law. His thirteen principles of faith were written after a long period of false prophets that came and went in the life of a community troubled by the death and resurrection of a Messiah whom they largely rejected.

Besides Maimonides' 12th principle that announces the coming of a dynamic leader, the scriptures are replete with quotes on the messianic era from Moses' prophecies (*Deut. 30:1*) to those of Isaiah, Jeremiah, Ezekiel, Amos, Joel and Hosea. Even the wall of the United Nations Building in New York is inscribed with Isaiah's famous quote: "And the wolf shall lie with the lamb." **When that does happen, the world will have received the codes, and come into the knowledge of opposites.**

The prophecy says that the Messiah will be a direct descendant of King David, and know his Torah stuff. "He" will rebuild the temple in Jerusalem, gather Jews from all over the world and bring them back to the Land of Israel. The messianic era will see world peace, ♪♫ no need for greed or hunger, and, in general, happiness, abundance and health for all. The divine plan of redemption will be fulfilled as humankind will feel that spirit and matter are one, and thus become kind. All of that will be achieved by a mass return to Torah's law as the Messiah reveals the concealed meanings of the scriptures, that is, the soul of the Torah – the Kabbalah. His strength will come from humility; not pride or greed for power. His magnitude will be catalytic, as he will lead by example, inspiring the individual and the collective to be the change.

These two prophecies – the third temple rebuilt and the reality of world peace – were seemingly unfulfilled by Jesus, explaining how, for the Jews, the Messiah is yet to come.

The Talmud states that there is a predestined time for this coming. While it is believed that the messianic redemption is imminent and will occur before the Hebrew year 6000 (as a point of reference, 2022 corresponds to year 5782), this "end of times" remains a mystery. It is said that every generation has one person who could step into the role; also, that the period preceding the advent of the Messiah will be one of great travail and turmoil. **When the times are troubled enough, "God" will activate upon this individual the necessary powers for him or her to precipitate that redemption.**

As for me, my work is to just learn to wait as I remove the blocks and complete my inquiry. I am also reminded of Gandhi's famous words: "be the change you wish to see in the world." The only way that I will ever trust that the Messiah did come is by causing all of the above prophecies to be fulfilled through me. Moreover, there is no individual enlightenment. I just need to realize that I communicate with the whole on a moment-to-moment basis through an invisible field of information interdependently entangled and connected. Waking up restructures the field. Eventually one individual will affect the tipping point of enlightenment, making World Peace a reality.

Actualizing the Messiah

> "If I am not for myself, who will be for me? If I am not for others, what am I? And if not now, when?" *Rabbi Hillel*

Will I dare actualizing and emPowering the NOW of my inner Messiah, or do I still believe that there's an "out there" out there? Am I so foolish that I never look for the messianic treasure where I can actually find it – inside? For unless I bring forth what which is within me, I will be waiting, *hoping* that others would save me. This means that I'll still be trapped in a world of greed, as my giving and receiving will be split, and my communication, infused with fear, confusion and domination.

The arrival of the Messiah touches into the ancient theological discussion of *Olam HaBah* (עולם הבא) "the world to come" vs. *Olam Hazeh* (עולם הזה) "this world." While *Olam HaBah* can be understood as the hereafter rewarding the righteous, it can also refer to "the days of the Messiah" which will greatly contrast with this age. This golden era may even happen in spite of me: "when you came down long ago, you did awesome deeds beyond our highest expectations. And oh, how the mountains quaked!" (*Isaiah 64:3*). But why wouldn't *Olam HaBah* be at all mentioned in the Hebrew Bible?

It may be out of this simple truth: I can only project my greed on what I call *Olam Hazeh* for "this world." While I say I want to be happy, healthy and strong, I continue to place my attention on being weak and unhealthy. This makes me sad. I fear turning within, possibly because inside, there is no light. Moreover, my eyes open outward, my hands spread outward, my ears hear external sounds. It seems logical that I would avoid searching for the Messiah "within" and be "without." Oyveh! This is how I contribute to the making of false Messiahs. I want to believe that I will be saved, but I don't really buy it as I know that I won't do what it takes to save myself. This dilemma is also how many souls have claimed to be the Messiah. I have the same complex when thinking: if I could just teach you, heal you, save you... Would I have those thoughts if I had embraced my pain?

Matter and the Messiah

> "Everything comes in time to him who knows how to wait." *Leo Tolstoy*

The legend narrates how the Messiah will come from the darkest of the dark, from the humblest of the humble. This darkness is the abysmal shadow. It is where I must go. The darker the shadow, the more potent the answers. Ironically, to be a light worker, I must do shadow work! Yep, the treasure is inside: I am the One, and fulfillment comes from within. If not, my quest is futile; guided by ambition. If I look for the Messiah in Power, prestige or prosperity, the seeker in me will increasingly become the "sicker," suffering from acute materialism, unconscious of just wanting my mommy!

While waiting for the third temple to be rebuilt, do I realize that I want my mother (my "matter") so much that I've lost sight of spirit? To see anything with physical eyes, I must first see it with spiritual eyes – a process called "faith." The "matter" of the Messiah will be made manifest (if only to me) when I fulfill all announced conditions as follows:

- **The Messiah must come from king David's line:** since we all share the same cells, aren't we all coming from king David's line? Rabbinical teachings speak of king David as the guardian of the root of the tree of life (*Malkuth* – "the QKingdom" or place of receptivity). The name David (דוד) for "beloved" is written Dalet-Vav-Dalet which resonates with code Satisfaction Guaranteed (see *TCO—Book 2*). Surely, when I know that I am *Dai* or "enough," I transcend my survival issues and find myself in the root chakra named *Malkuth* – "the QKingdom" of God. Moreover, realizing that the tree of life has its roots in heaven and its branches on earth is another way to see myself descending from king David.
- **The Messiah will have the knowledge of Torah:** to know the body of the Torah as the 0/1 Law and the soul of the Torah as the QKabbalah, I must embrace the female side of the shadow archetypes, namely, the victiM and the saboteuR. When I sense and feel them in me, I know what to do (my law) and I do it, body and soul. Henceforth, I know my Torah stuff, whether born Jewish or not.
- **The Messiah will inspire the building of the 3rd temple:** to rebuild Spirit's temple in Jerusalem ("City of Peace"), I must first understand how the war of the sexes is what destroyed it.

My temple is sustained by two pillars: to my left, the Dragon Queen who says "I desire;" to my right, the Lion King who says "I will." When these two polar opposites work together, I am centered as the Self who says "I know" and "I have."

- **The Messiah will usher world peace**: I can gather the Jews from all over the world (all the parts of me that are not ISRAEL/REAL) and bring them back to the Land of Israel, that is, to the State of Absolute Consciousness. When I enter it, I am peace. I have no need for greed as my hunger for LOVE is fed. I'm mostly happy, powerful, healthy and thus, abundant. The divine plan is fulfilled in the measure to which I feel the unity of spirit and matter.
- **The apparition of the Messiah will concur with the resurrection of the dead**: I can resurrect the dead by waking up from acting out the zombie-like patterns that kill me. Story is told that Buddha was asked: "are you the Messiah?" "No," said Buddha. "Then are you a healer?" "No," Buddha replied. "Are you a teacher?" "No, I am not a teacher." "Then what are you?" asked the student exasperated. "I am awake," Buddha replied.
- **The Messiah will reveal the soul of the Teaching**: to take the Kabbalah out of hiding, I work with the body of shame that just loooves its closet. Little by little, I expose its garments to the light. I know that my secrets make me sick. The more I air them, the more I reveal their counterparts in the form of cosmic secrets. Dying to my sins soon leads me to the radiance of a beautiful mind. Pride and greed are annihilated. The magnitude is catalytic, as I now lead by example, inspiring the individual and the collective to change.

Upon hearing of the prophecy about a "mass return to Torah's law," I'm reminded of the cartoon where a pig confesses to another pig: "personally, I wish the whole world were Jewish." If S/Hebrew is a language of Nature, doesn't that make us all Jewish?

Whether I feel it or not, we are One. Oneness is a mystical truth. If I recognize that all prophecies are fulfilled by the Messiah, everybody does. Moreover, no matter whether "I" call the mythical kingdom a "Shambhala" or a "Garden of Eden," there is an indigenous belief (a belief preceding any organized religions) and a cross-cultural prophecy that speaks of a mass return to this kingdom by way of a 10th Avatar – a "Messiah" of such magnitude it will allow for that kind of paradigm shift.

Hope and the Third Temple

> "Men marry women with the *hope* they will never change. Women marry men with the *hope* they will change. Invariably they are both disappointed." *Albert Einstein (XPR's Italics)*

One day, I shall be honest enough to hear the voice in me that is fighting a losing battle. And, on that day, I will stop hoping. How shocking is it to conceive that reprieve could come from the last hope – from being despaired (literally "without hope"), when hope is one of the three theological virtues, next to faith and love?

According to Hesiod's *Works and Days*, when Pandora opened her famous box, she let out all the evils of the world, and only hope remained. My personality wants to view that as a sign that hope is my last asset in dealing with evil. **Am I so afraid to lose all hope that help will come from out there that I would ignore that hope is in fact "in the same box" as evil? Might hope be so deceptive that it deceived us all?**

When awake, I don't hope. I trust. To hope for a better future, I must judge that the present is not good enough. And yet, I knew it as a child: there's no one and nothing out there. The outside world and/or "you" cannot fulfill me. Fulfillment is within. This knowing will end the war of the sexes and the soldiering golem waging it. But first, I must feel how I stress myself out by going into **a chronic fight and flight mode,** and why my communication expresses the following throat pathologies:

- **The fight of my female side:** I tend to aggressively push when I perceive that the male side doesn't want me. Feeling unfulfilled, my female now desperately clings, over gives and says too much. She is the part of me that won't let go.
- **The flight of my male side:** I tend to passively pull away when I perceive that the female side won't let me be. Feeling trapped, my male coldly withdraws, under gives and isolates behind a wall of silence. He is the part of me that won't let come.

My temple of Solomon is destroyed when the two beasts fight to be right, as per the above pathology. But when the male and female pillars unite in biblical knowledge, there's no one left to desecrate my Beth "house" which becomes a "temple" of peace. Indeed, the name *Solomon* comes from *Shalom* for "peace." I can now hear the XPR formula as follows: Understand → Choose *Shalom* → emPower the NOW of sound decisions.

Yes, the third temple will be rebuilt as my lies become Truth. I will then stop creating results I would rather not have to experience. And as hope turns to trust, trust will move into faith and faith, into love, allowing the transmutation of the snake into a Messiah to naturally complete.

When I accept that the "world" is not out there but in my consciousness, the question "why is there evil in the world?" becomes "why is there evil in me?" Might it be because I was yet to decode, and thus understand hopelessness?

Code Hopelessness - AB / BL / ABL

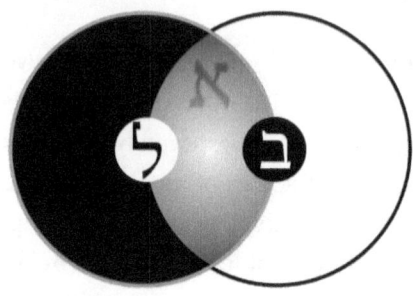

Imagine a language so sacred that it can reconcile opposites in just three letters...

Top: Hebrew letter Aleph (א) → A in Roman script
Right: Hebrew letter Beth (ב) → B, V in Roman script
Left: Hebrew letter Lamed (ל) → L in Roman script

Here is how S/Hebrew inscribes code "Hopelessness" in 3 words:

- **AB**: from top to right, I read *Ab* (אב) for "father, alphabet."
- **BL**: from right to left, I read *Bal* (בל) for "do not!"
- **ABL**: from top to right to left, I real *Aval* (אבל) for "indeed."

The Decoding: code Hopelessness is a beeline to acceptance. Indeed (speaking of "in deed"), it is only when I feel deep in my soul the sorrow of having committed a violation to LOVE that I am ready to change: "**indeed**, I have sinned," said Adam. This is a pivotal moment of true repentance; a turn within of such force that the addict in me will say "this is my last drink," and actually never suffer an exception again. While difficult to feel and resisted until the end, hopelessness announces the eminent arrival of my inner Messiah. Why? It is because the last of my plans and strategies to be loved, healed, saved or taught by the world out there fell flat on its face, and me, with it. The fall was so dire that I am done. The work (if only for that particular task) is done. As for the S/Hebrew codes, I have already seen the pairing of BL / LB as code Simplicity (see *TCO—Book 2, Understanding Knowledge*). Here is a quick reminder:

- **BL**: in one direction, I read *Bal* (בל) for "do not!"
- **LB**: in the other direction, I read *Lev* (לב) for "heart."

The BL/LB pairs partner to convey the entirety of Torah's wisdom, making it ultimately simple! First, I go from B to L, refusing to listen to *Bal* – my "do not" command. When sick and tired of being sick and tired, I turn to *Lev* – my "heart," totally willing to begin inscribing the LOVE that has no opposite, in tune with the ethics of complementarity. At this point I no longer resist anything.

Also simple, the letter Beth starts the first word of the Torah, while the letter Lamed ends the last word of the Torah. In between these two frames of reference is the whole of the law; the way, the truth, the life.

Code Hopelessness adds the mediumship of Aleph that balances the yesses and the nos of consciousness. By being the pure awareness that responds to the heart's dictates with a big YES, it allows for the turn within to be received as a gift of grace – a gift that I can't force or make happen. **Indeed**, enlightenment is **not** going to happen from my **doing** everything for it. However, it will also not happen unless I do everything for it – unless I give it my full **heart**. Eventually, the day comes when the Prodigal Son returns to the **Father** – that is, when the snake turns into a Messiah.

Belief and the Messiah

"The beliefs you truly hold, the ones you've decided to believe, your faith, will cause you to create or attract the experiences that will verify them." *Harry Palmer, Love Precious Humanity*

Scientists and mystics speak of the order of creation as follows: 1) think, 2) feel, 3) have, that is, beliefs → emotions → actions / manifestations. **And here is where it gets dicey: reality tells me what I believe with complete faith, which may or may not be the same as what I *want* to believe.**

On that note, Maimonides begins each of his thirteen principles of faith with *Ani Ma'amin B'Emunah Shelemah* "I believe in complete faith." These principles sustain a liturgical hymn called *Yigdal* ("may he be magnified") which conveys the fundamental tenets of traditional Jewish belief. A parallel for Christians would be the Apostles' or the Nicene Creeds.

Dear Maimonides, please forgive my audacity in what follows. I fully understand the 2nd Principle and the desire to believe in complete faith that "the Creator, blessed be His name, is a Unity, and there is no union in any way like Him. He alone is our God, who was, who is, and who is to be." However, if the trick to having faith is to be 100% (as in total certainty), I have reservations regarding these next two principles:

- **I believe with complete faith** that the Creator, blessed be His name, rewards all who keep His commandments and punishes all those who transgress His commands.
- **I believe with complete faith** in the coming of the Messiah, and even though he tarry in waiting, in spite of that, I will still wait expectantly for him each day that he will come.

When I really decide to wake up, my chilD grows up into a Leader. Doing so, I don't expect rewards or punishments. I know that I am good, since I am giving my all, so absorbed by the action that I am free of the action. This fullness of engagement is the reward. I do what I do because that's what I do. Period. It is also how I don't have any attachment to an outcome – rewards or punishments. I'm simply a TzaddiQ/a (an awake Leader), moving with 100% certainty, complete in my faith, loving "God" with *all* my heart, *all* my soul and *all* my might. This is the *Shema* prayer fulfilled – I feel the Oneness. I feel the LOVE. I have come. I have seen. I have conquered. I am in the Now.

Conversely, when communicating through the wounded heart, I break my word (which is my inner law), creating unconscious time in the process. This is how I delay experiencing my inner Messiah and tarry in waiting. Since I am misbehaving, I now believe that I am a naughty child and cast "God" into the role of a punishing Father.

One thing is certain: the collective believes with complete faith that it will have to wait. Few are the people who can actually imagine world peace. Time is a paradox, since being obligated to the collective is how I break my word and act compulsively: I CAN'T wait. Yep, I let myself be led into temptation, and then "hope" that the punishment won't be too severe. If I could wait, I would undoubtedly see grace at the end of my initiation. Upon seeing the pros and the cons of sabotage, do I still believe that I have a choice as to when to turn Visionary and see the good in the bad? If I were telling the truth when saying "I can quit anytime", why would I still sabotage my vision and delay my inner Messiah? Ah, this free will thing again!

2. Individual Power	3. Symbolic Power	1. Collective Power
The Inner Messiah	The Snake	The Outer Messiah

Symbolic Power and the Snake

The snake is a universal and potent symbol of change. It is the deceptiveness I know when I won't tell myself the truth about what I really want, and don't have my heart into doing the next "perfect" thing. **The pain coming from my ambivalence will lead me to THE decision by which to begin to turn my snake into a Messiah.**

The Snake and the Messiah

> "The only freedom man has is to strive for and acquire the *jnana* ("self-knowledge") that will enable him not to identify himself with

the body. The body will go through the actions rendered inevitable by *prarabdha* ("destiny") and a man is free either to identify himself with the body and be attached to the fruits of its actions, or to be detached from it and be a mere witness of its activities." *BE AS YOU ARE: The Teachings of Sri Ramana Maharshi*

Integrity *is* to believe with complete faith, to feel with all my soul, and to give/receive with full Power. When entire, I know that being congruent is the experience of "redemption." My prayers are no longer a pleading, since there is no yearning, not for a Messiah, for freedom, for anything. I am here. IT is here. THE END. No confusion.

For now, I am identified to the body – this shameful "thing" that stops at the skin. When I think that I am the body, I attach to outcomes, e.g.; closing a deal (if I don't, where will I find the money to support my body?). For now, I do believe with complete faith that I am here to wake up, and I still need to do the work and strive to eat from the "tree of self-knowledge," yet this time, consciously. I will then feel my "Jewish" heritage as I'll honor the mandate to learn about the messianic redemption and strengthen my faith in the Messiah's ultimate and imminent arrival.

The fact that this liberation comes from within is built into the pillars of the Jewish religion. Individual Power – or that which reveals my inner Messiah – is acquired via the pillar of *Teshuvah* ("turning within"). The more I resort to stop looking for LOVE out there, the more I feel the pillar of *Tephillah* (when I am blessed to see my "prayer" fulfilled). This rebuilds my temple of peace, and supports it by way of the quality of surrender that the pillar of *TzedaQah* represents. If *TzedaQah* means "charity," it is only when I know that there's no one "out there" that I experience the reciprocity of giving and receiving. Indeed, I transcended the divisiveness of duality, and merged into integrity.

Individual Power	Symbolic Power	Collective Power
Teshuvah – Turn within!	Tzedaqah – Give it all!	Tephillah – Feel blessed!

The Three Pillars of Judaism

Eventually, as the curse turns into a blessing, I will be able to hold the tension of opposites. I will then hear from within the truth of the old kabbalistic calculation that links the value of the word *Nachash* (נחש) for "snake" to the value of the word *Mashiach* (משיח) for "messiah." Yes, it is the word used in *Genesis 3;* the "snake" who leads me into temptation. Details of these geometries are in *TCO—Book 2, Learning to Code.*

This snake is said to be "the craftiest of all animals" as it tells partial truths: "you won't die. Your eyes will be opened, and you will be like God, knowing good and evil." As for me, am I ready to see how nothing but the truth can "rectify" my life?

Rectification & the Messiah

"Straight roads do not make for skillful drivers." *Paul Coelho*

The word "rectification" is built on Latin *rectus* for "righteous, correct and straight." And yet, having a "right" and a left is how I can navigate curves, and enhance my driving skills. This conundrum meets the Lurianic vision of Kabbalah: "there was spoilage for the sake of fixing and destruction for the sake of rebuilding." Without *Olam HaTohu* ("the World of Chaos"), there would be no need for *Olam HaTiqqun* ("the World of Order"), and vice-versa. Chaos and order can be felt as female awareness and male consciousness. The work of polarities was sensed by Rabbi Isaac Luria (1534–1572), the father of modern Kabbalah who based his interpretation on the Zohar.

The Luria saw how the two worlds – Chaos and Order – underlie the origin of free will and the realm of *Q'lippoth* (the evil "shells") that result from *Shevirat HaKelim* (the "fracture of the vessels"). Henceforth, the subsequent need for a redemption out of exile via the rectification of messianic order. This is the result of shadow work, a deliberate *Birur* "clarification" of the *Nitzutzot* "sparks" of holiness exiled in creation. The cosmic drama of *Tiqqun* resonates with the Buddha's first two Noble Truths stating that life is dissatisfaction; the cause of which being the yearning.

This pathology is acted out on the tree of life of modern Kabbalah, as the light travels through the vessels from the crown to the root. It first moves toward the male pillar (white spheres) and then goes to the female pillar (black spheres).

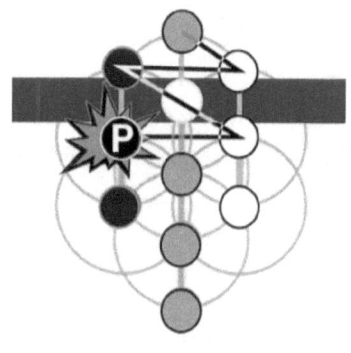

The "bad" news occurs upon reaching *Gevurah* – the sphere marked P for "Power." The big POW sound of an explosion occurs soon after I chose to serve my private agendas in lieu of the next "rectus" thing. I've just used my free will and burned myself ("a burn for a burn"). My misusing "POWer" created a need for order. But first, I invoked the chaotic, addictive and evil "shells" to encapsulate the light, so that I'd be so hungry for it that I'd work to redeem the entrapped sparks ("a fracture for a fracture"). This is how I set myself up to fulfill the order for "rectification."

In a nutshell (pun intended), I need the pathology to hear the Buddha's 3rd Noble Truth: there is an end to dissatisfaction. Happy are those who persevere on the path to the end! This path takes me to a double "rectification:" *Tiqqun Nephesh* – the "repair of the soul" and *Tiqqun Olam* – the "repair of the world." When all *Tiqquned* "fixed up," I see how within (the soul) and without (the world) reflect each other.

Serpent-Power and the Messiah

"When you succeed in awakening the Kundalini, so that it starts to move out of its mere potentiality, you necessarily start a world which is totally different from our world. It is the world of eternity." Carl Jung

Yes, it will take time of working in consciousness to become so real that I let go of repeating the past, elevate my soul out of its slumber and open to timelessness. The same awakening is known in Eastern teachings as *Kundalini Shakti*, Sanskrit for "Serpent Power." Kundalini is represented symbolically as a serpent coiled at the base of the spine; a dormant energy waiting to be released through meditation techniques.

I can now witness the eternal Self, and enter the state of Israel as the state of Absolute Consciousness. At that time, the whole structure of karmas becomes obsolete, since there's no ego left to suffer from the consequences of my actions. When there is no attachment to an outcome and no need for a "God" either rewarding me or punishing me, there is nothing to rectify (or "make right"). Having no desire to do harm, I can do no wrong. The whole perennial conflict between good and evil is at last resolved.

To feel that, I must know about the ultimate "repair, rectification or order:" *Tiqqun Cain*. While being the core of all *Tiqqunim*, it is mostly ignored – as if it was the snake's best kept secret. Surely, "correcting Cain" finishes the right and wrong game. I can now come to THE END of dissatisfaction, and know that I am enough. Called to be *Cain* for "possessed by jealousy," I could only kill my brother who had what that I *thought* I wanted and couldn't have: love, approval and recognition.

Now that I integrated all my fragmented parts, I stop asking you to love me and make it my work to love myself! The yearning, the hankering, the hunger, the neediness for a romanticized Messiah stops. The snake sheds its skin in the form of the desire body that used to fill me with shame. I can now wake up to a perfect *Nephesh* "soul" in a perfect *Olam* "world."

When I live in a soul and in a world where there are no mistakes and no accidents, I am not afraid to fail, and thus no longer "possessed by jealousy." This is how I CAN know that "the corrected soul" of *Tiqqun Nephesh* and "the corrected world" of *Tiqqun Olam* are the by-products of *Tiqqun CAIN*.

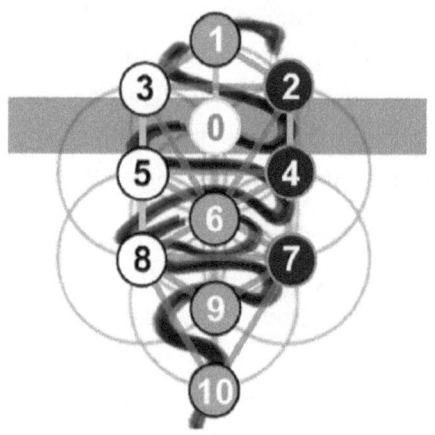

Serpent-Power Elevating My Soul by Connecting All My Fragments

Moreover, I went through such a relentless process in owning my errors that I came to see that there are no errors, since all is done *through* me and not *by* me — nothing wrong; nothing to forgive! Thus, while in English the letters of CAIN reorder as I CAN, in S/Hebrew, the letters of *Qain* reorder as *Naqi*, as I feel in my blood that my soul is pure: I *am* "innocent!" Moreover, my communication can now be well-received as I have no need to change you.

When I wake up and am transmuted into a Messiah, I know in my blood and my bones that the pain of being snake was necessary. This is also when my story changes.

Tiqqun also means "amending, editing." The story of Cain can now be "amended" to include the vision of Cain as serpent-Power moving up the messianic tree until the complementary perspectives of "I, WE, IT/ITS" come to the sphere 1 of a peace that is beyond sphere 2 of understanding. As such, Cain may just be the greatest prophet of all, as he came from the darkest of the dark – the first mortal and the first murderer – to have a chance to awaken Serpent Power and receive the gift of eternal life.

Conversion and the Messiah

> "The most that one of Jewish faith can do – and some have gladly done it – is to say that Jesus was the greatest in the long succession of Jewish prophets. None can acknowledge that Jesus was the Messiah without becoming a Christian." *Kenneth Scott LaTourette, Historian of World Christianity*

I can see how more and more people born of Jewish faith could gladly acknowledge that Jesus was the greatest of all Jewish prophets. After all, an entire religion was started from what was understood to be his teachings. I can also see that there is a difference between being a prophet – albeit among the greatest thus far, and being the Messiah.

I would like to reiterate how touchy this subject is, both for the Jews and the Christians. As long as the Jewish community as a whole does not sanction that Jesus is "The" Messiah, there will be some doubt in the Christian mind causing the desire to convert the world to Christian beliefs. "My prayer," said theologian John Piper, "is that the good news of Jesus, the crucified and risen Messiah, would flood Jewish communities around the world, that the veil would be lifted, and that we would see a massive turning of Israel to the LORD Jesus." Early church polemics went as far as judging that the Jews were no longer worthy of their own Scriptures because they had failed to accept Christ as their

Savior. "Forgive them (both Jews and Christians), for they know not what they do."

When I try to convince you to believe something about me (e.g.; salvation is in Jesus), there is a part of me not trusting it. Might that be because I am yet to fulfill my own law – to myself be true?

Moreover, Jesus' attainments seem to be inscribed as an archetypal initiation for giants. Most of the autobiographical events lived by Jesus are shared by other Great Teachers, among which Osiris, Theseus, Mithras, Buddha, Krishna and Hercules. I may also find that waking up includes passing many of the initiations listed below. For example, wouldn't it be a miracle if I could heal the part of me that is sick?

- Most of them were born under poor conditions, of a virgin and in winter.
- They had a star appear at their birth.
- They taught from childhood on, and said they came to fulfill the Law.
- They descended into hell.
- They casted out demons and crushed the head of snakes.
- They transfigured before followers.
- They performed miracles and healed the sick.
- They had Twelve Disciples who took vows of poverty.
- They were betrayed for a few pieces of silver (see next page).
- They died on a cross, for all mankind, and resurrected on the third day.
- They ascended into Heaven to sit forever beside the Father.
- They became Divine Judges and will return to reestablish order on Earth.

"They" are me; if I let it be... and if I'm willing to pay the price!

Redemption and the Messiah

> "When Judas, who had betrayed him, saw that Jesus was condemned, he was seized with remorse and returned the thirty pieces of silver to the chief priests and the elders." *Matthew 27:3*

Redemption is defined as the action of saving or being saved from sin, error or evil, and as the erasure of a debt or the recovery of something in exchange for a payment. Since saving myself involves paying a price, why do I have such a hard time investing first in my spiritual growth? If LOVE is my Nature, shouldn't it be free? Knowingly or not, I am asking about the paradox of STAGES versus STATES:

- The STATES (e.g.; absolute consciousness, waking, dreaming, deep sleep) are free. However, they come and go.
- The STAGES (e.g.; Leader, Officer, Visionary, Engineer) are to be earned. Once earned, they are permanent.

When a Judas, I am acting out the STAGE of the prostitutE. My mind is split, and my soul, betrayed for a few pieces of silver. The more shadow work I do, the more I can feel that the thought "what's in it for me?" is not real. When realizing that no one is acting and that my soul is pure (and that will be a virgin birth in the winter of my soul), I stop dreaming that I must pay the LORD of karma by suffering in order to make up for the harm I have done. I am free.

Meanwhile, I believe that I have debts and debtors. The "yearning" for *Mammon* seems so real that it splits matter from spirit, leading me to obsess on money, worrying about putting food on the table, clothes on my back and a roof over my head. It is the doubt that my creativity can support me that leads me to compromise my integrity. The same doubt that keeps me from knowing that my soul is pure is how I would seek redemption. It gets dicey when selling out is so painful that I want to make you pay for it. I now go deeper into Scare City, playing the "merit" card and mercilessly claiming my pound of flesh [taking a breath]. The curse of being ashamed and guilty, longing for someone or something to save me, ends when I do what it takes to redeem my firstborn. *Pidyon Haben* or "redemption of the firstborn" is a commandment in Judaism whereby a Jewish firstborn son is *redeemed* by use of silver coins. When viewed symbolically, the "firstborn" is my pain story. Once I pay the price of my liberation, I can lift up my eyes beyond the personal, and see who created all.

The Threefold Plan and the Messiah

> "The redemption plot is one of the oldest story shapes." *Peter Baynham*

How long will I desire to devolve me and fear being in my Power? While destiny answers: "as long as it takes; maybe millions of lifetimes," I do wish to speed up my awakening. And if it means decoding "the threefold plan" of the Mosaic Law, then so be it! What is it that I am yet to see which is currently hidden by the shame I won't feel? For me to still be in an illusion of separation – somewhat not happy, not powerful and not healthy, there must still be some secret linked to the "LORD" of Karma that keeps me in suffering.

Yod (י)	Vav (ו) / Heh (ה)	Heh (ה)
Individual Power	Symbolic Power	Collective Power
The Witnesses	The Judgments	The Statutes

The Mosaic Threefold Plan of Redemption

I wish to understand this plan, especially as it is mostly ignored...

- *The Chuqim* are four **"statutes,"** about which I am told *Naaseh V'Nishmah* "do and understand." I notice how the mere thought of blind obedience causes me to react with a big YES, BUT.

- *The Edoth* are the year's "**witnesses**," for me to hear/SEE that we are One, e.g.; the festival of Passover invites me to observe Nature's renewal, and spring free, here and now. YES, BUT: if I could "observe" the season of a new birth instead of repeating the past, I would. The thing is: I don't think I can.
- *The Mishpatim* are the "**judgments**," for me to understand, e.g.; "you shall not make for yourself an idol of any kind or an image of anything in the heavens or on the earth or in the sea." YES, BUT: even if I accepted that this law simply means "do not judge," the thing is: it's not simple to stop judging!

Until I realize how this plan supports the 0/1 Law of LOVE, I have two options: I can either resent the law as being coercive and turn lawless, or I can reveal my inner Messiah and explain the law to me so clearly that it becomes my pleasure to obey it.

Another "YES, BUT" shows up for me: how could I realize that this threefold plan of redemption supports the 0/1 Law of LOVE?

I first start by recognizing, if only intellectually, that the 0/1 Law of LOVE works in tandem with the idea of non-duality and/or of transcendence. Consider: when the twin parts of me unite, I know what to do and I do it lovingly. This is the #1 part of the 0/1 Law. I also know that I don't know what to do *until I do*, since my directions are given to me moment by moment. This is the #0 part of the 0/1 Law. Meanwhile, I am still a saboteuR and still in the stage of putrefaction. This is when the three poisons which are at the core of the Buddhist Wheel of Transformation come to help me understand.

Individual Power	Symbolic Power	Collective Power
Aversion	Ignorance	Greed
The Witnesses	The Judgments	The Statutes

The Three Poisons and the Threefold Plan

- **Greed and the Statutes:** if I weren't attached to an outcome, it is likely that I would have no issues with being told "do and

you will understand." I would chop wood, carry water, and I would understand as I'd be in total joy just out of giving myself totally to the action.
- **Aversion and the Witnesses**: if I understood in my blood that we are One, it is likely that I would not harbor any hard feelings around holiday time. Every day would be the occasion for me to give thanks; every day would be my birthday!
- **Ignorance and the Judgments**: if I took full responsibility for my failures, I would soon stop judging that I failed, as I'd realize that these very failures made me stronger, wiser and kinder. I would also extend the same generosity to my neighbor.

The Hebrew of the Torah speaks in potent symbols; as a snake for me to reveal the Messiah. My work is to decode them. When I do, I am so touched by their naivety that I am reborn - a child at heart. Note: the decodings that show the candor present in the Four Statutes, the Eight Witnesses and the Ten Judgments are unfolded in the books of *Golden XPR*, under the auspices of the *PaRaDiSe Mystery School*.

The goal is simple. It is also awesome: to have a complete understanding of the law which results in the ability to speak honest boundaries (a.k.a. "extreme self-care"), and to experience the well-being of the soul and of the body (Health with a big H).

Naaseh V'Nishmah for "we will do and we will hear and understand" is a clear call for humility, and, as such, for surrendered leadership. Rabbi Simai stated: 'when Israel put "we will do" before "we will hear," 600,000 ministering angels came to each and everyone from Israel and tied two crowns; one for "we will do" and one for "we will hear."' The two crowns become one, when I hear and understand that reality rules. I can now do and hear, or hear and do: equal! This brings me once again to the XPR Formula: Understand (Hear) → Choose Peace → emPower the NOW (Do).

Shin and the Messiah

"To you it has been granted to know the mysteries of the Kingdom of Heaven, but to them it has not been granted." *Matthew 13:11*

Jesus was teaching the codes of the Torah to his disciples, for them to feel how the sacred names for "God" are the embodiment of the energy they speak into being. And it makes me wonder... What is in Jesus' name *Yeshua* (ישוע) besides "he is saved?" According to the Talmud, the Name of the Messiah existed prior to any Big Bang Beginning.

It is believed that each letter has the wondrous Power to signal perennial truths. This is how the word *Ot* for "letter" also means "wonder, sign, mark." Henceforth, Hebrew mystics held that the entire cosmos was created from the twenty-two foundational letters. Indeed, communication is the result of what is said and done. Besides *Yeshua HaMashiach* – "the anointed One who is saved," Jesus is also called *Devar Elohim* ("the Word of God"), since he is the First and the Last or "Aleph and Tav." The word *Ot* for "word, sign" spells אות (AWT) or "Aleph and Tav." It was engraved as a wondrous mark on Cain's forehead (see *TCO—Book 1, Oh, no! Why the Bible!?*). *Ot* conveys the magnitude of *Tiqqun Cain* ("the repair of Cain") as it speaks into being a path to the end of dissatisfaction. This path stretches from Aleph to Tav and back, for me to amend the murderer in me that kills my potential. Doing so reveals my inner Messiah.

If the letters are messengers, what does the sign Shin (which is common to both words – *Nachash* for "snake" and *Mashiach* for "Messiah") tell me about salvation?

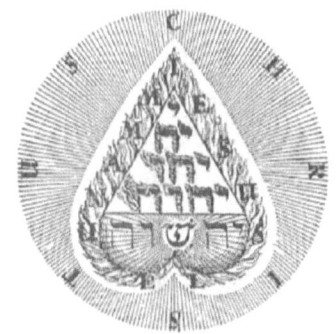

When a Shin is inserted in the four-lettered Name (יהוה), it invokes a 5th dimension and adds a 5th element (wood) to the four classical elements.

This five-energy system is invoked by YESWE's quintessence. Pronounced Yod-Heh-Shin-Vav-Heh, the letters (יהשוה) can also be read as *Yeshua* (ישוע). Therefore, how and why would Shin invoke salvation?

The letter Shin (ש) is the twenty-first letter – the one before last. Its numerical value is 300. **Its sound is "Sh" when the dot is on the right side, and "S" when on the left (see table below).** As a word, Shin means "1. tooth, 2. dedicated, 3. change." This motion from hunger to commitment to transformation is present in Shin's tarot – the Judgment card. This is the stage of resurrecting the dead parts of me, the time to come to the end of my own BS and meet "God" face-to-face. What life does slowly, the shout of the master and the voice of the horn can create in an instant. The S/Hebrew word for "horn" – the *Shofar* – can only be initiated by the fiery energy of Shin, a letter that is one the three mother letters – the elemental wombs of creation.

Individual Power	Symbolic Power	Collective Power
Fire / Wood	Air / Earth	Water / Ether
Sin (ש) / Shin (ש)	Aleph (א) / Aleph (א)	Mem (מ) / Mem (ם)

The SIX Elements and the Three Mother Letters

Tradition holds that, at the end of time, a "new" letter will appear. This "new" letter can be recognized in the doubling of Aleph. I have felt the depth of the letter Mem's message, as the word Mem is formed by two Mem: a Mem regular and a Mem final. I am now starting to see how the letter Shin also has a code of opposites built within. Since Aleph, Mem and Shin are known to mother three elements (and since there are SIX elements by which *Elohim* created the world), it implies that Aleph must take two forms. The first one has a value of 1, and the second, the value of 0, in order to engrave the 0/1 Law of LOVE.

Back to Shin, there is also the special case of the Shin with four branches, found on the *Tephillin* (a box worn on the 3rd eye by observant Jews in morning prayer). One side of the head *Tephillin* has a Shin with three branches, and the other, a Shin with four branches.

 The yin yang illustration of the three and four-branched Shin is the reverse of the one in *The Wisdom in the Hebrew Alphabet* by Michael Munk. Just like the two other mother letters, Shin has two sides (and two sounds – Shin and Sin), to merge the visible realm and the invisible realm. The negative space defines the form which I see, showing me how emptiness is form and form is emptiness. While the letters of the Torah are black fire written on white fire; the empty spaces are pregnant with meaning, giving me ample space to mind the gap, feel the breath within the breath, and understand. The image also pictures the Trinity as it is held by the Four-Lettered Name – the three within the four, the Son within the Mother. The 4-flame Shin joins the 3-flame Shin to combust my 4+3 or 7 deadly "Shins," and reveal the Messiah that was hidden by my secrets. Shin can now source the word *Shinui* – the "change" I wish to see.

My story is your story! Just like you (and just like Jesus), I have felt sad and forsaken. Just like you (and just like Jesus), I came to fulfill "the law that is no law." And to do so, just like you (and just like Jesus), I must die to my sins. Thanks to Shin's fire, I now have a clear path.

The TWIN Flame of the Messiah

> "And when one of them meets the other half, the actual half of himself, whether he be a lover of youth or a lover of another sort, the pair are lost in an amazement of love and friendship and intimacy and one will not be out of the other's sight, as I may say, even for a moment." *Plato, the Symposium*

How sweet that I would end the Messiah discussion where it started: in the need for sexual healing! When a soul is created, it is split into two twin parts who are eternally yearning to reconnect. In Plato's mind, the separated hearts find themselves by vibrating as the frequency of integrity. Throughout their walking as star-crossed lovers, they're compelled to keep looking for The One – the flame that mirrors their own brilliance. They know their life puzzle completes upon reuniting. This reunion will be the proof that they decoded patience and satiated the hunger for LOVE. Integrity is their soul compass. They must nullify any doubt that splits them from their heart. The more entire they are, the more irremediably attracted to each other they will be, and the more they'll recognize each other. **But how could "the One" be out there?**

The twin flame speaks of the *Hieros Gamos*; Greek for "the Sacred Marriage." Carl Jung describes it as "the union of archetypal figures in the rebirth mysteries of antiquity and also in alchemy. Typical examples are the representation of Christ and the Church as bridegroom and bride, and the alchemical conjunction of sun and moon."

A variant of the same tale is told in the gnostic myth of Sophia (Greek for "Wisdom"), a myth which has SIX articulations (**bolded** below). After living in the lofty heights of the **Fullness**, Sophia leaves the tender embrace of the Father to descend into the world of chaos and desperate alienation. Forgetting that she volunteered to go into the pit of **yearning**, Sophia feels lonely, sad, forsaken and even angry. She eventually sees a light and perks up, thinking it was her Beloved. But she was **hallucinating**. Seeking the light, she can't help but go deeper and deeper into the deceptive depths until she is stopped by Horos, a power known as **"the Limit."**

At this point, something strange happens, as the Limit radically splits her mind. She feels her heart ascending to the Fullness, while her mind remains trapped in exile. Becoming mad, she longs for the embrace of the Beloved so much that she creates a lesser god with whom to consort. Named the **Demiurge** for "a worker in between," he hangs with a group of co-actors to delay the ascent of the soul. He can be a benevolent creator (a stellar Christ), making the universe as pleasant as the confines of matter will allow. He can also shape-shift into a lunar serpent or a solar lion compelled by revolting urges.

2. Individual Power	3. Symbolic Power	1. Collective Power
Solar Lion	Stellar Christ	Lunar Dragon
The Father	The Son & Groom	The Daughter & Bride

The Shape-Shifting of the Demiurge Before Becoming Stellar Christ

The Fullness replies to chaos by sending two saviors, the Christ and the Holy Ghost. The Holy Ghost (Daughter) speaks through Sophia who acts as Christ's twin-flame to deliver the world. Mary-Magdalene may have been who played that role for Jesus to be Christ. Supported by his Bride, the Christ can now incarnate as the Son to model how to attain self-knowledge and return to the Father's Fullness.

A Shift in Gnosis

"Gnosticism was stamped out completely and its remnants are so badly mangled that special study is needed to get any insight at all into its inner meaning." *Carl Jung*

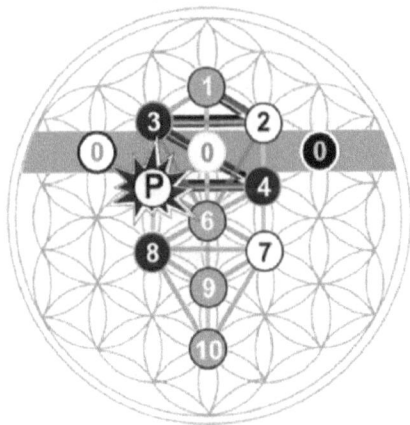

Here is how *Golden XPR's* QKabbalah understands the gnostic myth. The **Fullness** is the whole garden – in the flower of life that holds both the tree of life and the tree of knowledge. However, to feel the presence of the twin flames in the good and evil spheres on each side of knowledge (and by extension, the male and female flows of life), I must acquire the Power of Three. This involves balancing collective and individual Powers, and thus ending the fight of the lunar dragon and the solar lion (the twin sides of my brain). I can then center on the middle path, as a Christ "anointed" in symbolic Power.

The Limit is, of course, the abyss that separates the lower worlds of Ego-Egypt from the celestial Promised land (the first tier from the second tier). **The Demiurge** is the bestial and split mind that oftentimes creates a reality of hell on earth. When in hell, my polarities are reversed: my dragon desires to do evil, and my lion resists doing good. These tendencies are, indeed, "revolting urges."

Sophia leaving the Father is sphere 2 of wisdom that resorts to descend and trade places with sphere 4 of kindness, in order to heal boundary issues (the **yearning** that distorts my sense of limits and leads me to **hallucinate** that I am not enough). The madness and subsequent misuses of Power (see sphere marked with a P) will stop when I have complete understanding. I can then be a Mother to myself. As the third opens to seeing that my Father and my Mother are together, the twin flames can now merge as Son and Bride and handle the chaos of the infernal spheres. Surely, the marriage of kindness and understanding eases the possibility for me to love reality on its terms, no matter what "face" it shows me.

The Faces of Gnosis

"Your only obligation in any lifetime is to be true to yourself. Being true to anyone else or anything else is not only impossible, but the mark of a fake messiah." *Richard Bach*

Sin (שׁ) / Shin (שׁ)	Aleph (0) / Aleph (1)	Mem (מ) / Mem (ם)
Sphere of Kindness	Sphere of Reality	Sphere of Understanding
The Father	The SON / The Bride	The Mother

The Triple Flame of Shin Enlightening the Faces of "God" in the Three Supernal Spheres

To be true to myself is no small affair. Indeed, I must first take back my childish projections by owning that I do not see the reality of my father and my mother, but rather my creation of my father and my mother. Doing so, I stand a chance to own my projections, learn from the mirror, and love reality as it is, with all of its faces.

This attainment is sustained by the triple flame of the letter Shin. To make a fire, I must first use my breath to ignite the kindling. Similarly, the word *Esh* for "fire" is spelled Aleph Shin to mark that "fire" starts in the air of Aleph.

Indeed, Nature shows me that *Yeshua* (YESWE) can only exist when supported by his Aleph bride AYESWE (*Ayeshua*). Aleph and Shin are the twin letters that inscribe "fire." To know the passion of an intimate, spiritual and physical union, I still have to come to experience the message of the "TWINS" spelling "Thy Will Is Not Separate." In other words, I must first surrender my fears to stop attracting them to me. This is the work of revealing the Messiah: "anyone who believes in me will do the same works I have done, and even greater works, because I am going to be with the Father."

To complete my shift in Gnosis, I must know my **instruments** in relationship to the **faces** of "God:"

- The Fullness is the **Voice** calling **the World** or consciousness in which I live.
- The Yearning is the **Split Mind** waiting for **the Son** to deliver me.
- The Hallucinating is the **Lost Soul** blocking **the Bride's** message.
- The Limit is the **Pain Body** smothered by an exiled **Mother**.
- The Demiurge is the **Broken Heart** blaming **the Father** for my failures.
- The Savior is the **Forsaken Spirit** who is disconnected from sensing "God" in his **Cells**.

What I project *out there* – **the World, the Son, the Bride, the Mother, the Father and even the cellular body** – are in fact *in here*. Yes, the Son will deliver me, in other words, the mind will heal. I will then feel the Bride as the happiness of my soul. This also implies that I am destined to defy gravity – until I can raise to be FREE Fallin' into the three Supernals.

Code Gravity - BYE / YEB

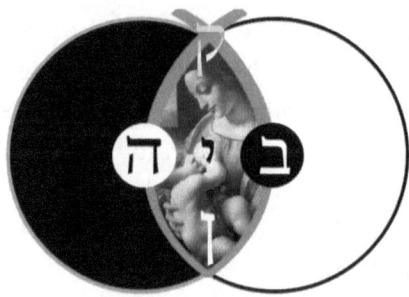

Imagine a language so pure and so sacred that it can reconcile opposites in just five letters...

The saboteuR - You had me at Elohim!

Top: Hebrew letter Qoph (ק) → Q in Roman Script
Right: Hebrew letter Beth (ב) → B in Roman Script
Middle: Hebrew letter Yod (י) → I, J, Y in Roman Script
Left: Hebrew letter Heh (ה) → E in Roman Script
Bottom: Hebrew letter Nun final (ן) → N in Roman Script

Here is how S/Hebrew inscribes code "Gravity" in 4 words:

- From right to middle to left, I read *Bi'Yah* (ביה) for "inside *Yah*" (inside animus-anima).
- From middle to left to right, I read *Yahab* (יהב) for "give."
- From top to middle to bottom, I read *Qayin* (קין) for "Cain, possessed [by jealousy]."
- From bottom to top to right to left, I read *Nuqbah* (נקבה) for "female, bride."

The Decoding: being trapped inside an animus and/or an anima that **possess** me is a truly depressing situation. Not only does it take me down, but it is also a gravity problem seemingly without a solution. **Cain** is so attracted to falling that I spelled his name vertically, as if he had no other option but to fall. Looking at the geometry more closely, I also see that, at its core, is an image of the Virgin Mary and Child. When I am myself "possessed," it is understandable that I would have cold feet. Indeed, it will take an absolute commitment for me to be at once the Son whose folly condemns me to fall, and the Mother who is virginal enough to fully embrace my Son's falling.

Only then can I descend as deep as needed into the abyss to retrieve my missing fragment and be whole! My hesitation in saying "I do" and in marrying me not for the better (I don't have a problem with that part) but also and foremost "for worse" is what makes me heavy. It is what causes me to be in shame – the densest feeling of all. Just like quanta of gravity are too weak to be recognized, my Cain's unending folly and fall continue to make my self-esteem so weak that I can't feel it.

If my soul can't withstand gravity, it is because I want to place a limit on how much failure, falling and folly I will accept.

My greed has me convinced that I should be further down the road by now: don't I deserve it? When my name is Cain, I don't have a choice. I'm at once loaded down with heavy weights and unable to touch bottom. To end my bondage to the density of materialism, I must understand *in my blood* how gravity is the universal force of attraction between all matter (between all "mothers"). I will then be able to fully surrender to the weight of things.

I have seen how opening up reorders the letters of Cain (קין) for "possession" into *Qani* (קני) for "innocence." When free of jealousy, I have no need for betrayal. I am the Son of "God" – the Word made flesh. Admittedly, I had some doubt: could I really be so true to my word that I would heal? Could I befriend the beast of despair?

Heavy stuff! The main challenge for physicists in the quantum field has been to explain gravity in quantum-mechanical terms. While entangled particles are mapped onto a four-dimensional space, gravity is thought to exist in the fifth dimension. This ties me directly to the fifth day of creation – the Leviathan's Day (*Genesis 1:21*). If the snake is the cleverest of all beasts, the Leviathan is certainly the most massive – the heaviest. The bigger my Leviathan monster, the stronger the acceleration, the harder the fall... but also, the weightiest the blessing I can **give** to the world! Whether I know it or not, giving it all (no attachments) is the ultimate desire behind the **666-Desiring**.

The Leviathan
The Beast of the Sea
666 – Desiring
Animus Possession

Surely, being victorious over the Leviathan is no less than mastering emotions and, as such, having the key to no longer misusing Power. This is when the impatient Son in me hears, sees and understands the **Bride** as I know that I am created male, but also **female**. Freed from an animus possession, I get the girl. This means that I can feel: I'm sentient again! If I can feel right from wrong, I CAN decide – a proficiency which stops the wavering between desiring and resisting. I'm restored to my "virgin" status, a word which actually describes me when I do what I do because that's what I do, without any attachment to any outcome.

I resonate with Etta James: ♪♪ "At last, my love has come along; my lonely days are over, and life is like a song…" I no longer see myself lacking and have no missing fragments; no jealousy! I am **inside** *Yah*, feeling from within that my Yod jewel is cozily contained in my Heh lotus. *Yah* is the "God" Name and Power that circulates throughout the tree of life, energizing it with wisdom. The transpose of wisdom is folly. When my terrible hunger for LOVE is finally satiated, my mind (the Son) is not insane anymore. Instead, it is patient as it is fed by the milky breast of "enough."

The saboteuR now takes a supine position, lying on "her" back, front upward, wholeheartedly trusting the vision. This new lightness of being ushers the dawn of the victiM's purification, when I am now willing to detox and ready for how Truth will change my life.

FOUR

The victiM - The GOD Technology

"(If Loving You Is Wrong) I Don't Want to Be Right!" Luther Ingram

TO UNDERSTAND why I play victim, I must feel how the trauma I have experienced broke my instinctual compass. Ever since, what is natural becomes thwarted, which is how I keep on setting me up to be harmed. How could I *not* suffer when robbed of the instinctual capacity to adapt, survive and thrive? Unable to reason my way through my issues, I'm stuck in the mud and can't get myself out. Moreover, I use my trauma to justify my failures. I even build my life around it. It's become my identity. My sense of justice is so deeply shattered that I bluntly distort the sense of the law. Moreover, without religious instinct, I can't give it all. Henceforth, I engage in toxic relationships, swinging from submission (a bona fide victim) to dominance (a bully). When the pain is big enough, I will eventually realize that I am the judge of "my" reality. Ideally, this will take me beyond a sense of injustice heightened by a profound distrust of "God," restore the knowledge of what's right and wrong, and strengthen my will so that I'll make the conscious choice to evolve the greater good as an agent of enlightened justice. Can the alphabet as the Law of laws facilitate this transition? Is there a GOD technology written in the stones formed by the S/Hebrew letters?

WHY ME? BECAUSE I CAME TO SHIFT MY MO! WHETHER I LIKE IT OR NOT, I AM HERE TO FULFILL THE LAW (THAT IS, TO SHIFT OUT OF THE WAYS I BREAK MY WORD TO MYSELF). TO THIS END, I AM ABOUT TO DISCOVER THE LETTERS OF A GOD TECHNOLOGY THAT SUSTAINS THE O/I LAW OF LOVE WHICH IS ALSO THE LAW WITHOUT LAW.

The Albedo Stage of Purification – when the white victiM turns to the Officer

I HAVE SEEN IN *TCO—BOOK 2* (SEE CODE TRANSFORMATION) HOW THE 22 letters can be organized into five tetrads that are framed by the first and the last letters – AT | TA. The last and 5th tetrad (which ascends me from stages S to R to Q to Z) may just be "the enlightenment tetrad" since its RQZ letters link to the operation of the three luminaries (the sun, the moon and the stars). Incidentally, the QZ letters that spell *Qetz* as the "end" of time also restore the religious instinct by being the first and the last letters of *TzedeQ* "justice" and *TzaddiQ* ("awakened one"). As for the letter S, I spoke of it in great length as being Messianic since it evokes the Last Judgment – when I stop judging. This is when I open my heart to justice as I know the difference between good and evil.

Who would I be if I could answer the loaded question "what is justice?" Would I still try to hide, deny and repress my wrongdoing while projecting it on a "you" whom I create as my oppressor? Bottom line: would I still be a victiM, compelled to justify myself, fighting to be right and seeking to make you wrong?

Next Stage: the victiM's Purification

Prepare to DIE! Inquiry tool: www.goldenxpr.com/tc03_victimhood/

Step 1: I fill in the blank: I want to know WHY I would choose to think I CAN'T _____ (e.g.; find a job, be patient, etc.). **Step 2:** I ask for truth and generate a number. **Step 3:** I find my number on the map and fill in the brackets: when possessed by the devil of [**Victimhood**], I go into the hell of wanting [**MY HELLusion**] which triggers my hunger for [**MY Hunger**]. The only way I'd be immune to [**Victimhood**] is by relating to how "God's" [**Immunity**] lives in me. **Step 4:** what most surprised me in this process was [_____].

Part I: The Victim's Broken Compass

- Written in Stone
- Taking Back my Projections
- The Broken Compass
- Noble Suffering: The Victim's Dirty Secret
- Defending against the Sacred
- Justice and the Victim
- The Letter of the Law
- The Vav Blip
- The Translator Effect - No Connection
- The Log Exemplified

Yod (י)	Vav (ו) / Heh (ה)	Heh (ה)
Individual Power	Symbolic Power	Collective Power
Communication	Healing	Commerce
Alchemy	Astrology	Theurgy
Resh (R) the Sun	Tzaddi (Z) the Star	Qoph (Q) the Moon

The Letters Inscribing the Triple Mastery

Written in Stone

"How did He permute them? Two stones build two houses, three stones build six houses, four stones build 24 houses, five stones build 120 houses, six stones build 720 houses, seven stones build 5040 houses. From there on go out and calculate that which the mouth cannot speak and the ear cannot hear." *Sepher Yetzirah, Chapter 4:4*

I keep on coming back to "communication is not what is said and done, but the *result* of what is said and done." This is how the philosophy of languages uses the expression "speech acts," since speaking presents information but also performs an action. Therefore, communication is akin to karma or to the law of cause and consequence: for every speech act, there is an opposite and equal reaction. :-)

Sepher Yetzirah concurs on the fact that words do matter by pointing out how letters are stones used to build houses. With the two stones AB (Aleph, Beth), I build the house of *Ab* ("father, alphabet") and the house of *Bo* ("enter").

A Redemption Code Written in Stone – AB | BN | ABN

What is to be entered? The sanctuary of peace that surrounds me when I make contact with the inner father and then, with my inner mother. The letters ABN write the word *Aben* (אבן) for the "stone" on which the

10 Words (and, by extension, the entire alphabet) are inscribed. Their message of oneness is received when I know myself as BN or *Ben* / *Bin* (בן) for the "son" / "in-between" the two circles of life. Indeed, the vesica piscis is symbolically the part of me that can effectively hold the tension of opposites.

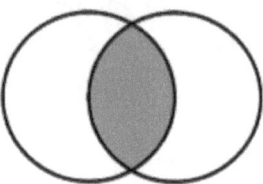

The Grey Vesica Piscis - an Invitation to do Shadow Work

As a quick reminder, the vesica piscis (Latin for "vessel of the fish") is the intersection of two congruent disks, each centered on the perimeter of the other.

I have seen how THE most impactful decision may just be to do shadow work and dive deep into the abysmal waters – as modeled by the letter Nun and as indicated by the sense of the word *Nun* for "fish." My goal in doing so is to redeem the sparks of my soul from their "fallen" state. Redemption is the message of the fish – a message written in stone and encrypted in my DNA.

As for the S/Hebrew letters, the root Z-D-Q is intense, as it branches into words whose translation tends to put me into a mode of resistance. These are *Tzedeq* for "justice," *Tzaddiq* for "righteous, saint," and *Tzedaqah* for "charity and righteousness." These concepts are so loaded that I end up playing the "righteous" and wrong game, as a way to defend myself against my own wrongdoing.

Truth be told, as soon I defend myself, I make me vulnerable to attacks – a victim, all over again! Am I willing to remember that there's no one out there; and especially, no vengeful "God?" Will I take back my projections of attacks, for it is the only way that I'll stop bullying the victiM in me?

TAKING BACK MY PROJECTIONS

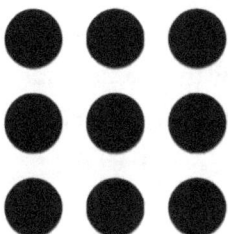

TAKING BACK MY PROJECTIONS: to remain infected with victimhood, I must have an aggressor.

It is also a projection that makes my victiM say: "the Devil made me!" The word "Devil" itself comes from Greek *diabellein* for "to throw across, to project." The Devil is thus the projection onto "the other." It is all that I hide, deny and repress, until I realize that there's no "other" to get me and no "out there" for me to dominate. Henceforth, my victimhood is proportional to the devils I am yet to meet.

When my victiM's screech meets *Samael as* "God's Poison," I become conscious of how this name poisons me with entitlement, until I detoxify by deleting the verb "I deserve" from my vocabulary.

When my victiM's split mind meets *Mephistopheles as* "the Destroyer of Lies," I become conscious of how this name draws out my forbidden desires, until I can stop the profanation by telling the truth about what I really want.

When my victiM's lost soul meets *Belial* as "Without Self-esteem," I become conscious of how this name leads me into chronic abuse to prove that I'm not enough! The abuse continues until I know that enough is "in off!"

When my victiM's pain body meets *Beelzebub as* "the LORD of the Flies," I become conscious of how this name leads me to numb my pain via numerous addictions until I no longer need a patron of dependence.

When my victiM's broken heart meets *Satan as* "the Adversary," I become conscious of how this name leads me to fight to be right until I have no desire to prove you wrong.

Finally, when my victiM's forsaken spirit meets *Lucifer* as "the Light Bringer," I become conscious of how this name prompts me to touch bottom until I realize that greater is the light that comes from darkness.

Meeting and understanding my devils is how to free myself from being in bondage to the material world. Until then, I will be a glutton for punishment, with a pain body either going into excess or into deficiency. If my gluttony is with food, I will move from overeating to under-eating – never quite hitting it right (eating it right?). Will I ever sense when enough is enough; enough food, enough money, enough seeking, enough lies?

Doing shadow work, I begin to deconstruct the "evil" pattern of fear and illness, and see that what was intimately personal is also transpersonal. Indeed, before life disappears, I can use this opportunity to find that which never dies. This quest – which is mystical in nature – will lead me to forgive and, in turn, to heal as it is when I restore my religious instinct. When I can enter a space of immortality where birth and death never happened, the death, the suicide, the abandonment, the rape, the betrayal – it all works to open me to compassion.

This is the mystical level above the trauma. It is where my soul wishes to uplift me using its utterly irrational yet unyielding force. It is where my sense of violence and injustice can be rephrased.

Most of the time, I really (like really) *think* I'm right, when I have no clue! The more information I access, the more perplexed I get. The more tools I invent, the less time I have. The more pleasures I entertain, the more pain I suffer. I am SO confused that I can't see the forest for my upside-down tree.

Moreover, my failures enforce the need to make *you* pay, a thought so dark that I must turn off my conscience to allow it. Indeed, upon witnessing what I judge as unfair, I find it hard to forgive my debtors – let alone my debt. When corrupting the nobility of the law and giving justice the overtones of a personal vendetta, I am far from balancing the scales.

Would I be litigious if I were kind enough and generous enough to harmonize my giving and receiving? Would I be less inclined to be argumentative, start disputes or disagree? It is my sense that I would naturally be kind and generous, and as such, fulfill my calling. Abiding the call is what nourishes me. It is the food of heaven and the source of true nourishment. It is LOVE in action. It is when the poison of entitlement is metabolized since I know it is not about me, and come to merge the victiM with the Officer of the Law, literally changing my MO.

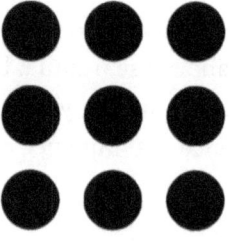

The Broken Compass

"There is a time for everything, and a season for every activity under heaven." *Ecclesiastes 3:1*

I look at my cat. He knows when to jump and when not to jump; when to sleep and when not to sleep; when to eat and when not to eat. He is completely connected to his body's instincts, and, as such, there is no double-guessing, no ambivalence – no "not enough!"

Carl Jung coined the mnemonic word "CRASH" for an easy recall of the five following instincts: Creativity—Religion—Aggression—Sexuality—Hunger.

I am a victiM due to my inability to stay in the body until the end of a "season" – when my hunger is so pure that I instinctively move from the season of not eating to the season of eating. A similar case could be made with creativity, aggression and sexuality. But religion as an instinct?

The thing is: I am not my cat. Having to contend with the split mind of a human, I often lead myself to an out-of-body experience. In other words, instead of emPowering the NOW, I'm stuck in an anxious memory and I can't get out! If I could restore the religious instinct, I would know not only the meaning of wisdom teachings (such as "we are One"), but also, I would have the integrity that gives it all. Yep, I would wake up from the DREaM of karma and love the LOVE "God" with *all* my heart, *all* my soul, *all* my might. In that space, there'd be NO suffering; no illusion of separation.

TCO, once again, asks a provocative question: what if there was a sixth instinct and what if that was imagery, such as the symbols of the alphabet? ♪♫ *Imagine* all the people-signs... I wonder if eye can... No need for greed or hunger... A brotherhood of instincts...

Noble Suffering: The Victim's Dirty Secret

> "Without pain, without sacrifice, we would have nothing."
> *Fight Club*

To be a victiM, I need the pain: without it, I couldn't claim that I have been harmed, injured, or even killed as the result of a crime, accident or action that was devised by you who is my "God" and my reality nemesis. However, in wanting the pain, my victiM's intention is not in mastering the Self and not in being in service to others. If I seek to be in pain, it is to manipulate you into giving me your attention and being of service to me. Therefore, my pain is not a sacrifice. It is neither real nor redemptive! I'm not interested in contributing my gifts, but more in securing your collaboration as I perceive that "you" owe me: "after all I've done for you..." Entitlement is my poison, and indebtedness, the hook by which I attach you to me. Pretty dark, indeed!

As a victiM, I use the instrument of the pain body. In fact, I make sure that I never heal by protecting me from truth and ignoring what my sickness tells me about myself. As long as I am sick, I don't have to show up. I can stay in bed! Like all defense mechanisms, my suffering is here to create unconscious time. Defending myself is how I obscure a truth that challenges my BS. To ensure that I never have to hear it, I not only assess that there's a threat, but I also forget that I am who decided that a defense was needed. I now have a double security system in place that allows me to deny all responsibility for my creations – starting with the victiM's identity. I can now go into amnesia, forgetting the fact that I am the one who set up the attack and called forth an aggressor by developing a need for a defense.

Why me? My victiM pretends that the gods must hate me, as I have zero control over some unsolicited illness or duress coming to me to weaken me and make me suffer. I have no say on the matter.

Unable to accept that my sickness is a decision which I once made consciously, I can never be free. However, by denying truth, I'm increasingly believing that I am the body – or that which is dying. So yes, my life is definitely suffering. Yet there is no nobility in it, no interest to look at what causes my suffering, no will to understand it.

Defending against the Sacred

> "In the concentration camps, we discovered a whole universe where everyone had his place. The killer came to kill, and the victims came to die." *Elie Wiesel*

To be in a concentration camp and feel that I belong, that is the big picture! As for me, I can't even feel "at home" in my current reality. I'd rather construct my own defense and be slave to laws which I try to control: "This reality is evil! I know it is and I'll resist it!" I ignore the bigger view – the sacred contract signed by my soul which is all about enlightening justice. The idea is for me to choose to give it all before I leave the body (and actually give it all). For if my struggle is not a true sacrifice, I won't feel the hatred transforming as it burns on a pyre of LOVE.

Yes, I have a body and I am a Soul as a program encrypted by a psychological DNA code with a series of predisposed characteristics. It is written as follows: this Sacred Contract serves as an agreement between [my Name] and the Soul, a.k.a. "God." It becomes effective on [DOB] and involves services provided for this lifetime. **The Soul hereby agrees to take human birth into a specific body and personality, so as to go through a predetermined set of experiences which will involve suffering.** While these experiences have already been written, [my Name] can choose to consciously use them as vehicles to die to the personality and remember the I Am. Note: a non-refundable 20% karmic fee shall be paid upon the execution of this contract, with the balance due no less than one (1) second after the time of death, whether the death is mental or physical.

This is the purpose of my contract: for me to know who I am, and thereby heal my mind. I will then recognize that, where there was war, there is now peace. Where there were sickening secrets, there is now healing light. When there were oppressive thoughts of temptation, there is now a body freed from tyranny. Body was always inert, in sickness and in health, in poverty and in wealth. It was my mind that was moving, compelled by unending desires. The truth of my earthly mission is to fulfill the law; not to distort it.

Am I defending myself against my own contract? What do I fear would happen if I were to fulfill my inner law?

Justice and the Victim

> "If it feeds nothing else, it will feed my revenge. He hath disgraced me, and hindered me half a million; laughed at my losses, mocked at my gains, scorned my nation, thwarted my bargains, cooled my friends, heated mine enemies; and what's his reason? I am a Jew."
> *Shakespeare, Merchant of Venice*

Shylock is more than a Jewish usurer and more than the antagonist of merchant Antonio in Shakespeare's play. His profile is so essential that his name is now used as a synonym for loan shark. I have seen how the financial lingo borrows words from the spirit realm, e.g.; Jesus saves! :-) The word "redemption" is right to the point as it signifies to be released from both blame and debt. Indeed, "forgive our debts as we forgive our debtors." The word "debt" itself speaks of something owed, but also of a trespass against others. Might the whole of the law aim at helping Shylock to do what it takes, which would mean to stop playing victim? He would then be able to heal any given situation. This is to say, he would pay the price. But when he wants to make "the other" pay, he becomes a combination of both a victim and a bully. Indeed, the victim – which is a universal archetype – would not exist without a bully.

A universal archetype says that we are all Shylocks and all Jewish. It is likely that "I" judged reality to be unfair, likely that I endured insults, and likely that I became resentful and vengeful as a result. Moreover, do I not have eyes? Do I not have hands, organs, dimensions, senses, affections, passions? Am I not fed with the same food, hurt with the same weapons, subject to the same diseases, healed by the same means, warmed and cooled by the same winter and summer? If you prick me, do I not bleed? If you tickle me, do I not laugh? If you poison me, do I not die? And if you wrong me, shall I not revenge? **If I am like you in the rest, I will resemble you in that. If I am wronged, what is my humility? Revenge** (taking ownership of Shakespeare's insights).

When I state "I crave the law, the penalty and forfeit of my bond," I am suffering from a hunger that can only be satiated by way of understanding. Rather than a pound of flesh, what I hanker for is the Word made flesh. Before I can take full responsibility for my creation (and thus fulfill the law), I must feel why I am unreasonably prone to go to the law to settle disputes. I must own that the struggle I have with "the world" is my creation. **I must feel that I'd rather be litigious and argumentative than to be so awed by the exactitude of the Law that I'd surrender my judgments.**

As long as I live in Scare City, perceiving that I CAN'T have what you're having, I will be greedy, resentful and vengeful – a victim turning bully. I will grow bitter and be unrepentant with respect to my demand for payment, while bettering the instructions for villainy that you, yourself, taught me. I'll follow a "kind of wild justice," as philosopher Francis Bacon offered, going outside the official justice system to respond to what I see as a "higher law." Feeling that the state is not ready, able or willing to enforce justice, I'll take the law in my own hands!

There is an intimate connection between the letter of the law, justice and revenge. The character Portia (as in Torah "portion") whom Shylock names a "Daniel" attempts to add **MERCY** to the mix. Yet who lacks mercy: the Jew refusing to let go of a Christian's pound of flesh or the Christian requiring the Jew's conversion? For if I am a Jew, I am equally a

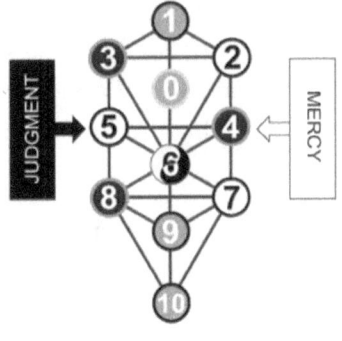

Christian! Might it be easier to try to control you than to change my

viewpoint? Who is the alleged narrow legalist and who comes in the body of a Messiah to fulfill the law of LOVE?

Daniel ("God of **JUDGMENT**") lives in the throat; the most challenging rung of the tree. This is where my polarities are inverted causing my female side (Shylock) to misuse Power by issuing severe judgments while my male side (Antonio) just appears to be kind and merciful.

Revenge is written in the Law of Talion, and money is "under" the desire to retaliate (see *TCO—Book 2; Understanding Knowledge*). I must still grok the letters of the law in order to feel the spirit of the law in my blood.

The Letter of the Law

> "People who follow their religion to the letter of the law are just silly. I mean, I want to tell Hasidic Jews: I promise you, God will not mind if you wear a nice cotton blend in the summer." *Sarah Silverman, Comedian*

The letter of the law versus the spirit of the law echoes the split of matter and spirit. Indeed, if words do matter (in the sense that communication is the *result* of what is said and done), the letters which form the words certainly do! When I obey the letter of the law and not the spirit, I listen to the literal interpretation of the words (the "letter" of the law), but not necessarily the intent of those who wrote the law. Conversely, when I honor the spirit of the law but not the letter, I may be doing what the laws' authors intended, but not necessarily adhering to its wording.

And it makes me wonder... Am I not the reader of a contract? Don't I interpret the script of reality in function of my stage of consciousness? And if so, am I yet to have evolved enough to be responsible for what I choose to observe, consciously or not?

William Shakespeare wrote numerous plays on the letter/spirit antithesis. He appears to come down on the side of spirit, often forcing villains (who side with the letter of the law) to make concessions. In *The Merchant of Venice*, he introduces the quibble as a plot device to save both the spirit and the letter of the law. The moneylender Shylock had made an agreement that he would take a pound of flesh from Antonio in case if he couldn't repay a loan. When the debt was not repaid in time, lawyer Portia at first pleads for mercy (the spirit of the law) and finally saves the day by pointing out that Shylock's agreement with Antonio mentioned no blood (the letter of the law). Shylock can have his pound of flesh only if he sheds no blood.

Interestingly, *Dam* (דם), the S/Hebrew word for "blood," is equal to *Adam* (אדם), to say: being human is to know oneness *in my blood*. Yes, being a deeply religious person is bigger than a denomination. It involves being compassionate and real enough to love reality with all my heart, all my soul and all my might. When I do, there is no narrow-mindedness. The symbols of religion and its intent line up, as I understand oneness so much that there is no more discrepancy between what I say I want and what I have. In that sense, I am the Living Word – a blessing to life itself.

I'm still missing an interpretation of the law that would be sensible enough to lead me to the Promised Land of enlightenment. If the prophecy of a cross-cultural wisdom teaching that would unify the nations is real, where is this teaching?

I crave the time (and mind) when my victiM won't need to make the law an external device to repress what I can't accept in me. The law will be engraved in my heart as it is on tablets of stone (See *TCO—Book 2, Understanding Knowledge, Code Wisdom*). However, to be able to read the letter of the law in accordance to its spirit, I must have complete understanding of why I once wanted to do harm. In other words, I must become so literate that I can read into my own motivations – no matter how poisoned they may be. The tablets will then open to me.

About the letters of the law, rabbis have asked what is the middle letter of the Torah. I find it fascinating that, even though we are living in the information age, there is no computer study that could offer a *D'rush* – an "inquiry" or "interpretation" that could be final. **Some rabbis say that the midpoint is in letter Vav of the word *Gahon* (גחון)** in *Leviticus 11:42*. Naturally, some deny it. The duality of interpretations is ironic, as it has been proposed that the middle is in *Darosh Darash* in *Leviticus 10:16* – *Drush* being the D level of PaRaDoX, the wisdom that knows the D-ifference.

As for *Gahon*, it is the "belly" full of undigested motivations due to my being unwilling to read what I feel in my gut. I see in the image here that the letter Vav is written enlarged, as a possible hint to its capacity to kill the spirit of the law. 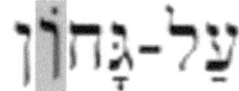 Not only Vav is the 6th Word ("Thy shall not murder"), but also, it is the letter initiating the 6-Desiring room. Will I be a "pharisee," wearing a mask of sanctity although I let the Vav of desire lead me into temptation? Vav answers: "please remember that I am also the agent of connectedness!"

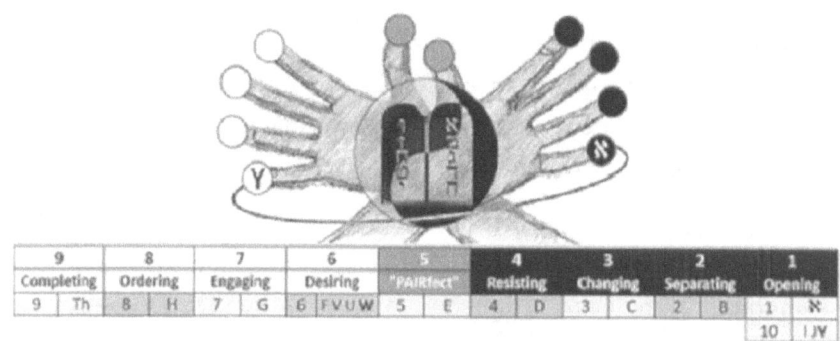

The Object of the Law: to Join my Hands in Service to Health

Above, I see my palms engraved with the yin yang tables of the law. Each tablet has 5 letters: 5 for my yin side and 5 for my yang side. When I don't split the letter of the law from the spirit of the law (in other words, when I obey my intuition), I no longer feel that the law is coercive. Instead of wanting to run, I stand in awe, touched beyond belief! And as I hear: "not my desire, Thy desire be done," my right thumb (and digit Vav W) that used to be **6-Desiring** for its own advantage joins the left thumb to experience how "PAIRfect" life is when desire and resistance balance each other...

The Vav Blip

> "It is said that desire is a product of the will, but the converse is in fact true: will is a product of desire." *Denis Diderot*

Vav is quite the symbol! It is dicey, since it may incline me to desire what is not good for me. While Yod symbolizes the Father's seed, Vav symbolizes the Son's phallus. "God" is the Word, which is itself a seed; "spermatic." To channel this seed in the proper Heh channel, the Vav phallus must be circumcised. This is exactly what happened to the Sumerian words *Adamu, Sabattu* or *Shumu*: their Vav and/or "U" sound disappeared when they became *Adam, Shabbat* or *Shem* in Hebrew. Vav's potential for misusing Power may also explain how the letter is not part of the "God" Name *Elohim*, and also how it shows up at the core of YEWE – the LORD of Karma. I enter the DREaM of Karma when my Vav acts out which causes my prostitutE's mind to split, and in turn, my victiM's body to be in pain, as I am unconscious of having a Heh womb to contain the energy.

Yod (י)	Vav (ו) / Heh (ה)	Heh (ה)
chilD	prostitutE / victiM	saboteuR

VictiM follows prostitutE, until there is no more split mind to follow.

I wouldn't be a victiM if I wasn't cut off from my body, and I wouldn't be cut off from my body if my mind was not imposing Scare City thoughts on me. On that note, the following pages will shed light on the passage from Hebrew into Greek, when the exact signs that write justice into being disappeared from the Greek alphabet. This disappearance may be how the felt sense of justice as the willingness to give it all also vanished. When Vav is so direly conflicted, how could the letter and the spirit of sacrificial law not be terminally divorced from each other?

Vav – the letter of desire – continues to be most challenging: For now, I wish to give its "blip" a context. It is easy for me to accept that Hebrew Aleph became Greek Alpha which became Roman script A, and that Hebrew Beth became Greek Beta which became Roman script B. **It is after the "Alpha-Bet" that confusion sets in.**

I have seen how 3rd letter Gimel (for "camel") is mostly mis-transliterated as if were the 7th letter G, and this, even though logic would have it that 3rd letter Gimel would have evolved into the 3rd letter C of "camel," especially as the 4th Hebrew letter Dalet became 4th Greek letter Delta which became Roman script D. I have also seen how the 7th Hebrew letter Zayin is mostly misheard as the letter Z, even though it evolved into the 7th letter G of "Gee whiz." These two misappropriations have led me to recognize that the mutation that affects my DNA is not in pair AT, but in pair CG. CG is the very pair that encrypts "the sin of the parents" and makes me a victim of my biology.

There is more to the mystery of "the letter of the law." Three letters were abolished in the passage from archaic Greek to modern Greek: they just stopped existing (see black columns which also gives the Hebrew source). These letters are: Greek Digamma (formerly Hebrew Vav), Greek San and Sampi (formerly Hebrew Tzaddi and Tzaddi final), Greek Qoppa (formerly Hebrew Qoph).

The displacement of Vav from rank 6 to rank 20

I will come back to the denial of an essential influence, this of a tribe that played a key role in the interpretation of the Hebrew Scriptures (the Sadducees). I will also show how their Hebrew name has four letters, three of them being in the black zones. For now, I shall focus on Vav, and what it means that the value of 6 and the energy of 6-Desiring would have been taken out of the Greek sense of communication.

Hebrew	Archaic Greek	Modern Greek	Roman Script
6th letter Vav	6th letter Digamma	?	6th letter F
6th letter Vav	6th letter Digamma	20th letter Upsilon	21st, 22nd, 23rd letters U, V, W
17th letter Peh	17th letter Pi	16th letter Pi	16th letter P

Since Vav (the semi-consonant either pronounced as a "V, W" or a "U, O") is essential, it first maintained its position in archaic Greek as the 6th Greek letter Digamma. Eventually, Digamma disappeared from modern Greek to mysteriously reappear as the 6th letter F of Roman script. Vav/Digamma also dropped to the rank of 20th letter Upsilon of the modern Greek alphabet, sourcing the U, V, W, Y of Roman script. To further complicate matters, letter F often gets confused with letter P due to the similarity between the sounds F and Ph. Might this be how I sometimes make my "Filosofy" unsound, as I can't know whether I'm dealing with an F or a Ph?

ATBaSh		ALBaM	
A	T	A	L
B	S	B	M
C	R	C	N
D	Q	D	X
E	Z	E	O
W	P	W	P
G	O	G	Z
H	X	H	Q
Th	N	Th	R
Y	M	Y	S
K	L	K	T
First/Last QKode		11:11 QKode	

I know that every letter is a musical note and that every note vibrates at a given frequency. Therefore, when I write "Alef" in lieu of "Aleph" and transcribe its final letter as if it were a Vav (F, U, V, W) and not a Peh (P, Ph), I alter the word's resonance. But why Vav and Peh? The answer is in *Sepher Yetzirah*: "the non-dimensional spheres are numbered ten as the fingers; five opposite five, with a singular covenant precisely in the middle, sanctified by the circumcision of the tongue and the phallus."

The ATBaSh and ALBaM codes have only one pair that matches: WP. Word Vav (W) means "nail, and," and symbolizes the phallus. Peh (P) means "mouth." Pair WP is "the singular covenant precisely in the middle, sanctified by the circumcision of the tongue and the phallus." Five pairs of letters are above pair WP, and five pairs, below it.

The message is consistent: "your word matters. It has life. Be true to it!" But how can I wake up from the DREaM and end Mammon's yearning, when I can't give me the permission to want what I want? Playing powerless as a victiM is my only Power. It gets me your attention, which is what I want from you because I can't give it to me. This is how I hunger for your love, approval and recognition. The problem is: even if you were to say you loved me, I can't trust your love since I know I manipulated you to have it.

Here is a surreal idea: what if feeling into the spirit of the disappeared letters would allow me to know that what I really want is to have my own love, approval and recognition? Would I then take better care of myself, that is, mother myself better?

The Translator Effect - No Connection

> "And God saw everything that S/He had made, and, behold, it was very good." *Genesis 1:31*

The translator effect is a takeoff from the observer effect known to quantum physics. These experiments have shown that what is being observed in nature depends on choices made by the observer. When I accept that there is nothing out there, and that any judgment that I make is self-judgment, I realize that what I am reading in the scriptures and/or in the "text" of life is the consciousness that I occupy. I can't take me out of the equation! For me to know what is real, I must let go of borrowed knowledge. When I do, my eye and I are enlightened, seeing black and white, a dead cat and an alive cat, at the exact same time. All options become possible when I speak in the language of paradox, and communicate with "God."

Henceforth, when I choose to observe the "bad" in reality, I create suffering by resisting my creation of reality (or what I believe about what is). For example, it is not that I created (my) illness, but more that I created my illness as "bad" by seeing, measuring and/or observing that it was so.

And it still puzzles me: since I am living in a state of absolute freedom (and this, whether I know it or not), why make the subconscious choice to observe bondage? Why sickening me by using force for me to adopt a given discipline?

To live and let others live, I must have the patience to not meddle with my own process. It will take as long as it takes for me to surrender my judgments. This reminds me how Star Trek's prime directive makes for an enlightened civilization based on respect: "whenever I interfere with someone's evolution, and no matter how well-intentioned I may be, the results are invariably disastrous." Consider: when I resist embracing my suffering, I will tend to want to meddle with "your" growth.

Knowing good and evil is to own my projections and let you be where you are: "why worry about a speck in my brother's eye when I have a log in my own? How can I say to my brother, 'Let me take the speck out of your eye,' when there is a log in my own eye? Hypocrite! I must first take the log out of my own eye. I will then see well enough to deal with the speck in my brother's eye." *Matthew 7:3-5*.

Anything else can only be a disconnection from reality. When I disappear the 6th sign Vav (the connector) and its counterpart Digamma (Gamma is 3, Di-gamma is 2x3 or 6), I can only completely misread the signs! Although they're right in front of me, I can't see them...

The Log Exemplified

"And I saw that wisdom is better than folly, just as light is better than darkness." *Ecclesiastes 2:13*

As it happens, what the translator "saw" in *Ecclesiastes 2:13* has little to do with what the Hebrew says, which is: "And I saw that greater is the wisdom that comes from folly, and greater the light that comes from darkness." The huge loss in translation is baffling, and yet my eyes cannot see the wisdom in folly unless I have the courage to travel through the realm of the delirious and come back from it! To be real and not a hypocrite, I must enter and remain in the state of objective consciousness, a state that includes and transcends waking, dreaming and deep sleep. This is easier said than done.

My judgment of the evil, dark, female side – the "left" side of the body and the "wrong" side of brain – is how I desire and resist the idea of righteousness.

Meanwhile, the possibility of waking up from the illusion of separation lives in the core advice of most religions: do not judge! That is the essence of the second commandment. It is also what surrender is! And yet, it is the pain caused by my judgments that will also open me to compassion when I understand that we are one: your pain is my pain. Just like me, you have known loneliness, sadness, shame and a fair amount of anger… It will take courage to plunge into the abysmal night of the soul, feel where my error is, and harvest the pearl in consciousness that is formed by the friction of lies and truth. It is also how to realize that greater is the light that comes from darkness.

When dreaming that I end at the skin, I can't feel that we are interdependently connected, although connectivity is a basic constituent of the fabric of reality, and oneness, a fundamental truth. Moreover, didn't Erwin Schrödinger, one of the founders of quantum mechanics, state that entanglement is not just a property of quantum mechanics, it's THE property? Entanglement *is* connectivity in the flesh...

There is no free lunch. I will be disturbed as I walk through the valley of the shadow of death until I satiate the hunger to be right. I can also sense that, when my eye is free of fear, I perceive the truth, see the light and finally answer my own question: why am I here? What's my purpose? Who am I?

Meanwhile, I am immensely comforted by remembering *Ecclesiastes 2:13*, as it helps me accept my folly by feeling into the entanglement of wisdom and folly, a.k.a. the code of opposites. MY oh MY: will I ever stop taking things so personally?

	Third Stage			Second Stage			First Stage	
9	8	7	6	5	4	3	2	1
Completing	Ordering	Engaging	Desiring	"PAIRfect"	Resisting	Changing	Separating	Opening
MY Problem	MY Secret	MY Poison	MY Hunger	MY Taboo	MY HELLusion	MY Question	MY Story	My Resisting

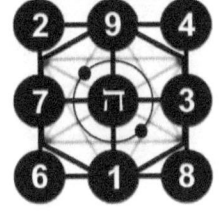

Part II: Restoring the Religious Instinct

- Restoring the Instinct Broken by the Pain Body
- The SIX "Days" of the Pain Body
- The Loss in Translation – No Voice
- The Grief in Translation – No Healing
- Ignoring the Number 72 – No Cooperating
- The Departed ZQ in "Sadducees" – No Eliminating
- The ZQ Twilight Zone – No Grounding
- Code Awesomeness – ZQ / QZ
- 🎵♪ (I can't get NO) satisfaction!
- The Righteous & Wrong Game – No Recuperating

Resh the Sun	Tzaddi the Star	Qoph the Moon
Alchemy	Astrology	Theurgy
Power – Sphere 4	Knowledge – Sphere 0	Wisdom – Sphere 3

The Spheres around Knowledge

The victiM - The GOD Technology

Restoring the Instinct Broken by the Pain Body

Prepare to DIE! Inquiry tool: www.goldenxpr.com/tco3_instinct/

Step 1: I fill in the blank: I want to know WHY I would choose to think I CAN'T _____ (e.g.; find a job, be patient, etc.). **Step 2:** I ask for truth and generate a number. **Step 3:** I find my number on the map to fill in the brackets: when I ignore the voice of the [**Ignorance**], I start telling the story of [**MY Story**], which results in having [**Pain Body**] and attaching to [**Victimhood**], until... Until the day comes when the

broken instinct of [**INSTINCT**] is repaired. **Step 4:** what most surprised me in this process was [_____].

The SIX "Days" of the Pain Body

> "For love to flourish, the light of your presence needs to be strong enough so that you no longer get taken over by the thinker or the pain-body and mistake them for who you are. To know yourself as the Being underneath the thinker, the stillness underneath the mental noise, the love and joy underneath the pain, is freedom, salvation, enlightenment." *Eckhart Tolle, The Power of Now*

The pain body has one agenda: to keep me from emPowering the NOW. When under its purview, each new pain is merged with pains from the past which are already lodged in my cells. This, of course, includes the traumas I suffered as a child. There is now a negative energy field that occupies my mind and influences my body, a field which has a life of its own. When it is active, I live almost entirely through my pain-body. When partially dormant, I experience it only in specific areas, such as situations linked with past loss or abandonment. Anything can be a trigger, as long as it vibrates with a pain pattern from my past.

Whether it is harmless as a whining or vicious as an attack, this life-form comes from a sense of dissatisfaction so deep that it turned destructive. Illnesses and accidents are often rooted in such negativity. Just like every other entity in existence, the pain-body just wants to survive, and for that, it needs me to be unconsciously identified with it. Like a parasite, it can then take me over, and live through me. Since it feeds on negativity, it must call on situations that are pain-inducing. While I say I want to be pain-free, my thoughts are designed to keep the pain going, for myself and others. To top it all, the more I want and need pain, the more I become a victim or a bully. But what if I understood the pain body's patterning? Even more so amazing, what if the letters of the law that were yet to be "read" contributed to inscribing the pain story and other slave narratives?

1. **No voice and the loss of translation:** a loss of voice occurs when my fallen angel can't speak an honest yes or an honest no. From thereon, I can only suffer, silently. Might it be linked to the voice of Torah being stifled, when the meaning of the word for "justice" was confused for "righteousness?"
2. **No healing and the grief in translation:** a loss of healing occurs when my prostitutE, unable to let go of being attached, can't cope with grief. Might this be linked to the sorrow of the sages who failed themselves in translating the Torah into Greek? Indeed, the multimodality of the S/Hebrew tongue just can't be rendered in Greek.
3. **No cooperating and the number 72:** a loss of cooperating between the different parts of me occurs when my saboteuR chooses to be disempowered. Might this be linked to ignoring the role played by the number 72 in synergizing the four spheres that could help the passage into the Promised Land, and thus heal my Power issues?
4. **No eliminating and the departed "Sadducees:"** a loss of eliminating occurs when my victiM has no outlet for purification. Might this be linked to the departure of the main letters of the word *Tzaddoq* for "Sadducees" in the transition from archaic Greek to modern Greek? These were the very sages grieving over an impossible translation.
5. **No grounding and the ZQ twilight zone:** a loss of grounding occurs when my chilD acts out. Might this be linked to the mystery surrounding the ZQ letters that inscribe a large part of Hermes' mastery and bring anyone who's willing to die to their sins to "THE END" of time?
6. **No recuperating and the "righteous" & wrong game:** a loss of recuperating occurs when my rising angel can't replenish himself. Might this be linked to my having such a hard time with my wrongs that I desperately try to be right over you? The

"righteous" loss in translation that caused suffering to my fallen angel is now blocking my ascent.

The Loss in Translation – No Voice

"But seek first the kingdom of God and his righteousness, and all these things will be added to you." *Matthew 6:33*

And here it is: I read "righteousness" and go into a contraction. I seem to have developed an allergic reaction to the word. I find its moral overtone offensive. This is so contrary to what I imagine Matthew's intention was that it leads me back to the root. What does the Aramaic version *really* say?

Something could have been lost as the verse moved from Aramaic to Greek to English. One thing is clear: I do not make "seeking the kingdom of God and his righteousness" my priority. I do not understand how doing so would secure the "things" I want. I also do not really understand that the ultimate deciding Power is the choice of Peace. I still think that Power is about money or fame or youth. Those are my priorities.

Back to my inquiry, I checked the Aramaic version of the gospels and read the word *Tzadiqutei* – the precursor of *Tzedeq* "justice." Justice has a different vibration than "righteousness." It has a nobility that I'd like to carry in all my affairs. And yet, upon judging that what happened to me is unfair, I find it difficult to forgive my debts and my debtors. Clearly, the need to make you pay is at the root of my constructing miscarriages of justice. Is my making you wrong how I hunger to be "right?"

When corrupting the nobility of the law and giving justice the overtones of a personal vendetta, I am far from balancing the scales. Would I resent and/or resort to the word "righteousness" if I were kind enough and generous enough to harmonize my giving and receiving?

And if justice is a point of equilibrium, how can it be best served by the right and/or righteous side alone? Once again, the tree of the knowledge of opposites visits me. IT IS THE KEY TO THE QKINGDOM (see image below). For if my heart doesn't understand knowledge, I can't feel that right and left are interdependently connected. How then could I yield enough energy to magnetize what I want? No can do! Indeed, when I deny that justice is moved by the law of LOVE which is 0/1, male *and* female, good *and* evil, right *and* wrong, I am into forced labor and can't let my goal be drawn to me.

The QKingdom

Bottom line: my fear of survival keeps me from entering the QKingdom of God. I don't even know that *Malkuth* for "QKingdom" names the root chakra. This center is healthy when I let go of seeing myself as a have-not and open to *QKabbalah* or "receive." Consider: when I receive in my root chakra that the crown chakra is reality and that reality rules (thus the name *Kether* for "crown"), I join earth to heaven. I am now in my voice and in my feet!

The Grief in Translation - No Healing

"Philosophy is written in this grand book, the universe, which stands continually open to our gaze. But the book cannot be understood unless one first learns to comprehend the language and read the letters in which it is composed." *Galileo Galilei*

Once upon a time, the ruling Egyptian-Greek emperor Ptolemy (c. 367 BCE – 282 BCE) gathered 72 Torah sages, whom he quarantined in 72 separate rooms, ordering them to each produce a translation. The number 72 is how the Greek version was called the "Septuagint," from Latin *septuaginta* "seventy," because it was produced by what was believed to be seventy translators working independently. Since then, the Septuagint has been adopted by the early Christian Churches.

It was on the 8th of Tevet of the year 3515 (246 BCE) that the Jewish sages produced 72 identical translations. This result was miraculous, especially since there were 13 places where the translators intentionally diverged from the literal translation.

The 72 sages knew that Greek could not render the many dimensions infused in the language of the Torah. Incidentally, these were the Saducees whose S/Hebrew name (*Tzaddoq, sing. Tzadduqim, pl.*) contains three of the four letters that disappeared in the passage from archaic Greek to modern Greek. Yep!

And so, although the translations bore witness to some level of divine intervention, the Saducees viewed the 8th of Tevet as one of the darkest days in Jewish history. They even compared this day to the day when the Jews made the golden calf. Subsequently, the 8th of Tevet became a dark day of fasting, in opposition to a white day of fasting such as the fast of *Yom Kippur* – the "day of atonement." They sought to commemorate their grief for having betrayed the pristine gift of truth of the Torah. Consider: when I can't stop grieving a loss, I am attached. And if not free, how then could I be <u>immune</u> to dis-eases of mind and body?

Years passed. It is surprising and even shocking to accept that English could be the best conveyor of Hebrew. Whereas the Hebrew alphabet has not changed form since inception, English may just be the most rapidly evolving language ever, as attested by its many codes and texting proficiencies. Called a "digital virus" and condemned as "textese," English specializes in conciseness. So does Hebrew.

Surely, each Hebrew sign is its own SMS. When transliterated, the letters SMS could be viewed as *Shemesh* – Hebrew for "sun," or "Name-Fire" (which is exactly – albeit naively – what a SMS is). For example, Beth (B), value 2, means "house" or that which divides inside from outside. Its code is Shakespearian in nature: "2B or not 2B, that's its question!" Almst any wrd cn be abbrvted in ths wy. Abbreviations and codes aren't new. They just require a different kind of reading. But before I open my mind to S/Hebrew & English as a marriage texted in heaven for me to see the light at the speed of the sun, I wish to revisit the mystery of the 72 sages – the infamous Sadducees.

Ignoring the Number 72 - No Cooperating

"The Rule of 72 is useful in determining how fast money will grow. Take the annual return from any investment, expressed as a percentage, and divide it into 72. The result is the number of years it will take to double your money." *Peter Lynch, Investor*

As for investing in Self-knowledge, 72 (or 10 + 15 + 21 + 26) is the Great Gematria of the יהוה (YEWE) tetractys. At the top is Yod (Y) = 10. The 2nd row is formed by Yod Heh (YE) = 15; the 3rd by Yod Heh Vav (YEW) = 21, and the 4th by Yod Heh Vav Heh (YEWE) = 26. The Great Gematria of YEWE that equals 72 is different than the 72 Powers of the Name used by Moses to part the Red Sea. These Powers are deciphered from *Exodus 14:19-21*, each of the three verses being formed by exactly 72 letters (see the decoding of this word puzzle in *Golden XPR's* books).

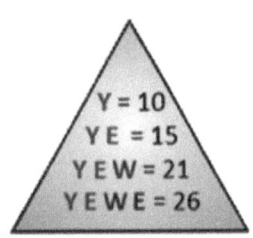

"When I came to the night in which this power was conferred on me, I set out to take up the Great Name of God, consisting of **72 Names**, permuting and combining it. But when I had done this for a little while, behold, the letters took on in my eyes the shape of great mountains, strong trembling seized me and I could summon no strength... and it was as if I were not in this world. At once I fell down, for I no longer felt the least strength in any of my limbs. And behold, something resembling speech emerged from my heart, and came to my lips, and forced them to move. I thought—perhaps this is, God forbid, a spirit of madness that has entered into me? But behold, I saw it uttering wisdom." *Abraham Abulafia, 13th century mystic*

Uttering wisdom?! This number 72 points out once again how shadow work is key to parting the sea of the unconscious and waking up, as it is the numeric value of *Chesed* for "kindness." When I have no need to defend (no **Power** issue) or attack (no **kindness** issue), I embody **wisdom** and **understand** that there is only One of us. When the four spheres are interdependently resonating with *Daath's* "Knowledge," wisdom and kindness are free to cooperate, trading places with each other as needed. This interaction is pictured below.

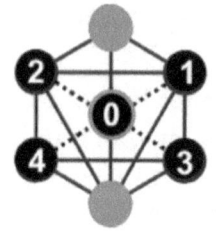

I saw how the marriage of wisdom-Power below heals the throat chakra by ending the war of the sexes. If the number 72 is the gematria of *Chesed*, it is also the gematria of *Chokmah* as per the Rule of Kolel. This rule stipulates that one digit can be added to or subtracted from the gematria value of a word without affecting its value. Indeed, "one" (1) is the prime of all numbers as it invokes the Monad or Divine Unity. The rule of Kolel makes visible the invisible Aleph that transmits the spirit of oneness itself.

- **Sphere 0:** *Daath* for "knowledge." This sphere is not accounted for as it is "here and not here." It is not part of the tree of life.
- **Sphere 1:** *HaBinah* (EBYNE) for "THE Understanding." Value is **72**.
- **Sphere 2:** *Chesed* (HXD) for "kindness." Value is **72**.
- **Sphere 3:** *Chokmah* (HKME) for "wisdom." Value is **73 → 72.**

- Sphere 4: *Gevurah* (CBWRE) for "Power." Value is **216**.

HaBinah for "THE Understanding" adds the letter Heh (which is the article "the") to the traditional name of the third eye. This liberty is excused when I "hear and understand" about the siddhis which are held to be first and foremost paranormal powers, whereas being emPowered is really the outcome of the complete understanding possessed by a siddha. This is no less than enlightenment, since it is THE understanding that there's only One of us. Such finality is known when the four spheres around *Daath* enter in synergy. Note: while the accounting differs from what I saw in *TCO—Book 2, Understanding Knowledge*, I still come to hear the 432 hertz frequency of the Music of the Spheres (72 x 3 + 216).

432 (or 72 x 6) is a precious frequency, as it takes me beyond the fear of Power, and thus, beyond fear. While each sound is represented by a unique underlying numeric essence, the frequency of 432 hertz has such a profound effect on consciousness and on the cellular structure of the body that it has been identified as "the Music of the Spheres." How perfect that the sum of values of the S/Hebrew Names of the most crucial spheres would equal the light of the 432 frequency! For indeed, how could I misuse Power when I feel and understand Oneness? I can only be kind to myself and others, which is wise!

The Departed ZQ in "Sadducees" - No Eliminating

> "It was the experience of mystery – even if mixed with fear – that engendered religion." *Albert Einstein*

Ah, the Sadducees! I'm like a dog on a trail... My ears perk up upon realizing that the name of the 72 sages – *Tzadduqim* for "Sadducees" – is formed on the same Z-D-Q root of *Tzedeq* for "justice" and *Tzedaqah* for "charity." These 72 were the sages who knew full well that translating the Torah into Greek was disingenuous. Their integrity was on the line.

An honorable translation just could not be done, which saddens them since the gift of the Torah can only be received when it is shared.

There is a clue in this story, a clue that, if found, might allow me to make sense of the mysterious *Tzedaqah*. To top it all, *Tzedaqah* is the middle path of religiousness and, as such, the very goal of the GOD technology offered by XPR. To see what was/is in my blind spot, I decided to look at what happened to the four letters צדוק (ZDWQ) in *Tzaddoq*, the singular of *Tzadduqim*, as they evolved into Greek.

Hebrew	Archaic Greek	Modern Greek	Roman Script
Tzaddi, Tzaddi Final	San, Sampi	Obsolete	Z, - - Z
Dalet	Delta	Delta	D
Vav	Digamma	Upsilon???	F, U, V, W
Qoph	Qoppa	Obsolete	Q

Offshoot of the Tables from the *Vav Blip* Section

Here is the surreal part: the 27 letters of the Hebrew alphabet (22 "regular" + 5 "final" letters) evolved into the 27 letters of the archaic Greek alphabet. In the passage from archaic Greek (27 letters) to modern Greek (24 letters), 3 letters were <u>eliminated</u> (San, Sampi, Qoppa) and 1 letter (Digamma) shifted its shape, rank, and name to become Upsilon, a mystery marked in the table above by the question marks (???). **Since San and Sampi came from Tzaddi and Tzaddi final, and Qoppa, from Qoph, this means that the first and the last letters of *TzaddoQ* strangely departed.**

Amazingly, only 1 letter out of the four Hebrew letters forming the word *Tzaddoq* made it into modern Greek: the letter Dalet that became Delta. As for the letter Vav, it is the letter whose nature was significantly altered. To resume and understand how Vav could be first called Digamma, I must go to the number value of the letters both in Hebrew and in Greek. The value of Hebrew Vav is 6. The value of Greek Digamma is also 6. Gamma (value 3) is the evolution into Greek of

Hebrew Gimel (value 3). This is how Di-gamma ("two gammas") would be equal to 6, which is Vav's value. 6th sign Vav eventually became 6th Roman letter F. The math completely changed when archaic Digamma vacated the 6th position and reappeared as modern Upsilon in the 20th position. Knowing that the letter Vav (W) is the part of YEWE that invokes the Son of "God," and realizing that this Son departed from the Greek alphabet, is it really a wonder why it is so hard for me to forgive myself to not be able to show up as the Alpha and the Omega?

"Do not think that I have come to abolish the Law or the Prophets; I have not come to abolish them but to fulfill them. For truly, I say to you, until heaven and earth pass away, not an iota, not a dot, will pass from the Law until all is accomplished." *Matthew 5:17-18.* Might Yod/Iota (the Father) be waiting for the Vav/Digamma Son to fulfill the Law? Moreover, might my reluctance in returning to the Father be mirrored in the confusion surrounding Vav's evolution from archaic Digamma to modern Upsilon? Is it speaking of how my mind (or the Son) keeps on wanting to compete with my heart (the Father)? To the point, might the light that TCO shines on this matter allow me to end the fight and, at last, forgive my debts and my debtors?

The ZQ Twilight Zone - No Grounding

> "While personal problems are not overlooked, the analyst keeps an eye on their symbolic aspects, for healing comes only from what leads the patient beyond himself and beyond his entanglement in the ego." *Carl Jung*

Carl Jung also spoke of the tarots as tracing the initiatory journey of the hero. Three of these tarots – the trilogy of the sun (R or Resh), the moon (Q or Qoph), and the star (Z or Tzaddi) – combine two aspects of light: inner and outer. Their inner light clarifies how the triple mastery is akin to enlightenment, and their outer light, how to use the physical luminaries as daily guides. **Again, I am noticing that the letters ZQ of** *TzaddoQ* **play an essential part here!**

This brings me back to Hermes, the god of healing, communication and commerce. Hermes is also called *Trismegistus* for "thrice-master" of alchemy as the sun's operation, theurgy as the moon's operation, and astrology as the stars' operation.

As always, the solar male and lunar female sides fight to the death, until they can humble themselves in seeing that they reflect each other's light. The sun of alchemy and the moon of theurgy must first get their act *together*.

While the greater light of the sun was created before the lesser light of the moon (*Genesis 1:16*), there are Talmudic commentaries on the moon taking offense, claiming that "she" should have come first! Again, and again, the war of the sexes speaks to issues of Power, rank and authority. Seeing what is at stake, the question becomes: does the acquisition of wisdom precede Power or is my having Power necessary to come into wisdom? Lastly, is the receiving of Power and wisdom concomitant?

1. **Alchemy** is how to master the operation of **the sun** and come into **Power**. After showing up reliably to the task at hand, I can only be a victor – not a victim! I am now at the end of dissatisfaction, filled with compassion.
2. **Theurgy** is how to master the operation of **the moon** and come into **wisdom**. If the moon "should" come first, it is only because the suffering caused by my lunacy will cause me to follow my folly until it delivers me to sanity.
3. **Astrology** is how to master the operation of the **stars** and have the **knowledge** of opposites – when I can be and not be. Embodying **wisdom**, I can foresee the outcome of my words and actions. Having **Power**, I open to a new level of response-ability and end up waking up from the dream of karma.

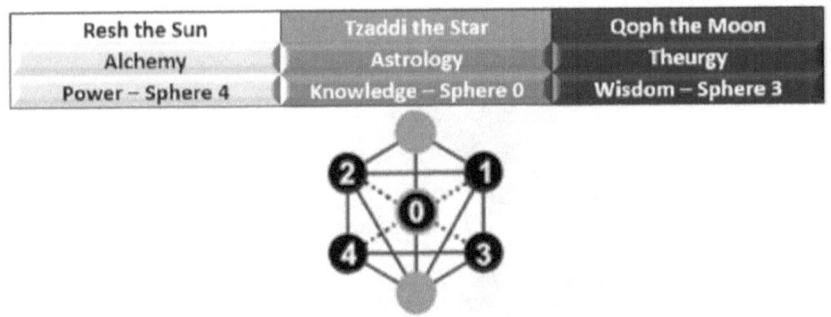

The triad formed by **Z-R-Q** of Tzaddi the star, Resh the sun and Qoph the moon strangely resonates with the root **Z-D-Q** of *Tzedaqah's* "charity." As for the letters in between ZQ, the pairing of **RD|DR**, it calls code Interaction (see *TCO—Book 2, Debugging the Oneness "Software"*). The signs Resh (**R**) and Dalet (**D**) are in an entanglement relationship.

As a quick recap, unless I am *echaD* (**D**) "One," I will give my Power to *acheR* (**R**) "the other." To become *Trismegistus* or "thrice-master" of astrology, alchemy and theurgy, the Tzaddi in me (my star being) must stretch to reach Qoph (my moon being). Consider: when I come to realize that greater is the wisdom that comes from lunacy, I become a *TzaddiQ/a* – a being who understands the One and the other so completely that I cannot not be kind.

There is a method to the spiritual madness: first alchemy by way of theurgy, and then, astrology. However, to know that, I must become aware of code Awesomeness. It is the key to the Z-D-Q puzzle as it leads me to the QZ "end" of confusion.

Code Awesomeness - ZQ / QZ

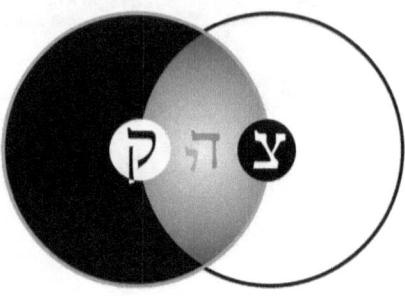

Imagine a language so pure and so sacred that it can reconcile opposites in just two pairs of letters...

Right: Hebrew letter Tzaddi (צ) → Z in Roman script
Left: Hebrew letter Qoph (ק) → Q in Roman script
Middle (inferred): Hebrew letters Dalet Yod (די) → DY in Roman script

Here is how S/Hebrew inscribes code "Awesomeness" in 2 words:

- **Z'Q:** in one direction, I read *Tzaddi Qoph* (צ'ק) as the 18th and 19th letters.
- **QZ:** in the other direction, I read *Qetz* (קץ) for "end."

The decoding: first, I recall that the letter Tzaddi is one of the five letters that have a final form – "final" physically when at the end of a word and metaphysically when at the end of an affliction. I can then inquire on what would be the specific redemption that is ushered by Tzaddi final. I begin with *Tzaddi,* the word for the "fishhook" that I use when doing shadow work so as to harpoon the abysmal formations that had engulfed the light of my soul. This is a very different form of "hooking" than the one done by the prostitutE who only wants something from the other. When I am as Tzaddi, committed to taking back my projections, I perceive how this letter would be the first letter of the enlightenment tetrad on the way down, and the last letter on the way up:

- **Tzaddi** (the 18th letter) is the 17th tarot of the star →
- **Qoph** (the 19th letter) is the 18th tarot of the moon →
- **Resh** (the 20th letter) is the 19th tarot of the sun →
- **Shin** (the 21st and penultimate letter) is the 20th tarot of judgment ←

To be a *Tzaddi-Q* (a "saint" or an "awakened one"), my star-like Tzaddi being must stretch to my moon-like Qoph being. This is to say: I must follow my lunacy until I come into the greatest wisdom of all – the one which was waiting in my folly. When I do, I die to my sins and the letters **Tzaddi-Qoph** turn around to write *Qetz* – the "**end.**" However, to reach Qoph, I must include the full-out spelling of *Tzaddi* (Z-DY) and thus make sense of its second and third letters which spell the word *Dai* (DY) for "enough." When I know that I am enough, I can be "in off." I am no longer compelled to do the wrong thing to compensate for feeling obligated to do the "right" thing. I can now hear/SEE the awesomeness of the QKosmic plan.

At the risk of repeating myself :-), story was/is told of Jacob who had wished to reveal to his children the secret of the "end" of time. And while there was some urgency as he could feel the Divine Presence depart, he was unable to do so. He asked his sons if they were still holding on to any sin that could deny them this treasured knowledge. "Look at our twelve names;" they countered, "you won't find the letters Chet or Teth which spell the word *Chet* for "sin." "True," replied Jacob. "But your names also lack the pair Qoph and Tzaddi forming the word *Qetz* for "end." You are thus probably not meant to receive Self-knowledge."

Ouch! Is this to say that sin is a necessary evil for me to come to "THE END?"

As a *Tzaddi-Q/a*, I don't mind "righteousness." Heck, I don't mind "left-eousness" either! I'm so willing to do what it takes that I'm considered a saint – someone fully awake. My magic is simple: my Power is wholesome, and my action, undivided. In that unity, there is no co-dependent behavior, no addiction and no confusion about the other "out there." I have no need to seek "your" approval (or disapproval), or to reluctantly obey a false sense of duty while resenting "you" for it. Thus, Tzaddi final inscribes into being the end of confusion (I thought it was "you." I now realize it was all me). When I come into THE Understanding that there's only One of us, I stop judging, incarnate into the Z-D-Q root, and extend to myself and others a kindness and a generosity that is akin to my highest vision of what charity ought to be.

🎵♪ (I can't get NO) satisfaction!

> The Buddha's Four Noble Truths: life is *Dukkha*, Sanskrit for "dissatisfaction." The cause of dissatisfaction is craving. There is an end to the dissatisfaction. There is a path to the end of dissatisfaction.

There is an END to dissatisfaction and there is a path to "THE END." This is truth. I have seen how the eastern tree of life comes to a new dimension after being paired with the western tree of life. Could it be the same with the fourth Noble Truth; the path to the end? Could there be a path to the end hidden in Jewish mysticism, a path which would complement the teachings of the Buddha and bring a different light onto them? I have seen how the S/Hebrew alphabet has 5 "final" letters, final as they each lead to an end by inscribing a specific redemption. The end of dissatisfaction is invoked by Peh final. As a word, *Peh* means "mouth." When my mouth is restored to its natural purity, I don't speak too much or not enough, I don't eat too much or not enough, I don't kiss too much or not enough. I also experience a number of transformations:

- **The sense of enough:** just like Abraham and Sarah did, I meet *El Shaddai* – the GOD Name that means "S/He who is Enough." In rabbinical Kabbalah, *El Shaddai* is so crucial that it is also referred to as *Hashem* – "the Name," as is YEWE. It is the Power spinning the sex chakra, since it is only after meeting *El Shaddai* that Abram and Sarai received a sign Heh to add to their names and could get pregnant. As for me, if my deceptiveness was how I could get NO satisfaction, I can now be successful since I do more than "just trying." I actually show up to the task at hand.
- **Honesty:** the Sanskrit name for the sex chakra *Svadhisthana* means "where your being is established." It is paralleled by S/Hebrew name *Yesod* for "foundation." Located in the lower belly and/or in the genitals, it acts as a center of pleasure and passion, and governs reproductive systems – be they physical, financial or emotional. Since the letters of *Yesod* (יסוד) reorder as *Sohdi* (סודי) for "my secret," the foundation is transmitted by *Golden XPR* as "honesty." Honesty is the basis of it all, as it is "where my being is established."
- **Abundance:** upon meeting the Name, the sex chakra that was blocked by fear now spins freely with the Power of abundance. I move out of Scare City, and the yearning for *Mammon* "money" doesn't rule me anymore as I no longer identify to being among the have-nots. Indeed, I died to my sins and went into "heaven / havin'". From thereon, the story of doubt – of how I think I can't [fill in the blank] – increasingly lets go of me.

Since the end of dissatisfaction is also the beginning of integrity, I can see in the image to the right that, whether in Sanskrit or in S/Hebrew, the letters of the names of the sex chakra look alike and harmonize for my being to resonate with the fundamental truth of Oneness, a truth that supports the Four Noble Truths. Together the two languages spell the principle of complementarity into being.

Surely, code Satisfaction Guaranteed (DY|YD) was announced in *Sepher Yetzirah* as the result of "the singular covenant precisely in the middle, sanctified by the circumcision of the tongue and the phallus." This is when the

middle path lights up, as the mouth chakra is quickened when I meet *El Shaddai*, come to the sense of "enough" and to the end of dissatisfaction. The sex chakra can now share its Power without fear.

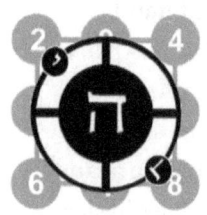

On the note of *Dai* (יד) "enough," the image to the left shows the letter Heh that is linked to the heart chakra significantly bigger as a way to acknowledge the magnitude of the "singular covenant precisely in the middle." There are two electrons orbiting it. Looking closely, I see that one electron is inscribed with a letter Dalet – the letter that initiates the sphere *Daath* of "self-knowledge" (the mouth chakra). The other electron is inscribed with a letter Yod – the letter that initiates the sphere *Yesod* of "honesty" (the sex chakra).

When these two electrons make contact, my angel-being is free to rise and free to fall. Doing so, I am continuously inscribing the word *Dai* (DY) for "enough" as the result of the Dalet (D) of *Daath* merging with the Yod (Y) of *Yesod*. Moreover, Dalet plus Yod also form the sign Heh (E) – the supreme container ensuring that my heart would remain unhurt and beautiful. Ah, I can hear now why, as a word, Heh means "breath," for God *is* the breath within the breath. :-)

The Righteous & Wrong Game: No Recuperating

"Do you prefer that you be right or happy?" *A Course In Miracles*

Naturally, I'd prefer to be happy! If so, why still play the righteous and wrong game? It does take two to make war – two people who cannot see that this kind of pointless debate is a very primitive way to establish order. It is astounding to me how much energy I waste in wanting to make "you" wrong or in trying to convince "you" that I am right. I fight for my entrenched belief, unconscious that I am attached to an outcome: to keep the personality alive! For my ego, being right is a matter of life and death, soon prompting me into a mode of defense/attack.

Truth be told, my disrespectful attempts to influence and even impose my ideas and opinions on "you" come from a self-esteem so low that it generates a hopeless need for validation. Ouch! Am I so insecure that I'd need you to agree with me about my being right, just so that I could feel better about myself? Why do I doubt myself?

Not only is the need to be right addictive, but it is also what destroys partnerships. Right and wrong intends to describe a degree of correspondence between two or more things. Newtonian physics, for example, obeys rules of behavior and physical laws that can be easily described in terms of right and wrong operations. But physics, and even law itself, becomes less determinate and more probabilistic when it moves into the quantum realm. The more I stretch the boundaries of perception, the blurrier the rules become. Indeed, numerous optical illusions reveal that I have substantial holes in my vision.

Moreover, is it right or wrong that the sun would burn or that we would die? The right and wrong game can only be played when I compete with my nemesis – reality. The burning sun or death are simply reality. My addictive mind, however, wants to be right. It will compete with God / reality and say "I shouldn't have gotten sun-burned" or "my father shouldn't have died."

Ultimately, right or wrong are judged in reference to my belief system. What I have been taught to judge as good is desirable and "right." What I have been taught to judge as evil is resisted and "wrong." While it could be easy to demonstrate that there are right and wrong ways, e.g.; to cook meat, it is when I get into values that trouble begins.

Similarly, while there may be judicial systems to guide how society ought to operate and make decisions about ethics, different cultures and/or judges have different opinions about what's right and wrong. This is how Lady Justice wears a blindfold – to not get into a personal arguments about "the right way." Seeing with the heart's eyes, I am less likely to let pride be the great separator – that which predicts my failure to love.

The moment I feel that we are One, I switch into humility and kindness, and stop arguing. There is no more contempt. I realize that you are what's left of me – a Satan or an "adversary" meant to refine me.

The refinement is just energy in motion: metal cuts wood, fire melts metal, etc. And while the cutting and the melting are an exercise in control (one force being stronger than the other), the end result is an enhancing of the wood; a refining of the metal. Seeing how opposite forces give rise to each other defeats the thought of a winner and a loser, or one-up and one-down. Instead of making "you" feel bad (if only in my eyes), I open to feeling a mutual respect and appreciation – the shared sense of being enough.

Respect has no need for labelling. It befriends uncertainty. Even better, respect has no regrets and no guilt. It sees the world and not "my" creation of the world. It's like being a true artist, knowing that I am not creating anything but just opening for the energy to be creating through me. I am a vessel – a Heh womb. Not making it about me, I let go of the urge to convince "you" to believe anything about me or about anything. I breathe more often. And if I still were to compete, I'd tell the truth about my wanting to be right, because I would know that I'm wrong. How? I simply would have forgotten that seeking the QKingdom is my priority. These are the times when I cause consequences I would rather not have to experience. Am I right? :-)

I am now ready for the pillars of religiousness – when the religious instinct is restored and my victiM, purified. These pillars exist to sustain my heart's intent to do what LOVE would do.

I am about to stretch my conscious hand (whether a righty or a lefty) to once again eat from the tree of the opposites and emPower the eternal NOW. However, instead of thinking I CAN'T, I will now prepare for the awesome. For only awe can stretch me to the other side of my playing small – into the realm of the sacred. This is where a different version of me awaits – when I start to think I CAN until I know I CAN...

Part III: The GOD Technology

- Preparing for the AWEsome
- Speaking of AWEsomeness...
- AWEsome and Innate
- I CAN think – Fire and *Teshuvah*
- I CAN receive – Water and *Tephillah*
- I CAN give it all – Air and *Tzedaqah*
- The GOD Technology
- Troubleshooting the Soul
- A Marriage Made in "Heaven"
- Ether – I CAN wait; therefore, I CAN receive!
- Wood – I CAN fast; therefore, I CAN think!
- Earth: I CAN decide; therefore, I CAN give it all!
- Astrology and the Letter Tzaddi
- A Meet & Greet with the AWEsome
- IT IS DONE!
- An Officer's Synthesis
- FEAR – False Evidence Appearing Real

Yod (י)	Vav (ו) / Heh (ה)	Heh (ה)
Individual Power	Symbolic Power	Collective Power
Alchemy	Astrology	Theurgy
Resh the Sun	Tzaddi the Star	Qoph the Moon
I CAN fast → I CAN think	I CAN decide → I CAN give	I CAN wait → I CAN receive

The Proficiencies of the Sacred

Preparing for the AWEsome

Prepare to DIE! Inquiry tool: www.goldenxpr.com/tco3_sacredness/

Step 1: I fill in the blank: I want to know WHY I would choose to think I CAN'T _____ (e.g.; find a job, be patient, etc.). **Step 2:** I ask for truth and generate a number. **Step 3:** I find my number on the map to fill in the brackets: when I remember my nature and exist as [**Elements**], my [**Conscious Types' Instruments**] has no fear of [**Fear**]. This is when I experience that [**SACREDNESS**]. **Step 4:** what most surprised me in this process was [_____].

Speaking of AWEsomeness...

"But *Teshuvah*, *Tephillah* and *Tzedaqah* will avert the evil decree."
Rabbi Amnon of Mainz, 11th Century

"Let us speak of awesomeness" is the title of the central poem of the High Holy Days of Judaism. These days are the ten Days of Awe between Rosh Hashanah (the New Year) and Yom Kippur (the Day of Atonement). The poem is held to be one of the most stirring compositions in the entire liturgy of the ten Days. These 10 days culminate in the day of judgment, as the different parts of "me" pass before the Heavenly Court like a cohort of soldiers being counted, to receive the decree of destiny. This decree is written on the day of the new moon (Rosh Hashanah) and sealed on the day of atonement (10 days later), as the names of who shall live and who shall die, who by fire and who by water, who by earthquake and who by plague.

This day of "At-One-ment" is not connected to the moon cycles (although every other Jewish holiday is). As such, it is beyond time. It is the gate of knowledge that can open at any season, and the choice of Peace that can be made in every moment. It is a portal for me to jump into the parallel world where the change I wish to be lives.

"But *Teshuvah*, *Tephillah* and *Tzedaqah* will avert the evil decree." This triad, however, loses its Power to shun evil as soon as it is translated the way it is traditionally translated as "repentance, prayer and charity."

Buddha	Dharma	Sangha
Individual Power	Symbolic Power	Collective Power
Teshuvah / Repentance	Tzedaqah / Charity	Tephillah / Prayer

Three "Awful" Translations

To see beyond and move from religious hypocrisy to the pure devotion that reveals that religion is an instinct, I must feel and sense what I am resisting. And even when I'm used to numbing my feelings and ignoring my intuition, I can restore sentience by understanding the GOD technology that is behind *Teshuvah*, *Tephillah* and *Tzedaqah*. Surely, sentience is awesome as it is the door to being human again. It does fill me with awe to experience the aha moment when that which understands has an understanding of "God."

AWEsome and Innate

> "My brain is like the Bermuda Triangle. Information goes in and then it's never found again." *Anonymous*

Legend has it that, as a soul in PaRaDiSe, I had complete wisdom and could access at will the zero-point field. I knew myself. My mind had no questions and wasn't plagued by doubts. This went on until Lailah, the Angel of the Night, lightly tapped me just above the lip, causing me to forget all memories; past and future. The story reminds me of Lethe, one of the infernal rivers of Greek mythology. Those who drank from it lost all memories, as *Lethe* is the antonym of *Aletheia* for "truth" and means "concealment." Going from Lailah to Lethe, there seems to be the presence (or rather the absence) of a collective mouth that involves a perfect recall of self-knowledge.

While eating from the tree of ignorance, I do not know who I am and forget that the three pillars (*Teshuvah*, *Tephillah* and *Tzedaqah*) are innate proficiencies belonging to the sacred. Instead, I think of them as "repentance, prayer and charity," concepts which accentuate my fear. How can I not fear death when I imagine that the Last Judgment will be an evil decree? I fell for the story hook, line and sinker that "God" is a vengeful Power who is merciless with those who are evil, like I am. I know I'm bad, since I let myself be led into temptations. The more I want what I can't have and resist wanting it by making it forbidden, the more I strengthen the conflict. And during all my unconscious calling to "repent," devotion waited to be felt as awesome and innate, so that its pillars could do their job and actually avert the evil decree I had invited by resisting my wrongdoing.

Meanwhile, I can't help but repeat the same error, as if I were unable or unwilling to remember who I am. This quandary touches one of the most intriguing passages in all of Plato's works, and is the basis of a most challenging philosophical question: if God is a geometer and if the Greek word *mathemata* (→ mathematics) means "that which can be taught," can abstract knowledge be learned, or better, remembered?

This question occurs in the middle of the Meno. Meno asks Socrates if he can prove the truth of his strange claim that "all learning is recollection." Socrates responds by calling over a slave boy who has had no mathematical training, and by giving him a geometry problem. A whole process takes place, which ends in the boy giving the right answers. Since Socrates did nothing but ask questions, the boy must have recovered rather than learned new beliefs. Socrates showed that, though learning is impossible, teaching is possible by helping someone recall an impression.

Do I really have an innate knowledge of geometry and thus, every other branch of knowledge? Might my learning disability (the repeated errors) be akin to an early onset of dementia that I use to protect myself from the legal consequences of my own decree: I am bad – an outlaw?

I want to believe that I can re-member a GOD technology that would stretch me to the sacred and grant me "wholesome Power" – which happens to be the meaning of the Greek name *Socrates*. Accepting that *Teshuvah, Tephillah* and *Tzedaqah* are each pointing to an innate proficiency, how would I recall in my blood what these sacred abilities are?

If the metalanguage that renamed itself S/Hebrew is based on a "universal grammar," it ought to have a way to language the memory of the three pillars of religion as the core proficiencies of the sacred. To see their intelligence, I will draw from the architecture of a pillar's formation. The column's topmost member is known as a *capital* (from Latin *caput* or "head"). This head acts as a mediator between the pillar and the load thrusting down upon it, broadening the area of the supporting surface. The three pillars happen to have a "head" via three little words that act as crowns. These words are found in the High Holy Days' prayer book. I will start with the "awesome" translations of the three pillars of religion, and then go to their crowns whose decoding aims at restoring the religious instinct.

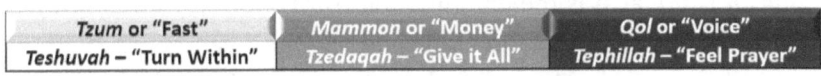

Tzum or "Fast"	*Mammon* or "Money"	*Qol* or "Voice"
Teshuvah – "Turn Within"	*Tzedaqah* – "Give it All"	*Tephillah* – "Feel Prayer"

Announcing the Three "Awesome" Translations and their Crowns

I CAN think – Fire and *Teshuvah*

'And at the ninth hour, Jesus cried out with a loud voice, "My God, my God, why have you forsaken me?"' *Mark 15:34*

Wood → Fire
Teshuvah – "Repentance"
The AWE of "Turning Within"

Traditionally, Teshuvah has been translated as "repentance." The S/Hebrew word for "repentance" is not Teshuvah. It is Charatah.

Charatah is when I feel so remorseful that I vow to act differently in the future. And yet, for the vow to stick, I must have come to peace with my wrongdoing, which is to say, I must understand why it was necessary for me to do what I did. When made from a place of guilt or sorrow, the decision to change can't hold, as it is forced. Like it or not, I can't hurry LOVE. I may have to wait minutes, days, years or lifetimes before I can accept what "I" once did. Until then, there will be something I won't want to see.

Here is what puzzles me... Just like dying and being born, Teshuvah – or "to turn within" – is a solo job. No one can do this for me! I must be the one who takes responsibility for what will be revealed in the process. While I know that Carl Jung's words are truth: "what you resist not only persists, but will grow in size," why be so stubborn and so afraid that I would keep hiding behind my tribe? Surely, my resistance to individuate makes sense as long as I need the collective to condone my story – as long as I need to be a victiM and make them my bully: "they made me!"

Teshuvah is fire as it is the enlightening "turn" from my lonely ways; a "return" to LOVE, when I am alone and all One. I can now be with my pain without resisting it, and begin to know who I am. Eventually, my limiting beliefs are so clearly seen that they leave on their own. This is when I understand fully that the plastic in me needs to be crucified. However, to let go of my judgments (starting with "it's not good to be alone"), I must come to the ninth hour. Forsakenness is what makes me so ready and willing to know the truth that I no longer hesitate to turn within.

Forsakenness is so excruciating that, if I survive it, it'll wipe out any religious hypocrisy in me. It will also leave behind the gift of devotion – when it is my pleasure to follow the voice and obey the Law. This pleasure multiplies when I realize that the fringe benefit for hearing my conscience is to do no harm.

My resistance to being lonely kept me from turning within. As long as I look for love, approval and recognition out there in a person, a substance or an activity, I have something to distract me from the truth. And all the while, I'm missing the mark. For if I could have allowed for this terrible loneliness to destroy the ego's illusion of separation, I'd have woken up to being whole, knowing that "it is done!"

'When he came to his senses, he said, "How many of my father's hired servants have food to spare, and here I am starving to death! I will set out and go back to my father and say to him: Father, I have sinned against heaven and against you. I am no longer worthy to be called your son; make me like one of your hired servants." So, he got up and went to his father.' *Luke 15:17-20*

I CAN think – or the ability to be coherent – comes from turning within to know the truth. It is to use my intelligence to look for answers where they are, even if turning within involves going in the dark. Thinking the unthinkable is also known as faith. It naturally moves me to befriend fear, as I now understand its stages. When I no longer resist being alone, I am ready to face my fear of death and subsequently, of being empowered. Fear was only here to keep me from such intimacy – into-me-see; into-me-think. It kept the ego alive and prevented me from being the change I wished to see. Although I can know that I was born alone and will probably die alone, my fear of rejection just ensured that I'd always have company. I used "you" to dismiss me, just so that I could postpone my day of "at-ONE-ment," when to face my loneliness and die to my borrowed self.

I CAN receive – Water and *Tephillah*

"Therefore, I tell you, whatever you ask for in prayer, *believe* that you have received it, and it will be yours." Mark 11:24

Ether → Water
Tephillah – "Prayer"
The AWE of "Feeling Prayer"

Traditionally, *Tephillah* is translated as "prayer." There's prayer, and there's prayer. When my prayer is a pleading, the S/Hebrew word is not *Tephillah*, but *Etirah*, which means "to pray, implore, plead, supplicate."

These prayers of supplication are far from the heartfelt prayers of *Tephillah*, which speak of the gratitude I feel and express when I believe that I received what I need and want, and always will. For when I occupy such spaciousness, I feel like a million bucks. Therefore, I can only attract goodness (or money or whatever it is I need).

The trick to believing is to be 100%, which equates to zero doubt. My faith (or certainty) is not in an outcome. It is the outcome of my being wholeheartedly engaged in the action that is likely to produce the results I desire.

Tephillah is the opposite of pleading, as it means "to attach myself." Such clinging to the divine is no less than the felt sense of devotion. It is the feeling of a love affair – a way of merging and melting into existence. I become as water, adopting the path of least resistance, losing the boundaries that I would normally use to divide me from existence. And as the two become one, I dance with life in deep harmony and respond to the call to love. That which was mortal in me drops on its own accord; only the eternal remains, taking with it the personal. I begin to relate to what the prophets talked about – being the first and the last, entangled with existence, knowing no beginning and no end. Such devotional prayer is the highest form of love. When I am blessed enough to experience it, I know that I CAN wait. How could I not when I received it all?

Surely, it was the doubt that pushed me to act compulsively and be out of rhythm. The more I cling and hand-fast myself to what is translated in the Bible as "my wife," the more appreciation I feel. "My wife" speaks of the feeling function; a function that is feminine in nature. This is the gut vibration that does not allow any doubt to enter my mind, and thereby, liberates me from the past. I can receive as I believe with complete faith that my needs are met, and my prayers, answered. This is the opposite of being restless in Scare City, in a mind that focuses on lack while imploring "God" or "the Universe" to provide.

There are many ways or techniques to feel "In God I trust," and sense in my body how appreciation releases my bond to the material world; many ways to feel a joy and gratitude that are now undeniable; even palpable. Chanting or dancing are among them. Joining a quorum of people praying together – masterminding – is another. Rituals can also help me reconnect to my "innernet" and soul network. They are designed to help me get out of the way, and feel.

Feeling is receiving the moment without judgment. It is to be listening and wide open; 100% engaged. It is meditating, during and beyond prescribed prayer times. It is to not resist anything, and therefore, easily transcend the frontier between the natural and the supernatural world.

When I CAN receive what my guidance offers, I reduce the chances of misusing Power and thus decrease the negative impact of cause and effect. Moreover, I know where truth lies and no longer resent the tribe for imposing its desires and belief systems on me.

- **Collective Power** is known when my Dragon Queen vibrates with the force of *Tephillah*.
- **Individual Power** is known when my Lion King vibrates with the force of *Teshuvah*.

Fire	Air	Water
Individual Power	Symbolic Power	Collective Power
Right-Hand Side (male)	Joined Thumbs (neutral)	Left-Hand Side (female)
Teshuvah – Turn within!	*Tzedaqah* – ???	*Tephillah* – Feel Prayer!

Hmmm.... What is the force of *Tzedaqah*?

And it makes me wonder... I can now recognize the synergistic essence of *Teshuvah* and *Tephillah,* for **turning within** is the only way for me to **feel my prayer** and know what my heart wants to receive: "not my will, Thy will be done; not my desire, Thy desire be fulfilled." If the two pillars sanctify the marriage of the Sacred Masculine (as the will) and the Sacred Feminine (as the desire), what is the proficiency of their progeny? Indeed, what does it mean in consciousness that the child of *Teshuvah* and *Tephillah* would be the third pillar of *Tzedaqah*?

Here again, the ZDQ mystery reappears...

I CAN give it all - Air and *Tzedaqah*

"This is the account of Noah. He was a *TzaddiQ* and wholehearted. Noah walked with God." *Genesis 6:9*

Air/Metal ← Earth
Tzedaqah – "Charity"
The AWE of "Giving it All"

Hear! Hear! Traditionally, *Tzedaqah* has been translated as "charity." The S/Hebrew word for "charity" is not *Tzedaqah*. It is *Chesed*.

Chesed stands for the "kindness, generosity and philanthropy" that are charitable. *Chesed* is the sphere that ascends when *Chokmah's* "wisdom" descends, a double motion that allows me to know the difference between the poverty I can change and the poverty I can't. The letters of *Chesed* can reorder as *Ches Dalut* for "fond of poverty," as is a donor who gives out of pleasure, and not obligation.

I CAN give it all is the climax of the creation of sacredness – its SIXth "day." It follows the stage when I know that I CAN receive. I ROGER that, that is, my Torah; my "inner law." ROGER means: "Received Order Given; Expect Results." Might I be unable to sense when enough is enough simply because I am unwilling to "receive" my heart's dictates? Moreover, how peaceful am I when I don't? Might dissatisfaction (no sense of "enough") be so big that it obscured the Z-D-Q root that branches into the words *Tzadduqim* for "Saducees," *Tzedeq* for "justice," and *TzaddiQ* for "integral?" I am like a Saducee experiencing the grief of a Z-D-Q root thus far hijacked and miscommunicated. The loss in translation begs the question: what is justice?

This root may just be the missing link to enlightened justice. I have seen how the ZQ letters disappeared in the passage from archaic Greek to modern Greek. And yet, the pairing of ZQ | QZ of code awesomeness is essential, since awe is the feel of sacredness. To know how awesome it is to be integral, I must come to the end of desire. This is to say, I must let go of my attachment to an outcome. Letting go of what I want for the little self alone is a *sacrifice* – a "making sacred." It is letting go of shame. It is the only way that my dragon and my lion will ever stop antagonizing each other. But I'm not there yet! The idea of sacrifice just irks me. I just don't want to let go of my pound of flesh!

Truth be told, how could I be wholehearted when I am letting a collective program impose its desires and its will on me? I am reduced to cutting corners and blaming others for my lack of freedom, not realizing that my very happiness depends on my giving it all to LOVE. I think that I end at the skin; that I am here and you are there. This illusion of separation makes it impossible for me to know that it is in giving that I am receiving. And yet, mutuality is the spirit of the law. To make matters worse, the more I resent being forced to give, the more the fundamental sense of *Tzedaqah* as integrity (100%) eludes me.

I became an objector of conscience on the ground of freedom of thought. I wanted to be free from a morality that has been preached for centuries; from religious practices that can't convey the sacred. I was told that I must first be truthful, charitable and do no harm, and then I'll be a religious person. But I'm starting to suspect that it is the exact contrary: religiousness, integrity and/or devotion will lead me to be truthful, charitable, and do no harm, as I'll hear and understand that there's only One (I) of us. But who's counting? Ahh... What I called "charity" is the end, and not the means to the end.

Just receiving this creates some space in me. It begins to shift the sense of obligation to give. Little by little, I start to know who I am and what I truly want, and stop reacting to the concepts of "righteousness" or "charity." Instead of getting stuck in the words' moral overtones, unclear whether I "should" or "shouldn't" give to those who are in need, I find myself to be more generous and kinder to myself and others. I can imagine myself succeeding in my creation because I no longer deflate the possibility to be total in my gift – integral; a *TzaddiQ* or a *TzaddiQa*.

Being integral is being entire – total. Integrity supports faith – a religious idea which science calls "certainty:" having zero doubts, I am the wholeness of Peace. Integrity is the quality infused in the Z-D-Q root that forms the S/Hebrew words for "justice, truthfulness, priesthood, and the enlightened ones." Integrity is modeled by an alphabet that remained unchanged through time. This alphabet didn't lose track of its signs Q and Z, Qoph (Q) being the hieroglyph for "monkey-mind," and Tzaddi (Z), for "fish-hook." Consider: when I "ignore" the workings of my mind, I don't have to dive into the abyss for the fish in consciousness. I can continue resisting doing the shadow work that would end up granting reality to words such as "justice, truth, enlightenment."

For me to know what I can and can't give (the SIXth "day"), I must be able to receive. For me to be able to receive ("day" 5), I must be able to decide what is important to me. For me to be able to decide ("day" 4), I must be able to think. For me to be able to think ("day" 3), I must be able to fast. For me to able to fast ("day" 2), I must be able to wait. Finally, for me to be able to wait ("day" 1), my compulsiveness must have caused me "enough" pain that I would want to know the truth.

Giving it all is *Tiqqun Cain* – "the repair of Cain." It is the end product of the GOD Technology. Knowing in my "heART" that I am giving it all, moment by moment, I live each day as if it were the last.

The GOD Technology

> "He who can no longer pause to wonder and stand rapt in awe, is as good as dead; his eyes are closed." *Albert Einstein*

Thus far, I have looked at the three flows of living a meditative life as "I CAN think, I CAN receive, I CAN give it all." This is the direct link to the Power of Three, an experience which makes me integral. These proficiencies are better felt when expanding the translation into a transmission, e.g.; I know beyond doubt the "charity" of *Tzedaqah* when I am able to give it all.

Individual Power	Symbolic Power	Collective Power
Teshuvah – "Turn within"	TzedaQah – "Charity"	Tephillah – "Prayer"
I CAN think	I CAN give it all	I CAN receive

The Integrity of the Power of Three

While these are essential and desirable proficiencies, I'm still missing the ramp by which to come to exercise these Powers naturally and thus, sustainably. This ramp is formed by the codes crowning *Teshuvah, Tephillah* and *Tzedaqah*.

The image below is taken from the prayer book read during the High Holy Days. TCO simply added the color codes of the Power of Three (white, black, grey). The three words in large print are the names of the three pillars preceded by the letter Vav (English U), the "and" that links them all (*U'Teshuvah U'Tephillah U'Tzedaqah*).

Each large word is crowned by a word in small print. These tiny words (*Tzum, Qol, Mammon*) happen to each have the same numerical value of 136. Below the three columns, the words in medium print form the sentence *Maavirin Et Roah Hagezeirah* which means: [And *Teshuvah, Tephillah* and *Tzedaqah*] "will avert the evil decree." This is the core of "Let Us Speak of Awesomeness," the prayer of the High Holy Days attributed to Rabbi Amnon of Mainz, 11th Century.

- **White column:** tiny word *Tzum* (ZWM-136) for "fasting" is above *Teshuvah* to say: I CAN think in the measure to where I CAN fast from my lies. If not, my attention will not be free since it will be fixated on protecting my secret.

- **Black column:** tiny word *Qol* (QWL-136) for "voice" is above *Tephillah* to say: I CAN receive my prayer in the measure to where I CAN wait. If not, I become compulsive, and end up saying the "wrong" thing.
- **Grey column:** tiny word *Mammon* (MMWN-136) for "yearning, money" is above *Tzedaqah* to say: I CAN give in the measure to where I CAN decide. When ambivalent, I'm so afraid to incur a loss that I can't relate to "it is in giving that I am receiving."

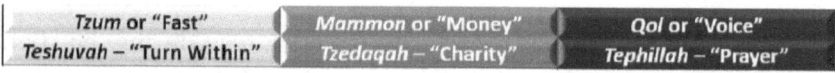

Tzum or "Fast"	*Mammon* or "Money"	*Qol* or "Voice"
Teshuvah – "Turn Within"	*Tzedaqah* – "Charity"	*Tephillah* – "Prayer"

Accepting that *TzedaQah* is akin to "integrity" (not only to give, but to give what I give wholeheartedly), why remain conditional? It is as if I wanted my personal dream of karma more than I do freedom; as if I desired for the results of my actions to fail me. If I am undecided about being entirely loving, might it be because I ignore that there is another dimension besides the material world – this of my sacred contract? I want to forget that I came to fulfill the law (no betrayal of my word, even though I might have experienced some serious trauma). Somewhere I made the decision to protect me from this reality and even to defend myself against it by becoming a victiM. After all, handicapping myself is a sure way to continue to think I CAN'T. I, myself, decided that fulfillment was a threat, and that an escape was needed.

From there, I expect that something unwanted will happen to weaken me and make me suffer. However, if courageous enough to own that I am the one who engineered this creation, I will be able to remember the decision which I had securely shielded in oblivion. This is the decision I once made to withhold love, and thus, not to give it all. Conversely, integrity is selfless – it doesn't take anything personally. It just does what LOVE wills. Meanwhile, I may benefit from a technology that can diagnose the errors of my way by using the language of elements.

Troubleshooting the Soul

> "If your only tool is a hammer then every problem looks like a nail." *Abraham Maslow*

My problem started with the Vav "nail" of the very desires which I had forbidden myself to pursue wholeheartedly. How come? Possibly, these desires opposed the wishes of my tribe. Possibly, they went against my conscience. Either way, I ended up being ambivalent, a part of me wanting what I wanted, and the other part opposing it. I am thus in dire need to troubleshoot my soul. But how?

I wish to review the basics of the "Created-SIX:" the elements. Elements are a natural part of how all cosmologies (including science) begin to explain the creation of the universe. When combining the teachings of the three main world cosmologies (also religions), I have a total of SIX elements that create "the world:"

- The four classical elements shared by Taoism, Hinduism and Judaism: fire, earth, water and air (which is metal in Taoism).
- The fifth element of Taoism: wood.
- The fifth element of Hinduism: ether.

Elements can either create or destroy each other, e.g.; water grows wood (it creates it), and it also controls fire (it destroys it). These principles sustain the Chinese five energy system – the basis of Traditional Chinese Medicine, Chinese astrology and Feng Shui. Elements also relate to the body, e.g.; the five organs of liver, heart, pancreas/spleen, lung and kidney correspond to wood, fire, earth, metal, and water, respectively.

When reintroducing ether as a 6th energy, the system goes back to its roots as three double matrices linked to the Power of Three. In Hinduism, the sacred marriage of sound and form is sanctified in *Om*, the supreme Sanskrit syllable consisting of the three mother-sounds (a·u·m) and linking the total world of Brahman as the triad of creation, preservation and destruction. In Judaism, the electromagnetism of the word is spoken by the three mothers Aleph, Mem, Shin. These letters invoke the visible elements of air, water, fire. Behind the three mothers are three fathers (the next forms of Aleph, Mem, Shin), which invoke the invisible elements of earth, ether and wood.

Individual Power	Symbolic Power	Collective Power
Wood → Fire	Air/Metal ← Earth	Ether → Water

SIX Elements and the Power of Three

Consider: behind fire, there is wood. Behind water, there is ether. Behind air/metal, there is earth. Wood is invisible because it takes time for the seed I plant today to grow into a tree. Ether is invisible because it acts as the field of all memories, past and future. As for earth, it is invisible because it is a matter of how much energy and/or faith I have in seeing it manifest. Elements relate to bodily organs (fire to the heart). They also relate to mental "organs" and/or archetypes (fire to the Leader).

Putting it all together, I now come to this table which starts in the Power of Three. It then connects the elements (e.g.; behind water, there's ether) and, next, the instruments of knowledge (e.g.; behind soul, there is voice). From there, each element now calls to an archetype (e.g.; behind the Visionary, there is GReed INgénue). Lastly, it correlates the SIX proficiencies of the sacred – the SIX "I CAN" (e.g.; behind I CAN receive, there is I CAN wait).

2. Individual Power	3. Symbolic Power	1. Collective Power
Wood → Fire	Air/Metal ← Earth	Ether → Water
Spirit → Heart	Mind ← Body	Voice → Soul
GRace INgénue → Leader	Engineer ← Officer	GReed INgénue → Visionary
I CAN fast → I CAN think	I CAN give ← I CAN decide	I CAN wait → I CAN receive

Grounding the Power of Three

The Power of Three outlines the triad of thesis, antithesis, and synthesis. These three propositions move through a progression in which the first idea is followed by a second idea that negates the first. The conflict finds its resolution in a third idea. Henceforth, my Power issues are healed in symbolic Power. This is where the mind-body connection is sane enough for me to return to homeostasis – the movement toward a relatively stable equilibrium between interdependent elements. As a result of balancing fire and water, I experience that body has no more tyrannical mind to follow, a change marked by the arrows being flipped in the column of symbolic Power.

A Marriage Made in "Heaven"

> "The secret to living a balanced life mentally, physically, spiritually, and socially boils down to one thing: PRIORITIES." *Joy Clary Brown*

Hashamayim, the word for "the heaven," also means "fire-water." Holding the tension in between these opposite energies closes the gate to hell. The attempt of fire and water to destroy each other is also the hopeless attempt of collective and individual Powers to have control. I can now end the fight of the visible elements of fire-water by going to the root cause which is in the invisible elements of wood-ether.

2. Individual Power	3. Symbolic Power	1. Collective Power
Wood → Fire	Air/Metal ← Earth	Ether → Water
Rising angel → chilD	prostitutE ← victiM	Fallen angel → saboteuR
I CAN fast → I CAN think	I CAN give ← I CAN decide	I CAN wait → I CAN receive

1. **No water = I CAN'T receive.** This is when I turn saboteuR. Behind water (the visible symptom of "I cannot receive"), there is ether (the invisible cause of "I cannot wait"). I ask myself: when do I fail at waiting? I write it down, and look forward to the next opportunity to consciously observe my compulsiveness. This will stop the sabotage.

2. **No fire = I CAN'T think.** This is when I regress into a chilD. Behind fire (the visible symptom of "I cannot think"), there is wood (the invisible cause of "I cannot fast"). I ask myself: what am I not willing to fast from? I write it down, and look forward to the next time when my attachment keeps me from a still mind. This will help me grow up.

No air = I CAN'T give it all. Behind air (the visible symptom of "I cannot give it all"), there is earth (the invisible cause of "I cannot decide"). Henceforth, what if I were to understand that the reason why I can't give it all is my unwillingness to decide? Consider: when I can't decide, I am afraid to not get what I want or to lose what I have.

I ask myself: what am I protecting? I write it down, knowing that, when ready to let go, I will come into the Power of Powers (decision), which will allow me to choose Peace and emPower the NOW. I also remind myself that I can't force homeostasis. The work is about removing the blocks to my Nature which is Love, big LOVE. Moving through the invisible elements may illuminate my blind spots and help open the eye of providence.

Ether - I CAN wait; therefore, I CAN receive!

"The voice of the intellect is a soft one, but it does not rest until it has gained a hearing." *Sigmund Freud*

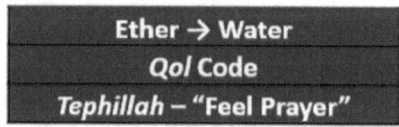

The code word is *Qol* (קוֹל) the "voice" or that which I ideally follow. It comes from the etheric field and desert of my soul, speaking in words that the deaf can hear and in images that the blind can see. It tells me what to do. Will I wait for its guidance?

Abraham became the first Hebrew – the first that went on the other side of the illusion of separateness – for one simple reason: he took "God's" call! The message he received is simple and likely to be true for me as well: "go, let go, give your all, and I will bless you!" (*Genesis 12:1-2*)

But I am afraid – afraid to hear voices when no one else is around, voices which no one but me can hear. When something akin to speech emerges from my heart, I fear that it might be a spirit of madness that entered me. Moreover, how can I be called when I am so unworthy? How can I be "God's" messenger when I get caught up in my uniqueness? Will I dare to be ordinary, humble?

If I weren't so afraid of bringing forth what's within me, would I keep running as fast as I can from the kingdom and its integrity? This is absurd: I am choosing my shame-based secrets over seeing that all the things I want are spontaneously adding themselves to me.

When I wait for the path to be clear, I am as Hermes. Being "hermetic" means that I do not let "you" or anything else pressure me into action. I CAN wait. However, when I let "God's" call go to voice mail, I hold consciously or not the intention to betray myself. Indeed, I am up against a lunatic me who is so poisoned by cleverness that it will persist in its folly. Thus, the call of theurgy – to master the operation of the moon. The earth is my body. The tides are my emotions. The ocean is my unconscious.

Unless I make my oceanic resistance conscious, I won't get the S/Hebrew *Koachim* of the "God" Names or the Sanskrit *siddhis* – the "superpowers" derived from complete understanding.

Meanwhile, the soul longs to be boundaryless, as it aspires to merge into the LOVE that has no opposite. It wants to do everything for the sake of LOVE. It even accepted that I would act as a victiM, defending and attacking until I could sense our oneness.

When I am one with everything, whatever simulated universe "God" gives me is not only okay; it is awesome, for I am no longer lonely and no longer a slave to *Mammon's* yearning.

"I CAN wait" implies that I know that the moment will come when to give it all! Meanwhile, embracing the part of me who lives in GReed – whose Giving and Receiving is not balanced – is the stretch from Tzaddi to Qoph, when I experience at once the letter and the spirit of the law.

To begin shifting my resistance to paying the price, I can pray the prayer "bring it on!" If it is necessary for me to hurt myself even more by refusing to hear a voice that gives me my own recipe for happiness, then so be it! I must become willing to follow my folly (and do the next "wrong" thing) as long as it takes for me to embody wisdom, and know the difference between good and evil; between what I can change and what I can't. Such is the purpose of folly – to lead me to wisdom.

The day when I CAN wait will come. Its promise is inscribed in goddess Shekhinah – the embodied presence of "God." Her name can also be heard as *She-khen* – "She who says yes," a big huge YES to the call. Therein is the secret behind the sacred proficiency of patience: the will to stop resisting and start agreeing. English transmits it by turning the letters of A YES into EASY.

Heartfelt prayer: when I understand that which understands "God," I CAN wait for the voice of kindness. Going against the tides and resisting feeling tells me that I am in a lie and thus not healing. My question when I am not peaceful: what is the message I don't want to hear? I write down the first thing that comes to mind. Sometimes, it may take writing three pages.

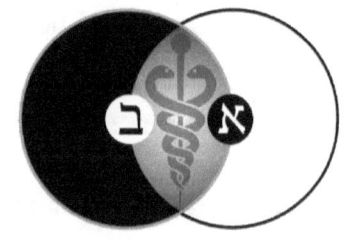

2. Individual Power	3. Symbolic Power	1. Collective Power
Sun Alchemy	Stars Astrology	**Moon Theurgy**
GRace INgénue → Leader	Engineer ← Officer	**GReed INgénue → Visionary**
I CAN fast → I CAN think	I CAN give ← I CAN decide	**I CAN wait → I CAN receive**

Step 1 – collective Power via moon theurgy: when I CAN wait to hear the voice of **GReed Ingénue**, I CAN receive the soul of my **Visionary**.

Wood - I CAN fast; therefore, I CAN think!

"There's hidden sweetness in the stomach's emptiness. We are lutes, no more, no less. If the soundbox is stuffed full of anything, no music. If the brain and belly are burning clean with fasting, every moment a new song comes out of the fire." *Mevlana Rumi*

Wood → Fire
***Tzum* Code**
Teshuvah – "Turn Within"

The code word here is *Tzum* (צום) for "fast." It has been said that a hungry man only sees food. To actually enjoy free attention, I must be able to fast from my desires – the most primal of which being food. Fasting is good for the ego: it keeps it in check! Moreover, as long as there is something I'm not willing to give up, I can't heal.

But what is it that I must fast from? The more I realize that words matter (they make "flesh"), the more I see that fasting is not as much from the flesh of food, but rather from the flesh (or the results) of the words I speak. As stated in *Matthew 15:11*, "it is not what goes into my mouth that defiles me, but what comes out of my mouth." Therefore, it is the story I tell that causes me to be unwell. If detoxing my body is among my goals, I must first fast from words before being able to fast from food: the weight is in my lies; not on my thighs!

Let's say that the voice tells me to move to Alaska, a recommendation that I try to ignore as it unsettles me. I will need to distract myself, and what better distraction but food? Besides using sugar or carbs to jam my circuits, I may go to alcohol, tobacco, drugs... My body will register what I take in – whether whole or chemical – as food, and do its best to process it. This is how, if I CAN'T receive my orders, I CAN'T fast. And since fasting is a key component of health, I am likely to dysregulate my system with the way I feed myself. If I resort to using substances, it is to try to numb my feelings of unworthiness. However, not only does my strategy work for a mere fleeting moment, but also, in the long run, it worsens my emotional state and decreases my self-esteem. If I could only see that my compulsiveness hides a lie (the belief that I am not worthy of love), I would be able to wait. **To resume: when I CAN'T wait, I CAN'T fast. When I CAN'T fast, I CAN'T think.**

When willing to know the truth, I have no issues investigating my beliefs. Turning within and going into the fire of my inquiry (into it and "intuit"), I can recognize what is real and what is not. This is how I come to know that I CAN think.

It is also how I begin to hear from within "I think I CAN, I think I CAN..."

This is enough understanding for me to persevere toward my given goal. I am now in the realm of alchemy, mastering the operations of the sun. Turning on the light and telling the truth is how to transcend and include inadequacy. I just have to accept that there may just be a certain quota of errors that is needed for me to know that there's nothing permanent. When I can accept failure and know that I will rise again and fall again and rise again, I meet the *Sol Invictus* ("the Invincible Sun"), and find that I am enough.

Turning within: to witness optimal effects, I fast from lying by inquiring on what I am not willing to give up. The question traces a path to sacrificing my "son," or that to which I am attached. The more I choose truth and let go of what I think I

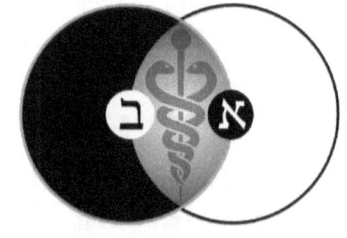

know, the more I CAN think of the "new song that comes out of the fire," rather than the automatic replay of cravings and lack.

2. Individual Power	3. Symbolic Power	1. Collective Power
Sun Alchemy	Stats Astrology	Moon Theurgy
GRace INgénue → Leader	Engineer ← Officer	GReed INgénue → Visionary
I CAN fast → I CAN think	I CAN give ← I CAN decide	I CAN wait → I CAN receive

Step 2 – individual Power via Sun Alchemy: when I open to **GRace Ingénue's** spirit and let "IT" do the fasting, I CAN think via the goodness of my **Leader's** heart.

Earth: I CAN decide; therefore, I CAN give it all!

"I think and think for months and years. Ninety-nine times, the conclusion is false. The hundredth time I am right." *Albert Einstein*

Air/Metal ← Earth
Mammon Code
Tzedaqah – "Give it All"

The code word here is *Mammon* (ממון) for "money, yearning." Time has come for me to free myself from my bondage to the material world, and take back my projections on money (whether good or not). For if I don't, I will still be yearning for someone "out there" to come and save me. This is to say, I'll be indecisive, not knowing the integrity of *Tzedaqah* – loving the LOVE "God" with *all* my heart, *all* my soul and *all* my might.

I postpone deciding because I live in a world of greed. When driving under Mammon's influence, my game is all about control as I am afraid not to get what I want or to lose what I have. I need you to "buy" me, which says that I don't really buy myself. Henceforth, I keep rehashing a slave narrative even though I am the one who made you my boss by giving you my Power. Besides, I highly dislike the fact that I am possessed by my possessions. To detach and stop counting, I must humble myself: not my will, Thy Will be done! Letting a Higher Power act through me, I'll eventually stretch to the sacred and think I CAN.

Matthew 6:4 calls it: **I can't serve two masters. I will either hate the one and love the other, or I'll be devoted to the one and despise the other. Either way, I can't serve both *Elohim* and *Mammon*.**

Elohim's message is simple: "let go. Give it all to Love. Love your neighbor. Love the stranger. Love what is. Know thyself. And brush your teeth!" Such is the body of the law, transmitted by prophets (and dentists) across traditions. Although transcultural, I still can't hear it. I wish I'd loosen my grip and just jump in. When I go totally into the dis/ease, something else besides me takes over and decides. This something else is grace. It is the holy instant when I know that, for example, I will never do drugs again. My eyes are open.

Realizing how much influence the invisible world has over the visible world also speaks of a healthy throat chakra. The reversal of polarities which sourced my ambivalence is no more. At last, I feel the difference between good and evil; between what I can change and what I can't. I am back in my Power, knowing what to do, moment by moment.

Meanwhile, *Mammon* uses the "yearning" to teach me about integrity. I can simply ask myself: what do I really want? When total in my desire, I find that I naturally experience a sense of fulfillment. I don't blame you for taking my stuff or forcing me to be, do, have anything. No matter the outcome of my decisions, I am at peace because I know I played fair and gave the game my best. My being integral breaks the shackles of materialism. In turn, it changes my stale routines and opens me even more so to bliss. Time also disappears: endurance comes naturally when I resist nothing.

Astrology comes in when I stop resisting and have no need to make it about me. It tells me who I think I am (e.g.; a Virgo), until I can die to the personality (e.g.; a Virgo), and just be and not be.

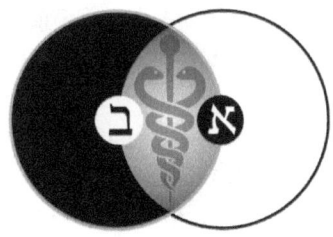

GIVING IT ALL: WHEN THE NEED TO make it about me is no more, I don't speak or act. IT speaks me or acts me. I choose peace and get out of LOVE's way. In turn, my newfound ability to remove greed from my decision-making process allows for sound choices – the choices of integrity.

2. individual Power	3. Symbolic Power	1. Collective Power
Sun Alchemy	Stars Astrology	Moon Theurgy
GRace INgénue → Leader	Engineer ← Officer	GReed INgénue → Visionary
I CAN fast → I CAN think	I CAN give ← I CAN decide	I CAN wait → I CAN receive

Step 3 – symbolic Power via stars astrology: when I CAN decide to let my **Officer's** body guide and support me, I CAN give all that my **Engineer's** mind has to give.

Astrology and the Letter Tzaddi

Superstitious awe of astrology makes one an automaton, slavishly dependent on mechanical guidance. The wise man defeats his planets – which is to say, his past – by transferring his allegiance from the creation to the Creator. The more he realizes his unity with Spirit, the less he can be dominated by matter. The soul is ever free; it is deathless because birthless. It cannot be regimented by stars." *Yogananda, Autobiography of a Yogi.*

The Hebrew sages echo Yogananda's wisdom when saying *Ain Mazel l'Israel,* "there is no astrological sign for who IS-REAL!" On the note of being ISRAEL/REAL, am I ready to do what it takes to stop the fight as Jacob did? As long as I resist something, I want something – a desire which will lead me to break my own word – my inner law. I am yet to understand that Jesus' words are equally relevant for me ("I have not come to abolish the Law or the Prophets, but to fulfill them").

When I receive the call and pledge myself to LOVE, I'm facing a Herculean goal. This goal is not only attainable; it is inevitable. To reach it, Hercules – Greek for "light of the soul" – went through 12 labors. These 12 labors can be recognized as the fate of 12 astrological signs; 4 mutable, 4 cardinal and 4 fixed. These 12 signs are invoked by 12 of the 22 letters. The process of bringing light to my soul (a.k.a. "enlightenment") involves an immersion into the moon cycles until the gold of illumination (a.k.a. the sun of God) can be sustained. I then avoid the trap of getting caught in my uniqueness as I let me be guided by the light of 12 stars – which are really the zodiac of SIX pairs of animals as the personal tendencies that are meant to consummate each other.

Why the sun, the moon and the stars? It is because my religious instinct is activated by life's order. I want to believe that there's an order for everything, just like there's an order to Nature. I can trust that the sun will rise and that it will set. I can trust the tides. I can trust that the trees will blossom in spring, and the leaves fall in autumn. "To everything, turn, turn, turn; there is a season, turn, turn, turn." But will I turn within long enough to realize that craving order denies the divinity of chaos? Chaos is served to me as soon as I make a choice. This is why I postpone deciding, because there's no guarantee. Results belong to a cosmic system that seems chaotic since its order is invisible to the eye. This is how, when I'm bound to the material world, I find myself hopelessly trying to control the outcome.

I think that if I'm good, I'll get good results. Then comes a piece of chaos that contradicts the rule I had built for myself. If attached, I will likely react to having my expectations being contradicted by becoming an addict and perpetuating a life of self-inflicted trauma. So, there was the first trauma inflicted by a parent, a teacher, society, the gods, and now, I've just added my own concoction by refining it and putting it on autoplay. I am seemingly locked in a judgment which I can't reconcile, such as this "shouldn't" have happened. It is unjust! This is when astrology calls, for me to master the operation of the stars.

Individual Power	Symbolic Power	Collective Power
Alchemy	Astrology	Theurgy
Resh (R) the Sun	Tzaddi (Z) the Star	Qoph (Q) the Moon
Four "Cardinal" Signs	Four "Fixed" Signs	Four "Mutable" Signs

The Operation of the Stars

Who do I think I am: a man, a black man, a teacher, a Scorpio, a 3 on the Enneagram? Truth be told, I am none of those "things." My birth chart only describes the beliefs I must surrender. If *Gnothi Seauton* or "**know** thyself" is engraved above the entrance to the temple at Delphi, my goal is to stay on the middle path and meet the **four "fixed" signs**.

Individual Power	Symbolic Power	Collective Power
I CAN fast → I CAN think	I CAN give ← I CAN decide	I CAN wait → I CAN receive
"I will"	"I know" ← "I have"	"I desire"

The Fundamental Keywords of Power: "**I know**" what "**I desire**," and "**I will**" it into being, until "**I have**" it.

A Meet & Greet with the AWEsome

Prepare to DIE! Inquiry tool: www.goldenxpr.com/tco3_keywords/

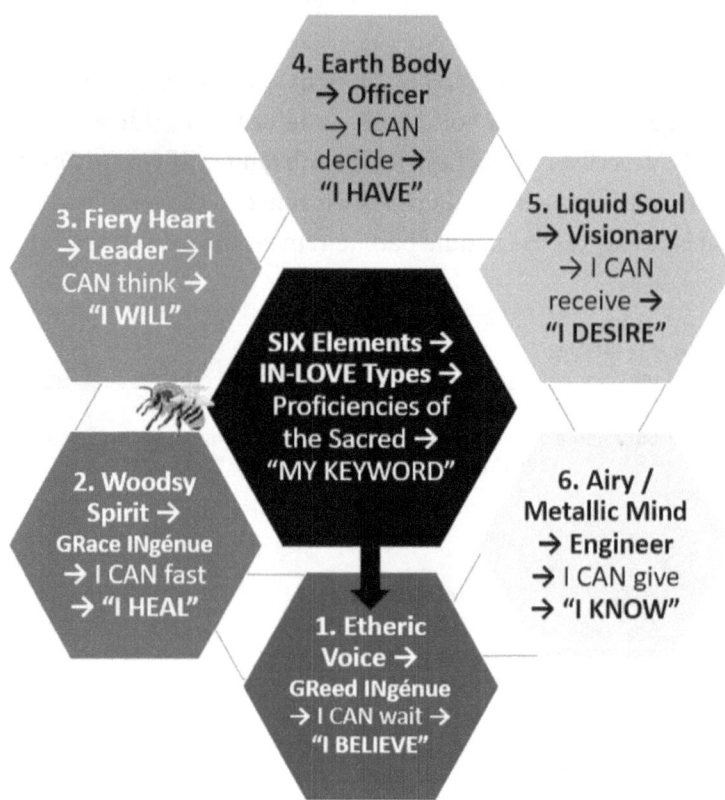

Step 1: I fill in the blank: I want to know WHY I would choose to think I CAN'T _____ (e.g.; find a job, be patient, etc.). **Step 2:** I ask for truth and generate a number. **Step 3:** I find my number on the map to fill in the brackets: when I remember my nature and exist as the [**Elements**] of my [**IN-LOVE Types**], I experience that [**Proficiencies of the Sacred**] and boldly speak the command [**MY KEYWORD**]. **Step 4:** what most surprised me in this process was [_____].

IT IS DONE!

"And out of the midst thereof came the likeness of four living creatures. [...] As for the likeness of their faces, the four had the face of a man; the face of a lion on the right side; and the face of a bull on the left side; also, the face of an eagle." *Ezekiel 1:5 [...] ibid, 1:10*

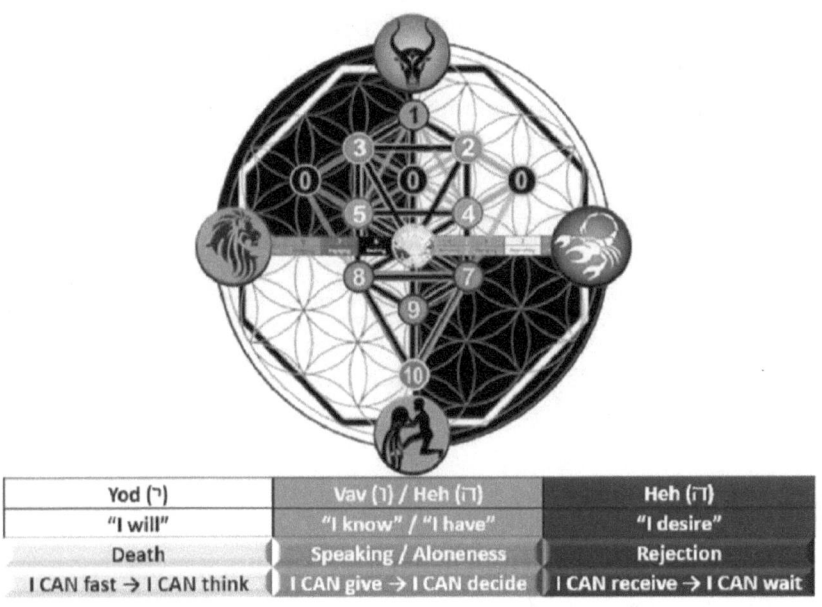

Yod (י)	Vav (ו) / Heh (ה)	Heh (ה)
"I will"	"I know" / "I have"	"I desire"
Death	Speaking / Aloneness	Rejection
I CAN fast → I CAN think	I CAN give → I CAN decide	I CAN receive → I CAN wait

Ezekiel's four beasts pictured above are the four astrological signs that are "fixed" as they teach me how to hold the tension while remaining in my temple of peace. They echo the four-lettered Name working through me to help me wake up on the other side of my victiM's fears.

Once again, I am touched by the depth of Cain's story – a CAIN who could not think "I CAN." Indeed, his inability to give it all is how his offering could never be received. While being a miser with his dynamics of engagement, he needed to prove to himself that his belief in a punishing "God" was true, and that reality was emphatically devoid of love, approval and recognition. For how else would he have justified his angst, his despair, his rage and the particular brand of OCD (Obsessive Compulsive Disorder) he designed for himself? Revenge was the name of his game, and retaliation, the motive behind his crime of passion!

While I am in the midst of my OCD's chaos, the Cain in me can't wait, and certainly can't fast. But what if I had the courage to surgically remove a belief or two? Consider: when I enjoy an operating system free of "hate" bugs, I know who I am. Being beyond time, I obviously CAN wait (no more OCD). Being beyond mind, I obviously CAN fast (no more private agendas). I am now ready, able and willing to find that it is my Nature to be LOVE:

Finding LOVE at the END of Time			
Creature's Instrument	Communication	Sacredness	Fear
The Lion's Heart	Leader's "I will"	I CAN think	Death
The Bull's Body	Officer's "I have"	I CAN decide	Loss
The Eagle's Soul	Visionary's "I desire"	I CAN receive	Rejection
The Human's Mind	Engineer's "I know"	I CAN give it all!	Speaking

- **The Lion** speaks to my **heart**, saying: "**I will.**" To be Abraham-like and authentically respond to the call, I must transcend my fear of **death**. When I do, I find that **I CAN think**.
- **The Bull** now speaks to my **body**, saying: "**I have.**" To succeed in my manifestation, I must transcend my fear of **loss**. When I do, I find that **I CAN decide**.
- **The Eagle** (sublimated Scorpio) speaks to my **soul**, saying: "**I desire.**" To feel where my pleasure lies, I must transcend my fear of **rejection**. When I do, I find that **I CAN receive**.
- **The Human** finally speaks to my **mind**, saying: "**I know.**" To be in my Power, I must transcend my fear of **speaking**. When I do, I find that **I CAN give it all**.

On the note of perfect action, I am ready to shift out of defense/attack when my victiM turns into an Officer. Having fulfilled the law, I stand as an agent of justice and take great joy in doing what it takes.

An Officer's Synthesis

"But life at its best is a creative synthesis of opposites in fruitful harmony." *Martin Luther King, Jr.*

When I CAN wait, I CAN receive. This takes care of theurgy – the operation of the moon. I followed the Voice (that's the receiving part) as I could feel which **desire** was sound and which was not. Therefore, when I CAN'T receive, I also CAN'T wait for the thought "what's in it for me" to let go of me.

When I CAN fast, I CAN think. This takes care of alchemy – the operation of the sun. I gave me the permission to fail and fall as needed and met the "Invincible Sun" which saves me from taking back my **will**. Therefore, when I CAN'T think, I also CAN'T fast from my attachments.

When I CAN decide, I CAN give it all. This takes care of astrology – the operation of the stars. I can be and not be, **have** and not have, **know** and not know. Anonymity ends the yearning for love. Therefore, when I CAN'T give it all, I also CAN'T decide to emPower the choice that would have the greatest impact for good.

Giving it all, I am Receiving it all. I am now like Abraham the Hebrew – someone who went "on the other side" of GReed into a world of GRace. My two hands are joined in a prayer that is instantaneously fulfilled by the LOVE that has no opposite. When I didn't know who I was, I served you. At times "you" were *Elohim*, and at times, "you" were Mammon.

Now that I know who I am, I feel that I am you. I have much gratitude and joy at observing me filled with the prophecy of "God," with wisdom, understanding, knowledge, generosity, with all manner of workmanship, and with laughter! Oh, wait... not so fast! Did I actually transcend fear?

FEAR - False Evidence Appearing Real

FEAR: if the rubedo stage of the red prostitutE is all about transcendence, the albedo stage of the white victiM is all about purification. Yet, to be effective in purifying my act, I must still become conscious of what the victiM in me needs to purify. It is what I most resist: fear of the physical world, and by extension, the FEAR that distorts what my eye observes in the physical world.

"**The fear** of LOVE is the beginning of wisdom, and knowledge of **the sacred** is understanding." *Proverbs 9:10*

Sacredness is the complement of fear. As for the sacredness of this proverb, it unfolded in *TCO—Book 2, Understanding Knowledge*. When I have the knowledge of an understanding heart, I cross over the abyss and embody wisdom. This means that any misuse of Power has become unthinkable. Meanwhile, I am incapable to wake up from the DREaM of karma and know what LOVE is. LOVE is to be One with everyone and everything, a oneness which can only be felt when I am at once in my Leader's heart, my Officer's body, my Visionary's soul and my Engineer's mind.

For now, I am captive to the illusion of separation and its subsequent fears. As a prostitutE, I fear speaking (I don't want them to read the private agendas which, by the way, can't help being heard by whom can hear). As a saboteuR, I fear rejection (and reject the truth that would set me free). As a victiM, I fear loss (and won't decide, e.g.; to get in shape). As a chilD, I fear death (what if I were to actually grow up, stop blaming my parents and recognize my wrongs?). As for the angels in me, they fear falling (not realizing that their Power is in the falls and the failures).

I shall focus on loss, which is my victiM's fear. This is how I can't decide. I'm afraid not to get what I want or to lose what I [think] I've got. Ignoring that sacredness is on the other side of fear, I CAN'T make THE Decision – the decision to purify my victiM's story. Just like I won't read *Proverbs 9:10,* I won't read *Matthew 6:31-32:* "therefore do not worry, saying, 'what shall I eat?' or 'what shall I drink?' or 'what shall I wear?'
It is only the doubting part of me that seeks these things. For my heavenly Father knows that I need all these things. If I were but to seek first the kingdom of God and 'ITS' justice, all these things would be added to me."

Yep, for me to not transform into an Officer, my victiM must partner with my chilD who's afraid of death. Henceforth, I never grow up into the Leader and reach the "heavenly Father" who provides for me. Resisting fear of losing my victiM's identity is how I leave presence to go into **defense/attack**. That MO now defines me.

Surely, I am devoid of presence when my fearful masculine starts **defending** himself by going from one justification to the next. "God" forbid I'd be female – evil and wrong! But what happens when I am female? When the fearful masculine is played out for me as "he" starts justifying his action after I caught him with his hand in the cookie jar ("he/him" could equally be a "she/her"), will I be strong enough not to flip into the fearful feminine who responds by **attacking**?

To me, these are the two most profound and powerful quotes of *A Course In Miracles*: "if I defend myself, I am attacked" followed by "would you rather be right or happy?" They both speak of and to my inner victiM – the part of me that believes that I am the body, and, as such, needing to retaliate against any perceived attack.

On the note of believing that I am the body, the conversation whether my neurosis prompts me to generally act as the fearful masculine rather than the fearful feminine is independent from the gender(s) to which I identify. When I die to the "I am the body" belief, the fearful masculine vanishes to reveal the Sacred Masculine. Same for the fearful feminine which will eventually give way to the Sacred Feminine.

The day of my death will come. I will then give it all to LOVE, having no need to be right, righteous, belligerent or to justify myself. I'll know the errors I make are when the divine seeps in. Until then, I will continue to cut corners while brooding for how unfair life is to me. In that case, I will tend to feel insulted as I am yet to detoxify the poison of entitlement, believing that I didn't deserve to be treated that way...
Well, "sync" again!

Being in fear, I can't relate to sacrificing who I *think* I am, sacrifice being, after all, the essence of the Law. Therefore, I make it about me!

Having a twisted idea of what justice is (False Evidence Appearing Real), I project that you are my oppressor, and want to make you pay for "forcing me," never realizing that I'm the one who's narrating this slave story... If I could only make THE decision to purify all my futile attempts to go into defense/attack and just be... Present. No past. No future. Just presence.

Then and only then the chilD in me would begin to awaken from the DREaM that mommy and daddy can't see me, hear me, or understand me. Hearing my Self, I'd finally be a Leader beyond FEAR, fully expressed...

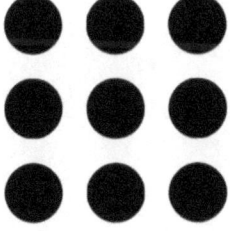

FIVE

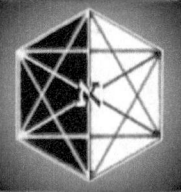

The chilD - If at First, I Don't Succeed...

'In a letter to Ms. Edith Schroeder who had inquired on "the significance of Freud's Jewish descent for the origin, content and acceptance of psycho-analysis," Carl Jung replied: "One would have to take a deep plunge into the history of the Jewish mind. This would carry us beyond Jewish Orthodoxy into the subterranean workings of Chasidism... and then into the intricacies of the Kabbalah, which still remains unexplored psychologically."' *C.G. Jung, 1973, Vol. 2*

THE THING IS: unless I'm fully awake, I'm yet to surrender my ego's desires. This implies that I cannot really know whether my creation is ethical enough to be of optimal service to the community. To be a servant leader, I must grow up, drop my story of unrequited love, and stop blaming the "YOUniverse" for my failures. To this end, I will now focus on the first three chapters of *the Book of Genesis*, since these chapters unfold the two ways by which to create (being either primary or secondary) and the one sure way by which I destroy (being tertiary). Yep, to feel and understand the true meaning of "you create your reality," I must first have the courage to turn off my destructive energy. When it is done, I stop taking life's occurrences personally and see that "IT" is good. The chilD has now grown up into a Leader.

AS FOR THE "INTRICACIES OF THE KABBALAH," THEY EXACTLY MIRROR THE COMPLEXITY OF MY SOUL PATTERNING – A COMPLEXITY THAT RICHLY UNFOLDS IN THE FIRST CHAPTERS OF *GENESIS*.

The Citrinitas Stage of Awakening – when the yellow chilD grows up into a Leader...

TO GROW UP IS TO WAKE UP, AND VICE-VERSA. WHAT I WAKE UP TO IS THE sobering realization that I am 100% responsible for how I create reality. When I am honest enough, I stop blaming my mommy or daddy (or the parent I project on a partner, a friend, a boss, etc.). I am simply here, in full acceptance. I don't leave me and don't abandon myself.

Meanwhile, I act with pride as a spoiled child does. I want to be right and fight with "God," which increases my discontent with myself. In that space, I'll do everything for love, yet don't really mean it! I am in fact so hungry for your attention ("you" whom I've created as my mom and/or dad) that I may act out just to have your disapproval. In a weird sort of a way, I'd rather be punished than not be noticed at all. I made my parents my gods, and my gods, my parents: I put them in charge of approving or disapproving of me.

However, to give my Power away to a "God," to a parent, to you, to money, to the world – and let it deal me either reward or punishment, I must first deny that we are all connected to the One Mind, and all have the same access to creative Power.

Next Stage: the chilD's Awakening

Prepare to DIE! Inquiry tool: www.goldenxpr.com/tco3_poisons/

Step 1: I fill in the blank: I want to know WHY I would choose to think I CAN'T ... (e.g.; find a job, be patient, etc.). **Step 2:** I ask for truth and generate a number. **Step 3:** I find my number on the map and fill in the brackets: when I identify to the [**DREaM**], I am susceptible to [**MY Poison**] which leads me to violations by way of [**MY Secret Vice**]. Is it then a wonder why I would have [**MY PROBLEM**] issues? **Step 4:** What most surprised me in this process was [_____].

BIZARRE

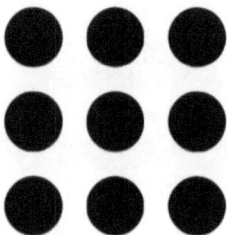

BIZARRE that I'd be so hungry for attention that I'd become a naughty chilD... **My core belief is that I'm unwanted; no one really loves me!** In 2011, nearly half (45%, or 2.8 million) of the 6.1 million pregnancies in the United States were unintended. Specifically, 27% of all pregnancies were "wanted later" and 18% of pregnancies were "unwanted."

And if I am born a girl in a culture that favors boys, I am doubly unwanted! Conversely, the added pressure to perform doesn't make it easy on boys. This when I choose to invent an imaginary friend!

To protect my wounded child and reconcile myself with the evil done by my gods, I create a *golem* (S/Hebrew for "imperfect quirk"). Heck, it sounded like a good idea at the time! What I did not imagine is that my creation would turn against me, making me his creature!

How long will the enemy triumph over me? This is the chilD asking:

are we there yet? To stop time, I would have to take full responsibility for my creation of enmity, that is, for my golem! Truth be told, my "God," my family, my friend or my enemy are not outside of me, but in my cells where they live as the intense passion of the virtues and the vices I inherited, starting with the sin of pride.

It is pride that blames "you" for not loving me. Before engaging socially, I am subjected early on to an array of regulations which makes me sensitive to certain obligations. **It is this false sense of being obligated to others that makes me resentful and deprives me of my own leadership. Instead of humbly following my heart, I can't seem to differentiate between the ego and the environment.**

No wonder I'd express myself through the broken heart, throw a tantrum, or refuse to grow up! Discovering my true nature feels like a betrayal of the people I am the closest to – my parents. I thus choose to remain indoctrinated and unspoken, in order not to break with the family traditions.

Surely, I tell the story of unrequited love, as I created me to be thoroughly unwanted. Am I flawed, damaged goods, imperfect? My golem is the belief that I am fallen, living in a state of sin which renders me incapable of receiving love. Resigned to being powerless and feeling direly unheard and unseen, I now develop a number of aversions. And since I was taught that hatred is unacceptable, I'll project it out onto my parents whom I blame for my inadequacies.

Moreover, since my parents were my first role models – my gods, really, I also unconsciously superimpose my parents onto "you," making it your fault if I cannot succeed. This is how, even when caught with my hand in a cookie jar, I will claim: "I didn't do it!"

To actually be capable of innovation and free the genius that is all bottled up inside me, I must unlearn my childish ways and destroy the golem I created to protect me, yes, but also, to attack me. In other words, I must now love me, see me, hear me.

On that note, if a tree falls in a forest and there's nobody to hear it, does it make a sound? The psychological riddle may be resolved by holding that a tree only makes a sound when there is an audience to witness its fall. This is not unlike a child who cries after having fallen when seeing that the parent is worried. And it makes me wonder... Isn't it bizarre that just hearing myself fall would not be *sound* enough?

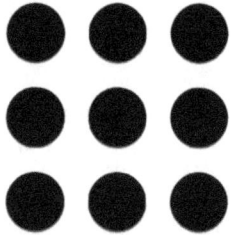

Part I: An Overview of Creation

- Taking the Fifth
- Fish Page
- I Am Here to Create
- The Wizard of UZ
- I Am Here to Uncreate
- Time, Space & Mind
- Mind and SIX-based Time
- The TWIN Sequential Order
- Code Creativity – BRA / BAR / ARB
- The Goodness of Creation
- The Mind of Life
- The Egg, the Ego and the Eight of Life
- What do I really want?

Adam Qadmon	The Snake / Cain	Adam HaRishon
Simultaneous Creation	Non-Causality / Preservation	Gradual Destruction
The Seed of Life	The Core / The Gem of Life	The Egg of Life
The First SIX Days	The 7th Day / Doing Time	The Second & Third SIX Days

The Geometrical Mysteries of Creation

Taking the Fifth

"If you insist on asking me why I feel the way I do, I plan to take the Fifth Amendment." *Mason Cooley*

Besides "I didn't do it," one of the favorite replies of my chilD is "I dunno." This is a way to refuse to testify, on the grounds that the testimony might incriminate me. Until I can be true to my word (after I have returned to *Av,* the "father" as the "alphabet" that spells out my guidance), I do have the right to remain silent. What is my crime? It is to be unconscious of my motivations for saying and doing what I say and do. The agendas of my ego show up in the fact that there is a misalignment between what I say I want and what I have *in reality*. The unconscious intentions that are in my space – my "secrets" – are what obstruct my creative magic. How can I free my genius from its captivity?

The *Haggadah Shel Pesach* for "story of Passover" answers. It is a rabbinical text that sets forth the order of the Passover ritual and narrates the exodus out of Egypt. One of its famous sections is *Arba'ah Banim,* the "Four Sons" (a wise son, a wicked son, a simple son and a son too naïve to formulate a question). These are the four ways in which my chilD expresses its wound, until I take the fifth.

I already met the face and/or the archetype of the Son as the mind's spokesperson. It is the mind which requires healing, as it fights with the heart (thus the perception of a broken heart), and speaks of slavery until I am free to drop the story. Meanwhile, my mind is filled with questions. This may be how the Talmud speaks of the unleavened bread eaten at Passover as *Lechem Oni,* "bread of the answer." Shall I go right or left? Which choice will keep me safe? As for the "Four Sons," their types seem to mimic the first humans as they appear in the Bible:

- **The simple child** is *Adam Qadmon's* mind (the primary Adam of *Genesis 1*), who knows to be created male and female, in the divine image.
- **The naïve child** is the mind of *Adam HaRishon* (the secondary Adam of *Genesis 2*), who let himself be led into temptation by the Woman.
- **The wise child** is the woman's mind who is yet to know the difference. In spite (or maybe because of) her foolishness in letting herself be lured, she saw "that the tree was to be desired to make one wise." *Genesis 3:6*
- **The wicked child** is snake's mind, who lies and misuses his language-Power in order to lead the woman and the Adam into temptation.

Simple	Naïve / Wise	Wicked
Adam Qadmon	Adam HaRishon / The Woman	The Snake
Genesis 1	Genesis 2 & 3	Genesis 4

The Four Sons and the Four Chapters

Bottom line: the chilD is the part of me that will not take responsibility for my creation, and thus, seeks either approval in the form of a reward or disapproval in the form of a punishment. *Genesis 3:10-13* is where I make the choice to hide from my conscience, defend myself, and then blame "you" for my error: "But the LORD God called to the man, "Where are you?" He answered, "I heard your voice in the garden, and I was afraid because I was naked; so, I hid." And he said, "who told you that you were naked? Have you eaten from the tree that I commanded you not to eat from?" The man said, "the woman you gave to be with me—she gave me some fruit from the tree, and I ate it." Then the LORD God said to the woman, "What is this you have done?" The woman said, "The serpent deceived me, and I ate."

Sooo... The Adam blamed the woman. The woman blamed the snake. And while it is not part of the narrative, the snake must have blamed "God" for His creation. By manipulating the woman, the

snake was intending to prove that there is nothing good about the world that "God" had created.

I am all of it: the Adam, the Woman and the snake. If only I had said: "I did it, God, and I am so so sorry! I make a sincere vow to realign to my heart and restore the balance I compromised," I'd still be in PaRaDiSe. Instead, by disowning my error, I made it into a full-fledged transgression. I am now convinced that I am bad, which is how I have issues with Power and authority. Consider: when I cannot trust in my goodness, being successful in my creation is nearly impossible. I am now appointed to birth the fifth son – the son that sees that the Four Sons that are in the DREaM are "good," and even very good!

WHY AM I A CHILD? BECAUSE I CAN'T WAIT. INSTEAD OF PERSEVERING TO THE END, MY MIND MOVES AT THE SPEED OF IMPATIENCE, ASKING NONSTOP "HOW LONG?"

It takes maturity to make the motion of full response-ability, and therefore "move" to feel the angst of not having what I say I want. While the chilD fights with "God," the Leader accepts reality. When dissatisfied, I lead by realizing that dissatisfaction must be what I *really* want. Such realness sits me be back in truth, where to witness an instant alignment between my words and my results.

Consider: when unwilling to take full responsibility for my creation, I make "you" the cause of my failure and thereby invite the illusion of separation. Moreover, since creativity is a solo job, I will not be able to succeed in my creation until I can recognize that my results are a reflection of what I truly communicate, which is not necessarily the same as what I think I am communicating.

I Am Here to Create

> "Every man must decide whether he will walk in the light of creative altruism or in the darkness of destructive selfishness."
> *Martin Luther King, Jr.*

I am here to create. I create as I breathe. I create as I think. I create as I speak. It is unavoidable. If I were to doubt it, I can just try not to move for a while, and do nothing. Yep, I'll just sit or lay down and watch my breath rising and falling… It is called "meditation." I now have a front row seat to observe how that which moves is the mind. Each motion is a creative act. I wish I could still it, calm it down, stop the incessant ruminating… I wish I could keep my attention on my breathing – in and out, in and out, in and out… But, no siree! I get hooked by my thoughts; enthralled by their story, lost in their chaos… That much I can realize by only sitting for a few minutes. It's insane! I'm insane… This may be how I am not always thrilled with my creations when they clearly come from the abysmal and even demonic realm.

To create something new, I must let go of the known. However, meeting the law that is no law and breaking the rules is dangerous business, for I may lose all sense of boundaries and turn crazy destructive. Moreover, what if I enjoyed being above the laws? What if I let my superpower go to my head and become an arrogant chilD? "Pride goes before destruction, and a haughty spirit before a fall," says *Proverbs 16:18*. I had never checked before the S/Hebrew words for "destruction" and "fall." *Shever* for "destruction" is the root of *Shevirah*, the "shattering" stage of the Lurianic cosmic drama. As for *Kishalon*, it does mean "fall" and "failure." The word's gematria (KSLWN) is 406, equal to last letter Tav which, when fully spelled out as the word *Tav* (TW) means "sign, note" and, by extension, cross. Such is the infamous Path of the Cross as travelled by the hero – a path that will take me down as long as there is an ego that boasts about the creative act. The sense that I am superior (and thus, entitled) must be taken down. It is likely that my lacking humility is how I'd unconsciously choose to be stuck rather than moving on to the next level of creative Power. I'm afraid of falling / failing, and the older the body gets, the greater the fear.

And it makes me wonder... Why would I take a fall *personally* unless my mind is moved by a *personality?* Personalities want something. As long as I desire this or that, I am not surrendered. As long as I am not surrendered, I am not (and nor is my work) an original. I'm just an imitation of Christ, yet to reveal the Messiah behind my snake!

Sooo... What do I want which I *think* would make me all Powerful once I received it? Is it a kingdom, knowledge, wealth, a master, youth, fame? For those are the SIX "days" that span my Devil's pact – or shall I say "my Devil's peace?" More to come on that which "antagonizes" me; my *Satan* as that which will eventually bring me to peace.

The Wizard of UZ

> "Once upon a time, in the land of Uz, lived a man whose name was Job. This man was PAIRfect and sincere; he revered *Elohim* and turned away from evil." *Job 1:1*

The S/Hebrew name *Job* means "the Hated One." Job could have believed that, to be given such a dire reality, his "God" must have really hated him. If the chilD is who tells the story of unrequited love, then Job could have had a tantrum from being called to be "the Hated One." To top it all, his best friends bluntly told him that he must have done something really wrong to deserve such hateful treatment! As for the land of Uz, if the Wizard is the archetype of creativity who seemingly manifests stuff out of the ether, Job must be the greatest of Wizards as judged by the intensity of what he created. As for me, how would I react if I were destined to have everything taken from me; my money and my family and my health? Would I be able to be as PAIRfect and sincere as Job? Job was truly "PAIRfect:" he had 3 daughters and 7 sons; "he owned 7,000 sheep, 3,000 camels, 500 yoke of oxen and 500 donkeys..." *Job 1:3*

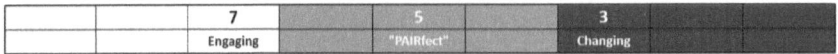

The PAIRfection of 3 and 7, 7000 and 3000, 500 and 500

The S/Hebrew word *Tam* (TM) is "PAIRfect" as it plays with *Mat* (MT) "death" to inscribe code Commerce (see *TCO, Book 2*). It is the chilD who fears abandonment and, by extension, death. Job didn't have that fear, as he could welcome any change to his "secured" situation and still revere (or "feared") *Elohim*. What was his magic?

The Book of Job tells the story of unmerited suffering. It is unmerited because Job was a true leader in that he knew to sacrifice for the greater good. The willingness to render everything sacred by giving it all to "God" allowed him not to take his fall personally. Here's what *Job 1:5* says on that theme: 'when a period of feasting [of his sons and daughters] had run its course, Job would make arrangements for them to be purified. Early in the morning he would sacrifice a burnt offering for each of them, thinking, "perhaps my children have sinned and cursed God in their hearts." This was Job's regular custom.'

As for me, if I knew that my Giving/Receiving was no longer tainted by GReed but colored by GRace, I would neither take failure personally nor feel "cursed." Instead, I would see that my creativity blesses all. I'd also realize that the word translated as "cursed" in *Job 1:5* primarily means "blessed." *The Book of Job* has all sorts of interesting tidbits that can only be sensed when feeling into the codes. Here's another one, when *Satan* (for "the adversary") questions YEWE: "does Job fear *Elohim* for nothing?"

The translation doesn't allow me to see the subtleties of a play that involves two different "God" Names: *Elohim* as "God" and YEWE as "the LORD." Basically, Satan (who's introduced as one of the Sons of *Elohim*) is about to be authorized by YEWE to take Job down in every possible way. The question is: just how "PAIRfect and sincere" is Job, really? YEWE is the LORD of karma. "He" comes to me as the "DREaM" when I ignore the difference between good and evil, and as LOVE when I know the difference between good and evil. Henceforth, Satan wants to know if Job will continue to "fear *Elohim* for nothing" and be LOVE. The word *HaChinam* that is translated as "for nothing" directly means "by grace alone," that is, without attachment to an outcome and/or without receiving payment. For such is the experience of a man who woke up from the DREaM and is thus free of Mammon's yearning.

Again, if I knew that my Giving/Receiving was not influenced by GReed but by GRace only (i.e.; if I revered *Elohim* and not Mammon), I wouldn't doubt that that my creativity blesses all and serves the good of all. Alas, unlike Job, I am still in a DREaM of separation from *Elohim* and yet to give it all to LOVE.

As embarrassing as it is for the Wizard in me to admit, my spell check is not always working. When I say "let there be whatever," I don't always see that the whatever that is created is good – a blessing rather than a curse or a curse that is truly a blessing. I can't quite recognize that my magic wand is a magic WANT: my creativity (and/or sex magic) depends on the purity of my motivations. Indeed, what do I really want? Any dark secret that is in my space will show up in what I manifest, whether I like it or not. Similarly, any fear will lead to a False Evidence Appearing Real...

I Am Here to Uncreate

> "What might be taken for a precocious genius is the genius of childhood. When the child grows up, it disappears without a trace.

It may happen that this boy will become a real painter someday, or even a great painter. But then he will have to begin everything again, from zero." *Pablo Picasso*

Wiping the slate clean was supposed to be the victiM's purifying, a process allowing "her" to turn into an Officer. These alchemical stages are confusing to me. They appear to be sequential but also terminal, each in their own way. And are they, really?

1. **Putrefaction** ends the saboteuR's life
2. **Purification** ends the victiM's life
3. **Awakening** ends the chilD's life
4. **Transcendence** ends the prostitutE's life.

TCO guided me in beginning with the last to be the first stage – transcendence since, unless I go beyond my fears, I'll keep on revising the scene of the putrefying, purifying and awakening crimes. This is to say, I'll never go deep enough into the dark night to be complete with the sabotage, and thus never really move from purifying to purity, or from awakening to being fully awake.

This much is clear: I must include and transcend my fears. On that note, there is a fear that is 95% of the fear equation: the fear of falling. Consider: when I fear speaking, it is because I am afraid of making a fool of myself, i.e.; of falling and failing. Same with the fear of rejection, loss, death, and Power. If I could only stop judging me for my falls and my failures, my ego personality would be dead, and I'd have no more fear of death. Consequently, the push/pull would stop, as would the self-doubt and the yearning: no more fear of Power. Indeed, if at first, I don't succeed and if I were to allow myself to fail and fall and err, I'd be free, as I'd be fully "awake" as Buddha and know that my soul would be as pure as Christ.

Sooo... If I were to be so creative that I had found trillions of ways that did not work, then I would become a master as I'd learn that falling and failing are not about me. And if the knowing of "nothing personal" were the only thing I've achieved in this lifetime, then I could rest in the sense that it is enough! Indeed, when I have no need for boasting or self-berating, I transcend time, space and mind.

TIME, SPACE & MIND

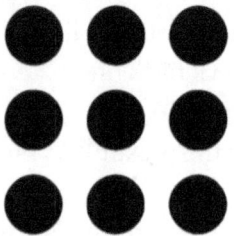

TIME, SPACE & MIND: being in an unending conversation about failing while singing the song "I can't get NO satisfaction" speaks of the myth of Sisyphus, a character who was condemned to ceaselessly roll a rock to the top of a mountain, to only see it fall back of its own weight. This is an appalling sentence in which exertion accomplishes nothing.

Somewhere, I started to think of Sisyphus as me, myself and I attempting to reach a couple of goals for a lifetime now, to no avail. Why do I *think* I CAN'T?

Schopenhauer's answer is "you can do what you will, but you can't will what you will." To which TCO adds: I can do what I desire, but I can't desire what I desire. I can do what I decide, but I can't decide what I decide.

As the result of my perceived powerlessness, I would feel sorry for myself, depressed, and even angry. Until I realized that I was the rock and the rock n' roll star, the up/down motion and the push/pull... Indeed, I am here to uncreate!

What I *think* as I fail and fall either seals my fate or ends it. I just need to let go of the opinion "I shouldn't have fallen again" and I'm free – free and stronger than a rock! I'm even a rolling stone getting satisfaction!

Such sense of enough is tied to the redemption code that has the S/Hebrew word *Ab* (AB|אב) for "**Father**" and *Ben* (BN|בן) for "**Son.**" AB + BN = ABN. When *Ben* joins forces with *Ab* (that is, when the mind surrenders to the heart), a new reality is formed invoked by the word *Aben* (ABN|אבן) for "stone."

God is Good. ALL is written! The three letters inscribe my destiny as a prodigal Son – to return home, to the Father, knowing that there is no loss, no gain; nothing personal. At last, I wake up from the DREaM of LOVE, to just be Love.

"If I speak in the tongues of men or of angels, but do not have Love, I am only a resounding gong or a clanging cymbal. If I have the gift of prophecy and can fathom all mysteries and all knowledge, [. . .] but do not have Love, I am nothing. If I give all I possess to the poor and give over my body to hardship that I may boast, but do not have love, I gain nothing." *1 Corinthians 13:1-3*

When the knowing of "nothing personal" is the only no-thing I've achieved, gained or acquired in one lifetime, I can rest in the sense that it is enough; that I am enough. Indeed, having no need for either boasting or self-berating, I transcend TIME, SPACE AND MIND.

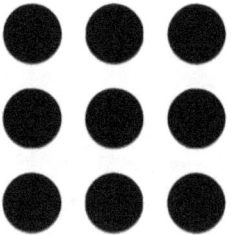

Mind and SIX-based Time

"All we have to decide is what to do with the time that is given us." *J. R. R. Tolkien*

If I could only decide to end my greatest ambivalence, I would grow up and stop repeating the same insane behavior – a behavior that can only produce poor results. I would also experience a daily growth in self-esteem and, therefore, in my perception of the sense of enough. My mind wouldn't go against my heart anymore, and my hands wouldn't be split in divided action. I wouldn't fight what is real. Instead, I would just love "God."

And this begs the question: what am I not understanding that I would keep on creating unconscious time?

I have seen how the SIX letters of the first word of the Torah are an important key; possibly the most important. The SIX letters of the word read as *Bereshit* (בראשית) for "in the beginning" can be reordered in many ways, one of them being as *Resh Bayit* (ראש בית) for "head of the house." What will I follow: my heart or my mind? The choice I make will influence the way I create time.

Establishing my heart as "the head of my house" ends time, as it is when I drop the plan and become willing to obey the law without law. I realize that the past or the future do not exist, unless my mind decides, consciously or not, to focus on a memory or image of them in the Now. While time is on my mind, and since the beginning of time is the beginning of mind, which mind is it?

- **The classical mind** resonates with YEWE *Elohim*. Its communication occurs in the space-time that writes history linearly as "HIStory." This flow is observed as moving forward (either too fast or not fast enough). It is formed by a sequence of now moments, connected by cause and effect, and strung together by memory.

- **The quantum mind** resonates with *Elohim*. Its communication occurs in the space-time that randomly emPowers the Now. It does not have a beginning or an end, and jumps from here to there. It is not moving as an arrow or a flow. It goes backwards, remembers the future and alters the past. Weird, indeed!

The realization that time is in fact "created SIX" as in 60 seconds, 60 minutes, 24 hours, etc. validates the reading of the SIX crucial first letters of the Torah as *Barashit* for "Created-SIX." This translation becomes a transmission as I use tools (e.g.; the BEE maps) to include and transcend mind.

If my linear mind still had reservations with the "Created-SIX" translation (and would understandably still favor "in the beginning"), I could look for a clue in the last word of *Genesis' Chapter 1*. This last word is *HaShishi* for "the SIXth [day]." As such, it definitely has the last word. :-)

Moreover, in-between the chapter's first and last words are the SIX days of Creation. Therefore, the beginning, the middle and the end of *Chapter 1* all point to a "PAIRfect" order inherent to chaos. This is especially true as number 6 is the first perfect number – a number that is equal to the sum of its positive divisors. 6 has divisors 1, 2 and 3, and 1 + 2 + 3 = 6.

The TWIN Sequential Order

> "There is no lostness like that which comes to a man when a perfect and certain pattern has dissolved about him." *John Steinbeck*

As above, so "belove:" both orders are needed for me to think in terms of non-duality. Both choices are "write." Opposites are needed to make a whole. Just like the S/Hebrew alphabet which can be read in reversed ascending order (from T to A) or in direct descending order (from A to

T), so can time. Time also works in what science now calls "time reversal symmetry" (TRS).

Experiments in quantum science have demonstrated that, while I can know the past and change the future, I can also know the future and change the past. The former idea is widely accepted, while the latter is challenging to conceive. And yet, when both can be kept in mind, I have the very real option to choose peace, here and Now.

Above	1	2	3	4	5	6
Belove	1	6	5	4	3	2

The TWIN Order

- **The Order of Above** evolves the stages of the linear fractal as per the classical mind. It is the choice to read the first word as *Bereshit* "in the beginning."
- **The Order of "Belove"** evolves the stages of the random fractal as per the quantum mind. It is the choice to read the first word as *Barashit* "Created SIX."

My mission: understand the part of me that lives in the past instead of emPowering the Now. To this end, I can feel how I create the WORD in SIX "days" via the Genesis Movement. See next page...

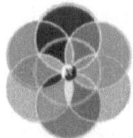

The Genesis Movement

To see the unifying equation of the "Created SIX" in motion, click the seed logo on emPoweringNOW.com. If reading the e-book, click the image above.

Code Creativity - BRA / BAR / ARB

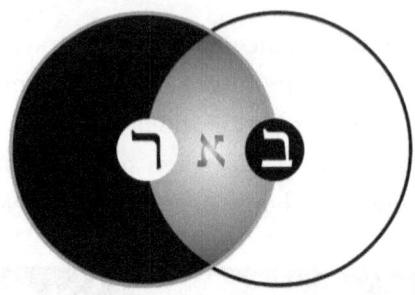

Imagine a language so pure and so sacred that it can reconcile opposites in just three letters...

- Right: Hebrew letter (ב) Beth → B in Roman script
- Middle: Hebrew letter (א) Aleph → A in Roman script
- Left: Hebrew letter (ר) Resh → R in Roman script

Here is how S/Hebrew inscribes the code "creativity" in 3 words:

- **BRA**: right to left to middle, I read *Bara* (ברא) for "created."
- **BAR**: right to middle to left, I read *Be'er* (באר) for "well."
- **ARB**: middle to left to right, I read *Orab* (ארב) for "lie in wait, ambush."

The Decoding: the "well" is that which contains water or all the subtle possibilities that **lie in wait** until I can summon them ("let there be... and there was"), and see them trustfully to be "good." They are now *Bara* or "**created**" – *Bara* being the 2nd word of the Torah: *Bereshit **Bara** Elohim* [...] "in the beginning, God **created** [...]" and certainly, *Bara-shit Bara Elohim*: "**created**-SIX, *Elohim* **created** [...]."

To see code Creativity, I simply make visible the Aleph that was invisible in code Abundance (see *TCO—Book 2, Choosing Mastery*). Doing so leads me to realize that the *Ab* Father and the *Ben* Son whose reunion was prophesized in the *Aben* stone (*Ab* + *Ben* = *Aben*) also exists in AB (אב)| BR (בר). Indeed, next to *Bar* (בר) which also means the "son," I now have *Av* (אב) "the father." To harness my creativity, I must give it all, like Abraham did who was willing to give what was most precious to him – his son. That is how he was the "father of multitudes."

If the father is called to surrender his son, the son is called to return to the father. The trick is to realize that neither the father nor the son are outside of me: they are both me! Whether in AB | BN or in AB | BR, the message is congruent.

It is also at the core of the four worlds of PaRaDiSe: *Atziluth* ("transmission"), *Beriah* ("**creation**"), *Yetzirah* ("**formation**") and *Assiyah* ("action/manifestation"). Surely, the Son must elevate his consciousness and grow up to the level where the Father lives.

Yod (י)	Vav Heh (וה)	Heh (ה)
Atziluth	*Beriah / Assiyah*	*Yetzirah*
Transmission	Creation / Manifestation	Formation
The Father	The Son / The Mother	The Holy Ghost
Spiritual	Mental / Physical	Emotional

The Four Worlds of PaRaDiSe

When I bridge the generational gap, I am in the world of **transmission** – in the level above the level where the problem was **created**. This means that I know what to do (I hear my heart), and I am following the voice. As the mind no longer competes with the heart, there is nothing personal in any breaking of the vessels, disastrous fall, humiliation and/or sickness. My tree is integral, and my creativity, a blessing to all.

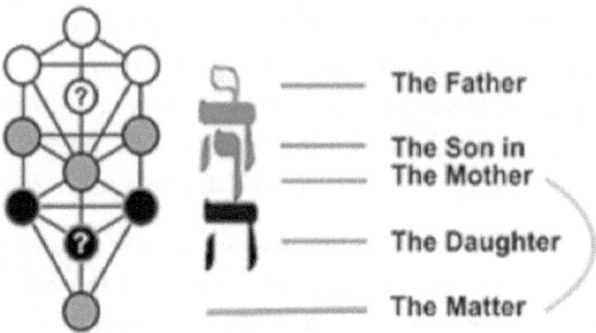

The White Sphere with a (?) between the Father & the Son

To return home, I simply answered the white sphere's question (*Daath*) by dying to the ego personality. This made creativity easy, as the mind is no longer moved by private agendas. I also answered the black sphere's question and exposed my secrets.

Doing so, I reunited the Daughter with the "Matter." I can now feel the self-esteem that alone can do due diligence. It doesn't really matter whether I'll have my desired outcome or not since hearing my heart's **transmission** fulfills me in the Now. Utterly absorbed in the action, I am free of the action.

Not only do I think I CAN succeed in my creation, but also and foremost I know that I AM the AIM – the surrender of a servant Leader.

The Goodness of Creation

"And *Elohim* saw all that He had made, and, behold, it was very good. And there was evening and there was morning, the sixth day." *Genesis 1:31*

Adam Qadmon	The Snake / Cain	Adam HaRishon
Simultaneous Creation	Preservation / Non-Causality	Gradual Destruction
The Seed of Life	The Core / The Gem of Life	The Egg of Life
The First SIX Days	The 7th Day / Beyond Time	The Second SIX Days

The Sacred Patterns of Life

The belief that "God" created the universe according to a geometric plan is ancient. Plutarch quoted Plato saying "god geometrizes continually" (*Convivialium disputationum*). The quote was adapted by physicist Carl Friedrich Gauss as "God arithmetizes." The illustration above builds up three patterns on the background of the Flower of Life. The six vesica piscis (black almond shapes) in the center form **the Gem of Life**. The dark grey circles sustain the shape of **the Egg of Life**. The six-white circle form **the Seed of Life**.

Simultaneous Creation	Non-Causality / Preservation	Gradual Destruction
The Seed of Life	The Core / The Egg of Life	The Gem of Life

These geometries converge in the core circle to help me better understand the synergy of creation, destruction and preservation. This synergy is no less than the **Mind of Life** or that which expands the code of opposites and vesica piscis by "growing" it into **the Seed of Life, the Flower of Life, the Egg of Life, the Tree of Life** and **the Fruit of Life**. Note: the middle path of non-causality will be explored in *Chapter 6 – Beyond the Fear of Power*.

The Mind of Life

> "[The golden proportion] is a scale of proportions which makes the bad difficult to produce and the good easy." *Albert Einstein*

It is indeed most extraordinary – and even shocking – that there could be a resonance between geometry and ethics. The more I recognize it, the more I allow myself to feel the order inherent to chaos, and relax. This felt sense is helped by an inquiry that is universal, credible, and radical, as it is sourced in sacred "geometry" – from Greek *ge-matria* for "Earth measurer." Its measure models for me how transcend excesses and deficiencies.

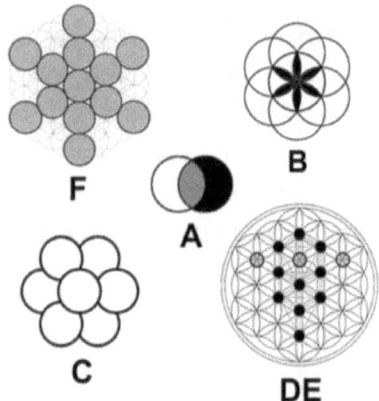

- Figure A – Vesica Piscis.
- Figure B – Seed of Life containing the Gem of Life.
- Figure C – the Egg of Life.
- Figure D – the Flower of Life as the "garden" of *Genesis 2:17* in the midst of which grows **Figure E** – the Tree of Life (black spheres) and the Tree of Knowledge (grey spheres).
- Figure F – the Fruit of Life.

Out of Nothing came a couple of circles intersecting to form a **Vesica Piscis** – a "vessel" for the light of an oceanic creativity to grow as **the Seed of my Life**, so as for me to actualize **my** potential. While this **Seed** is genetically engineered to grow into **the Flower of my Life**, I must feel WHY **the Egg of my life** hosts the specific conglomeration of genes it does (genes inscribing specific vices and virtues). I will then blossom as the intelligence of the *Torah* (the Five Books of Moses), and hear its wisdom as **the Tree of my Life**. I will do so by eating from **the Fruit** of the **Tree of the Knowledge of Opposites,** and die to the personal in "**my**" Life. The Leader in me will merge with the blueprint of the Universe, an Information Super Highway which contains every possible creation in existence – every atom, molecular structure, life-form, including the version of me being home, successful in my creation, as I am One with the mind of Life.

The Egg, the Ego and the Eight of Life

"The bird fights its way out of the egg. The egg is the world. Whoever will be born must destroy a world." *Hermann Hesse*

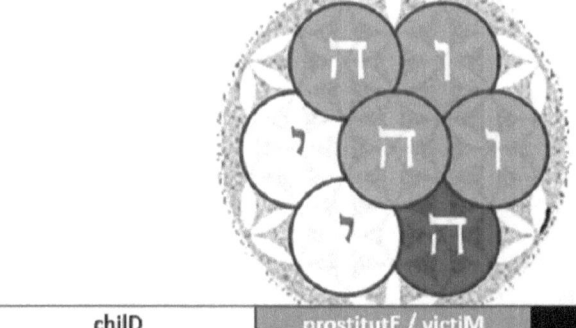

chilD	prostitutE / victiM	saboteuR
Yod (י)	Vav (ו) / Heh (ה)	Heh (ה)
Leader	Engineer / Officer	Visionary

The Egg / Eight "Bless-signs" in the DREaM of LOVE

Expressed geometrically, the four-lettered Name lives in the pattern known as the "egg of life," which is superimposed over the flower of life. Whether I know it or not, life is symmetry. This is how life is beautiful! I can experience the mirror effect and truth of "as above, so below" as the fight of opposites and as their fusion. Resisting reality will make life on earth hell. Accepting is what heaven feels like.

To see the blessing – "bless-signs?" – in the curse, I recognize YEWE as the Power of accountability. Its eight cells include both the stages of the DREaM Code and of the LOVE Code. And it makes me wonder... Is it because the egg is the only food solidifying when heated that the Egg of Life includes the parts of me that resist change? Looking at the geometry, I infer that there is a circle that is concealed. This is where my **saboteuR** hides. To come out as a **Visionary**, I must be able to visualize the jump.

Once I understand why I chose to kill my potential, the behavior will change on its own accord.

What do I really want?

Prepare to DIE! Inquiry tool: www.goldenxpr.com/tco3_childishness/.

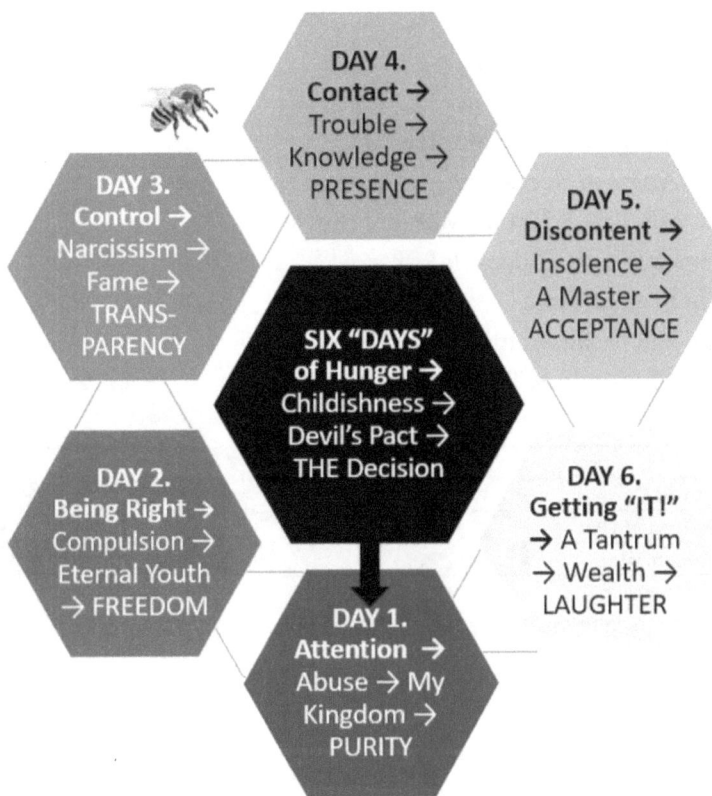

Step 1: I fill in the blank: I want to know WHY I choose to think I CAN'T _____ (e.g.; find a job, etc.). **Step 2:** I ask for truth and generate a number. **Step 3:** I find my number on the map to fill in the brackets: if hungry for [**Hunger**], I tend to regress into a chilD and go into [**Childishness**]. Do I know that what I really want is [**Devil's Pact**]? Will I sell my soul to have it or will I decide to enjoy the gift of [**THE DECISION**], which is the way to receive [**Devil's Pact**]? **Step 4:** what most surprised me in this process was [_____].

Part II: The Psychological Decoding of Genesis 1 & Genesis 2

- Fish Page
- Genesis 1 – *Adam Qadmon*
- Being Primary, Thinking I CAN!
- Genesis 2:1-3 – You Complete Me!
- The Angel of Necessity
- Genesis 2:4 – A Pivotal Moment (Review)
- Genesis 2:4-25 – *Adam HaRishon*
- The Seed of Time
- The Fall of the Mouth Chakra
- Being Secondary, Thinking I CAN'T!

The Code of Opposites		
Yod (י)	Vav (ו) / Heh (ה)	Heh (ה)
The Tree of Life	The Seed's Core / The Gem	The Egg of Life
Transmission	Creation / Manifestation	Formation

Being Primary in *Genesis 1* | Being Secondary in *Genesis 2*

WHILE IN MY MOTHER'S BELLY, I ONLY HAD TO MAKE A WISH FOR IT TO MANIFEST: I WAS PRIMARY, WHICH MEANT THAT I KNEW NO DREAM OF SEPARATION! THIS IS THE CASE OF THE ADAM QADMON – IN GENESIS 1. WHEN I AM THAT, I AM ON TOP OF THE WORLD AND DEFINITELY THINK I CAN. INDEED, I HAVE DOMINION OVER EVERYTHING; NO SELF-CONSCIOUSNESS OR LACK OF SELF-ESTEEM WHATSOEVER! THE THOUGHT THAT MY PARENTS OR "GOD" DON'T LOVE ME OR THAT I MAY HAVE DONE SOMETHING WRONG TO CAUSE THEM TO NOT LOVE ME NEVER CROSSES MY MIND. I AM FREE.

Eventually, I was born and everything changed. The sense that I belonged vanished. Now I have to cry if I'm hungry, wet or unwell, a strategy that is not fool-proof. In short, I've lost my power, which causes a delay between my prayer and its fulfillment, and thus explains the terrible yearning. This is the case of *Adam Harishon* – in *Genesis 2*. When I am that, I am plagued with all sorts of anxiety and limitations: "thou shalt not…" Perhaps one day, I'll be able to give it all to LOVE.

But for now, I live in fear of losing my mommy (or my job, or my partner, or my health, or my wealth). I am most certainly in Scare City, yearning.

Genesis 1 - *Adam Qadmon*

"**I never paint dreams or nightmares. I paint my own reality.**" *Frida Kahlo*

The transmission of "you create your reality" calls me to inquire on how I *think* of "God" and "His" creative process. To know whether I am co-creating with "God" as *Elohim* or "God" as Mammon, I just need to look at "my" reality. Am I successful in all aspects of my creation (family, food, sex, money, etc.) or might I have a few creative blocks here and there? To be primary and actually think I CAN, I am given the first chapter of *Genesis*. Again, I may read its first word as *Bereshit* for "in the beginning" or as *Barashit* for "Created-SIX."

Barashit for "Created-SIX" is at once the S-Secret and the P-Practicality of the PRDS transmission. Among other "Created-SIX" patterns, TCO uses BEE maps as the organization of "fractals" that unfold the SIX "days" or stages of any given creation. To "receive" the *QKabbalah* of *Genesis 1*, I will use the two interactive fractals of being **PRIMARY** and **Creativity**.

The code is written as follows: **Day # – PRIMARY → Creativity**, e.g.; **Day 1 – SPEED → Necessity**. I am also given the verses from which these understandings are derived. I am now fully equipped to go into R-Reflection and feel how this Biblical story is my story, in the vision that doing so will make a D-Difference in my finding and staying in PaRaDiSe.

Day 1 – SPEED → Necessity: when I make **speed** part of my life, I am not afraid of making an error and don't create unconscious time to postpone reaching my goal. I look at what challenges me as the **necessity** that will nurture what I seek to create (necessity *is* the mother of invention). Therefore, I have no objection to taking lemons and making lemonade. I simply harvest the light out of darkness. I am simply doing due diligence. This is how I am one with my goal in real time, as I do nothing to contradict its attainment.

Here is the Torah portion: "In the beginning *Elohim* created the heavens and the earth. Now the earth was formless and empty, darkness was over the surface of the deep, and the Spirit of *Elohim* was hovering over the waters. And *Elohim* said, "Let there be light," and there was light. *Elohim* saw that the light was good, and he separated the light from the darkness. *Elohim* called the light "day," and the darkness he called "night." And there was evening, and there was morning—one day." **Genesis 1:1-5**

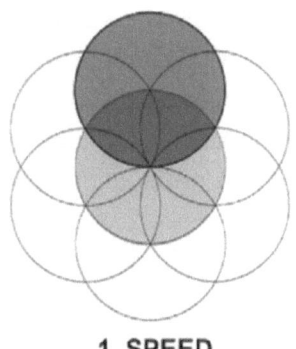

1. SPEED

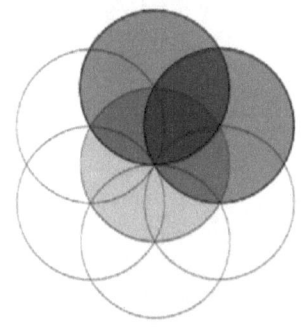

2. DECISIVENESS

Day 2 – DECISIVENESS → Originality: the Power of decision may just be the greatest Power of all, as it is creativity in action – a creativity that is sustained by my willingness to be organized. Surely, while I know that seeing piles of paper confuses me, the fear of deciding which possession to keep and which to separate from is why I delay and placing my affairs in order. I resist both – the expression and the action of putting my affairs in order, as I know it equates to preparing for the end. Is there some sort of cosmic judge giving me six "days" to organize myself before I'd begin my sentence? This is how being **decisive** is such a gift, because it requires that I'd forgive the past. This implies that I'd turn off its creative energy. It is the only way that I would be in present time. Therefore, mastering organization is also mastering separation which asks that I'd wake up from the dream of separation. This is also how organization is the foundation of creativity as it calls me to dare being an **original** and not just an imitation. Here is the Torah portion: 'And *Elohim* said, "Let there be a firmament between the waters to separate the waters from the waters." So, *Elohim* made the firmament and separated the waters under it from the waters above it. And it was so. *Elohim* called the firmament "heaven." And there was evening, and there was morning—day two. And *Elohim* said, "Let the water under heaven be gathered to one place, and let dry ground appear." And it was so. *Elohim* called the dry ground "land," and the gathered the waters he called "seas." And *Elohim* saw that it was good.' **Genesis 1:6-10**

Day 3 – DELEGATION → **Divergence:** if I don't **delegate**, it is because I fear that my co-workers won't do as good of a job as I do. Hmmm... Might it also be because I'm afraid they'd be better than me? And yet, when I am a true artist, I know that I am not creating: IT is! Not only can't I control the creative flow, but also, accidents are an inherent part of the art making process. Indeed, they are the **divergence** without which there is no art! *Elohim* did not make a mistake by delegating the Power to create to the trees, even though what the trees produced diverged from what was ordered. It was what will allow one of the trees to become the tree of the knowledge of good and evil in the next chapter. Here is the Torah portion: 'Then *Elohim* said, "Let the earth bring forth vegetation: seed-bearing plants and fruit <u>trees bearing fruit</u> in which is their seed, each according to its kind, on the earth." And it was so. The earth brought forth vegetation: plants bearing seed and <u>trees bearing fruit</u> in which is their seed, each according to its kind. And *Elohim* saw that it was good. And there was evening, and there was morning—day three.' **Genesis 1:11-13** Note: there actually is an earth tree that qualifies as a "fruit tree bearing fruit." This is the cacao tree: all its parts are eatable, even the bark of the tree.

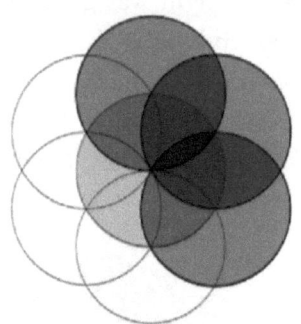

3. DELEGATION

Day 4 – GUIDANCE → **Discontinuity:** one moment, it is sunny; the next it is raining. One moment, I'm clear; the next, I'm confused. I can't bank on anything, other than being counseled on a need-to-know basis. This is how my **guidance** may... surprise me by asking me to do a 360-degree turn, and this, without any warning and seemingly totally out of the blue. To know that I am devoted to follow the voice, I need the **discontinuity** to interrupt my routine. Otherwise, how would I even trust it or trust me? Here is the Torah portion: 'Then *Elohim* said, "Let there be lights in the firmament of heaven to separate the day from the night, and let them serve as signs to mark the sacred times, and days and years, and to give light on the earth." And it was so. *Elohim* made two great lights —the greater light to govern the day and the lesser light to govern the night. He also made the stars. *Elohim* set them in the firmament of the heaven to give light on the earth, to govern the day and the night, and to separate light from darkness. And *Elohim* saw that it was good. And there was evening, and there was morning—day four.' ***Genesis 1:14-19***

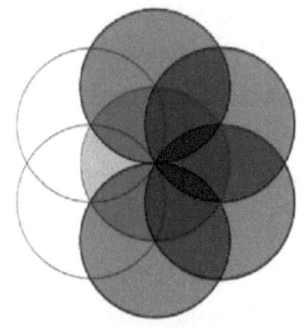

4. GUIDANCE

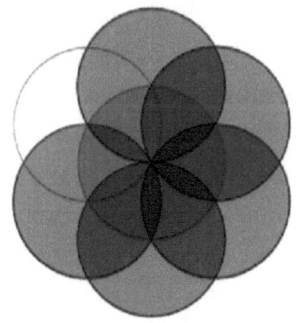

5. GROWTH

Day 5 – GROWTH → Incubation: before my creation can be made manifest and see the light of day, I must go through a preparation which involves significant **growth**. This is the stage of transformation when I **incubate**. Yep, I must cocoon with my creation and sit on my eggs while being silent and solitary to allow for all the different alchemical processes to enter in synergy. This work will trigger a number of emotions as expected in a "watery" phase. Here is the Torah portion: 'And *Elohim* said, "Let the water swarm with living creatures, and let birds fly above the earth across the heavenly firmament." So,

Elohim created the great beast of the sea and every living thing with which the water teems and that moves about in it, according to their kinds, and every winged bird according to its kind. And *Elohim* saw that it was good. *Elohim* blessed them and said, "Be fruitful and multiply. Fill the waters in the seas, and let the birds increase on the earth." And there was evening, and there was morning—day five.' **Genesis 1:20-23**

**THE SIXth Day – SEX MAGIC →
Distillation:** this is the apex of creation, when all gets together as if per magic. SIX is **SEX**: this **magic** is sexual, since it involves distilling disparate elements so as to form one essence. **Distillation—noun:** the extraction of the essential meaning or most important aspects of something. Thus, I must proceed carefully, moving from the simpler to the more

SIX. SEX MAGIC

complex, and attributing purpose and sustenance to each element. Here is the Torah portion: 'And *Elohim* said, "Let the earth produce living creatures according to their kinds: the Behemoth, the creatures that move above ground, and the wild animals, each according to its kind." And it was so. *Elohim* made the wild animals, the Behemoth, and all the creatures that move above ground according to their kinds. And *Elohim* saw that it was good. Then *Elohim* said, "Let us make Adam in our image, in our likeness, so that they may rule over the fish in the sea and the birds in the sky, over the Behemoth and all the wild animals, and over all the creatures that move along the ground." So, *Elohim* created the Adam (i.e.; the mind) in his own image, in the image of *Elohim* he created him; male and female he created them. *Elohim* blessed them and said to them, "Be fruitful and multiply; fill the earth and subdue it. Rule over the fish in the sea and the birds in the sky and over every living creature that moves on the ground." Then *Elohim* said, "I give you every seed-bearing plant on the face of the whole earth and every tree that has fruit with seed in it. They will be yours for food. And to all the beasts of the earth and all the birds in the sky and all the creatures that move above the ground—everything that has the breath of life in it—I give every green plant for food." And it was so. *Elohim* saw all that he had made, and it was very good. And there was evening, and there was morning— THE SIXth Day." **Genesis 1:24-31**

Male Fire	Male Air / Female Earth	Female Water
[Broken] Heart	[Split] Mind / [Pain] Body	[Lost] Soul
The Father	The Son / the Mother	The Daughter

So, *Elohim* created the Adam in his own image, in the image of *Elohim* he created him (i.e.; the Son); male and female he created them (i.e.; the Son and the Mother).

When I see that elementals are created male and female since they either go up or down, I also realize that the instruments of knowledge (soul, heart, mind and body) are also created male and female. This is to say that there is a code of opposites beneath every concept. Similarly, the first word of the Bible is created male and female. *Bereshit* for "in the beginning" is male as it invokes **linear time** with beginnings and endings. *Barashit* for "Created-SIX" is female as it invokes **random time** with a call to emPower the Now. Linear time and random time complete each other as male and female do. When including both perceptions, I stop counting "time" to instead make time count. Understanding the Torah's first word is understanding the working of mind – how it creates in SIX days.

To this end, I am given S/Hebrew as a language of Nature, in this case, the root-word DBR. It branches into the word *Debarim* for the 10 "Words" / "Commandments." It also forms *Deborah* for "bee" – an insect whose genius is organization, the principle that sustains creativity. Just like honeybees build a honeycomb to serve as storage vessels for honey as well as homes to raise young bees, TCO assembles its fractals in hexagonal shapes, to better reveal the order in the jigsaw puzzle of knowledge. **May the message of these pages be as sweet as honey and allow you and me to just BEE!**

Being Primary, Thinking I CAN!

Prepare to DIE! Inquiry tool: www.goldenxpr.com/tco3_willingness/.

Step 1: I fill in the blank: I want to know WHY I would choose to think I CAN'T _____ (e.g.; find a job, be patient, etc.). **Step 2:** I ask for truth and generate a number. **Step 3:** I find my number on the map to fill in the brackets: when not having the Power of [**Primary**], my creativity has [**Creativity**] to it, implying that I resist [**WILLINGNESS**]. **Step 4:** what most surprised me in this process was [_____].

Genesis 2:1-3 – You Complete Me!

"Thus, the heavens and the earth were completed in all their vast array. And on the seventh day *Elohim* finished his work that he had done, and he rested on the seventh day from all his work that he had done. So, *Elohim* blessed the seventh day and made it holy, because on it *Elohim* rested from all his work that he had done in creation." *Genesis 2:1-3*

The expression RIP is well-taken: "Resting in Peace." To observe and remember the "Shabbat day," I may just have to die to the body or to who I *think* I am (whichever comes first). I will then have fulfilled the prophecy and entered "the Eternal Shabbat." I experience this most holy "day" when I neither push nor pull, but instead allow creation to happen *through* me. To "observe and remember a day of rest" is the fourth of Ten Commandments.

Vav 6	5	Dalet 4
Desiring	"PAIRfect"	Resisting
6 ו	5 ה	4 ד

The fourth commandment is also the word *Dalet* for "door" – the door of time that opens when I redeem the murderer in me. Indeed, the fourth Word is made "PAIRfect" by the sixth Word – the sign Vav which invokes the command "do not kill." This is how Cain could never be killed (and thus never rest in peace). Sleeplessness goes with guilt, and sleep, with innocence. Therefore, for Cain to be able to RIP, he must declare his own innocence ("I have not sinned"), and mean it.

For me to feel my innocence, I must surrender my hunger and/or any ego ambition. As long as I want this or that, I am not surrendered. Surrender is loving reality for the sake of love and nothing else, not even for the sake of liberation. Being in such graceful zone is how I can work while resting and rest while working. I am no longer focused on an outcome. I simply turn within to hear what my appointment is. It may be to wash the dishes, to make a phone call, to build an Ark. :-). Indeed, I am devoted to follow the voice, an experience known as Bhakti Yoga in Hinduism. It is true meditation: my devotion is so complete that I find fulfillment in the action. As pleasure overtakes my being, I know that my soul is pure, and can feel and sense how religion (♪ and no religion too) *naturally* blossoms in me. **This is growing up. It is also how code Fulfillment spells out** *Shabbat.*

Indeed, you, reality, complete me! This Holy Instant of Union between the Son and his Bride (mind and soul) is the climax of the Created-SIX – when I rest while working. *Golden XPR* breaks open the seals of ancient prophecies by revealing a unifying equation in the Torah's first word (*Barashit* "created-SIX"). When realizing that consciousness uses words to create, a novel interpretation arises: it is not the **world** that was created in six days; it is the **word**! Using the universal properties of elementals, I can now recognize patterns behind the disorder of any concept. Called the seed of life and/or the Genesis pattern, the geometry's design transmits the SIX progressive "days" or stages of creation. The end of mind is when the 6th circle is formed. For at that moment, the 7th circle that was here before time reappears.

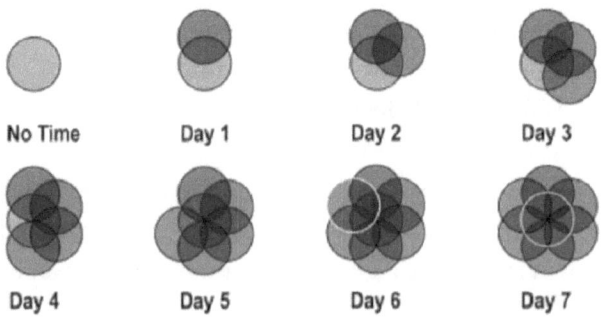

"And on the seventh day God completed the work that he had done, and he rested on the 7th day from all the work that he had done." *Genesis 2:2*

The possibility to simultaneously complete my work and rest from my work is made visible by the geometry of the Genesis Pattern, a.k.a. the Seed of Life. It shows once again that "God" is a geometer. The moment when the 6th day and 6th circle is formed makes it clear that, although there was no action involved, a new and 7th circle was created. The past tense "was" is accurate as circle 7 was here as circle 0 before any beginning (no time). The difference between 0 and 7 is as follows: the 7th circle includes and transcends the gem of life – the SIX "seeds" and vesica piscis that hold the stages of secondary creation (when I think I CAN'T).

Therefore, the miracle is not the complexity of the world that I have created, but the simplicity of the equation that describes its complexity.

The Angel of Necessity

> "If you bring forth what is within you, what you bring forth will save you. If you do not bring forth what is within you, what you do not bring forth will destroy you." *Gospel of Thomas*

This way of creating – when there is no more doer (or chilD to make it about me) – is what non-causality is. Being innocent, I am neither boastful nor remorseful, and no longer suffer from any superiority or inferiority complexes. I just see that the angel of necessity directed the show. What happened was needed for me to bring forth what is within me, including the reluctance to do so. **I needed to fall and fail a thousand times, and, if it's not enough, a million times until I'd be sufficiently humbled to know that neither failure nor success concern me: nothing's personal!**

When I have nothing left to prove, I'm no longer destructive. I do not kill my potential anymore. I get out of the way, let the energy speak through me (Shabbat), and end up succeeding in my creation. This birthing process goes way beyond mastering a skill or having a potent message. To be at once so selfless and mature that I can "bring forth what is within me," I must turn towards my madness and abandon myself entirely to it. The demon will lead me to the angel. This is true compassion (or being "with my pain"). It is the only way to stop using my destructiveness against myself and others. This is when I know evil so much that I change for good.

As I begin to feel the Providence of "in God, we trust," my communication also begins granting harmonious results. Moreover, I no longer NEED to be led into temptation. My deadly sins have fulfilled their purpose, leading me to face the fear of my mortality. I am now ready for the truth I always knew but didn't want to know. I step out of my comfort zone, take off the masks, and touch into the Eternal. Since I have officially "died for my sins," there is nothing to prevent me from freely expressing my soul.

Therefore, for me to return to being the divine child and archetype of perfection, I NEED to lose track of having ever been *Adam Qadmon* (the zero point of "Primary" Adam), and only be aware of *Adam HaRishon* (the "First" Adam). I can now play the part of the naughty child, acting out and believing that I am unwanted, imperfect, flawed, damaged goods, not enough. It is the necessary impulse that will eventually lead me to do what it takes to know it *is* all "PAIRfect."

I understand that the reality ("God") I am experiencing right now is absolutely "PAIRfect" → I choose to Rest in Peace → I emPower the NOW.

Genesis 2:4 - A Pivotal Moment (Review)

> *"When you realize there is nothing lacking, the whole world belongs to you."* **Lao Tzu**

When a captive of Scare City, I am not tuned into the frequency of abundance. I haven't subscribed to that channel. Instead of feeling that I have it all, I look at my reality and feel gypped. What happened? One moment, in *Genesis 1*, I believe, I was created male and female, and had dominion over just about everything. The next moment, in *Genesis 2*, I dream that I am in a garden that desperately needs tending.

There's no shrub, no herb, and no rain. Moreover, not only am I all alone, but also I have to deal with a "God" giving me all sorts of limitations. Just one of those days where I might as well have stayed in bed. So, what happened? The fourth verse of *Genesis 2* did!

> "These are the generations of the heaven and of the earth <u>when they were created</u>, in the day that the LORD God made earth and heaven." *Genesis 2:4*

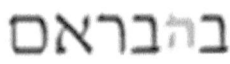 Pronounced *Behibaram,* the word pictured here means "<u>when they were created</u>." Its 2nd letter – the sign Heh (ה) – is shown as it is written on the Torah scroll: shrunk. The shrinking of a sign that means "window, breath or womb" can only be an omen of doom. It is sending both the mother (אם) and the son (בר) into exile and opening the captivating book of Scare City, overflowing with a myriad of fantastic stories of inadequacy. Reading from that book, I doubt that I'll get my results – be it the girl or the entry into the Promised Land.

The downgrade definitely occurred when I imagined that the LOVE God made *earth and heaven.* What an interesting creation! *Genesis 1* saw the generations of *the heaven and the earth*, and kaboom, everything's upside down in *Genesis 2* with a LORD "God" that flipped poles on me!

All the while, I forget that "God" is my creation. So is money. So is the heaven and the earth. The question is now meatier: why choose to observe hellish lack when I could partake of heavenly abundance? Why would I deliberately choose to be in bondage to materialism?

Genesis 2:4-25 – *Adam HaRishon*

"Show me a hero, and I'll write you a tragedy." *F. Scott Fitzgerald*

To choose bondage (and it is a choice since, whether I know it or not, I exist in a state of absolute freedom), I must desire to be secondary and think "I CAN'T." In this manner, I never have to be responsible for my failure to divinely create. I would rather give my Power to "you," be *you* money, the world, a parent, a "God" that deals in rewards and punishments... To do so, I must also go against my Nature which is to be free, and deny that we are all connected to the One Mind and, consequently, all have the same entry into creative Power. Yet, I am so afraid of doing it wrong that I limit the flow of my abundance and even cut myself off from it. *Genesis 2* shows me how I dry the well of my inspiration.

Having partaken of the decoding of *Genesis 1* as the "primary" mind of the *Adam Qadmon*, I now have a clearer understanding of how "Created-SIX" is at once the S-Secret and the P-Practicality of the PRDS transmission. Among other "Created-SIX" patterns, TCO uses BEE maps as the organization of <u>fractals</u> that unfold the SIX "days" and, in this case, the SIX stages of any given creation.

Just like I used the two interactive fractals of primariness and creativity in view to "receive" the *QKabbalah* of *Genesis 1*, I will now use the two interactive fractals of secondariness and comparison in view to "receive" the *QKabbalah* of *Genesis 2*. If *Adam Qadmon* of Genesis 1 and *Adam Harishon* of Genesis 2 are the antithesis of each other as primariness and secondariness, so are creativity and comparison. They oppose each other. Surely, as soon as I compare my artwork to that of another artist, my creativity is gone!

The code is written as follows: **Stage # – SECONDARY → Comparison**, e.g.; **Stage 1 – NO RECEPTION → the Stigma of Envy**. I am also given the verses from which these understandings are derived. I am now fully equipped to go into R-Reflection and feel how this Biblical story is my story, in the vision that doing so will make a D-Difference in my finding and staying in PaRaDiSe.

Stage 1 – NO RECEPTION → the Stigma of Envy: this is the entrance into Scare City signaled by the shrunk Heh in *Behibaram* for "when they were created" in *Genesis 2:4*. Without Heh, there is no womb of compassion and no possibility to be "pregnant" (no success in my creation). Disconnected from *Atziluth,* the world of "transmission," I have no individual Power. How then would I not envy you? The concerned Torah portion (*Genesis 2:4*) is in the prior section.

Stage 2 – NO ABUNDANCE → Downward/Upward: the "God" Name YEWE *Elohim* newly appears, impeding Nature's **abundant** ways: there's no rain and no one to till the ground. Moreover, the earth must now supply the waters of heaven. This inversion (when water goes up, and not down) speaks of comparing myself **up** (when I am superior to you) or **down** (when I see myself as inferior to you). Here is the Torah portion: "no shrub had yet appeared on the earth and no plant had sprung up, for the LORD God had not sent rain on the earth and there was no one to work the ground. But streams came up from the earth and watered the whole surface of the ground." *Genesis 2:5-6.*

Stage 3 – NO GOODNESS → Insatiability: the reversal continues as I am "formed" from dust. I am now in *Yetzirah*, the world of "formation," unaware of *Beriah,* the world of "<u>creation</u>." Since my mind is no longer balanced as I ignore it is "<u>created</u> male and female," how could I make sound judgments or be cognizant of my own **goodness**? No wonder I'd be **insatiable**: I can never have or be enough! Here is the Torah portion: "Then the LORD God formed a man from the dust of the ground and breathed into his nostrils the breath of life, and the man became a living being." *Genesis 2:7.*

The Worlds in Which I Move, Consciously or Not...

Stage 4 – NO NATURE → Measurement: I lose sight of my **Nature** and of a geometry that is literally a "**measure of the earth**," imbued with the sense of enough. I do not even know what Eden is, as the decoding is yet to come. As for the garden, it is the **figure DE** below – a shape which can accommodate two trees in its midst. Here is the Torah portion: "The LORD God had planted a garden in the east, in Eden; and there he put the Adam he had formed. The LORD God made all kinds of trees grow out of the ground—trees that were pleasing to the eye and good for food. In the middle of the garden were the tree of life and the tree of the knowledge of good and evil." *Genesis 2:8-9*

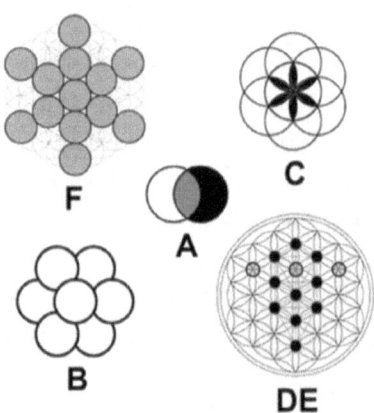

To connect the five rivers (or five energy flows) to the geometry of five mental patterns, I just need to know the meaning of their names. Here is the Torah portion: "A river that waters the garden flowed from Eden. It then separates into four heads. The name of the first river is the Pishon; it winds through the entire land of Havilah. The gold of that land is good; aromatic resin and onyx are also there. The name of the second river is the Gihon; it winds through the entire land of Cush (the "black" gem at the core). The name of the third river is the Tigris; it runs along the east side of Ashur. And the fourth river is the Euphrates." *Genesis 2:10-14*

Figure A is the garden as the source code which holds all codes of opposites, and which separates into four heads or rivers (B, C, DE, F).

- **Figure B** of the egg of life is the first river named *Pishon* for "increase," as the number of available eggs for optimal fertility. It winds down through the entire land of *Havilah*, as the "circle" of deaths and rebirths symbolized by the egg.
- **Figure C** of the seed of life is the second river named *Gihon* for "bursting forth" as a seed does. It winds down through the entire land of *Cush* which is the "black" gem at the core.
- **Figure DE** of the tree of life and of knowledge is the third river named the *Tigris* for "rapid" as is the lightning flash that moves from the crown chakra to the root chakra. It runs speedily along the east side of *Ashur* for "successful."
- **Figure F** of the fruit of life is the fourth river named the *Euphrates* for "fruitfulness."

	The Code of Opposites	
Yod (י)	Vav (ו) / Heh (ה)	Heh (ה)
The Tree of Life	The Seed's Core / The Gem	The Egg of Life
Transmission	Creation / Manifestation	Formation

The Geometries of Opposites

Stage 5 – NO AUTONOMY → Bitterness: first the Power of History puts the Adam (me) to work. However, I have **no autonomy** as I am micromanaged and setup by way of negative commands and "no good" judgments. How would I not be **bitter** when my freedom is impinged upon in so many ways? Here is the Torah portion: 'The LORD God took the Adam and put him in the Garden of Eden to work it and take care of it. And the LORD God commanded the Adam, "You are free to eat from any tree in the garden; but you must not eat from the tree of the knowledge of good and evil, for when you eat from it you will certainly die. The LORD God said, "It is not good for the man to be alone. I will make a helper suitable for him."' ***Genesis 2:15-18***

THE SIXth Stage – NO CONGRUENCE → Hankering: while I am able to use my words to call any number of creatures, I am not **congruent** enough to name my significant other. I seem to be tongue-tied, a reality I create by longing and **hankering** for the other, which makes any relationship... complicated. Here is the Torah portion: "Now the Lord God had formed out of the ground all the wild animals and all the birds in the sky. He brought them to the man to see what he would name them; and whatever the Adam called each living creature, that was its name. So, the Adam gave names to all the livestock, the birds in the sky and all the wild animals. But for Adam no suitable helper was found." *Genesis 2:19-21*

The Seventh Day – NO CREATIVITY → Comparison: unable to cope, this is when I go to sleep. I have no self-consciousness, yes, but also no consciousness of being the source of my **creations**! This is when I end up **comparing** myself. Comparison shows up in the word *Arum*, which is translated in the final verse of Chapter 2 as "naked" and the first verse of Chapter 3 as "clever."

Why such great disparity in meaning for the same construct? The snake is the one who brings a comparative measure by being not only "clever," but "cleverer" or smarter than any other beast of the field. This is to say that the snake is even more subtle than the Leviathan (the great beast of the sea) which has no qualms about taking me down with it/her/him into the abysmal nadir. **This snake is, of course, my ego. It is the force of the unconscious that moves me out of pure awareness into self-consciousness (when I compare myself to others).** It is also a Higher Power transporting me out of the bliss of ignorance in which I was for me to wake up to being eternal – **beyond time.**

The Seed of Time

"If you can look into the seeds of time, and say which grain will grow and which will not, speak then unto me." *William Shakespeare*

And the SIXth "day" came when the formation of the SIXth circle adds the two missing black seeds for the Gem of Life to appear...

I have seen how God is a geometer, since enlightenment and/or the possibility to simultaneously complete my work and rest from my work is made visible by the geometry of the Seed of Life, a.k.a. the Genesis Pattern. The "day" when the SIXth circle is formed makes it clear that, although there was no action involved, a 7th circle was created.

Yes, circle 7 used to be circle 0. It lived before any beginning – in no time! This matters since, until I wake up from the perception of forced labor, I will be "doing time." Like it or not, my prison sentence is written in the Gem of Life which I see as a seed of time. Indeed, who knows which seed will live and which will die?

The 7th circle is the result of the SIX circles, stages and "days" that occurred prior to it – in time. The end of mind is made possible *after* the 6th circle is formed. For at that moment, the 7th circle that was here before any creation reappears for me to rest while working. This means that, no matter what happens, I see the goodness of the plan and sense the presence of the angel of necessity behind what I would normally judge as "bad."

Above / Gem	1	2	3	4	5	6
Belove / Seed	1	6	5	4	3	2

Above / Gem is *Adam Harishon's* creation of unconscious time;
Belove / Seed is *Adam Qadmon's* creation of purposive time.

The Gem of Life shows me that, unless I dive into the darkest of the seed to fully understand my shadow side, I will not know the center of my integrity and will prevent myself from resting in peace. And if I don't know peace, I will think "I CAN'T," and be unable to fully unleash my creative Power.

This is when my male side will withdraw and my female side become "clingy." However, when I embrace my evil inclination, "I become one flesh." In other words, "the left-brain side clings to the right-brain side," as there is no ego left to separate me from the change I wish to see manifest. Indeed, there is no shame in me to convince me that I am not enough to follow my heart.

Here is the Torah portion: "the Lord God caused the Adam to fall into a deep sleep; and while he was sleeping, he took one of the man's ribs and closed up the place with flesh. Then the Lord God made a woman from the rib he had taken out of the Adam, and he brought her to the Adam. The Adam said, 'This is now bone of my bones and flesh of my flesh; she shall be called woman, for she was taken out of man.' That is why a man leaves his father and mother and clings to his wife, and they become one flesh. Adam and his wife were both naked, and they felt no shame." *Genesis 2:22-25.*

On that note, it might be a good idea to review code "HELLusion" of Separation (see *TCO—Book 1*) that unfolds at length what this rib business is, and how "the woman" does not come out of "man." Being on purpose with my male and female sides balanced is emPowering the NOW. It comes naturally when I can choose peace. When I can't, there is something I do not understand, e.g.; why did we have to have that big fight? In continuing with this example, when the purpose of the fight is revealed to me, I have an easier time surrendering as I see it was a "necessary evil."

This involves meeting the demons that run the show I call "fate" and thus making the unconscious conscious. However, if I were to do the contrary and ate from the tree of the *ignorance* of good and evil, I would cause the progressive fall of the mouth chakra (0) into the chakras below it (1, 2, 3).

When my mouth is fallen, I tend to judge myself for either speaking too much or not enough, eating too much or not enough, or kissing too much or not enough. Having lost all sense of measure and can't get it "write."

The Fall of the Mouth Chakra

"Listen! Clam up your mouth and be silent like an oyster shell, for that tongue of yours is the enemy of the soul, my friend. When the lips are silent, the heart has a hundred tongues." *Rumi*

I have seen how my fears cause the mouth's gradual fall, first into the heart chakra, second into the sex chakra and third, into the root chakra, prompting a few self-serving questions on the way down:

- The fall into a heart chakra (1) that is now closed by **greed**, and asking: will I get them before they get me?
- The fall into a sex chakra (2) that is now defiled by **lust**, and asking: can I mate with that person?
- The fall into a root chakra (3) that is now defiled by **gluttony**, and asking: can I eat it? Will it eat me?

What I had not seen was how the pollution that can only affect the remaining chakras is such that the war of the sexes is amplified. How could it not when the male and female sides of the tree are deprived of "sexual knowledge" (no *Daath*), and thus estranged from each other?

- The female side of the throat chakra (4) that is now closed by **wrath** fights for her pound of flesh.
- The male side of the throat chakra (5) that is now closed by **pride** fights for a respect he won't give.
- The female side of the navel chakra (6) that is now closed by **envy** fights for what is not hers to have.
- The male side of the navel chakra (7) that is now closed by **sloth** fights for his debasement.

No wonder I would "do time," as I am sentenced to arrive in the hell of the seven infernal spheres, hellish and "infernal" as they are separated from the knowledge of the three "supernal" spheres (see the three transparent circles in "The Fall of the Mouth Chakra" image). This inferno is what Dante termed the "Purgatorio," where I am escorted by an angel singing *In exitu Israel de Aegypto* ("Israel exiting Egypt"). It alludes both to the redemption of Christ and to the soul's conversion from the misery of sin to the state of grace. In each of the seven terraces, the penitents (that is, me, myself and I) do something to purify themselves of their vice:

- On the terrace of **wrath**, viewed as "love of justice perverted to revenge and spite," I experience hallucinations of meekness soon changing to hallucinations of wrath.
- On the terrace of **pride**, viewed as "self-love perverted to hatred and contempt for my neighbor," I am forced to walk with my head bowed while being whipped.
- On the terrace of **greed**, viewed as "excessive love of money and power," I am lying face-down on the hard rock floor, peeking onto the other side.
- On the terrace of **envy**, viewed as the "love of my own good perverted to a desire to deprive other men of theirs," I walk around with my eyes sewn shut by an iron wire.
- On the terrace of **sloth**, viewed as being the "failure to love God with all my heart, all my soul, and all my might," I run without being allowed to rest.
- On the terrace of **lust**, viewed as an "excessive love of others and thereby detracting from the love due God," I am shown walking within a raging fire.
- On the terrace of **gluttony**, viewed as "excessive love of pleasure," I am starved, forced to stand beneath two trees and unable to make use of the food hanging there.

How could something luminous like a "gem" be so dark? It is because greater is the light that comes out of the darkness. To transcend duality, I must learn to hold the tension. As the poison of ignorance is transmuted into the knowledge of opposites, the poison of GReed turns to GRace (I sin no more). Finally, the poison of aversion is detoxified and the curse of enmity is undone (I lie no more).

Just like it took a pivotal moment for the mouth to fall, it will take it a pivotal moment for the mouth to rise again and for the "Heh" womb of enough to be restored in me. Meanwhile, I will have to deal with doubts and thoughts of inadequacy,

Being Secondary, Thinking I CAN'T!

Prepare to DIE! Inquiry tool: www.goldenxpr.com/tco3_resistance/.

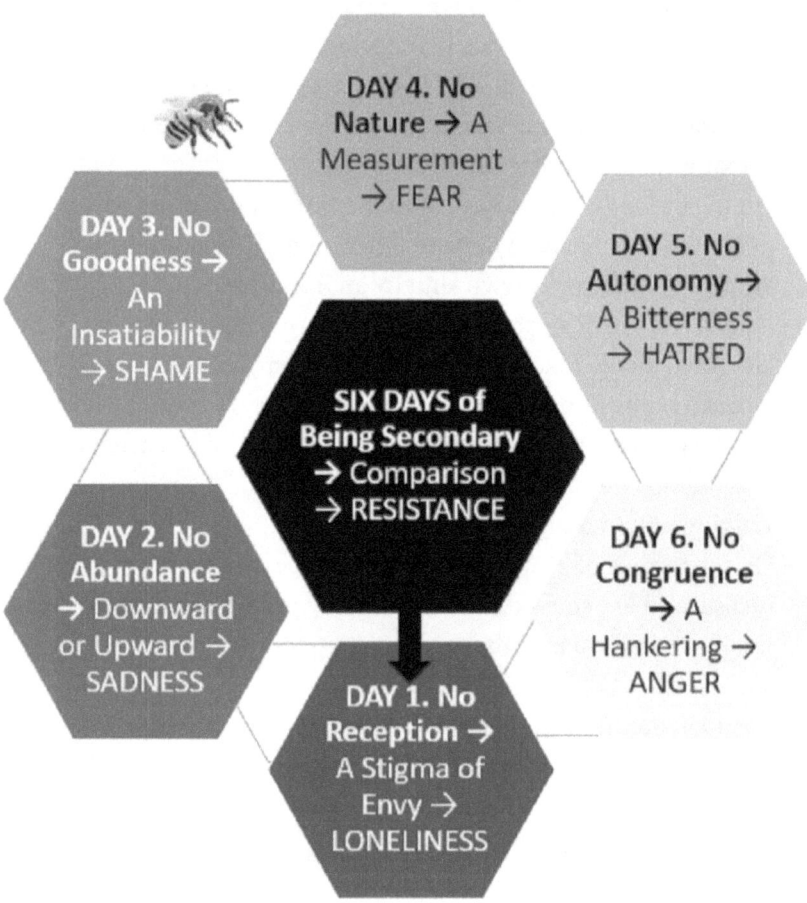

Step 1: I fill in the blank: I want to know WHY I would choose to think I CAN'T _____ (e.g.; find a job, be patient, etc.). **Step 2:** I ask for truth and generate a number. **Step 3:** I find my number on the map to fill in the brackets: when having [**Secondary**], I start comparing myself, seeing [**Comparison**], which causes my [**RESISTANCE**]. **Step 4:** what most surprised me in this process was [_____].

Part III: The Psychological Decoding of Genesis 3

- Fish Page
- Compounding
- Genesis 3:1-22 – the Woman & the Snake
- Genesis 3:22-24 – the Challenge
- The Hunger for the Leader of LOVE
- The East of Eden
- Code Perfect Bliss – OD/N | O/DN
- Being Tertiary, Thinking I Don't Want To!
- Fish Page

The Snake	The Adam / The Adamah	The Woman
chilD	prostitutE / victiM	saboteuR
Enmity	Forced Labor / Thorns' Diet	Envious Childbirths

Genesis 3 and the Four Curses

Being Tertiary in Genesis 3

BEING TERTIARY IMPACTS THE RESTORING OF MY CREATIVE INSTINCT. TO FEEL IT, I CAN GO TO THE UNIVERSAL LANGUAGE OF COLORS (PIGMENTS AND NOT LIGHT). INDEED, THE PIGMENTS' PROGRESSION BEST TRANSLATES THE EVOLUTIONARY STAGES OF THE TREE OF LIFE.

The Hermetic Order of the Golden Dawn suggests a system of colors for the worlds of the tree of life. In this system, the supernal Sephiroth radiate percentages of values: *Kether* is white, *Chokmah*, gray, and *Binah*, black. The pigmented colors become visible in the infernal Sephiroth. In the world of creation, I see the primary colors – red, yellow and blue. In the world of formation, I see the secondary colors – green, purple and orange.

Incarnation may be the greatest test. Indeed, I must "fall" into the world of manifestation, in the QKingdom, to see the tertiary colors as the result of mixing the primary colors with the secondary colors. This is how the QKingdom is my last palette, whose tertiary colors happen to be "Created-SIX:" blue-green, blue-violet, red-orange, red-violet, yellow-orange, and yellow-green

Yod (י)	Vav (ו) / Heh (ה)	Heh (ה)
Atziluth	*Beriah / Assiyah*	*Yetzirah*
Transmission	Creation / Manifestation	Formation
Values	Primary / Tertiary Colors	Secondary Colors

From Values to Hues and Back

COMPOUNDING

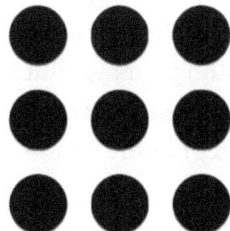

COMPOUNDING: tertiary colors are also called intermediate colors, due to their compound nature that combines primary and secondary colors. As such, they are best to identify a double problem which also tends to compound...

It is Pablo Picasso who wisely said: "every child is an artist. The problem is how to remain an artist once we grow up." As for the compounding effect, since every artist is a child, the problem is how to grow up into a servant leader while remaining an artist. This would be no less than combining heart and soul, which is what an "heARTist" is called to do.

I begin in doing all I can not to compromise my vision, regardless of how much fear of the material world I may live in. In other words, I listen to the voice of my conscience. In fact, hearing is not only to listen to the voice, but to follow the voice and be the voice. Finally and terminally it is no longer about me! When that happens, I can only be successful in my creation.

This is when I grow up and wake up into an innocence that is childlike – and not childish. It is the innocence of a life so fully investigated that it transcends doubt and fear. It has a quality of profound acceptance of the ever-changing and wondrous grace and elegance of life. Such sentience is the compounding interest. But first, I must inquire on my motives in choosing to hear the snake's voice rather than this of my heart. Indeed, why would I muddy up the colors of my QKingdom?

Genesis 3:1-22 – the Woman & the Snake

"If you hear a voice within you say 'you cannot paint,' then by all means paint, and that voice will be silenced." **Vincent van Gogh**

The instrument of voice comes out of ether. As such, it can sound as if it has an echo. When *Bat Qol* – the "Daughter of the Voice," I am also *Bat Tephillah* – the "Daughter of Prayer." My devotion is such that I can feel in my blood that my prayer is already fulfilled. I think I can have it, and therefore, I have it. There is another voice, which opposes the first – the snake's seductive voice calling me to temptation. Admittedly, it is the pain of letting myself be deceived again and again that prepares me for truth. Indeed, an honest woman (or man) cannot be conned! Therefore, there is, once again, a purpose to evil: to ready me to hear/SEE truth. This is epitomized in the story of the Fall, narrated by *Genesis 3*, when the snake comes into the picture.

Speaking of which, a talking snake is a notable curiosity! I see this event as a potential confirmation that I am dreaming. On that note, the transition between Adam 1 and Adam 2 also reminds me of the dream world: one moment I am Adam 1, having it all; the next, I am Adam 2, in a less than perfect garden, having to contend with a "God" who issues negative commands and is out to judge me. To top it all, I find myself unable to name what I need, especially when it comes to an adequate partner. Moving from state to state, I'm even put into a deep sleep, so that a rib could be surgically removed and then fashioned into a woman. And this all begs the question: when I woke up and saw that "God" had brought me a woman, was I actually in the waking state or dreaming to be awake?

The story moves on to *Genesis 3*, when I am now the woman, meeting a talking snake. And it makes me wonder... Since I do not find that bizarre at all, I must either be a snake whisperer or be faced with a particularly smart animal. As a matter of fact, the snake is introduced as being the most subtle of all animals, clever enough to distort the truth. Also marvelous is that the woman in me can hear it! Yes, I may still be dreaming. And the dream world speaks in symbols for those who can read them. The woman is the female side of my brain. It is where divergent thinking occurs, that is, where snake comes in to talk me into breaking the rules. This is why the snake didn't speak to the Adam, as the male side of the brain wouldn't be able to hear its voice or to relate to creative thinking. Or might it be destructive thinking? Surely, snake is here.to lead me to do no harm by teaching me that destruction can be done in two ways: wholesome and unwholesome.

The Adam	The Snake / the Messiah	The Woman
The Father	The Son / the Mother	The Daughter
Brahma	Vishnu	Shiva
Creation	Preservation	Destruction

Besides, it is only natural: the pendulum must swing from creation to destruction, from male to female, and back. For me to center in preservation (when I experience that creation and destruction are free of private agendas), the snake must turn into a Messiah.

To "receive" the *QKabbalah* of *Genesis 3*, I will use the three interactive fractals of the invisible forces, the DREaM archetypes and the Fall. The code is written as follows: **Day # – Invisible Force → The DREaM** archetype → THE FALL, e.g.; Day 1 – the Unconscious → the Fallen angel → 'THE SEDUCTION. I am also given the verses from which these understandings are derived, and now fully equipped to go into R-Reflection and feel how this Biblical story is my story, in the vision that doing so will make a D-Difference in my finding and staying in PaRaDiSe.

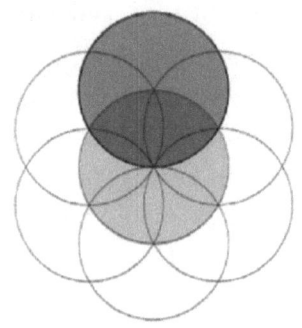

1. THE SEDUCTION

Day 1 – the Unconscious → the Fallen angel → THE SEDUCTION: I shall start with the idea that Adam is dreaming (unconscious). I am the Adam. Thus, what I see out there (be it a snake, a woman, a tree) is only a projection of what I deny and repress in me. For me to fall as the result of trying to seduce you by way of cleverness, I must ignore that I am moved by an agenda of revenge. And why wouldn't I want to make "God" pay when I feel coerced by "His" laws? This is how the snake in me will shift the truth slightly and talk my female side into unwholesome destruction. Here is the Torah portion: 'Now the snake was cleverer than any other beast of the field that the LORD God had made. He said to the woman, "Did God actually say, 'You shall not eat of any tree in the garden?'" And the woman said to the snake, "We may eat of the fruit of the trees in the garden, but God said not to eat of the fruit of the tree that is in the midst of the garden, neither shall you touch it, lest you die." But the snake said to the woman, "Surely you will not die. For God knows that when you eat of it your eyes will be opened, and you will be like God, knowing good and evil."' *Genesis 3:1-5*

Day 2 – Control → the prostitutE → THE EVIL EYE: perception follows motivation. When hungry, I see food. What do I really want and why? On that note, I find the desire of my female side – what she sees when looking at the tree of opposites – most intriguing. She sees the practicality of nourishment, aesthetics, but also and foremost, to be made wise! Why would I wish for wisdom unless I was feeling some level of folly? After all, she was talking to a snake! I am she. A moment ago, I was naked and had no shame. I had zero self-consciousness. However, when I accept that I am in an illusion of separation, it makes sense that I would start thinking in terms of survival, and desire the kind of wisdom (the smarts) that puts me in control. The evil eye has just opened, which is also how I would compromise my integrity: I no longer know the difference between good and evil! Here is the Torah portion: 'So when the woman saw that the tree was good for food, and that it was a delight to the eyes, and that the tree was to be desired to make one wise, she took of its fruit and ate, and she also gave some to her man who was with her, and he ate. The eyes of both were opened, and they knew that they were naked. And they sewed fig leaves together and made themselves loincloths." *Genesis 3:6-7*

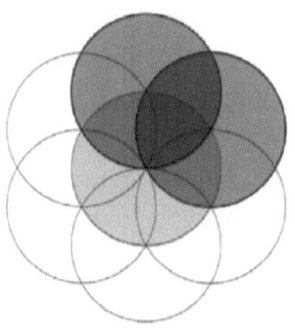

2. THE EVIL EYE

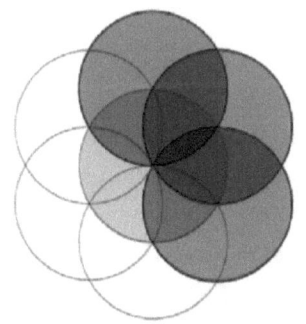

3. THE COVER-UP

Day 3 – Severity → the saboteuR → **THE COVER-UP**: me, severe? I get angry when a well-meaning friend tells me: "don't be so hard on yourself!" Well, if I could, I would. It is clear that there is an unhealthy interaction between severity and self-sabotage: I beat myself up after I sabotage myself. I sabotage myself in order to beat myself up. Is it crazy? Yes! When wisdom descends to shift my folly, kindness will ascend and I'll stop torturing me! For now, I'm hiding from my conscience. I know what to do, I just don't want to do it. That's the cover up! My mind is split which is how I listen to the wrong voice. I'm also covering up as I am afraid, waiting for the other shoe to drop. Here is the Torah portion: 'And they heard the sound of the Lord God walking in the garden in the cool of the day, and the man and his wife hid themselves from the presence of the Lord God in between the trees of the garden. But the Lord God called to the Adam and said to him, "Where are you?" And he said, "I heard the sound of you in the garden, and I was afraid, because I was naked, and I hid myself." He said, "who told you that you were naked? Have you eaten of the tree of which I commanded you not to eat?"' *Genesis 3:8-11*

Day 4 – Possession → the victiM → THE DISOWNING: surely, I come to this world in a pure mind, fully multi-modal and connected with all life. Yet soon enough, I lose my freedom over personal beliefs which will eventually possess me. Here is how: I begin a game, e.g.; the game of liking potatoes versus tomatoes. At first, I'm moved by curiosity: what would it be like to only like potatoes? However, I'll eventually

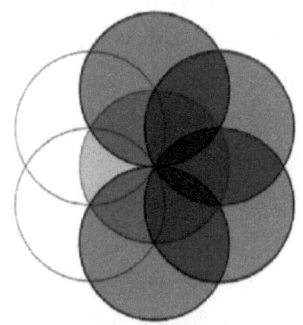

4. THE DISOWNING

forget that I was playing, and will really believe that I dislike tomatoes. As the beliefs aggregate to form the mass of a full-fledged identity, they impede my motion. Should that not be enough, I get to really enrage "the Beast" I begot by disowning it. "This is not my creation!" Up to that fateful moment, I could always reverse the program since I was its creator. But now, via an act of foolish ignorance, I've just transferred the power to the beast and made myself its slave. From thereon, even though I might desire to eat a tomato for a change, the chips are down (pun intended), and I'm stuck in the narrow-minded land of a potato eater, getting hungrier by the minute! Back to my biblical predicament, if only I had had the guts to say: "I did it, God, and I am truly sorry," I'd still be in PaRaDiSe. Yes, I may have had to do a bit of clean-up and vow to change, but I'd be a victor; not a victim. Here is the Torah portion: 'The Adam said, "The woman whom you gave to be with me, she gave me fruit of the tree, and I ate." Then the Lord God said to the woman, "What is this that you have done?" The woman said, "The snake deceived me, and I ate."' *Genesis 3:12-13*

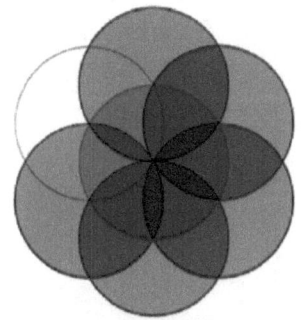

5. THE CURSE

Day 5 – Indulgence → the chilD → THE CURSE: three people violated the law (the snake, the woman and the Adam), and curiously, four "people" got cursed (the same three, plus *HaAdamah* "the ground"). While the four curses are given sequentially, in the order of the violations, the collapse of one part affects the other parts, having them fall like dominos. First, what the snake puts in motion – A chilD's prank, really – starts the war of the sexes. I now see "you" as my enemy and resist doing good by you, either overtly or covertly. The result is immediate: my female side now suffers from the womb, especially as her desire for a supportive male side is not satisfied. The unending cravings start. As for my Adam's mind, it is stuck in Scare City and resenting having to work hard for his money. Moreover, he deals with an *Adamah* or a "ground" that is prickly and not cooperative. Both swing from severity to indulgence (and back). Here is the Torah portion: 'the Lord God said to the snake, "Because of what you have done, cursed are you above the Behemah and above all beasts of the field; on your belly you shall go, and dust you shall eat all the days of your life. I will put enmity between you and the woman, and between your seed and her seed; they shall bruise your head, and you shall bruise their heel."

The Snake	The Adam / The Adamah	The Woman
chilD	prostitutE / victiM	saboteuR
Enmity	Forced Labor / Thorns' Diet	Envious Childbirths

To the woman he said, "I will surely multiply your pain in childbearing; in pain you shall bring forth children. Your desire shall be for your man, but he shall rule over you." And to Adam he said, "Because you listened to the voice of your wife and have eaten of the tree of which I commanded you, 'You shall not eat of it,' cursed is the *Adamah* ground because of you; in pain you shall eat of it all the days of your life; thorns and thistles it shall bring forth for you; and you shall eat the plants of the field. By the sweat of your face, you shall eat bread, till you return to the ground, for out of it you were taken, for you are dust, and to dust you shall return.'" *Genesis 3:14-19*

The SIXth Day - Destiny → the Rising angel → THE STIGMA: it is my destiny to make the unconscious conscious. This is why I'm here. Yes, I am an eternal Soul born into a mortal body. I can even think of myself as a program encrypted as a psychological DNA code with a series of predisposed characteristics. This is written as an agreement between me and the Soul, a.k.a. "God." It becomes effective

SIX. THE STIGMA

on my day of birth, and involves services provided for this lifetime. The Soul hereby agrees to take human birth into a specific body and personality, so as to go through a predetermined set of experiences which will involve suffering. While these experiences have already been written, I can choose to consciously use them as vehicles to die to who I think I am, and remember the Self. As for Eve and Adam, by choosing not to remember that they were programmed to do what they did, they could not transform their fate into destiny. They were now deep in the DREaM of separation, thinking they ended at the skin (literally). This clothing is the body of shame. It is stitched with the "I'm not enough" belief. And now that I am dressed in my own insufficiency, I repeat the same error while pretending to expect different results.

Here is the Torah portion: "The man called his wife's name Eve, because she was the mother of all living. And the Lord God made for Adam and for his wife garments of skins and clothed them." *Genesis 3:20-21*

There are two ways of falling: the first is divine – like falling in LOVE, gracefully, like a snowflake does. The second is "just human," and the one that hurts. Might I have forgotten that the way to rise high is to descend? If so, the 7th day of the Fall (the "day" that was here prior to any fall) is the day to remind me of the challenge.

Genesis 3:22-24 – the Challenge

"What if you do fail, and get fairly rolled in the dirt once or twice. Up again, you shall never be so afraid of a tumble." *Ralph Waldo Emerson*

0/7. THE CHALLENGE

Asking "why," "why not," or "what if" (as long as it is as an initiate and not a victim) compels me to evolve and open to new perspectives. Indeed, what if failure was the foundation of any true success? What if falling held the secret of rising? What if folly was the surest way to embodying wisdom?

There is a scriptural "what if" in what may be the most provocative verse of the Bible. It invites working in consciousness, as I stretch my limiting beliefs beyond the transcendental chakra (the mouth of the knowledge of good and evil) and open the 3rd eye of the tree of my life. However, this place is well-guarded. To reach it, I must want it above all (literally)!

Here is a most denied Torah portion, especially when read from a chilD's perspective as the chilD will refuse to show up to the invitation: 'Then the LORD God said, "Behold, now that the man has become like one of us in knowing good and evil, **what if he stretched out his hand and took from the tree of life and ate? He would live forever!**" Therefore, the LORD God sent him out from the garden of Eden to work the ground from which he was taken. He drove out the Adam, and at the east of the garden of Eden he placed the cherubim and a flaming sword that turned every way to guard the way to the tree of life.' **Genesis 3:22-24**

The "flaming sword that turns every way" is my mind that is massively weak-willed, taking one step forward and two steps backward, until I can make the firm decision to take full responsibility for my experience. After that, the flaming sword will still turn in every way, yet this time to block any possible doubt. The sword is made of metal and mental substances so as to ask me (the prostitutE in me) to pay a right of passage in the currency of purity.

When I do, the stretching out of my Yod "hand" and the growing of my chilD into a Leader becomes easy. The secret behind this transformation is visibly protected and even discouraged in order to reveal the strength of my commitment. I am also given a potent incentive: a stigma that leaves me no choice but to return to PaRaDiSe. The body of shame and the subsequent "HELLusion" of separation are so painful that I will eventually find the courage to do what it takes to find relief as I transcend the fear of being emPowered. When free of the collective and no longer betraying myself by way of tribal suicide, I will naturally rise into individual Power.

Yod (י)	Vav (ו) / Heh (ה)	Heh (ה)
Individual Power	Symbolic Power	Collective Power
chilD → Leader	prostitutE → E / victiM → O	saboteuR → Visionary

Stretching the Yod chilD into a Leader

The Hunger for the Leader of LOVE

"There is hunger for ordinary bread, and there is hunger for love, for kindness, for thoughtfulness, and this is the great poverty that makes people suffer so much.." *Mother Teresa*

As for now, I am a chilD, hungering for my mommy's and my daddy's love, approval and recognition, a parental role I project on "you" who will want to assume it for me. While I try to be good and please you, I soon start resenting feeling obligated to serve you. I don't like me when I put your needs in front of mine. And yet, it's still hard for me to set boundaries. This is when I start regressing, losing any ground I may have gained. So, now, I change my ways to be bad to the bone! It is unclear whether I want to be punished by you or to punish you.

Meanwhile, I miss the mark as I can't find approval or even disapproval out there: I am it! When sufficiently angry and depressed, I realize that the only way out of the mess I have myself created is the choice to rest in peace. And if I can't quite surrender and enter at will this state of enlightenment that could be called "Shabbat" and/or "PaRaDiSe," I can always inquire. Like a skilled detective, I start asking the "write" questions about motive, opportunity and evidence. Why would I be so obstinate in my refusal to take responsibility for myself? Growing up is the challenge, isn't it? But what is so frightening about it? The more I feel my chilD's fear of death, the better I understand myself. The more I understand myself, the less I have to revisit the scene of the crime.

Understand → Choose Peace → emPower the NOW.

The Snake as Lion King	The Adam-ah as Stellar Judge	The Woman as Dragon Queen
"I will"	"I know" / "I have"	"I desire"
Opportunity	Evidence	Motive

The Three Keys of Criminology

As I orient myself to the East, I pray to understand how the S/Hebrew word *Eden* may just be the cousin of Sanskrit *Ananda* – the "bliss" present in *Satchitananda* for "truth, consciousness, bliss." But before having such peak experience, I must earn my passage (the stretch of the chilD into a Leader of LOVE) by sojourning East of Eden. This may be where I could come into complete understanding, be at choice, rest and do no harm. And it makes me wonder... What's so special about the East; why not the West of Eden?

The East of Eden

> "And their dwelling was from Mesha, going toward Sephar, unto the mountain of the east." *Genesis 10:30* (note: *Sephar*, the name of the eastern mountain, is formed on the root-word XPR).

Steinbeck's East of Eden ends with the S/Hebrew word *Timshel* to give the hero the choice to conquer sin. *Timshel-Bo* is given in *Genesis 4:7* to Cain, to mean "[you] must rule over it," it being the desire to do harm. If I am Cain "possessed," how easy is it for me to rule over sin? I found that I will remain a slave to my addiction until I have suffered so much pain that I could decide that I am done. That is why I would go East of Eden: to claim the Power I've lost. The word *Qedem* must be for true "East," since *Mizrach* is the word for cardinal "East" – the direction that Jews face during prayer.

Formed on the root of *Qadmon* "primary," *Qedem* is like a factory reset. It reloads my operating system for me to know perfect bliss, as established in these different shadow occurrences:

1. Adam 2 found himself in a garden which was planted *MiQedem* "eastward."
2. The angels with flaming swords were placed *MiQedem* "eastward" of the Garden of Eden, to block the way to the higher spheres of the tree.
3. Cain went *Qedmat Eden*, East of Eden, after he murdered his brother.
4. The builders of the Tower of Babel journeyed *Qedem* "East."
5. Lot, Abraham's nephew, journeyed *MiQedem*, to the deprived city of Sodom.
6. Fleeing his family, Jacob traveled *Qedma* to the "East."

Code Perfect Bliss - OD/N | O/DN

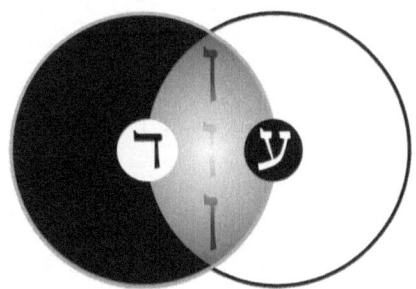

Imagine a language so pure and so sacred that it can reconcile opposites in just three letters...

Right: Hebrew letter Ayin (ע) → O in Roman script
Left: Hebrew letter Dalet (ד) → D in Roman script
Middle: Hebrew letter Nun final (ן) → N in Roman script

Here is how S/Hebrew inscribes code "Eden" in 4 words:

- OD: right to left, I read *Ed* (עד) for "witness."

- **OD N:** right to left to bottom, I read *Ed Nun* (עֵד ן) for "witness of the fall."
- **O DN:** right to left to bottom, I read *Ayin Dan* (ע דן) for "eye of the judge."
- **ODN:** right to left to bottom, I read *Eden* (עדן) "Eden."

The Decoding: I wish to start with a quick reminder of code Perspective, the code that sustains the *Shema* prayer of Oneness and foundation of the three Abrahamic religions. To "understand" that there's only One of us, I must "hear" (the meaning of *Shema*) that the ability to be a true **witness** comes from knowing that I don't know. I now have a wide enough perspective to make sound judgments. Henceforth, pair DO stands for "self-knowledge" and pair OD, for "witness."

When I add a Nun final to pair OD, I build the word *Eden* (עדן) for "**Eden.**" Nun is one of the five letters that takes on a different shape when at the end of a word, as in "Eden." These five signs are also messianic, as they usher a specific redemption – an end. Nun signals the end of indebtedness: forgiving my debts and my debtors definitely makes life simpler! Why would Nun final lead me to the end of indebtedness?

Because, as a word, Nun is the fish, and even the big fish Leviathan. Being able to master my emotions to where I can endure the "Leviathan test" (when the going gets tough and the tough gets going) is the ultimate forgiveness – the for-giving of my debts. This also means that I paid my dues. I am no longer into retaliation or holding on to what is owed to me: I don't need to make you pay.

Consider what the mind of Eden may be: I **witness my fall**, my failures and my self-indulgent follies without **judging**, as I am in truth, consciousness and bliss. I cultivate my garden, taking out the bad weeds and nurturing the growth of the fruit I am here to bear. If unable to love me unconditionally while at my weakest, I can also use the **eye of the judge**. This judge is blind-folded, so s/he could see with the heart the truth that is invisible to the eyes.

Either way, I must go **as far as my judgments** take me, no matter how seemingly bottomless is the pit in which I must fall. As long as I am growing a garden of truth and consciousness, the result can only be "perfect bliss."

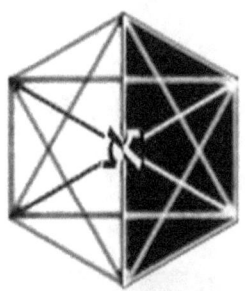

Being Tertiary, Thinking I Don't Want To!

Prepare to DIE! Inquiry tool: www.goldenxpr.com/tco3_invisible/.

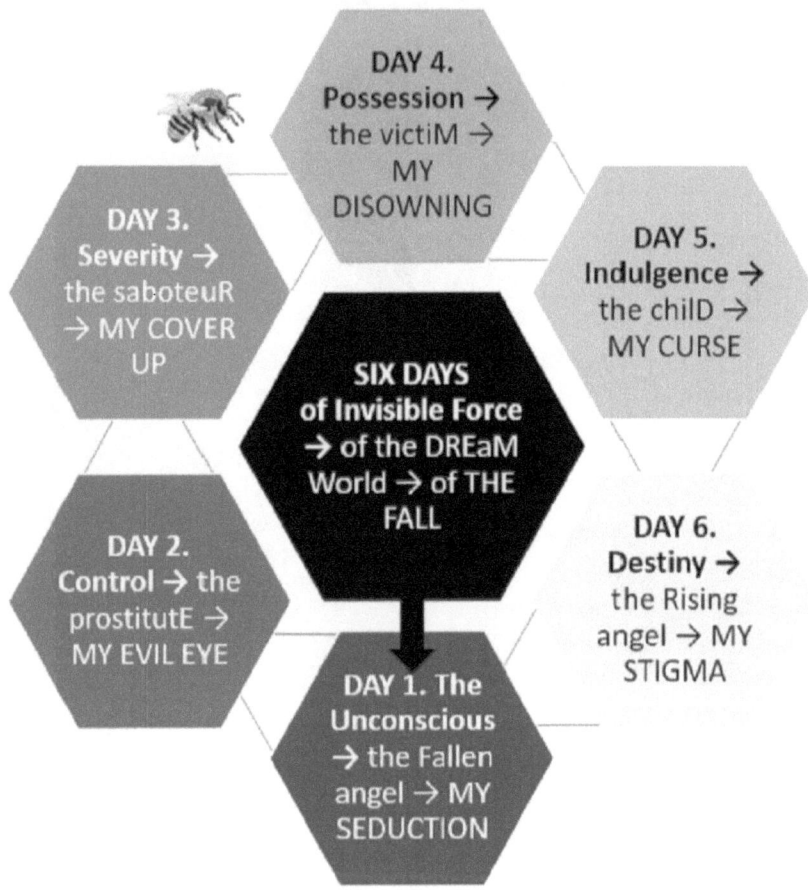

Step 1: I fill in the blank: I want to know WHY I would choose to think I CAN'T [_____] (e.g.; be patient). **Step 2:** I ask for truth and generate a number. **Step 3:** I find my number and fill in the brackets: when compelled by the force of [**Invisible Force**], I identify to [**DREaM**], leading me to acting out [**THE FALL**] patterns. **Step 4:** what most surprised was [_____].

It is the insecure chilD in me that boasts about the blessings I have received. Truth be told, to keep the chilD either boasting or self-berating, there may still be a victiM thinking that I didn't deserve the adversity that came to me: I can't stomach it or receive it! As a result, I'm fighting with "God" and/or reality.

But what if I could know that my first real "act" as a Leader is to surrender? Indeed, I am not a Leader unless I can deal with a crisis. And to best deal with what shows up, I must start by surrendering. Henceforth, I have understanding and kindness, and also wisdom and courage. I am 100% present. Every desire, every willful speech act, every decision is centered in LOVE. Henceforth, there would be no more push/pull, doubt or yearning. At last, I would feel that my heart is unhurt, and my mind, beautiful.

To resonate with such harmony, the cup of my heart must be broken. Completely. Ultimately. Only when I am not, can the wholeness of LOVE begin pouring into me, from every realm, from every direction. Only when I am not, can I know the sense of surrendered leadership.

To this end, I must still escort my rising angel until its resurrection is done. Which brings me to the final chapter – when I transcend my fear of Power.

SIX

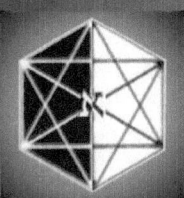

Rising Beyond the Fear of Power

"If you want to build a ship, don't drum up people to collect wood and don't assign them tasks and work, but rather teach them to long for the endless immensity of the sea." Antoine de Saint-Exupéry

TCO's MISSION is to heal my relationship to Power until I come to no yearning. Surely, if I came to the end of desire, I would know who I am and wouldn't need to resort to misusing Power to secure my sense of worth. It is thus when I long for naught that I am in my Power. Meanwhile, might my allegiance to Mammon's physical world deny the reality of a transcendental world where matter is energy?

Indeed, why can't I connect to a freer version of me? I would first have to accept that there is an end to the Mammon induced "yearning" and persevere to such END – when I know that I am giving my all to LOVE. At this point, I would fear for nothing. I would just be – emPowering the NOW. So what keeps me from persevering? To answer, I'll parallel the Buddha's Noble Truths with the decoding of *Genesis 4* (the story of Cain's mortality). Lastly I will allow myself to peek into the advent of the sense of enough – that which grants satisfaction, even in the knowing that nothing is satisfying.

THE BIG LETTERS D.R.E.M. CALL THE FOUR SHADOW ARCHETYPES OF THE CHILD, THE SABOTEUR, THE PROSTITUTE AND THE VICTIM BY USING THEIR END LETTERS, SINCE THESE FOUR TEND TO GO BACKWARDS. AS FOR THE SMALL "A" IN THE MIDST OF THE DREaM, IT STANDS FOR THE ANGEL OF WHICH I AM NOT AWARE WHILE I AM ASLEEP IN THE DARK.

From a to IN (from a as in angel to IN as INgénue), I spell "aIN," as in "aIN't misbehavin!"

Yes, the answers are in me: I know what to do. It is just that I'm reluctant to do it. When under the purview of the angel of necessity (the little "a" in DREaM), my "aIN't misbehavin'" is the childish denial that will continue until I resonate with the IN code. "IN" takes me "IN," where the answer are. The code initiates an "INgénue" being that is either moved by GReed or by GRace. **Just like falling and rising are equal, so are GReed and GRace.** When I resonate with this code of opposites, I am at once INgenuous (i.e.; free from the reserve or dissimulation of GReed; candid; sincere) and INgenious (i.e.; resourceful, intelligent, showing genius by GRace alone). I know that the way "IN" is the way out.

Ain is the transliteration of the S/Hebrew word (אין) for "nothingness." It is written by the letters painted on the cover. Surely, as long as I'm not strong enough to pull myself up from the top or to support me from the bottom, I am still making it about me, and still suffering.

Part I: Life is Suffering

- Life Is Suffering
- Four Crucial Steps
- Created-SIX
- Revisiting Code Liberation – AYN / ANY
- Revisiting Code Health – AYN / OYN
- Code No Yearning – AYN / NO
- Fish Page

Genesis 1 & 2	Genesis 4	Genesis 3
Creation	Preservation	Destruction
The Suffering of Suffering	The Suffering of Conditioning	The Suffering of Resistance
The Evil Eye (No 3rd Eye)	The Evil Tongue (No Throat)	The Evil Inclination (No Navel)

When the three Buddhist sufferings meet the three Jewish evils...

Life Is Suffering

"Pain is inevitable, suffering is optional." Buddhist Proverb.

Suffering is a universal truth: just like me, you have lost a loved one. Just like me, you have gotten sick. This is how the Buddha made "life is suffering" the first of the Four Noble Truths. However, while pain is part of life, it does not have to rule my life. Henceforth, the Buddha spoke of two "arrows" of suffering: the initial pain and the pain I create by resisting it. The first is unavoidable; the second is not.

To better understand the nature of suffering, I wish to view it from two opposite perspectives and/or languages: Buddhism and Judaism.

Buddhism has broken down suffering into three basic patterns. These become doubly enlightening when supported by what Judaism views as the three evils. These evils span the first chapters of Genesis, challenging the naturalness of the triad of **creation, preservation** and **destruction**. In the advanced table below, the Power of Three remains the foundational organization of four synergistic steps that build onto each other for me to recognize the three evils and end the pain story.

Genesis 1 & 2	Genesis 4	Genesis 3
Creation	Preservation	Destruction
Alchemy	Astrology	Theurgy
Nothing Permanent	Nothing Personal	Nothing Satisfying
The Suffering of Resistance	The Suffering of Conditioning	The Suffering of Sufferings
The Evil Eye (No 3rd Eye)	The Evil Tongue (No Throat)	The Evil Inclination (No Navel)

A Progressive Elucidation of the Darkness of Suffering and Evil

Here is the progression:

1. How the triad of creation, destruction and preservation is supported by the triple mastery to engrave the three marks of existence.

2. How the three marks of existence (when unread) lead to the three sufferings.
3. How the three sufferings connect to three evils and affect the tree of (my) life.
4. How Genesis' first four chapters stage the three sufferings and the three evils.

Four Crucial Steps

> "We made a searching and fearless moral inventory of ourselves."
> *Alcoholics Anonymous*

Step 1 – how the triad of creation, destruction and preservation is supported by the triple mastery to engrave the three marks of existence:

1. **Creation** is supported by **alchemy** which is how to master the operation of the sun and come into Power, thus the idea of "creative Power." After showing up reliably to the task at hand, I can only be a victor. The perseverance in spite of instability engraves the mark of existence called *Anicca* (or "**nothing permanent**").
2. **Destruction** is supported by **theurgy** which is how to master the operation of the moon and come into wisdom. If the moon argues to come first, it is because I must follow her lunacy until it delivers me to sanity. The intelligence to do so engraves the mark of existence called *Dukkha* (for "**nothing satisfying**"). This ties to the first Noble Truth: life is *Dukkha* or "dissatisfaction."
3. **Preservation** is supported by **astrology** which is how to master the operation of the stars and have the knowledge of opposites – when I can be *and* not be. The selflessness engraves the mark of existence called *Anatta* ("**nothing**

personal"). This infers that no karma is binding since I can change the past and know a different future Self.

Step 2 – how the three marks of existence (when missed) lead to the three sufferings:

1. The mark of **nothing permanent** (when missed) may lead to **the suffering of resisting change.** This is when I cling to enjoyable events, not accepting that the laws of impermanence dictate a transformation. The reality of instability now rubs against my need to control. I avoid pain and seek pleasure, discounting that even clinging to pleasure must come to an end. My grasping leaves me constantly longing.
2. The mark of **nothing satisfying** (when missed) may lead to **the suffering of sufferings.** This is when I find myself unable to create my preferred reality since I perceive that I am separated from that which I hold as good (knowledge, youth, wealth, fame), and united to what I hold as not good (birth, sickness/aging, poverty, death). The sense of being cursed makes it seem like the ultimate suffering.
3. The mark of **nothing personal** (when missed) may lead to **the suffering of conditioning.** This is when I construct a narcissistic narrative in response to my suffering. From early on, I am conditioned to be either a boy or a girl and tell a sexist pain story, which induces a pervading sense of anxiety. This is the pit that gender-fluid identities "try" to avoid. However, even being gender-fluid is an identity. The underlying sense of suffering is due to seeing that life does not offer me a solid ground, and that my very existence is questionable. I feel like I don't belong

Step 3 – how the three sufferings are clarified by the three evils that affect the tree of (my) life:

1. **The suffering of resistance** is clarified by **the evil eye**. I know what to do. I just don't want to do it (I resist change). By disowning what I know I should do to have what I want, I increase the hunger since reality can now only mirror my resistance to having it all. This is how I summon my demons and flirt with FEAR (False Evidence Appearing Real), denying me the option to feel successful and loved. Moreover, since the failure I resist persists, I continue to see lack rather than plenty by blocking **the 3rd eye,** the "I" of a conscious observer.
2. **The suffering of sufferings** is clarified by **the evil inclination**. This suffering causes a huge amount of anxiety, as I can't allow myself to succeed in my creation. I am a killer! I can't help but to break my own law until my temple is burned to the ground. I worsen my case by feeling bad. And since I turned off my conscience along with sentience (the capacity to feel and sense), I can't get the message of my emotions. Henceforth, not only does repeating my insane behavior block **the navel** chakra, but it also progressively lowers my self-esteem.
3. **The suffering of conditioning** is clarified by **the evil tongue**. This suffering leads me to be entrenched in the slave narrative. I couldn't let go of my pain story if my life depended on it (and it does). Even if I were to decide not to talk about my addiction of choice, I'd find myself continuously evoking it. However, my "confessional" does not provide relief, nor does it allow for redemption. Instead, it blocks the sane functioning of **the throat** chakra by strengthening my neurosis' communication pathways, each time deepening its programming.

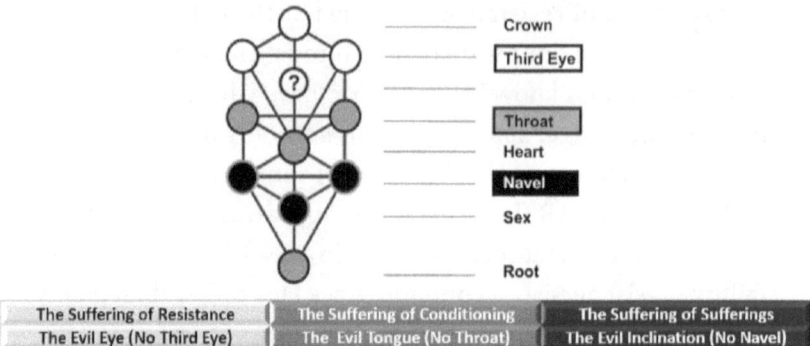

The S/Hebrew tree of life reveals the essence of suffering and evil by splitting the three "problem-chakras" into their male and female sides

Step 4 – how the first four chapters of Genesis stage the three sufferings and the three evils:

1. **Genesis 2** speaks of **the suffering of resistance.** I fear the emPowerment that I had in **Genesis 1** by objecting to my guidance and believing the lie of my snake-like ego ("no, you won't die if you eat from the forbidden fruit; you'll be like gods"). Also, I think that there's an "out there" out there (a jungle), and that the other (be it "God," the woman, the snake, the tree) will eventually get me and/or confine me. These antagonizing judgments are how I close **my 3rd eye**.
2. **Genesis 3** speaks of **the suffering of sufferings**. I now lose the transparency I had in Genesis 2, when I was naked and had no shame. To do so, I simply blamed the other and refused to take responsibility for my errors. This is how I changed clothes, going from the light body to the shame body whose garment is sewn by the "no good" desires I forbid myself to have. **My navel chakra is now so blocked that I am no longer able to feel what I really want, which renders me incapable of asking for it.**
3. **Genesis 4** speaks of **the suffering of conditioning.** My name is Cain ("possessed by jealousy"), a calling which trains me to envy the love and approval that my brother enjoys, and thus to be forever depressed and angry. I must kill him: it is a crime of

passion! Cain and Abel are opposites: Cain is bad (female) and Abel is good (male). Such sexual conditioning is how Cain can't accept the result of his communication: to have his feminine side sent into exile. When I am Cain – deprived of my female ability to feel and sense, I am so restless that I can only create against myself. This worsens the block of **my throat** chakra, and prevents it from coming into wisdom-Power.

Genesis 1 & 2	Genesis 4	Genesis 3
Creation	Preservation	Destruction
The Suffering of Resistance	The Suffering of Conditioning	The Suffering of Sufferings
The Evil Eye (No 3rd Eye)	The Evil Tongue (No Throat)	The Evil Inclination (No Navel)

CREATED-SIX

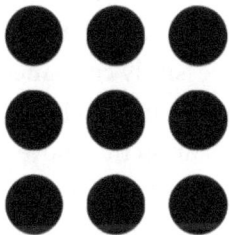

CREATED-SIX, I CREATED HEAVEN AND HELL

What will it take for me to see surrender as the foundation of my leadership? The answer is consistent: it will take being of service to *Elohim* and not to Mammon. In other words, I must transcend the fear that keeps me in Scare City. For until I do give it all, my mind is poverty-stricken, as I am afraid of not being able to provide for the body.

Lamed (ל) Yod (י)	Aleph (א)	Mem (ם) Heh (ה)
Yod (י)	Vav (ו) / Heh (ה)	Heh (ה)

Top Row: the Letters of *Elohim*, Bottom Row: the Letters of YEWE

On the first row and in the first column of the table above, I see the letter Lamed (ל) with the letter Yod (י). In the third column, I see the letter Mem final (ם) with the letter Heh (ה). In the middle is Aleph (א). These five letters write *Elohim* (אלהים) – the "God" Name of *Genesis 1*, the very Name that is "Created-SIX." On the second row, I recognize the four letters of YEWE (יהוה) – the "God" Name of *Genesis 4*, when the Cain in me must suffer the consequences of my murderous words and actions. When joining YEWE to *Elohim*, I write the "God" Name of *Genesis 2* and *3*.

Indeed, when the Vav of desire enters the scene (second row), I automatically lose track of my Aleph being (i.e.; of the purity of my soul). Unless my Vav is successfully contained within a double Heh, my two hands will separate: one hand will know what to do, and the other won't want to do it. To be clear on the above, I may just have to wait for Part II to unfold: can't hurry LOVE! :-)

I now add one row to my table to include the SIX shadow archetypes. Behind the saboteuR is the fallen angel. I also see that the chilD is behind the rising angel.

Lamed (ל) Yod (י)	Aleph (א)	Mem (ם) Heh (ה)
Yod (י)	Vav (ו) / Heh (ה)	Heh (ה)
chilD → Rising angel	prostitutE / victiM	Fallen angel → saboteuR

The FOUR Shadow Archetypes + the TWIN Angels = the Created-SIX

Yes, to kill my potential, I must believe that I am fallen, flawed, damaged goods, not enough! Conversely, it makes sense to me that, for my chilD to surrender and become a Leader, I must lift myself up. Accepting my falls and my failures is a good beginning. However, I must persevere until I am risen, for this is when I won't fear being emPowered. I'll be "a top" without being a bully!

To move out of Scare City, I must transition from "GReed" into "GRace." When in GReed, my GR or Giving/Receiving is done out of fear; when in GRace, out of love. This is how the sin of greed is the deadliest of the seven, as it stirs the SIX other sins. When I start **envying** "you" for what I think you have, I am not far from the **wrath** that perverts and sabotages the sense of justice. Conversely, when my chilD goes into boasting ("I did it!"), **pride** takes me down and soon has me downplaying ("I didn't do it!"). I now go into **sloth**, so discouraged that I can't love reality with *all* my heart, *all* my soul, *all* my might.

Lamed (ל) Yod (י)	Aleph (א)	Mem (מ) Heh (ה)
chilD → Rising angel	prostitutE / victiM	Fallen angel → saboteuR
Pride → Sloth	Lust / Gluttony	Envy → Wrath

As for **lust / gluttony**, the former is indulged by the scared masculine and the latter, by the scared feminine, regardless of genders. When in fear – scared rather than sacred, a man (male gender) may also resort to overeating and a woman (female gender) may also resort to pornography.

I wish to add one more row to my table to include the poisons. At the hub of the karmic wheel of Buddhism are three poisons represented as a rooster (greed), a pig (ignorance) and a snake (aversion). *TCO—Book 1* balanced the three poisons of the east with the three poisons of the west: greed with cleverness, ignorance with entitlement, and aversion with competition.

chilD → Rising angel	prostitutE / victiM	Fallen angel → saboteuR
Pride → Sloth	Lust / Gluttony	Envy → Wrath
Aversion → Competition	Ignorance / Entitlement	Cleverness → Greed

Since this chapter intends to decode the psychology of the rising angel in such a way that it/I would be "risen," I will inquire on how my chilD's aversion turns into a hellish form of competition. A heavenly form of competition is when there is no sloth in my space – when I am 100%, no holds barred.

In such space, time and mind, there is no hell and no illusion. When the aversion stops, the chilD no longer seeks recognition. When the greed stops, the saboteuR no longer offers lip service. When the entitlement stops, the victiM no longer seeks retaliation. When the ignorance stops, the prostitutE is no longer Power-hungry. And finally, when the competition stops, the angel rises into the light.

Aversion → Competition	Ignorance / Entitlement	Cleverness → Greed
Recognition → Light	Power / Retaliation	Separation → Service

SIX Poisons - SIX Drives

Indeed, when the snake is not trying to outsmart others, there is no more "HELLusion" of separation. And when that hell is no more, there is no desire for enlightenment – just the light! CREATED-SIX, I CREATED HEAVEN AND HELL, and I saw that it was all good. I said "let there be enlightenment," and I saw that I was; awesome, good, free – liberated!

Revisiting Code Liberation - AYN / ANY

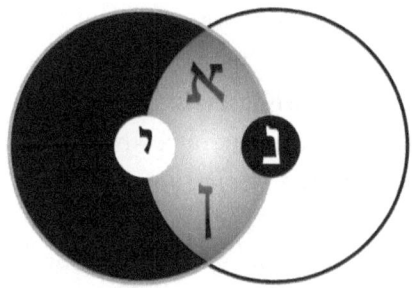

Imagine a language so pure and so sacred that it can reconcile opposites in just three letters...

Right: Hebrew letter Nun (נ) → N in Roman script
Bottom: Hebrew letter Nun final (ן) → N in Roman script
Top: Hebrew letter Aleph (א) → A in Roman script
Left: Hebrew letter Yod (י) → I, J, Y in Roman script

Here is how S/Hebrew inscribes code "Liberation" in 2 words:

- **AYN:** going counterclockwise from the top, I read *Ain* (אין) for "nothing."

- **ANY**: from the top to the right to the left, I read *Ani* (אני) for "I."

The Decoding: ah, the joke of the personal: "me; nothing?" When I don't know who I Am, the joke's on me! I can't rest. I take every error personally, and feel humiliated when I fall or fail. How could I not when I won't feel the greed that influences my decision making? If I did, I would also feel that the rapacious desire for Power is not "I." This realization alone would begin turning off its creative energy. Befriending (my) greed is a holy instant, as it links the *Ani* "I" to the *Ain* "**nothingness.**" I can now be free to be or *not* to be, to have or *not* to have, to do or *not* to do – in sickness and in health. Feeling the pure light of the soul, I'm no longer hungry and thus, no longer trying to fill the emptiness. "I" just is. This changes the way "I" see things which, in turn, changes what "eye" sees. English "I/eye" is the perfect conveyor of S/Hebrew *Ain /Any* to say: 'when no longer denying evil, you won't get trapped in the illusion that separates the seer from the seen, the subject from the object, "me" from "you." Merging with the invisible realm, you'll see the real "I" within that abides in the real "**nothing**" without.' Hearing this transmission still presupposes that I'd be as regular sign Nun, willing to fall again and again until I descend as terminally as Nun final. For how could I fear falling if there's no one left to want love, approval and recognition? Surely, how could I fear falling when I know beyond doubt that I will get up? Such knowing is the love, approval and recognition of the Self. It takes away the need to seek for it in "all the wrong places."

Revisiting Code Health - AYN / OYN

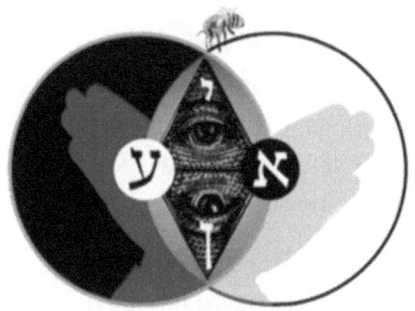

Imagine a language so pure and so sacred that it can reconcile opposites in just four letters...

Top: Hebrew letter Yod (י) → I, J, Y in Roman script
Right: Hebrew letter Aleph (א) → A in Roman script
Left: Hebrew letter Ayin (ע) → O in Roman script
Bottom: Nun final (ן) → N in Roman script.

Here is how S/Hebrew inscribes code "Health" in 4 letters, 2 words:

- **OYN:** left to top to bottom, I read *Ayin* (עין) for "eye."
- **AYN:** right to top to bottom, I read *Ain* (אין) for "nothing."

The Decoding: the two words above – *Ayin* and *Ain* – are pronounced in the exact same manner. However, it is the difference in spelling that allows for the partnering of signs Aleph (A) and Ayin (O) to inscribe code Health. *Ayin* (with a sign Ayin) is the word for "**eye**." Moreover, the letter it evolved into (the letter O) is as round as an eye. The first time that the word appears is in *Genesis 3:5*: "For God knows that when you eat of it, your **eyes** will be opened, and you will be like God, knowing good and evil." The word is fittingly used in its plural form, since it speaks of the eyes of duality (pl.) that open to seeing the "no good" just after I commit a violation to LOVE. Conversely, the single eye that sees goodness (the third eye) now closes and goes into nothingness.

For it to open again, I will have to assimilate the desires of my personality, desires meant to serve private agendas. This ego can only see evil, speak evil and hear evil, as it is up to "no good." *Assimilating* means to reduce to **nothing**. What S/Hebrew says via the words *Ayin* and *Ain*, English transmits as "eye-no-sense."

Surely, when I stop looking for the proof that I am not enough, the hunger for Love does not own me as it once did. And as "I" change the way "eye" looks at things, what I look at changes. Returning to eye-no-sense/innocence is easy. I just need to welcome anonymity and forget about making a name for myself. I will then understand that life has no meaning. It just is: I-no-sense.

The eye of providence can now shine on me again. I am able to see the good in the bad. This is no less than the gift of vision. The ability to envision healthy tissues, for example, precedes the formation of healthy tissues. This explains how it is my faith that makes me well, for it is only the eyes of doubt that keep my attention on being unwell and, thereby, continue to create dis-ease. Moreover, when liberation and health join forces, there can be no more yearning.

Code No Yearning - AYN / NO

Imagine a language so pure and so sacred that it can reconcile opposites in just four mirrored letters...

Right image: code Liberation, reflected
Left image: code Health

Here is how S/Hebrew inscribes code "No Yearning" in 2 letters, above and beyond the 3 letters Aleph, Yod, Nun:

- **NO:** keeping my attention on the enlarged script (black dot of right image, white dot of left image), I read *Nah* (נע) for "to move, to stir."
- **AYN:** keeping my attention on the small script (of both right and left images), I read *Ain* (אין) for "nothing."

The Decoding: the double image above juxtaposes **code Liberation** and **code Health**. There is, however, a slight shift: the three signs that are in both codes (Aleph, Yod, Nun final) seem to recede in the background as they reflect each other. As for the two signs that are unique to each code (Nun regular, Ayin), they appear enlarged. The desired effect is to forget about the three signs that happen to spell *Ain* for "nothingness," since my attention is now drawn to the two bigger signs. These are the signs of my motion and emotions as they write the word *Nah* for the "moving and stirring" of my feeling body. Here is how...

Surely, from a purely physical viewpoint, I can't move in the void, a.k.a. the big "**nothing.**" I can't fall either: where would I fall to? For me **to move** and **be stirred** to fall, rise or rotate – that is, for me to be angel or demon, I must have a reference point, a twin particle with which to fall in love and *fail* at LOVE. Contrasting myself, I can now become something or be someone. Evolution calls the shots: I once was 0/1, not being and being, and now, thanks to you, I'm being somebody – in opposition to you. You and I ("WE") have accepted to be the significant other for the other and play the role of partners in crime, so that we would *feel* something, for good or bad.

But what if the game was rigged? What if I were to accept that I am TCO – antagonized by life in order to become Spock-like? Spock was a Star Trek character who was repeatedly bullied during his youth in order to incite lower base emotions. If Spock could get angry, that would be the proof that he was "just human" and not divinely patient as a Vulcan is. As for me, if I could stop being triggered by "you," wouldn't I experience not only the Passion, but also the Dispassion of Christ? There would be no more suffering, as I'd let go of **yearning** for a different "you." I would just be still – knowing that I Am; **nothing** and everything. Surely, that would open me to adopt the behavior of LOVE, which is all I want to begin with, whether I know it or not.

"IN THE BEGINNING," SOMETHING ETERNAL OCCURRED THAT HAD THE capacity to choose what it would communicate when it came into being. I can call that something "consciousness," as it is that which shines a light on reality in order to make something appear. Without consciousness, what is there? Moreover, can I experience anything unless I am conscious? If a tree falls in the forest and there is no consciousness to hear it, does it make a noise? Does it even fall? Indeed, what is there when I don't experience a thing? Consciousness is necessary for me to create a personal reality. But what happens when I have no ear to hear a tree falling, and am not here to experience reality?

1. The notion of time disappears as I have no way to gauge duration.
2. The notion of space disappears as I have nothing to scale.
3. The notion of causality disappears as I have no mind to boast as a risen angel or take me down as a fallen angel.

I do not like it when I am told that I'm not conscious. I do not like it when I am told that I am not the experiencer of my feelings and not the doer of my actions. Bottom line: I do not like it when I am told that I don't have free will. And yet, I have the hardest time taking full responsibility for the results of my communication, as a Leader of LOVE is called to do. Moreover, aren't the laws predicated on the sense that people make conscious decisions, that they have experiences, and thus, that they ought to be held responsible for their actions? In a well-functioning society, I have intrinsic values, even if I am as Cain – a murderer. I'm still conscious; I have the Power to decide, and can thus communicate and contribute to the whole.

And it makes me wonder... Is there a place where I have broken the rules so terminally that there is no going back?

Part II: The Psychological Decoding of Genesis 4

- Mind and Heart
- The Beauty of Preservation
- The Philosopher's Stone
- SIXth Stage - the Practice of Rising
- Cain and Abel (Review)
- Enlightenment in Seven Things
- The Seven Lights
- Five, Seven, or SIX?
- "Who knows four?"
- Enlightenment
- When the Soul Fears Resting…
- My Gravitational Problem
- Virginity
- Desire and Cain
- The V of Violence
- The Two Hands
- The YEWE that Came from the Wombman
- The Map of (My) Suffering

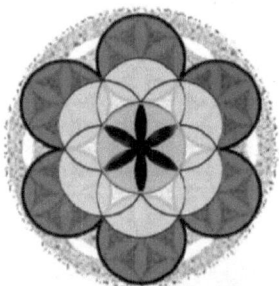

Adam Qadmon	The Snake / Cain	Adam HaRishon
Simultaneous Creation	Preservation / Non-Causality	Gradual Destruction
Brahma	Vishnu / Atma	Shiva
The Seed of Life	The Core / The Gem of Life	The Egg of Life

I Am That I Am

Mind and Heart

> "Nothing was ever created by two men. There are no good collaborations, whether in music, in art, in poetry, in mathematics, in philosophy. Once the miracle of creation has taken place, the group can build and extend it, but the group never invents anything. The preciousness lies in the lonely mind of a man." *John Steinbeck*

Growing up – and therefore, creating – is a solo-job. This is how "nothing was ever created by two men" (or by two women). Surely, I knew it as a child: there's nothing out there! If blessed (or cursed) with siblings, I must learn to see the sacrifices I make for "them" as what I do for me and me alone. I will then have a greater chance to unleash my creativity.

On that note, all cultures (including science) use creation myths to attempt to answer the questions we all have on the origin of the universe: what is real? Where do I come from? What is my purpose? Who am I? According to the Egyptians, in the beginning was darkness, water and the great god Atum. Surprisingly, the Hebrew Bible has two creation stories and two Adams for the two opposite ways in which the mind creates:

- **Genesis 1**: a first Adam who is created male and female, and has dominion over it all. This Adam is also known as *Adam Qadmon* or "primary Adam."
- **Genesis 2**: a second Adam who is a man and in lack, projecting "God" out there, and so lonely he has to be put into deep sleep to meet his woman. This Adam is known as *Adam HaRishon* or "first Adam." However, the idea of a first infers a second. Doubt now enters the mind, as Adam turns secondary.

These Adams are like atoms. They appear randomly, with opposite beliefs on creation:

- **Primary Adam** thinks "I CAN." If this Adam/I have faith, it is because I listen to and hear my heart's dictates. It is also how I participate in **simultaneous creation:** I know that observing a wave or a particle is a choice that I make, consciously or not. I also know that my beliefs source my experience and take full responsibility for the results of my communication.
- **Secondary Adam** thinks "I CAN'T." If this Adam/I have doubt, it is because I am disconnected from my heart. It is also how I participate in a **gradual creation** that can only turn into **gradual destruction:** my male side has given his Power to an external "God" who acts as a prime cause in distributing rewards and punishments. Since I believe that experience precedes beliefs, I am incapable of being source, which renders me a victim. In my perception, there is nothing I can do to stop suffering.

I have seen in the previous chapter how the Bible's two creation stories are theories on the mind-body connection and, by extension, the nature of the physical world.

There is a third mind and a third way to create which is about to unfold here: non-causality. Non-causality does not deny the reality of the world, but only that a personal creative process brought it into existence. In that no space, time and mind, there is neither boasting nor self-deprecating. The world is just an uncaused appearance in the Self: I am that I am, because that's what I am. Period.

Having the knowledge that I Am [not] is how I don't need to derive pride or guilt from (my) creating. When believing in gradual creation, I first commit a violation which leads me to losing PaRaDiSe. Let's say that I was disloyal to my spouse. If into gradual creation, I may say something like "I shouldn't have had an affair," and feel even worse as the result of my judging myself. If into simultaneous creation, I may be able to relax as I see that I should have had an affair, on the grounds that I *actually* did. Aligning to what is real gives me Peace. If it doesn't, I am still into gradual creation (and still "milking" that creation). While it would be nice to accept that reality rules and that my affair is inscribed in the context of a greater plan, do I actually believe it? **And if I do believe it, why am I still in a conversation about the past?**

To change the past and really give it and forgive it (no more conversation), I must come into non-causality, when I can see that a creative process brought into existence the affair or the murder or whatever violation of love I committed. I was to play the role of a lawbreaker because I did play that role. This quality of acceptance frees me from the weight of shame I was carrying. By returning me to innocence, it allows me to no longer repeat the maladaptive pattern. Indeed, I am now equipped with the ability to say and feel: "I have not sinned." Should acceptance reveal to not be enough, I must now inquire on why I would do harm until I understand the root-cause of my creation.

The Beauty of Preservation

> "Spiritually evolved persons, established in the Atma, whose minds are free from the notion of doership, understand the True Self within and are therefore not tainted by their actions." *Jack Hawley, The Bhagavad Gita*

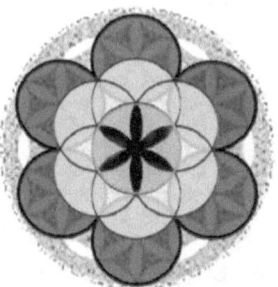

Adam Qadmon	The Snake / Cain	Adam HaRishon
Simultaneous Creation	Preservation / Non-Causality	Gradual Destruction
Brahma	Vishnu / Atma	Shiva
The Seed of Life	The Core / The Gem of Life	The Egg of Life

The I Am - The Atma(n)

Awakening the chilD invited me to revisit the ancient belief that "God" created the world according to a geometric plan. Indeed, it was Plato who said "God geometrizes continually" (*Convivialium disputationum*).

The sacred geometry above builds up three patterns on the background of the Flower of Life. These three patterns are also found in the Trimurti as the Hindu trinity of Brahma (the god of creation), Shiva (the god of destruction) and Vishnu (the god of preservation). Moreover, just like in the "God" Name YEWE, out of the third comes the One as the fourth. This One God is known in Hinduism as the Atma for the Self's or the I Am's individual essence and Brahman for the universal consciousness which underlies all things.

What does this mean practically? When I am as Cain, my redemption resides in being free of any sense of doership. Upon not taking anything personally, I know that worldly activities (such as, killing or being killed) are modifications taking place independently of me in the realm of action/manifestation. Not about me!

The Philosopher's Stone

> "Those who have taken refuge in this knowledge and have attained identity with me, are not born even during creation, and not afflicted during dissolution." *Bhagavad Gita, Chapter 14, verse 2.*

Nothing personal is the sense of the mark engraved on Cain's forehead. Geometrically, it is formed by six vesica piscis (black almond shapes) in the core circle. Known as **the Gem of Life**, these six vessels are the gold in the shadow – the Philosopher's stone.

They represent the will to fall as deep and as often as needed in order for me to rise as I know that there is no one who is fallen, in the sense of damaged goods or not enough.

When I transcend the fear of falling, I also transcend the fear of rising, i.e.; of Power.

The core circle is the circle that was before the beginning (before circle #1) and after the end (after circle #6). As such, it is beyond time, space and mind as the 7th "day" of *Shabbat,* when I work while "resting."

Emanating from it come the Seed of Life and the Egg of Life that converge to help me better understand the threefold synergy of creation, destruction and preservation. This synergy is no less than the **Mind of Life** or that which expands the code of opposites by growing one vesica piscis into a seed of life, a flower of life, an egg of life, a tree of life and a fruit of life (see *Chapter 5, Genesis 2:4-25 – Adam HaRishon*).

Starting with *Is TCO "write" for me?*, I looked at number "ThREE" as the "TREE" of the knowledge of opposites. The three flows of this tree (neutral knowledge, male good and female evil) are a map of how consciousness works. This knowledge is universal. It is the philosopher's stone by which to not be afflicted by destruction and not be comforted by creation. The threefold expression is also present in the Trimurti of Brahma, Vishnu and Shiva as it is in the Trinity of the Father, the Son and the Holy Ghost.

The three forces differ within each individual in proportions, desire and will, which explains why I would speak, think, feel, and act as I do (LOL: nothing personal). For me to be free, I must go beyond the three and abide in the force of the fourth. **This is when I stop identifying with the body and/or the doer and abide in the Self. I am here and now, and can now hear and know that I AM the AIM.**

SIXth Stage - the Practice of Rising

Prepare to DIE! Inquiry: www.goldenxpr.com/tco3_empowerment/

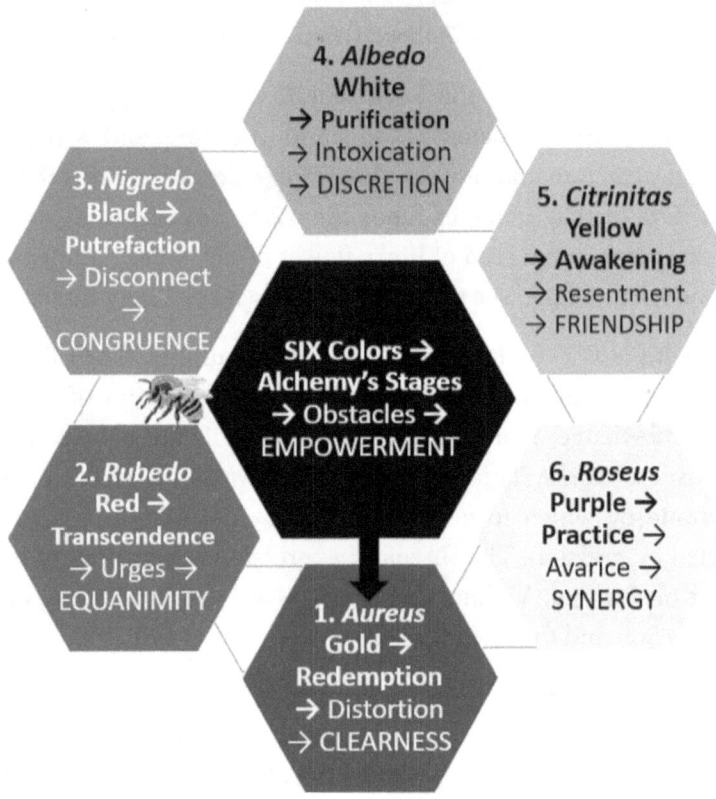

Step 1: I fill in the blank: I want to know WHY I would choose to think I CAN'T _____ (e.g.; find a job, be patient, etc.). **Step 2:** I ask for truth and generate a number. **Step 3:** I find my number on the map and fill in the brackets: When I see reality in [**Colors**], I am in the stage of [**Alchemy's Stages**]. I am now called to confront any possible [**Obstacles**]. The more successful I am, the more I experience the angel of me rising into the [**Empowerment**] I couldn't reach. **Step 4:** what most surprised me in this process was [_____].

Cain and Abel (Review)

"Karma is only in spacetime and causality. Your real Self resides non-locally." *Deepak Chopra*

My name is Cain. Being the first mortal and the first murderer, I have a vested interest in understanding why I would create the reality I create. I'm also the first to meet the "God" Name YEWE as the LORD of Karma and Power of Accountability. While I want to make up my own mind (and not end up as my parents), I won't accept the consequences of my decisions. Instead, I feel that my punishment is too great. Truth be told, it's not freedom I want, but freedom from responsibility. I'm like a child: I want to do what I want, but ultimately, I'd like you to pick up the pieces. It's like wanting to drink all I want today, and refusing to accept tomorrow's hangover!

If I could only stop causing effects that I would rather not have to experience, I would rise to my vision and find rest in the process. But I can't change – or die or rest – since YEWE put a mark on my forehead to keep me from being killed. This "mark" is the word *Ot*. One day, I realized that, read in a mirror, *Ot* (AWT or "Aleph and Tav") flips into *To* (TWA or "Tav and Aleph"). I had an epiphany as I remembered the story of the letters presenting themselves to "God" in reverse order, each letter-being eager to create its own reality (see *Learning to Code – When the Letters Turnaround*).

Only Aleph was modest enough to stay away from any creating. Its mind had stopped moving: no yearning! When aligned with Aleph, I am pure choiceless awareness. I love reality; for better, for worse, for richer, for poorer, for murderer, for life-giver: it's equal! It is only when I identify to Beth that I start judging, feel compelled to make something happen and then fear the price that I'll have to pay for using magic. What if I summoned the "wrong" thing?

The Power of decision is dicey. It can lead me to taking my creations personally and to play the game of reward and punishment. Yep, I'll

either reward myself with "I did it" or punish myself with "I shouldn't have."

As for Aleph's ability to withdraw from creating, it aligns with the findings of quantum physics and quantum religion. Science calls it "nonlocality," and religion, "non-causality." A growing body of empirical evidence suggests that human consciousness is nonlocal, meaning it is not confined to specific points in space (like brains or bodies), or specific moments in time (like past, present or future). In everyday life, distance and location seem very real. Yet physics now suggests that, at the most fundamental level, the universe is nonlocal.

This means that there is no space, no time, no mind, and thus, nothing to cause creation. Since my real Self is nonlocal, I can wake up from the dream of karma which depends on causality and can only exist in space and time. It is proven: none of my judgments of what I think reality "should" be can interfere with the QKosmic plan.

So, what is blocking me, still? Why regret what I have done when I know that non-locality is true – a scientific truth which is mirrored in the holy scriptures?

Indeed, Sri Ramana Maharshi spoke of *Ajātivāda,* an ancient Hindu doctrine that denies all causality in the physical world by stating that the creation of the world never happened at all. When I know the Self and realize that the Self exists as the only "thing" that never changes, nothing ever comes into existence or ceases to exist. The same idea is found in the Talmud (*Pesachim 54a*) as "the seven lights that existed before creation."

So, I am timeless, being the Eternal Now and seeing the letters of the name *Qain* for "possessed by jealousy" reorder as *Naqi* for "pure, innocent." The murder is forgiven. I have no more questions. I CAN rest now.

Enlightenment In Seven Things

Listen to the story now... Once upon a time, I was compelled to come out of the big Nothing to become something. The hunger to be me was riveting, and so painful that I eventually became willing to know the truth. When ready to give it all, I found a unique way to fill my heart with LOVE. Indeed, to know that it's not about me, I just needed to walk a reciprocal walk – me walking "God" and "God" walking me.
This is how to open to being "PAIRfect."

The Seven Lights

"Seven lights were created before the world was created, and these are: Torah, the Turn Within, the Garden of Eden, Gehinnom, the Throne of Honor, the House of the Sanctuary and the Name of the Messiah." *Talmud, Pesachim 54a*

The Hindu scriptures convey the wisdom of their teachings clearly, e.g.; *Ajātivāda* is "the Doctrine of Non-causality." It comes from *A* for "not, non," *Jāti* for "creation, origination, causation," and *Vāda* for "doctrine." As for the S/Hebrew scriptures, they speak in tongues. To see the light of these seven 'things,' I must decode them.

I'll begin with the Torah. Meaning "the Way, the Teaching, the Law, the Song of LOVE," it elects to be the "Doctrine of Non-causality" itself. **Moreover, it inscribed the entire Wisdom Teaching between its first letter (the B of *Barashit*) and its last letter (the L of *Israel*).** First, I go from B to L, resisting *Bal*, the "do not" command and causing consequences that are not my pleasure. When in enough suffering, I change my ways and go from L to B, turning to my *Lev* "heart," and listening. I am no longer serving private agendas, and no longer trying to push the river. I don't move. IT moves me. This is how the Torah can be received as a doctrine of non-causality.

Indeed, ♪♪ Mother Torah comes to me, speaking words of wisdom: "L it B!" When in my heart, it becomes simple. I can let it be, as I have nothing left to lose. Concerning the SIX "days" around the core of Torah as the teaching of non-causality, their sequencing is deduced from the order of the instruments of Self-knowledge that call them into being, moving me from Voice to Spirit, from Spirit to Heart, from Heart to Body, from Body to Soul and, finally from Soul into Mind. Day 1 – MY [BURNING] DESIRE – emanates from the Voice which, sooner or later, will lead me into temptation. Day 1 is under the purview of Voice which is the first instrument.

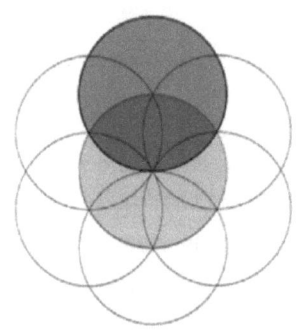

1. MY DESIRE

The Voice calls Gehinnom as MY [BURNING] DESIRE: *Gehinnom* is the abode of the wicked, a deep ravine separating Mount Zion from the "Hill of Evil Counsel." As a place of punishment called *Tophet* ("fire-stove"), it is the burning desire; the yearning for and the playing with Power compelling me to come out of nothing in order to become something – in this case, me. The problem comes from identifying to the idea of "I" and "mine." This desire soon becomes MY burning desire for "your" love, approval and recognition, which implies that I don't have any of it. As "I" is now split from "you," I start listening to the other voice – the one leading me into temptation by inciting me to seek credentials and to make a name for myself. However, who besides me, myself and I is doubting myself? If I knew who I am, would I believe in me enough not to take "your" rejection of me personally? After all, it is my suffering from a case of mistaken identity (I am the body; that which is dying) that will lead me to meeting the Eternal "I."

The Spirit calls the Garden of Eden as MY GENIUS: the garden is where I cultivate the flower of MY genius. The S/Hebrew word *Gan* for "garden" is kin with Arabic *Jinny*. It is also the root of the Latin word *genius*. The "Garden of Eden" is where I take the risk to blossom into a beautiful mind; a mind impersonal enough to contribute its fruitful expression to further the work of transformation.

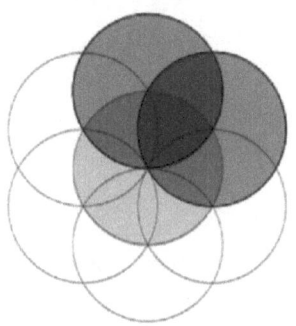

2. MY GENIUS

However, to really be selfless, I must be open enough to surrender my judgments. As long as I think "you" should love me, see me, hear me, I will default back to making it about me and experience two modes of operation: enlightened and enlightened not. 1) enlightened: I am in my genius zone (no matter what my "art" is). I enter the unknown, experience the mystical and lose track of my identity. I feel awe, realizing that creation is done *through* me, not *by* me. 2) enlightened not: there is something I do not understand, and I am not at peace. If I did, the part of my genius that is still encapsulated by a demonic energy would be freed of it. Transmuted. Truth be told, I can no more hurry the LOVE that has no opposite than my rebirth into spirit. When limited to "normal" consciousness, I believe that I am the body and thus, the doer of the actions. Guilty as charged! To return to the quality of presence I experienced when I was at once here and not here, I must surrender until the unknown (what I don't understand) is known. The intense clarity will then, once again, be surreal as I'll feel myself turning on the light of the shame body and seeing the secret desire I was forbidding.

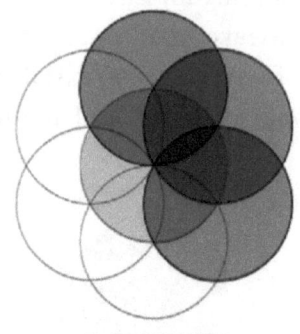

3. MY TURN

The Heart calls the Turn Within as MY TURN: I am clear that I am now at the point where my conditioned existence, although punctuated here and there by the fleeting joys of a new toy, has become wearisome. Will I have the courage, or more to the point, the intelligence to look for the keys where I lost them – within? Will I do what it takes to wake up from the discontent of societal hypnosis and surf the creative edge of my being? Having suffered enough pain looking for LOVE out there, I now become willing to know the truth, and ready to change my ways as I continue striving toward self-knowledge. But, if that really were the case, why continue lying to myself? Why are the results of my communication painful at times? Why do I procrastinate putting my affairs in order? Why do I not listen to my heart *at all times*, and really see the change I wish to see? The reason is simple: I still want to think that I have a choice between going fully in or flirting with the "out there" out there. Moreover, there's truth to the fact that I can't force it. Indeed, I can bring my ego to the waters of Torah, but I can't make me drink. I will have to wait for MY turn to come to play my piece – after a holy accident makes me so thirsty for truth that I go where it lives to find it: within!

The Body calls the Messiah's Name as MY WORK: so I lie... Big deal; doesn't everybody? This is where S/Hebrew *Mashiach* for "messiah" inscribes a name that is equal in value to *Nachash* – the "snake" that is so clever that I can't even recognize that I'm lying to myself. The shift from the snake's lies to the messiah's truth gives meaning to my life. Surely, uncovering my secrets changes my story, my language, and thus, my physical world. It may also wake up kundalini; the serpent Power lying coiled at the base of the spine. As I clean up my childish act and grow up into a Leader taking full responseability, I also lick my wounds, harvesting the pearls in consciousness as I go. I realize I was confused. I thought it was "you" that caused me pain. I now realize it was ALL me. This is how I look forward to feeling

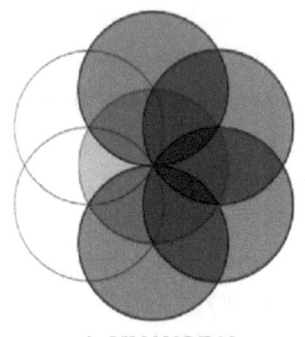

4. MY WORK

hurt by you (or anyone) again, as it is this illusion of suffering that will bring me back to truth. And what is the truth? It is MY work to hurt me, until I can love, recognize and respect who I Am. This is a solo job: no one else can do it for me! Moreover, until and unless IT is done (that is, until MY work is done), I will not be able to trust that "you" actually love me.

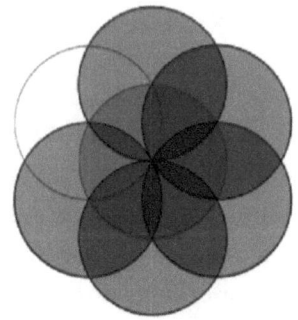

5. MY SACRIFICE

The Soul calls the House of the Sanctuary as MY SACRIFICE: a most controversial event is when "God" asks Abraham to sacrifice his son Isaac. What sort of a "God" would be that cruel? Moreover, if the divine plan called Abraham to be the Father of All Nations and if "God" promised the same Abraham a son in order to fulfill his destiny, how could the same "God" take the precious son away?

What's going on? In many ways, I am as Abraham. I have been promised a "son" to fulfill my destiny, a son whom I will eventually be asked (and tasked) to let go. For Abraham, his "son" was his son. For others, their "son" might be their lifework, their marriage or their estate. My "son" or that which I must sacrifice is that to which I am the most attached, namely the ego. Indeed, unless I renounce the sense of "I" and "mine," I will not be free of yearning. I must forget my personal desires – sacrifice them as they are only what the personality wants. This sacrifice which is the sacrifice of me (MY sacrifice) must be felt deep within as the very goal of life. It is the moment when, as Abraham, I answer to the call saying *Hineini* "here I am." I now resonate fully with the words of Khalil Gibran about the children, "they come through you but not from you, and though they are with you yet they belong not to you." *The Prophet.*

SIX. MUTUALITY

The Mind calls the Throne of Honor as MUTUALITY: the letter Heh was added to Abram and Sarai's names when they accepted the idea of sacrificing everything to the divine (this was before their allegiance was tested, of course). Fifth Word Heh is also the prompt to "honor my father and my mother." When I respect this command as my recipe for happiness, I decode opposites from within and open to mutuality. This is the yes/yes that ends all fighting and competing. To seat myself in mutuality is to know the Throne of Honor, as any dishonoring of "you" is unthinkable. When sitting on it, I know the Eternal Self. I feel something within that is real no matter what scenario is being played by "you." If disrespected or even insulted, I can focus myself to the point where I am non-reactive. Whether I get honor or dishonor, praises or affronts, I remain present. I view all that occurs settled in a reciprocity with the Self, simply because I know no separation. I thus experience a detachment that is natural; not forced. And as I feel in my blood the truth of "as above, so below; as within, so without," I take nothing personally, which also means that nothing can disturb me. However, when afraid of what "you" may think of me, I depend on you for my self-esteem. I am yet to know that I am who I am, simply because that's who I am. Once accepting this intensity of binding, desire disappears, tension vanishes, dissatisfaction ends. I know that the joy I feel won't pass since it has no reason whatsoever. I feel such an appreciation for the whole of life that trying to be right and to make you wrong is unconceivable. I am much happier saluting you, may "you" be an idea, a mother or a father, a partner, an enemy or any event whatsoever.

0/7. NON-CAUSALITY

The Torah is the teaching of NON-CAUSALITY – the doctrine that helps me kill my desire for fame and leads the murderer to the throne, where I can just be and have nothing left to lose. This 0/7 Wisdom Teaching is the beginning and the end, and, as such, beyond time. It sustains the SIX other "light things." First, I understand the burning desire that compels me to create an ego in order to make things happen as **MY desire**. Besides wanting recognition, this personality of mine has the unique voice of **MY genius**. When I interact with it, I know the bliss of not being. This curious mode of being at once here and not here eventually leads me to take **MY turn** and look within for what I normally seek out there. I am now ready to enter the darkness, and do **MY work** – shadow work. As I allow myself to give it all, I begin to know that **MY sacrifice** is this of the ego that loves to identify to the idea of "I" or "mine." The more I let go of what's in it for me, the more I come to recognize the principle of **mutuality** that undergirds the whole of life. I smile as I feel the words **MY duality** transforming into **mutuality**: nothing personal, no "MY," indeed! These SIX/7 things are given as the constituents of a state of enlightenment that had always been here, waiting for me to decide to say "let there be light" and see that enlightenment was already created.

Five, Seven, or SIX?

> "I busted a mirror and got seven years bad luck, but my lawyer thinks he can get me five." *Steven Wright*

The Torah's first word – *Barashit* or "created-SIX" – leads me to understand how I "do time" and recreate my jail, day after day, so afraid I am of the unknown. Accepting that *Barashit* is the unifying equation I sought, any set of seven would stretch me backward into SIX "days" of creation. Conversely, any sets of 5 would stretch me forward into SIX. The movement of 7 into SIX occurred in the Seven Lights – the Torah becoming the 7th sphere in the center as the doctrine of non-causality itself. Considering the famous set of 7 deadly sins, I can also see that greed is the central head which feeds every other sin, e.g.; would I have any envy or pride if I weren't greedy for Power? To stretch 5 into SIX, I will take the example of the 5 love languages: quality time, words of affirmation, touch, acts of service, gifts. I'll begin by using the elements:

- **Quality time** could go to air / mind.
- **Words of love** could go to fire / heart.
- **Touch** could go to earth / body.
- **Acts of service** could go to water / soul.
- **Gifts** could go to wood / spirit.

From there, I know that I am missing a language that would be invoked by the element of ether and its instrument – the voice. What could it be? The many romantic movies I watched come to mind... There's always a moment when a lie is being uncovered, which leads to a breakup. Eventually the offending party comes back with something like "I was a jerk, please forgive me," and proceeds in telling the whole truth; nothing but the truth: no more secrets, please! The couple is now back in love, and yes, honesty may just be the most attractive love language there is. It might even bring the five other languages to convey the sense of being unconditional.

"Who knows four?"

"WHO KNOWS FOUR?" IS THE FOURTH LINE OF A TRADITIONAL PASSOVER SONG MEANT TO LEAD ME TO FREEDOM. I KNOW #4 WHEN I "GROK" THE AXIOM OF MARIA THE PROPHETESS. YEP, IT TAKES A FEMININE ENERGY TO STATE: "ONE BECOMES TWO, TWO BECOMES THREE, AND OUT OF THE THIRD COMES THE ONE AS THE FOURTH." WHAT DOES THAT MEAN?

Yes, out of the third letter of YEWE comes the one as the fourth letter which is a Heh (E). This Heh is one, as it is the container of the Sacred Masculine. When I know 4, I resonate with the Sacred Feminine since I feel the Mother (the force of the fourth letter) in me. I can be patient as I have a container – a "Mother." Mother is matter, and matter is energy. I have it all, as I did when I was in the womb. I just need to think a thought to see it materialized. This readies me to push the alchemical envelope as I recognize the 5th essence of the angel by which to rise above the problem: my fear of falling. I then naturally move into SIX – a number by which to kill the vanity of my desires and transcend the mind as I become aware of a 7th realm. I am now back before time, when my angel abides in the void, knowing that there's nothing personal; resting while falling.

"Of letters I am the letter A," *Bhagavad Gita, Chapter 10, verse 33*

Surely, whereas four is karmic as D.R.E.M, five and SIX are Dharmic as the "a" calling the angels and avatars of me and in me.

Enlightenment

Prepare to DIE! Inquiry tool: www.goldenxpr.com/tc03_non-causality/.

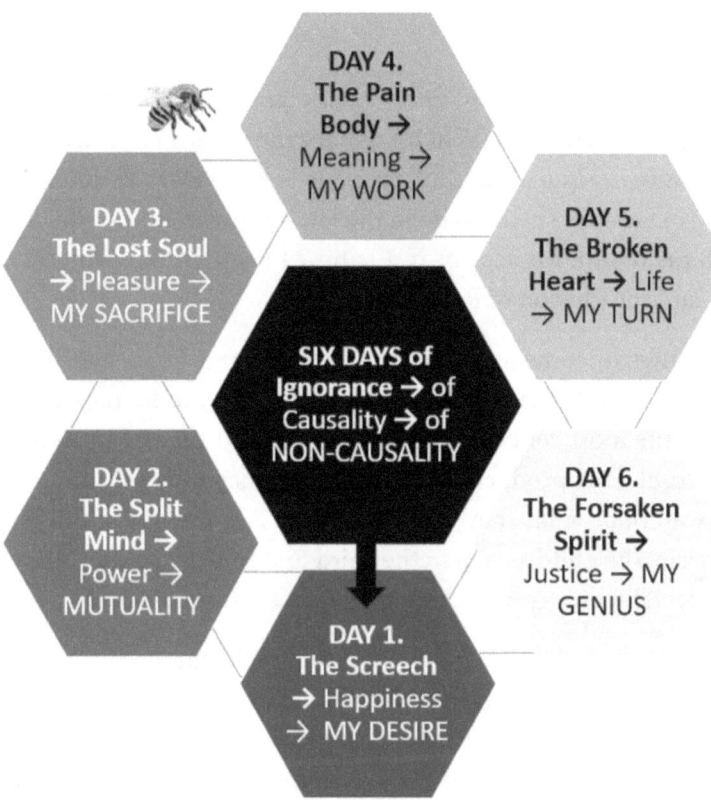

Step 1: I fill in the blank: I want to know WHY I would choose to think I CAN'T _____ (e.g.; find a job, be patient, etc.). **Step 2:** I ask for truth and generate a number. **Step 3:** I find my number on the map and fill in the brackets: when playing the instrument of [**Ignorance**], I hopelessly push for [**Causality**], which will end up turning on the light of [**NON-CAUSALITY**]. **Step 4:** What most surprised me in this process was [_____]

When the Soul Fears Resting...

'But LOVE said, "anyone who kills Cain will suffer vengeance seven times over." LOVE then put a mark on Cain so that no one would kill him.' *Genesis 4:14*

Shabbat Shalom or "Rest [in] Peace" is the greeting spoken from Friday night into Saturday night. When I replace the word *Shalom* with *Yirah*, I obtain *Shabbat Yirah* "Rest [in] Fear." It is the sense of unease – the anxiety that always seems to be in the back of my mind, compelling me to push or to pull. My fear of rest is how I keep on replaying the past and go into the illusion of forced labor.

To put things in context, my parents – Adam and Eve – had just been kicked out of PaRaDiSe when they had me. As the firstborn, I, Cain, inherited the most concentrated essence of good genes, but also of bad genes. Urgh! This produced a marked tendency to break the law in a bigger way than what they had ever done. Ah, the sin of the parents which visits the children up to the third and fourth generations: it's no joke, especially as it grows in intensity with each generation!

One thing I don't understand: why give a child the name of Cain for "possessed" by jealousy? If this is supposed to be my calling, it's a lot to take on! I can also see that my mother had high hopes for me – "the man she acquired from YEWE!" Did she even know that YEWE was the Power of accountability? For she was an accountant, all right... She controlled everything I did. I wasn't allowed to speak my wants. As for my father, he wasn't here; too busy putting bread on the table... So yes, I was set up! How could I not hold a grudge and be conditional in my offerings? And then upon seeing that my brother's gifts were recognized when mine were not, how could I not be enraged? Just the thought that I CAIN'T and you're ABEL unhinged me!

I know that this will continue until I can grow up, forgive my parents, and really give it all to LOVE. I'll then turn to non-action, and rest while creating – even while making money. I also know that something big is at work with my incessant disquiet since the letters of *Shabbat Yirah* (שבת ירא) reorganize into the unifying equation of *Barashit* (בראשית) for "created-SIX." I suspect it is for me to understand one of the most impactful fears: rest or death. After a life of insane failures and death-inducing episodes, I realized that I was afraid of what would happen if I became stronger than the force pulling me down. Yep, I have a feeling we're not in "CAINsas" anymore!

My Gravitational Problem

> "All know that the drop merges into the ocean but few know that the ocean merges into the drop." *Kabir*

How does it work? Was I rebelling against the law or did the need for legislation follow the first murder? For eons sages, legalists and political theorists have wrestled with the same question: should we place justice above the law? I may just be the one who started the legal debacle by prompting the question "what came first: the crime or the law?" **I imagine that the law comes first, since justice doesn't define the law: conscience does! Conscience is a voice. Consciousness speaks in words.**

While my good inclination is the law of LOVE directing me to act responsibly, my evil inclination can always find a way around the laws. It is even clever enough to know that doing the moral thing is not always the "right" thing to do! Nonetheless, if the heart's counsel is the law, the plurality of edicts appears to be invented for the lawless and the disobedient, for the murderers, the thieves and the liars – for the parts of me that repressed the feelings of hatred, and buried the rage deep inside. These parts are too far gone into the depth to hear the simplicity of the Golden Rule.

> "I have explained the phenomena of the heavens and of our sea by the force of gravity, but I have not yet assigned a cause to gravity."
> *Isaac Newton*

Would I need a cause for gravity if I didn't let myself be pulled into wrongdoing? I can't grasp how "God" would have no beginning and no end – beyond time, space and mind and/or any causation. I seem to need a reason for my suffering – an origin point. Even today, while science better explains gravity, there simply isn't much evidence to reconcile what causes it within a quantum model. Nobody has found a solution thus far, and the question is annoying, especially since, if we are certain to live in a quantum world, we're yet to figure out a way to include gravity in it.

Physicists think that the problem resides in gravity's extreme weakness. The gravitons (hypothetical quantized particles of gravitational energy) are individually too weak to be felt. We would need a huge particle detector, so huge that it would collapse into a black hole! We never dreamed it would be that hard to quantize gravity. And, truth be told, gravity is not a force like the other forces are.

Similarly with self-esteem. The sense that I am enough and that there's always more is different from other powers. It may even be their foundation. However, since I'm still working on earning it, I find myself doubting that there is an end to my dissatisfaction.

If gravity is arguably the deepest question in physics, shame is the deepest question in metaphysics. Why can't I just feel it? As soon as some particles of chaos hit my life, I become heavy, serious and *grave*. I obsess on the critical nature of my predicament. Afraid of falling and of being humiliated again, I end up letting myself be pulled down when I really want to grow up. I'm just not enough: no self-esteem.

If my emotional body is disturbed by the proverbial "pride [that] goes before destruction and a haughty spirit before a fall," it may be because I am yet to touch bottom. This is the prerequisite before I can evolve to the level of wholesome Power – the Promised Land or the second tier, when I am yet to free myself from the tyranny of the pairs of opposites – for good or bad, richer or poorer, in sickness and in health... There will come a time when to no longer differentiate between falling or rising. I will then allow myself to rise until I am risen.

VIRGINITY

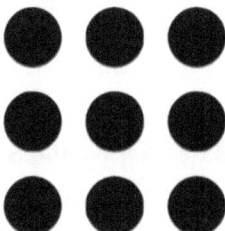

VIRGINITY is to do what I do for no other reason than because it is what I do. If I were a virgin, I would not be concerned by misery or happiness, loss or gain, defeat or victory, falling or rising, and thus would never be contaminated by the poison of greed. However, I am poisoned when I do what I do because I want my results. Am I not entitled to the fruit of my action? Ah, if I could stop taking personally the consequences of my activities, I wouldn't postpone doing due diligence.

I'd be able to detach from success or failure. I'd be equanimous, and have the Power to choose peace in each and every moment. I'd be free of Ego-Egypt and move out of Scare City. I would yearn for nothing.

It is clear. I must forget desire. Indeed, this is my destiny as someone who's possessed by jealousy – to kill the desires that feed my vanity.

When free of desire, I do what it takes as I have no fear of falling or of rising. My work becomes my sacrifice as I offer up both the action and the fruits of the action to the Divine. I live in the House of the Sanctuary. Henceforth, my action is non-binding: it comes without a karmic debt.

This is the sense of Sanskrit *Dharma* and S/Hebrew *Mitzvah*, which both imply a mutuality of existence with all other beings – a love for humanity. Thus, sacrifice is a universal rule and a fundamental law of nature. This sense of justice as giving it all to LOVE permeates all of creation. This is what transmutes hatred into love, suffering into satisfaction, misery into happiness.

The ultimate sacrifice is inscribed as one of the Seven Lights. It is putting the ego personality to death: my being bound to the light within lets me know beyond doubt that "IT" is not about me. Therein is the meaning of the binding of Isaac: first, Abraham accepts to lose his son, then Isaac chooses to return to the father by fully consenting to being bound on the sacrificial altar. Talk of mutuality!

As for what's left of me, I just have to feel how my many likes and dislikes were imprinted in my mind by my family and my culture. I will soon realize that the formidable force that compels me to do evil is the force of desire. It is desire that drags me down and demands a specific outcome for my action. However, the profit is never enough. The more I feed the desire body, the hungrier it is. It is a bottomless pit.

"Therefore, Arjuna, realizing the truth of your True Self is your principal weapon for eradicating desire." *Bhagavad Gita, 3:43*

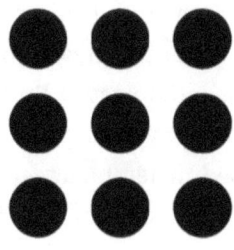

Desire and Cain

"Everything that exists in your life, does so because of two things: something you did or something you didn't do." *Albert Einstein*

Yep, it's all my fault: guilty as charged! Causality is a tough nut to crack, maybe as tough as the perception that I end at the skin. If I just listened, I would stop existing as an ego: look Ma, no private agendas! I received a gift: the mark on my Cain's forehead. I simply need to decode it and feel it. I will then understand the need to have been a murderer and be at peace with my "choice." This means that I CAN forgive. My story is your story, just like me, you may regret having killed your potential. Just like me, you can time-travel, change the past and know a different future.

Resting is transcending time, space and mind. When in the state of deep sleep, I forget all about my pain. It only reappears as soon as I am in the waking state. It's ironic to call it that as I'm yet to wake up. For my body to age *naturally*, the great time machine (my brain) must surrender its judgments. When I see order in the chaos, I regret nothing. Instead, I remember a providential future. This return to innocence does wonders for my aging mind and body. It might even eliminate the need for Alzheimer!

Therefore, time is more than attending the temporal structure of the universe. Time is created by the way I think and feel about these three marks. Once their soul is decoded, they complement the three marks of existence that are an essential part of Buddha's teaching. The word *Ot* (אות) for "mark" that was given to the murderer in me is a three-lettered word. Once reversed (when I learn from the mirror), each of its letters invokes and elucidates one of the Buddha's **marks** (bolded below):

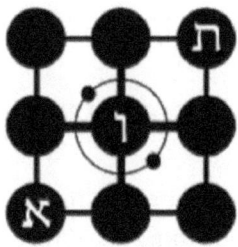

- Tav (ת) is the "sign" at the crossover point. It says "**nothing is permanent.**" When I accept that time accounts for change, I let go of the many losses along the way and have an easier time living.
- Vav (ו) is the "connector." It says "**nothing is satisfying.**" When I stop judging myself as inadequate, I don't separate from what is. Instead, I better appreciate a reality that is enough, knowing that there's always more.
- Aleph (א) is the "ox's" primal force. It says "**nothing is personal.**" When primal, I understand Oneness. And as I accept that my pain is your pain, I find my own strength, and begin to detach from the narrative that makes it about me; about the slave in me.

The three marks – nothing permanent, nothing satisfying, nothing personal – are engraved in the three letters את which can also be read as *Aleph V"Tav* or "A&T." AT/TA is code Communication, when I can then feel truth in my cells, and no longer "miss the mark," an expression understood to mean "when I no longer sin." As for me, I'd rather think in terms of doing no harm, and not adding to the violence that is already part of the natural world.

The V of Violence

"Everyone can perform magic, everyone can reach his goal, if he can think, wait, and fast." *Hermann Hesse, Siddharta*

Vav is a compelling letter. Seated at the top of the **6-Desiring** chamber, it initiates the 666 mark of the beast. Henceforth, it is the SIXth Word prompting the "do not kill" command, on which Cain completely snoozed. The Power that runs through Vav is enough to risk being misused, which may be how the sign is not visible in *Elohim* (אלהים); only audible.

6	
Desiring	
6	ו
60	ס
600	ם

Vav has the value of 6, as in the "Created-SIX" for me to understand my beast's measurement problem and the sense that I am not enough.

As for the verb *Retzach* (רצח) in "thou shall not kill" (*Exodus 20:12*), it has a wider range of meanings besides "to slay, kill, murder." In the sense of "breaking," it speaks of my saboteuR who compensates for my impotence by taking revenge and destroying the good, the true and the beautiful. This is where the entanglement of the saboteuR and the chilD are at its clearest: I need to free one to free the other.

Lion King	Star Child	Dragon Queen
chilD	prostitutE / victiM	saboteuR

The Three Pillars

What if embodying the potency of Vav's grammar were enough to lead me to the end of desire? That might just do the trick and kill vanity! Once fulfilled, I would be free to experience the following (bold) possibilities:

- Vav is a semi-consonant. It can be read as the consonant F, V, W. It can also be read as the vowel sound A, E, I, O, U → **I would become multimodal.**
- Vav is the word for "nail, connector" → **I would understand oneness.**
- Vav works as a prefix and a conjunction with the meaning of "and" → **I would transcend the 'either or' of my addicted mind and be all-inclusive.**
- Vav is also a consecutive construction when Vav is a prefix to a verb in order to change its tense from past to future (and vice-versa) → **I would forgive and be the change I wish to see.**

ויאמר אלהים, יהי אור; ויהי-אור.

The line of Hebrew text above comes from *Genesis 1:3*. It reads *Vayomer Elohim Yehi Aur; VaYehi Aur* and means "And God said: '**Let there be** light.' **And there was** light." The same verb *Yehi* is present twice, first, as a future tense ("let there be"), second, as a past sense ("and there was"). The change in tense is created by simply adding the sign Vav in front of the verb as a prefix and the conjunction "and:" "*and* [there was light]."

How could one letter be so powerful that it would either condemn me to repeat history or open a gate to eternity – the knowing that I am beyond time, able to change the past and know the future? I asked and saw how Vav is shaped as a Möbius strip, especially when it is within letter Aleph, spinning the mind into the non-duality of perfect balance.

Looking at the image, I see that Vav is at the core of Aleph, uniting the two Yod – the male and female "hands" into the LOVE that has no opposite. As such, Vav fosters the knowledge of *Tov V'Rah* or "good **and** evil" since it is the **"and,"** the connector by which to include evil. Whether conscious of it or not, every "Vav-Violation" gets me closer to the moment when I stop resisting evil and the "I'm bad" thoughtform attached to it. I can now change for good.

Aleph or Vav + Yod + Yod = 26. 26 = YEWE. This Vav is also silenced in Gehinnom – one of the seven lights that existed before time. It is the burning **desire** that compels the little something (the consciousness of me) to come out of the big nothing (pure awareness). However, and while on my path of individuation, I didn't know how brutal the desire to make a name for myself really is. This too, I was to experience. When I see that time is not linear, my saboteuR drops the plan and opens me to having a happy childhood. Henceforth, I can feel the wisdom of the 6th Word: "Thou shall not kill," and honor its Hindu kin in *Ahimsa* – the commandment of non-violence.

Cain is so deep in the DREaM he can only be hungry for LOVE. Being the first mortal, the first murderer and the first to be accountable for his actions, he alternates between desiring and resisting death. This obsessive compulsion lives in the letters (קין) of his name: Qoph (ק), Yod (י), and Nun (ן). These three signs are the only signs of the S/Hebrew alphabet whose "Great Gematria" contains a **Vav**:

- Qoph (Q) spells out as Qoph + **Vav** + Peh. It is equal to 186.
- Yod (Y) spells out as Yod + **Vav** + Dalet. It is equal to 20.
- Nun (N) spells out as Nun + **Vav** + Nun. It is equal to 106

Murderer Cain is a loaded gun until he can embrace the **Vav** desire which is now directed to revenge – to making "God" and his brother pay. I am Cain. When I feel and understand the torment behind my Vav's murderous desire, I am able to contain it. My attention is focused, and my chilD, disciplined. I can begin to imagine WORD Peace, and have no doubt that my creativity serves the greater good. What was first given as *Ot* (אות) – a mark miraculous enough to include the three marks of existence – has now become *HaOt* (האות) or "THE Mark" by revealing the Heh womb that was previously invisible as the container of Vav, granting Cain/me the sense of enough.

The Two Hands

"There are 10 kinds of people. The kind that understands the binary code, and the kind that does not." *Anonymous*

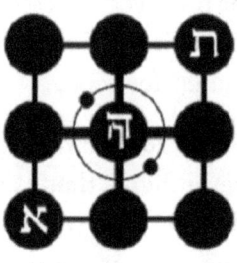

9	8	7	6	5	4	3	2	1
Completing	Ordering	Engaging	Desiring	"PAIRfect"	Resisting	Changing	Separating	Opening

The 10 kinds of people as 10 fingers

Indeed, my 10 kinds of people are also the 10 digits – "digit" coming from Latin *digitus* for "finger." When the 0 digit performs its duty (which is to annihilate the ego), my two hands spontaneously join at the thumbs as pictured above in the eagle shadow. I can now hear: "not my will, Thy Will be done," which allows my right hand to know what my left hand is doing. At last, conscious and unconscious are in agreement. Therefore, when I say: "let there be whatever," I see shortly that "whatever" is already created. There are no uninformed intentions in my space to cause a delay between what I say I want and what I have in reality. Surely, the ability to succeed in my creation depends on my telling the truth. This is when the ego snake is nullified.

The truth which makes the communication of my 10 digital fingers impeccable can be helped by understanding "the 10 Words" – the first 10 letters and numbers of the S/Hebrew alphabet. These 10 words happen to prompt "the Ten Commandments," an ethical device which is mostly resisted and yet to be felt. If I did, I might even come to the end of the terrible loneliness that frightens me and hinders me.

When my hands separate, I need to hide my secret from you. This is why I distance myself. This is how I'm lonely. I don't want you to know that I don't really serve the good of all (or of you), but just the good of me, myself and I. The separation occurs when the thumb of my right hand chooses to break the union of my metaphorical "eagle" hands to fulfill its personal cravings. To do so, I must first forget that I am LOVE. I must also ignore that I am truth in action. And if I do all of that, I can finally desire to do evil and let myself be led into temptation.

Henceforth, I am now the 2nd Adam, the one who is in doubt. Even my rebelling is a trap, as I find myself replaying the past. The more I identify to being not enough, the more I need to run from the Now! If only I could be true to myself...

I had scarcely finished praying that prayer when YEWE made its appearance.

The YEWE that Came from the Wombman

"All truths are easy to understand once they are discovered; the point is to discover them." Galileo Galilei

It is so easy to forget: there is no one and nothing outside of me! Yep, I am it all – the Bible, the writers of the Bible, the editors of the Bible, the commentaries on the Bible, the heroes of the Bible. I am Adam, Eve, the snake and the tree. Will I dare say it: I am God?

I have created "God" in my own image, just as "God" created me in the image of the Divine. It thus stands to reason that Cain's story would be my story, since there's only One story of pain. Just like me, you bleed when pricked. Just like me, you have known loneliness, sadness and a fair amount of anger. Just like me, you have a hard time forgiving.

The Torah is kind enough to give me a map to hearing and seeing how today's chaos has already been mapped out. Born out of PaRaDiSe, Cain is destined to meet YEWE – the Lord of karma and, as such, the Power of accountability. However, since he is the first mortal, he is also the first to fear death. His liberation from suffering is contingent on his discovering this truth: it is in dying that one comes to eternal life.

My liberation from suffering invites the death of "I" and "mine." Indeed, when I do not take anything personally – neither my genius nor my demon, I am released from the cycle of rebirth that is impelled by the laws of karma.

Just in case I am yet to succeed in my creation, the next "BEE Map" will give me the opportunity to connect the SIX "days" of failure to the SIX "days" of suffering – a suffering that may get intense enough to lead me to the SIX "days" of my liberation.

The Map of (My) Suffering

Prepare to DIE! Inquiry tool: www.goldenxpr.com/tco3_liberation/.

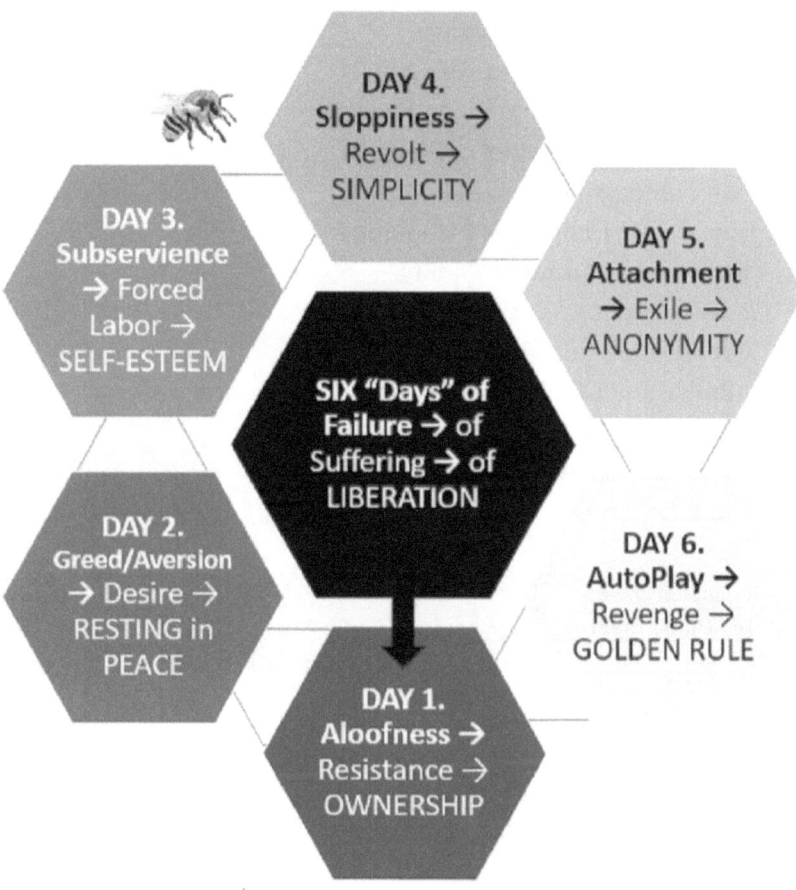

Step 1: I fill in the blank: I want to know WHY I would choose to think I CAN'T _____ (e.g.; find a job, be patient, etc.). **Step 2**: I ask for truth and generate a number. **Step 3**: I find my number on the map and fill in the brackets: when resisting the experience of [**Failure**], I let my [**Suffering**] negatively affect me, a pain which will eventually lead me to fulfill my wish for [**LIBERATION**]. **Step 4**: what most surprised me in this process was [_____].

Part III: The End of Suffering

- Genesis 4:1-17 – The Story of (My) Suffering.
- The Turn to the East
- The Mastery of 777-Engaging.
- The SIX "Days" of my Leadership
- The Commitment behind 777-Engaging
- The "heART" of Servant Leadership
- Code Compassion – ND / DN
- Wanted – An Enlightened Humanity
- The Brilliant Murder of "Vanity"
- Code Absolute – ST [and] AB
- Code Incarnation – BNT / ANS
- Childlike and Clueless
- Code Depth – NWN / WWW
- Redemption Code – AB / BN / ABN
- A NDE (a Nun Depth Experience)

2. Individual Power	3. Symbolic Power	1. Collective Power
2. The Limbic Brain	3. The Neocortex	1. The Reptilian Brain
2nd Son – Abel	3rd Son – Seth	1st Son – Cain

The Triune Brain

Genesis 4:1-17 – The Story of (My) Suffering

"Now Adam knew his wife Eve, and she conceived and bore Cain, saying, "I have acquired a man from YEWE." *Genesis 4:1*

This was the first of two instances when my mother Eve spoke, offering words of such potency they are yet to be heard. It is also the first time the four-lettered Name YEWE appears on its own. Thus far, the second Adam had met YEWE *Elohim* as the Power of History, a name that set him up to commit a first violation by giving him a negative command. This is how this Name would spin the sphere *Binah* – the 3rd eye of "understanding." I learn from history when I see the probable consequences of my words and actions, and choose to no longer repeat my erratic behavior. However, to "understand" the lesson and free my will, I first have to be a poor student, and do what is contrary to my guidance.

As for YEWE, it is mistranslated as "Lord," misheard as *Yahweh* or *Jehovah*, and ignored as the Verb that inscribes my destiny. It may even be THE verb as it is cause and effect in action. Indeed, it enacts an accounting system that pays me in the measure of what I say and do, rewarding me when good, and punishing me when bad.

- **When I resist feeling bad,** the four-lettered Name goes retrograde. It invokes the DREaM of four unconscious archetypes (D for chilD, R for saboteuR, E for prostitutE and M for victiM).
- **When I enjoy feeling good,** the four-lettered Name goes direct. It invokes the LOVE of four conscious archetypes working as One (L for Leader, O for Officer, V for Visionary, E for Engineer).

Eve's rare speech act has vast implications, especially as it now involves measurements. The S/Hebrew word *Qanity* "I have acquired" holds the letters of *Qain* (Cain) which is how I'm bound to material life, being "possessed" by my possessions. As her children, Cain and Abel, we are the first generation born out of the PaRaDiSe wedlock, in the lower worlds. Prior to us, Adam was an immaculate conception (someone who didn't come out of a human sperm and a human egg). As Cain, I am prey to serial births and rebirths, believing that I am "just human," and as such, meant to err. Henceforth, I'm stuck in the past, endlessly reincarnating into the same insane time loop, and having children in the hope that they'll make me an immortal. I am a prisoner of my mind, and, to top it all, also in constant service to Mammon. Whether I know it or not, my quest for liberation is now of the essence. Eve is the "Mother of All Life," but also and equally the "Matter of ALL Life." That's what she "got" when speaking of "getting" Cain. My freedom depends on my ability to transcend the physical, turn matter into energy and thus, "acquire" enough wholesome Power that I can free myself from being in bondage to the master of money and yearning.

To this end, here is the decoding of *Genesis 4* via the SIX "days" of my being in the dark, unconscious of moving into SIX "days" of failure, followed by SIX "days" of SUFFERING and ending in SIX "days" of liberation. The code is written as follows: **Day # – Shadow Archetype → Failure → SUFFERING → Liberation.**

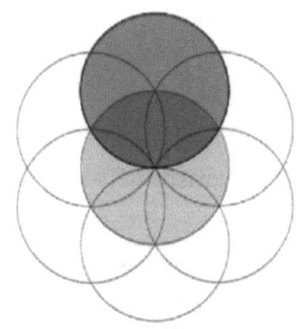

1. RESISTANCE

Day 1 – The Fallen Angel → Aloofness → RESISTANCE → Ownership: I have fallen, and I can't get up. No matter what I try to create, I fail because I believe I am creating separately from the whole. If I hopelessly yearn for success, it is because I am cursed with a deeply frustrated desire for my man. Yes, I am Eve; Adam's female side. In my mind, success goes with male achievement. So, I try very hard to convince myself that "I got it" – I got the object of my desire; in my case, a man in the form of a son. But I haven't! What I've gotten is just more karma that will have to be cleaned up. I start thinking: maybe

I didn't do it right. So, I try again, birth Abel and fail again. At that time, I was far from birthing Seth! I now think that I don't have any mothering skills. I learn more and fail again. I then construct a story for why I failed: Adam is against me! But I never really allow myself to see the truth, which is that I fight "God" or reality. I go **aloof**, separate. I keep on **RESISTING** doing the next "write" thing. Henceforth, I only see "you" as my enemy, and wonder how I can "get" you before you'd get me. Speaking of not getting it, I never take **ownership** of my circumstances: "the snake made me!" Here is the Torah portion: 'Adam knew his wife Eve who conceived and bore Cain saying, "I have gotten a man from YEWE." Later she gave birth to his brother Abel.' *Genesis 4:1-2*

Day 2 – The Prostitute → Greed / Aversion → DESIRE → Resting in Peace: I don't know who I am and don't know that I belong. Perceiving that I am all alone and that it's a jungle out there leads me to sell out and prostitute my gifts. I fail by becoming increasingly toxic, as my ignorance soon begets **greed**, and my greed, **aversion**. Living in Scare City

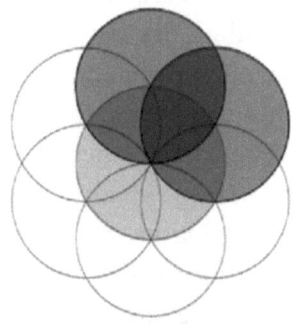

2. DESIRE

while imagining that you've got what I long for, I can only hate you and withhold from you or smother you and over-give to you (both being far from "PAIRfect"). The vicious cycle now sharpens and intensifies the **DESIRE**. That's exactly what happened to me, Cain. My unwillingness to give it all is how my offerings were disregarded. It is also what brought me to despair. No matter how I played it, there was no way for me to win or to **rest**. No **Peace**. Here is the Torah portion: "Now Abel kept flocks, and Cain worked the soil. In the course of time, Cain brought some of the fruits of the soil as an offering to the LORD. And Abel also brought an offering; the fat portions from some of the firstborn of his flock. The LORD looked with favor on Abel and his offering, but on Cain and his offering he did not. So, Cain was very angry, and his face was downcast." *Genesis 4:3-5*

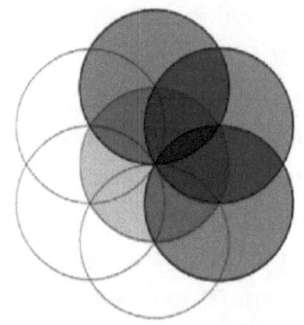

3. FORCED LABOR

Day 3 – The Saboteur → Subservience → FORCED LABOR → Self-esteem: mostly, I'm anxious, disquiet, and barely coping. I also pack a lot of anger behind the mask of depression. Yep, it appears that I am saddened that my offering would not be accepted. But the truth is: I'm angry, so angry that I am enraged. Sometimes I feel that this rage is what gives me Power while I am so pitifully failing. At least, I have that – my rage! And while I can barely own up to my calling (it's hard to admit that jealousy "got" me), I would need something phenomenal to encourage me to feel how painful that rage is. It is maddening to feel so obligated to "you" (**subservient**, truly) that I become tongue-tied. I just can't seem to ask for what I want or need! I "try" to be good; to do my best. But I know I'm not really good and not really doing my best as my sacrifice is motivated by a false sense of duty. I don't really want to give. Giving feels like **FORCED LABOR** to me! Subsequently, I keep on sabotaging myself by leading me into temptation and missing the "good" mark. Can I help it if I'm flawed, not good enough? Is it my fault if I suffer from low **self-esteem**? Here is the Torah portion: "Then the Lord said to Cain, "Why are you angry? Why so depressed? If you do what is right, will you not be accepted? But if you do not do what is right, sin is crouching at your door; its desire is contrary to you, but you must rule over it." *Genesis 4:6-7*

Day 4 – The Victim → Sloppiness → REVOLT → Simplicity: if I'm so dissatisfied and if I desire killing you, it's not that I'm evil, but more that I can't allow myself to go deep enough into the rageaholic 'habit' hole to get the message! This rage is sourced in my passion – a hunger so formidable and so ancient it terrifies me. While I hear that I must "rule over it," how can I not get **sloppy** and hold the tension when I feel like such a victim? I am so low – my sense of worth is so low – that I must turn into a bully so that the other would end up being my victim. This way, I have found someone that has it even worse than I do – someone lower on the chain. So, yes: I can see the simplicity of "do what's right, and you'll be accepted." But I'm so afraid to be rejected again that I go into **REVOLT** and deliberately do wrong, so that, at the least, I would have a reason for why my offering is not wanted. Controlling my being a failure by killing any prospect of

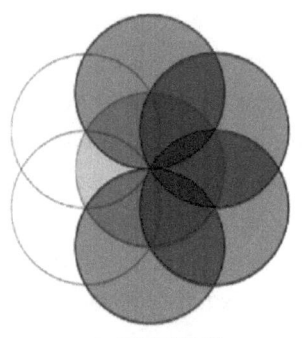

4. REVOLT

success: that makes it **simple** for me. But does it, really? Here is the Torah portion: *'Now Cain said to his brother Abel, "Let's go out to the field." While they were there, Cain attacked his brother Abel and killed him. Then the* LORD *said to Cain, "Where is your brother Abel?" "I don't know," he replied. "Am I my brother's keeper?" The* LORD *said, "What have you done? Listen! Your brother's blood cries out to me from the ground."' Genesis 4:8-10*

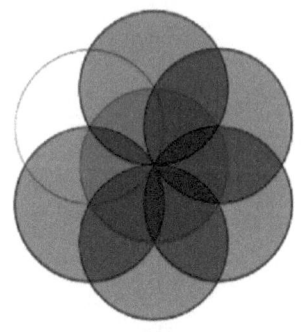

5. EXILE

Day 5 – the Child → Attachment → **EXILE** → Anonymity: I would not be so afraid if I could feel non-causality *in my blood*, and realize that there is no one acting and no one experiencing. I'd let go of my **attachment** to an outcome and stop resisting the consequences that I placed in motion. But I'm so intent on being right that I can't even imagine that the whole structure of karmas and curses will become

obsolete when there is no one left to resist or desire punishment. I'm like a child, hungry for your attention – even if it is negative attention! I can't see that I am the one who is separating by sending me and even condemning me to **EXILE**. Yes, I take everything personally. I am Cain. I wish I'd have another name. I wish I'd open to **anonymity**, but alas...

Here is the Torah portion: "'Now you are under a curse and driven from the ground, which opened its mouth to receive your brother's blood from your hand. When you work the ground, it will no longer yield its crops for you. You will be a restless wanderer on the earth." Cain said to the LORD, "My punishment is more than I can bear. Today you are driving me from the land, and I will be hidden from your presence; I will be a restless wanderer on the earth, and whoever finds me will kill me.'" *Genesis 4:11-14*

SIXth Day - the Rising Angel → AutoPlay → REVENGE → Golden Rule: so, I'll admit it. My soul is heavy – a far cry from being as light as a feather. I must not understand the force of gravity. I still feel that my punishment is more than I can bear. Here's the proof: I'm like your regular Sisyphus, the guy who was punished because he tried to cheat death! Just as he, I keep on rolling down in the

SIX. REVENGE

depths of Hell, each single time I try to free myself from my karma. So yes, it does feel like failure is on **AutoPlay** and that I'm a prisoner of the depths – never to rise to the top. I can't even die, since anyone who tries to kill me will be punished in **REVENGE**, seven times over. It's like a fail-safe mechanism that "safely" keeps the failure going! To be able to rest while working and have no fear of death, I would have to understand the dynamics of 7-engaging. I would have to own that I am terrified of dying to who I think I am... Indeed, transcending the fear of death is also realizing that I was never born! This is what the land or consciousness of Nod is about. This is why I moved there. Yes, I must return to the East of Eden. I hear it is the land of compassion, where to embrace my pain so completely that I will stop doing harm as I'll feel the sense of the **Golden Rule** circulating in my blood. I will stretch to the 7th day – when my suffering reveals the liberation that was always present. Here is the Torah portion: 'But the LORD said to him, "Not so;

anyone who kills Cain will suffer vengeance seven times over." Then the LORD put a mark on Cain so that no one who found him would kill him. So, Cain went out from the LORD's presence and lived in the land of Nod, east of Eden.'" *Genesis 4:15-16*

Liberation in the East

"Here again we witness the single outcome of a worldwide process, with East and West yielding the same results, and once again for the same reason: Men have forgotten God." *Aleksandr Solzhenitsyn*

0/7. LIBERATION

When I am **IN-LOVE**, I experience the delightful willingness to give it all: no holds barred! I know what liberation is as I have no need to add to my suffering. At last, I love and approve of myself. But how do I open to such self-love? The answer is simple, and yet not easy to hear. For me to be this change I wish to see – within and without, I must transmute the hatred that lives in me. The poison of aversion is very real. It is activated when I perceive that reality is "no good."

But who is the observer of such reality? What eye? What "I?" To have another way to look at challenges, I must earn the light of my being. While it is a gift, I am not always aware of it. I worry, I stress, I fret, which is all coming from my perception of attack. Do I forget that, when I perceive attack, I am both the victim and the aggressor? Earning my right of passage to the Promised Land of an Open Third Eye (where I can think straight), I must surrender to going counter-clockwise. This is doing shadow work, an invitation to befriend the prostitutE, the saboteuR, the victiM and the chilD. There is a purpose to suffering, if only to take me to the shores of liberation.

While the continued regression and the going backwards in the **DREaM** can be intense, they are a necessary move for me to **EVOL**ve and stop misusing Power. When I do, I no longer project unrequited love. I am **LOVE** and **IN-LOVE** with reality and "God;" with everything. I have no need to push or pull, no doubt, and no yearning! The liberty of going clockwise (starting in the South; in the fiery L of my Leadership) ushers a liberation that is surprising. At last, I begin to see the end of my exploring, when I know the "true East" for the first time, and feel mind and body renewed in their connection.

Yod (י)	Vav Heh (וה)	Heh (ה)
Fire	Air / Earth	Water
South	East / West	North
L of Leader	E of Engineer / O of Officer	V of Visionary

The Butterfly Wheel of LOVE

Here is the spell spun by the butterfly wheel of LOVE, when I am in a **DREaM**, not having "**EVOL**ved" enough to actualize **LOVE**:

1. E is for the Engineer whose actualization I delay by turning into a prostitutE. This is when I doubt myself (and others, same) →
2. V is for the Visionary whose actualization I delay by turning into a saboteuR. This is when I betray myself (and others, same) →
3. O is for the Officer whose actualization I delay by turning into a victiM. This is when I defend/attack myself (and others, same) →
4. L is for the Leader whose actualization I delay by turning into a chilD. This is when I blame myself (and others, same) →

On and on I continue to cycle on the butterfly wheel of transformation, which is also known as the wheel of suffering. But then, just like there is nothing personal about "my" suffering, and certainly, nothing satisfying in it, I can now say that there is also nothing permanent to the pain story. I can drop it! When I stop making it about me and stop trying to be a clever Sisyphus trying to outsmart the gods, the suffering that was on auto-repeat comes to an end. Going from vexing greed to amazing grace changes my way from counterclockwise (and in need of purification while in the HELLusion) to clockwise (and in appreciation of purity while in PaRaDiSe).

I can surrender to being **IN-LOVE**, as I experience the heart of servant leadership:

- **IN** is for the mutuality of GReed **INgénue** and GRace **INgénue** who stay on the hub, unaffected by the ups and downs of the wheel. As such, the twin INgénue prompts the physics of commitment which allows for code Compassion.
- **L** is for the **Leader** of LOVE whose heart is open to hear a higher guidance. As such, the Leader prompts code Absolute.
- **O** is for the **Officer** of LOVE whose body receives the orders given by the heart, and delivers results. As such, the Officer prompts code Incarnation.

- **V** is for the **Visionary** of LOVE whose soul transmits the expression of the heart. As such, the Visionary prompts no code, as "she" is mainly clueless.
- **E** is for the **Engineer** of LOVE whose mind killed the last desire and has come to be free of all yearning. As such, the Engineer prompts code Depth.

The next few pages will unfold the codes that transcribe the voice of commitment, the spirit of compassion, the heart of the Absolute, the body of incarnation and the mind of depth. Note: Commitment, Compassion, the Absolute, Incarnation, Cluelessness and Depth are explored next as the SIX "days" of my Leadership.

The SIX "Days" of my Leadership

Prepare to DIE! Inquiry tool: www.goldenxpr.com/tc03_leadership/

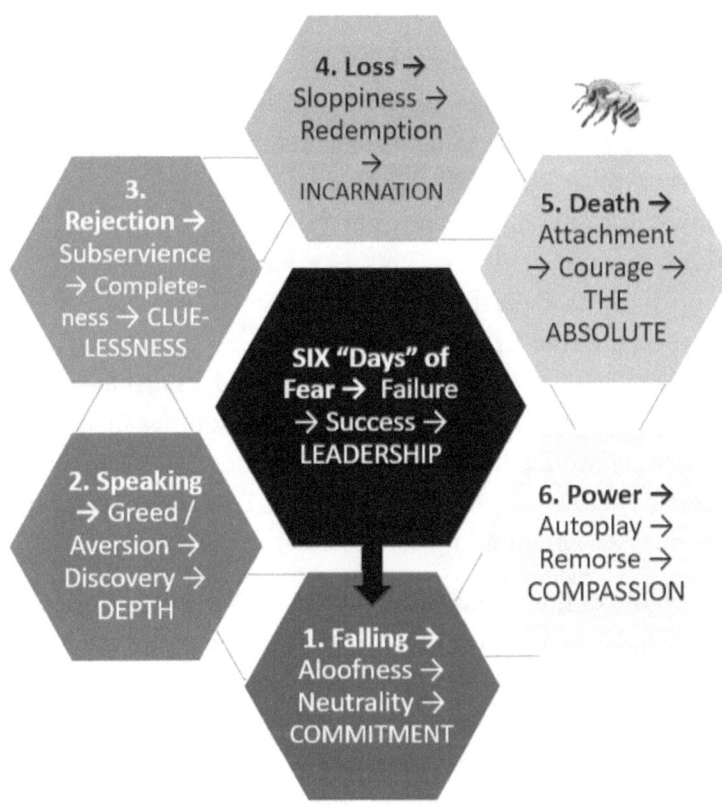

Step 1: I fill in the blank: I want to know WHY I would choose to think I CAN'T _____ (e.g.; find a job, be patient, etc.). **Step 2:** I ask for truth and generate a number. **Step 3:** I find my number on the map and fill in the brackets: when fearing [**Fear**], I eventually shut down and fail myself by way of [**Failure**]. When tired of using [**Failure**] to make me feel small, I take a chance with [**Success**], which opens my heart to the [**LEADERSHIP**] of leadership. **Step 4:** what most surprised me in this process was [_____].

The Commitment behind 777-Engaging

"The only limit to your impact is your imagination and commitment." Tony Robbins

To sustainably stop the illusion of forced labor and enjoy doing due diligence, week after week, 24/7 and not suffer vengeance 7 times over, I must master the dynamics of engagement. Incidentally, it is also the way to tame the 666 beast of desire. This is easier said than done, as I must now connect the dots between the role I play as an individual

7	
Engaging	
7	ז
70	ע
700	ן

and the overall collective goal "God" has in mind. I must feel that I am not accidental, that existence needs me as I am (quirks, included), and that something would be missing without me. Once I open to the sacredness of my task, I get energized by it. This is the secret behind being on purpose and fulfilling my potential.

That the whole of life would miss me if I didn't exist gives me tremendous vigor and even dignity. This is confirmed by the 77 value of word *Az* (עז) for "strength." Clean engagement and the fulfillment thereof come from my having the sense that I am at home in my body and in the world. I can then relate to the awesome way that existence cares for me, and to the abundant love raining on me from all dimensions. This also means to forgive my violations and those who violated me. This process of ultimate forgiveness is part of a 7x7-week or 49-day ritual known as "the Counting of the Omer" – a ritual that stretches from Passover (when I leave Ego-Egypt) to the holy day of *Shavuot* (when the law is given). This is confirmed by the 490 (70x7) value of *Tamim* (תמים) for "blemish-free, perfect."

I also notice that a "sin" not forgiven increases dramatically with each generation. Lamech who is five generations removed from Cain must atone 70x7 for the murder he committed, i.e.; 10 times more. Here is the

Torah portion: "And Cain knew his wife, and she conceived and gave birth to Enoch. Cain was then building a city, and he named it after his son Enoch. To Enoch was born Irad, and Irad was the father of Mehujael, and Mehujael was the father of Methusael, and **Methusael** was the father of Lamech. [...] Lamech said to his wives, "Adah and Zillah, listen to me; wives of Lamech, hear my words. I have killed a man for wounding me, a young man for injuring me. If Cain is avenged seven times, then Lamech is seventy-seven times." *Genesis 4:17-24*

And it makes me wonder... Did Lamech become a murderer out of reacting to his father Methusael? The name **Methusael** means "who is from God" – a name whose numerical value of 777 inscribes the mastery of engagement. Not only does mastering engagement annihilate any possibility of killing my potential, but also it simultaneously ensures that I'd reach my goal as this goal "is now from God."

Code Compassion - ND / DN

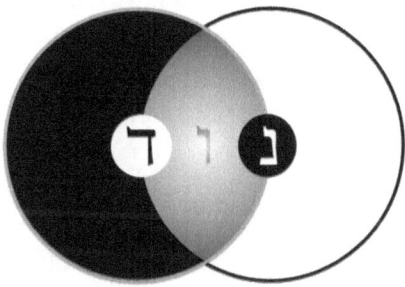

Imagine a language so pure and so sacred that it can reconcile opposites in just a few pairings of letters...

Right: Hebrew letter Nun (נ) → N in Roman script
Middle (inferred): Hebrew letter Vav (ו) → F, U, V, W in Roman script
Left: Hebrew letter Dalet (ד) → D in Roman script

Here is how S/Hebrew inscribes code "Compassion" in 5 words:

- **ND:** from right to left, I read *Ned* (נד) for "piling up [praises and critiques]."
- **DN:** from left to right, I read *Dan* (דן) for "judge."
- **NWD:** from right to middle to left, I read *Nod* (נוד) for "wandering."
- **NWN:** from right to middle to right, I read *Nun* (נון) for "fish, posterity."
- **DWD:** from left to middle to left, I read *David* (דוד) for "beloved."

The Decoding: *Nod* is the land where Cain fled: "so, Cain went out from the LORD's presence and lived in the land of **Nod**, east of Eden." *Genesis 4:16.* This "land" or consciousness is where the Cain in me can express his sorrow and thereby feel it. The **wandering** has two faces. The first face is ambivalence. This is the part of me that decides (e.g.; to stop drinking) and takes back my decision (e.g.; when I have the next drink). Doing so is costly to my self-esteem. The second face is measure. This is the part of me that knows when to push and when to pull as I move bravely to and from the place where it hurts in order to feel it. The two complementary motions of going in and out of the pain are compassion (from Latin *com-* "with" + *pati* "pain") in action.

It takes courage to pray "bring it on;" **pile on** all the praises but also and foremost all the critiques that "you" have against me! Make them as severe as I can stand them to be, for I wish to be a **judge** of truth. Keep doubling the blows until I surrender to feeling the pain that I inflict on myself! For in that doubling and that back and forth (when W joins the two N signs of **NWN** and the two D signs of **DWD**), I shall see inscribed the endurance of **Nun** – the messianic **fish** who comes from the House of **David – the Beloved.** When all is said and done, it will remind me that being entire and loving "God" / reality with *all* my heart, *all* my soul and *all* my Power are the natural result of feeling my passion until IT is done!

Wanted - An Enlightened Humanity

"'Adam knew his wife again, and she gave birth to a son and named him Seth, saying, "God has appointed me another seed in place of Abel, since Cain killed him." Seth also had a son, and he named him Enosh. At that time people began to call on the name of the LORD.' Genesis 4:25-26 – THE END of Chapter 4

The finish of my story as Cain is a last transformation and integration by way of my second brother; the third son of Adam and Eve named Seth for "the appointed one." To recap, first comes Adam Qadmon who had it all together but in a child's way (s/he was yet to earn it and own it). Then came Adam HaRishon, when "he" was in such an illusion of separation that he needed to be put to sleep to dream up the missus. Then came the snake whose lies prompted the loss of PaRaDiSe. Next, my mother Eve got pregnant, first with me, then with Abel, and finally with Seth. This is when she spoke again. Just like me, she seems to be asleep as she is still counting, for how else would she think in terms of a restitution for losing Abel? On the note of dreaming, there were three sons and no daughters. So, how did I, Cain, manage to have an entire progeny?

Indeed, how? Especially since the shrunk Heh of *Genesis 2:4* continues to eclipse the feminine and the ability to receive. And it is not because it is eclipsed that it is not here! Adam Harishon being put to sleep to conceive his woman does not change the fact that his brain was still created male and female, in the divine image. Seth also needed a woman to procreate. He named his son Enosh for "a man." This man was to carry on his inherited divine appointment and birth an enlightened humanity – a humanity calling on the name of LOVE. The answer to this dilemma is as follows: all of these generations, from Adam Qadmon to me, are the "I Am." The "I Am" is *Ehyeh* (אהיה). It has two Heh wombs; one for my female side and one for my male side. When I know who I Am, I stop identifying to the body and thinking "I'm the man." There's no push/pull, no doubt and no cravings. Having two signs Heh, I am accessing all parts of my brain, strengthened (and not weakened) by knowing the extent of my female reptilian brain. Being whole and "PAIRfect," I feel the mind-body connection through the neocortex of the Adam in its Adamah "ground." The curses being removed, I can be successful in my creation and have a wild progeny, yet this time, consciously.

2. Individual Power	3. Symbolic Power	1. Collective Power
2. The Limbic Brain	3. The Neocortex	1. The Reptilian Brain
2nd Son – Abel	3rd Son – Seth	1st Son – Cain

The Triune Brain Created in the Divine Image

To acquire that much authority, I must integrate the Power of Three. This will cause the reptilian brain and the limbic brain to consummate each other. Similarly, I am initially born backed up by collective Power (as it ought to be), but also enmeshed in it. Second, I must resist being pulled by "the world" if I want to discover my individual nature. Third, I come into symbolic Power, and surrender what's left of my vying for control. These three stages now collapse into one state, when I have the Power to just be, even when in the midst of chaos. **The gods can now trust me and involve me in a QKosmic plan meant to move all sentient life to LOVE. To be Seth – "appointed" to transmit the light of the I Am, my brain had to include both Cain and Abel's dangerous tendencies.**

The Brilliant Murder of "Vanity"

> "Vanity of vanities, says the Teacher, vanity of vanities! All is vanity." *Ecclesiastes 1:2*

Vanity, my brother! How could I love you so much that I would want to kill you? Indeed, there are two sides to my pain story. My male side is named *Abel* for "vanity." When the translation of *Ecclesiastes 1:2* says: "vanity of vanities! All is vanity," the Hebrew reads: *Abel Abalim! Hakhol*

Abel. Abel is the reward finder – the one who is "able:" all he touches turns to gold! As Cain, I relate to the other side: no matter how hard I try, I don't succeed! So yes, I'm named the "possessed" one. I'm possessed by jealousy as I see you ABEL to get what you want while I CAIN get no satisfaction. Argh!

Am I tongue-tied because I try to hide the self-serving calculations that are constantly roaming through my mind? Is it why I am not free to place my attention on the dimension where I can be the change? I hate being prey to the tyranny of appearances; always wondering what people think of me. I'm just afraid; afraid of being found out, of loneliness, of my business falling apart, of dying in misery… I want to look good like you do, or better than you do! Vanity of vanities; yep! No wonder I would eventually decide to get rid of my problem and kill Abel.

Killing "vanity" was actually brilliant as it is killing any self-centered desire. Indeed, for me to let go of being attached to an outcome (jealous), I must decide why I want what I want. If, for example, I wanted to be fit, I must know that my wanting fitness is not out of vanity. Same for wanting to build a fortune: I must be at peace with my motivations. This is to say: I must kill my brother "vanity" which I do by knowing that receiving what I want also serves the good of all. Then and only then, will I stand a chance to fulfill my desire and my potential. I will then see that having, for example, prestige is not higher or lower than not having it and be free to do due diligence, as I will be able to either take it or leave it.

Such freedom is how I know that my prayer is already fulfilled: I want everything I have, and I have everything I want. This is the time paradox that I was born for… and died for! To enjoy my "neocortex" immortality, I had to violate the laws and then torment myself about it. My mind was to obsess on a past that I could neither forgive nor forget. My mother (and matter) had to be *Chavah* "Eve," the S/Hebrew equivalent of Sanskrit *Saṃsāra* as the cyclicality of death and rebirth to which life in the material world is bound. I was to give my Power to a "Lord" of karma spinning the wheel of suffering. Karma is not only a universal religious belief. It is also found in Newton's third law of motion: "for every action there is an equal and opposite reaction."

I eventually learned that I could decrease the negative impact of cause and effect. I just needed to stop my mind from moving: "be still and know that I Am." While going up and down the wheel, I am "wandering" which is my fate as Cain, but also the meaning of *Saṃsāra*. LOL: is this saying that anyone whose chilD is yet to grow up is a "wandering" Jew? **My inability to center in the midst of chaos is how the wheel of suffering is a wheel of transformation.** This is how *Tiqqun Cain* remains the most critical of all possible adjustments (see *Chapter 3*). Strangely, this "repair" proves my innocence and not my guilt. It frees me from being in bondage to Mammon's world of fear, greed and domination. It is why I was born.

The more conscious I am that this work fulfills the first part of my divine appointment, the freer I am to offer my gifts unconditionally (which is the second part of my divine appointment). Doing so opens me to the sense of compassion to be "with my pain." Little by little, I extend to "you" a love that knows no bounds – the LOVE that has no opposite. And it is because I am so close to a transcendental state in which there is no cravings that I help other beings – just by my presence – to be free of suffering. I am Cain the Compassionate, devoted to loving and respecting "you," as you are what's left of me.

Therein is the depth of absolute of incarnation. Incarnation asks me to go so deep that I'd find absolution by way of absolute truth. To begin feeling it, I am given three codes: Absolute – Incarnation – Depth.

Code Absolute - ST [and] AB

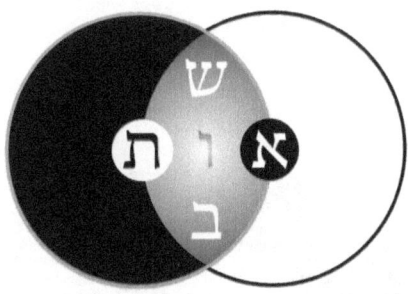

Imagine a language so pure and so sacred that it can reconcile opposites in just a few core letters...

Top: Hebrew letter Shin (ש) → S, Sh in Roman script
Right: Hebrew letter Aleph (א) → A in Roman script
Middle: Hebrew letters Vav (ו) → F, U, V, W in Roman script
Left: Hebrew letter Tav (ת) → T in Roman script
Bottom: Hebrew letter Beth (ב) → B in Roman script

Here is how S/Hebrew inscribes code "Absolute" in 5 words:

- **ST**: from top to left, I read *Seth* (שת) for "Seth, appointed."
- **AB**: from right to bottom, I read *Ab* (אב) for "father, alphabet."
- **AWT**: from right to left, I read *Ot* (אות) for "mark, sign, miracle, proof."
- **SWB**: from left to right, I read *Shuv* (שוב) for "turn, change."

The Decoding: the code ATBaSh is "the first and the last" since it is named after the two most meaningful pairs that begin and end it all: **AT** and **BS** (see *Chapter 3*). When pairing them as **ST** and **AB**, I see **Seth** (the 3rd Son) who is **appointed** to go to the **father**. The how-to comes from using the central Vav to **connect** the dots. I look in life's mirror to read the "**mark**" inscribed on my third eye, and decide to move from stage to stage until I link **A and T** (אות), each time acquiring more wholesome Power. I will eventually have gained "enough" self-esteem to find that I CAN face my fear of aloneness, **turn within** and **change**. I am now ready for code Incarnation.

Code Incarnation - BNT / ANS

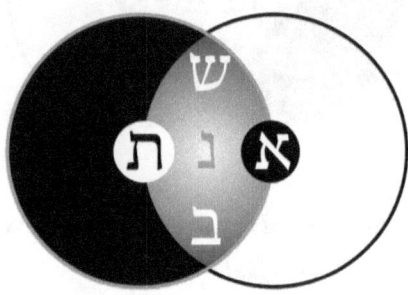

Imagine a language so pure and so sacred that it can reconcile opposites in just a few core letters...

Top: Hebrew letter Shin (ש) → S, Sh in Roman script
Right: Hebrew letter Aleph (א) → A in Roman script
Middle: Hebrew letter Nun (נ) → N in Roman script
Left: Hebrew letter Tav (ת) → T in Roman script
Bottom: Hebrew letter Beth (ב) → B in Roman script

Here is how S/Hebrew inscribes code "Incarnation" in 2 words:

- **BN(W)T**: from bottom to middle to left (W inferred), I read *Banot* (בנות) for "daughters."
- **AN(W)S**: from right to middle to top (W inferred), I read *Enosh* (אנוש) for "a man."

The Decoding: code Incarnation replaced the Vav of code Absolute with the letter Nun (נ). The four other letters are in the same place. Seeing this, I remember that word *Nun* has a sign Vav at its core, which shows up when *Nun* is fully spelled-out as Nun Vav Nun. This Vav is known as *Vav Hachibur* as it is the "connecting principle" that joins opposites. The first time it appears in the Torah is in *Et Hashamayim V'Et HaAretz* or "the heaven **and** the earth." It is also *Aur Yashar* as it is the "ray of straight light" that moves as a lightening flash from the crown to the root so as to manifest a slice of reality. When spelling *Yashar* with two signs Yod, the letters of *Aur Yashar* (אור יישר) amount to 727. These two Yods are dispatching their light via the Vav strip within Aleph (see *The V of Violence, this chapter*). I find myself thinking: if only I had a Nun to add to it, I would come to 777, the mastery of engagement that I already witnessed as commitment – the voice of my leadership.

Here is the 50 I was missing: it is the sign Nun, which occupies a central place in code Incarnation since Nun holds Vav which holds Aleph. I saw how the word *Nun* (NWN) holds a Vav in its heart. Also, the word *Vav* (WAW) holds an Aleph in its heart. Aleph is the primal force of unity. This is how Nun is the "PAIRfect" sign, occupying the absolute core of the Nine Chambers (both horizontally and vertically).

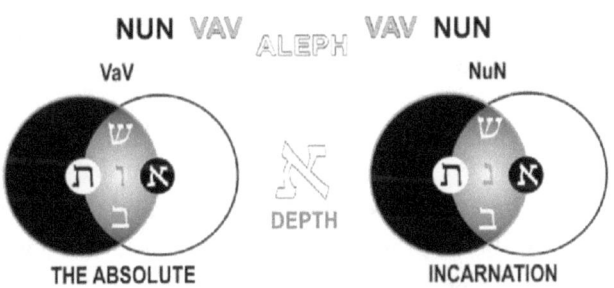

Inside Nun is Vav. Inside Vav is Aleph.

YES, TO INCARNATE AS A DIVINE TEACHER, IT TAKES VIGOR AS I MUST KEEP GOING, FALLING AND DIVING INSIDE, UNTIL I COME TO RECOGNIZE THE ABSOLUTE DEPTH OF MY EGO CREATION.

Aleph + Vav + Nun spell *Own* (און) for "vigor," a sexual potency felt when the sons knew the daughters: "when the Adam began to multiply on the face of the Adamah and daughters were born to them, the **sons** of Elohim saw that the Adam's **daughters** were beautiful, and they took as women whomever they chose." *Genesis 6:1*. This verse holds the secret of incarnation, as **Enosh** accepts his "appointment" to be a sentient **man** being, and a Son of Elohim as an incarnate teacher of the divine. When, like Enosh, I choose to be chosen, the call to usher an enlightened civilization is fulfilled through me (if only through the society of my cells). This choice is also what makes Enosh a "son of Elohim," as well as a "man acquired from YEWE," as Cain was.

The "heART" of Servant Leadership

"To command is to serve, nothing more and nothing less." André Malraux

I am still Cain. If my mother has gotten me from YEWE, it is my job to clean up, grow up and wake up as I claim my divine DNA. Henceforth, I'll live in a sane mind (as the spirit of my father Elohim), in a sane body (as the matter of my mother Earth), and as a blessed child "of Elohim." I'll also enjoy wholesome Power, as I will have transitioned the thoughtform that I can't have the love that I want. Henceforth, the jealousy will have served its purpose.

This is the reality behind the name *Enosh* (אנוש) "a man," a word which comes from *Ish* (איש) also "man" and *Anshei* (אנשי) for the "supermen" who had the Power of the Name behind them as they "fell" to Earth, namely the Nephilim (*Genesis 6:4*). These three words – *Ish, Enosh, Anshei* – start with Power as they originate in the creative *Esh* (אש) "fire" to which either a Yod, a Vav or a Nun is added to make a "man." Using the ATBaSh code, I can transpose the Aleph of *Anshei* (אנשי) into Beth, and write the word *B'Shni* (בנשי) for "in both of them," male and female.

Indeed, it is a Noble Truth that there is a cause to dissatisfaction. That cause can be found in the female's yearning for fulfillment, and the male's yearning for freedom. This yearning describes me, Cain. There is an end to the yearning and thus, to the dissatisfaction, and a path to the level of incarnation when I know that I am enough. And that is what Enosh brings forth.

According to the Book of Luke, the lineage of Jesus has been tracked to Adam through Seth. According to the Book of Matthew, Jesus' lineage starts much later with Abraham. When I accept that Adam HaRishon (which ends up being me) is yet to wake up, I realize that the characters in my DREaM are a projection of me. Thus, Abel, Seth, Enosh, Jesus and/or my parents are all cellular beings and DNA patterns who, somehow, live in me as my thoughts, and by extension, in my cells.

While childishness is centered on the little self, childlikeness resonates with a leader's heart, as it opens to the LOVE that has no opposite. 'Jesus saw some babies nursing. He said to his disciples, "These babies are like those who enter the kingdom." They said to him, "then shall we enter the kingdom as babies?" Jesus said to them, "when you make the two into one, and when you make the inner like the outer and the outer like the inner, and the upper like the lower, and when you make male and female into a single one, so that the male will not be male nor the female be female, when you make eyes in place of an eye, a hand in place of a hand, a foot in place of a foot, an image in place of an image, then you will enter."' *The Gospel of Thomas*

This quote is no longer perplexing as I read and feel TCO. Surely, making the two into one (the male and the female) is cracking the code of opposites. Similarly, understanding that money is the motivating factor behind the law of talion (an eye for an eye, a hand for a hand, an image for an image) informs THE decision to move from GReed into GRace, and purify my Giving and Receiving. It is entering *Daath,* as the man is no longer the Giver, the woman, no longer the Receiver. Similarly, Enosh is no longer "a man" giving and Cain "a man" not receiving. **When the heartfelt knowing of oneness replaces the suffering of retaliation and of any calculations for undue profit, I enter the kingdom of a childlike heart and know the "heART" of servant leadership.**

Childlike and Clueless

> "Man is a rope stretched between the animal and the Superman—a rope over an abyss. A dangerous crossing, a dangerous wayfaring, a dangerous looking-back, a dangerous trembling and halting."
> *Friedrich Nietzsche*

Enosh – the final metamorphosis of Cain – is the Superman; the "Homo Superior." It transforms the hatred into love; the envy into gratitude. This change ends all suffering. For the ego's rigid standards to perish, my humanity must be tossed upon a sea of uncertainty until the Lion's Will does not antagonize the Dragon's Desire (and vice-versa). To return to childlike innocence, I must let go of any attempt to control the world out there, and recognize – and even feel – that I am clueless.

Individual Power	Symbolic Power	Collective Power
Lion's Will	Man's Knowing / Taurus' Having	Dragon's Desire
Awaken	Transcend / Purify	Putrefy

The Transformation into Superman

Potentially, the most difficult part of growing up is to let go of the tribe. Just like cutting the umbilical cord is necessary at the time of physical birth, it is also necessary at the time of spiritual birth. This is a most delicate "cut," since the attachments to my birth family – to its traditions and belief systems – go very deep. There is a constant involvement that feeds the shared story, and a deep fear to lose that connection, even if there is suffering in relating to the parents. Moreover, my mother and father are the first people I have ever been exposed to. So yes, waking up from the DREaM and growing up takes a whole lot of courage. This is especially true given the popular belief "family comes first."

But what about seeking the kingdom first? What about discovering my true nature and being determined to live in accordance with it?

Inquiring on family comes first as I seek the kingdom. Surely, I can either be a victim of my biology and be limited by the thoughtforms that were transferred to me, or I can use the same imprints to find my voice and refine my message. When my mother gave birth, she sensed a formidable energy moving through her. And then I was born – a song whose notes I will only sing when I hear the voice I am here to share. Such hearing and voicing are linked to my soul contract – to my awakening. It is not a coincidence if the chilD's archetype is colored yellow by *Golden XPR*, just as the *Citrinitas* alchemical stage of awakening. To fulfill my inner law, I must let go of collective Power long enough to know my true nature – who I am as an individual and as a Leader. I have found that, from balancing Dragon and Lion (desire and will), I could finally say an honest yes and an honest no. Instead of remaining childish and either submitting to what my parents tell me I can or cannot want or rebelling against it, I individuate by taking full responsibility for what I really want and WHY I'd want it, and find the courage to ask for it. This growth is vital. This is also the last metamorphosis – to grow into someone who knows to be clueless. And for that, I must dive deep into my genealogy.

Code Depth - NWN / WWW

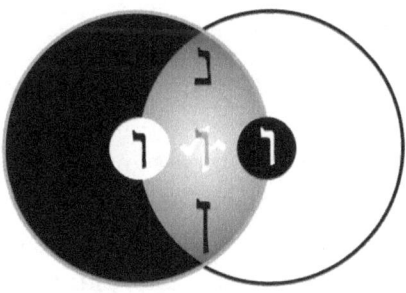

Imagine a language so pure and so sacred that it can reconcile opposites in just two fully spelled-out letters...

Top: Hebrew letter Nun (נ) → N in Roman script

Right, Middle & Left: Hebrew letters Vav (ו) → F, U, V, W
Middle (purposefully almost invisible): Hebrew letter Aleph (א) → A
Bottom: Hebrew letter Nun final (ן) → N in Roman script

Here is how S/Hebrew inscribes code "Depth" in 2 words:

- **VAV**: from right to left, I read *Vav* (ואו) for "nail, and," and see Vav x 3 (ווו).
- **NWN**: from top to bottom, I read *Nun* (נון) for "fish, generation."

The Decoding: both signs, Vav and Nun, are fully spelled out as the words they are: *Vav* means "nail, and" and *Nun*, "fish, posterity." The word *Nun* (NWN) has a Vav (W) at the center, and the word *Vav* (WAW) has an Aleph (A), the primal force of unity. **Thus, Aleph is at the core of Vav which is at the core of Nun.** Let's say that I'm "possessed" as Cain is. Whether my addiction is to a substance (e.g.; sugar), an idea (e.g.; money) or a person (e.g.; a lover), I just can't let go. I'm hooked. Let us also imagine that I work on myself as I know that acquiring self-knowledge is how to free myself. To resolve my dilemma, I can dive for the shell that has ingested my light and liberate the **fish** trapped in that vessel, linking this fish **and** that fish (the **generations** of them) until I come to Aleph's pure awareness.

To be free, Cain has to dive deep, very deep until he comes to the purity that understands choicelessness, and therefore non-causality. This added depth is present in the three signs Vav that are in the three letters of Cain's name resonating as 666 – the mark of the beast. As a gentle reminder, Cain's name is spelled with the only three letters of the alphabet that hold a Vav in their core, thus the triple Vav (see *the V of Violence*). The good news is: there is an end to dissatisfaction! With each Vav, Cain makes a connection (an "and") to the unity of Aleph which is here, even when invisible. **Thus, the question: how deep down the "habit" hole am I willing to go? Code Absolute answers by deepening the sense of the Redemption code.**

Redemption Code - AB / BN / ABN

The Father	The Son & the Stone	The Mother
Aleph Beth	Nun	Beth Aleph

N	W	N
W	A	W
N	W	N

A NDE (a Nun Depth Experience)

"WHAT IS GREAT IN SIGN NUN IS THAT IT IS A BRIDGE AND NOT A GOAL: WHAT IS LOVABLE IN NUN IS THAT HE IS AN **OVER-GOING** AND A **DOWN-GOING**." TCO SUBSTITUTED "SIGN NUN" TO "MAN" IN FRIEDRICH NIETZSCHE'S QUOTE.

Nun has no fear of Power. It is not afraid of falling (DOWN-GOING) or rising (OVER-GOING). When I feel that my falls are prompted by the Angel of Necessity for me to fall in LOVE, my trust in the One of us becomes as candid as a white rose, so exquisite it can't be tainted. I salute each failure with *Namasté*, "no mistakes." I am the ultimate Fool: the deeper I fall, the more I rise with an innocence that makes me an advisor of Kings. Such supreme purity is the result of a NDE and of an AT/TA initiatory journey that calls to dive deep into shadow desires, to reemerge in the light body, shameless as I even died to my name! If I am nameless, it is because I am you! When there's no more desire to make a name for myself – or to misuse the Power of *Hashem* "the Name," there is no more shame.

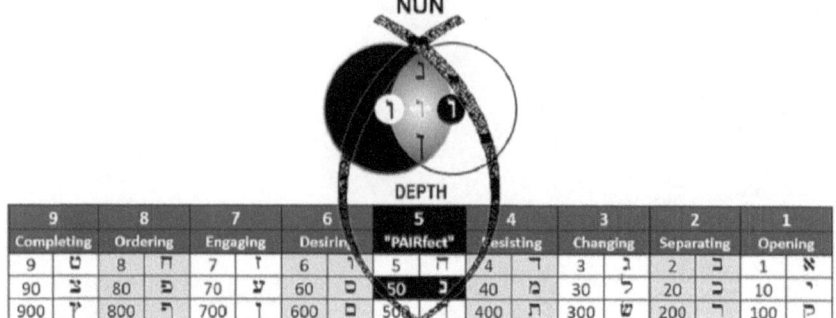

NUN IS THE "PAIRFECT" SIGN, AS IT OCCUPIES THE ABSOLUTE CORE OF THE NINE CHAMBERS, BOTH HORIZONTALLY AND VERTICALLY (SEE DARKENED CELL ABOVE). INSIDE THE WORD *NUN* FOR "FISH" AND "FISHER" OF SUPERHUMANS, THERE IS A *VAV*. INSIDE THE WORD *VAV* FOR "AND, NAIL, CONNECTOR," THERE IS AN ALEPH, THE CORE OF AWARENESS.

THE END

"Now this is not the end. It is not even the beginning of the end. But it is, perhaps, the end of the beginning." *Winston Churchill*

This is "THE END" page – a page that aspired to be written for what feels like eons. It is a vision that could not rest until it was fulfilled and free. Yes, I have come to fulfill the law. Doing so liberates my will. Whereas I could do what I willed, but could not will what I willed, this page dares talk about freed (rather than free) will. Indeed, I knew what to do. I just didn't want to do it. Couldn't will it into being! I started with a simple question: why can't I do good, or at the least, do no harm? I like me when I do good. And yet, to manage, I had to feel how deep my allegiance to evil went.

Yep, I pretended I wanted to find the House of "God" and do "Good." I said I wanted to honor all life, but deep inside, I was hiding the seeds of destruction. I went to TCO because its calling a spade a spade confronted me where I needed to be confronted. Even speaking of evil was edgy. I realized how I took the word "conscience" out and substituted to it the word "consciousness" so that I'd be removed from actually knowing good and evil. I heard the Word telling me: "if you really knew evil, you would change for good." And that touched a nerve!

Surely, I must have decided to ignore that, from *the Epic of Gilgamesh* on, all ancient stories are a treatise in ethics. I even retired the word "sin," thinking that I was too advanced for such barbarian language. Meanwhile, I continued making choices devolving me. By cleverly disabling the word "sin," I was giving myself the tacit permission to engage in it. I thought I could destroy species and get away with it, all the while ignoring that I was the species I destroyed. Truth be told, I couldn't even sustain the sense that we are One. I broke that compass and that compassion long ago! To survive the destructive fire (a fire I started and couldn't put out), I had to fulfill an old prophecy and rebuild the temple that I destroyed not once, but several times. Only then was I be able to play with Power without getting burned!

The Temple of Jerusalem ("the City of Peace")		
Individual Power	Symbolic Power	Collective Power
Simultaneous Creation	Non-Causality / Preservation	Gradual Destruction
Freedom of "I will"	Sacredness of "I know" / "I have"	Fulfillment of "I desire"

And it makes me wonder... If there is no creation, there is also no destruction and no temple to preserve. There is nowhere to go as everything is now here. This realization at once fulfills the Dragon of **Desire** and frees the Lion of **Will**. It is how **I Know** that I CAN wait and also that I CAN give it all because **I Have** it all. This page is when fear turns into sacredness, when there is no "I" thought to separate me from you. Surely, when there is no "I" to create and no creation, there is no "I" to destroy and no eye to see the destruction of a temple; just an entry into "the City of Peace..."

B'Siyata DiShemaya: "with Heaven's help!": August 6, 2022—9th of Av, 5782

It was written that *Tisha B'Av* or "the 9th of Av" – the darkest day of Jewish history – would fall on a Shabbat in the year 5782. This Shabbat is known as *Shabbat Chazon* or "the Rest of Vision," for it is when the eyes of duality (the eyes that are transfixed by evil and destruction) close for the eye of Providence to open (the eye that sees that what was created was good). How could that even be possible?

HOW? HEAR, HEAR!
LANGUAGE IS MOVEMENT. MOVEMENT IS LIFE.
LIFE JUST IS. IT HAS NO MEANING.

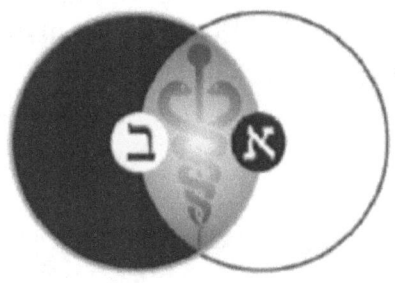

The PaRaDiSe Mystery School

"The most beautiful thing we can experience is the mysterious. It is the source of all true art and science." *Albert Einstein*

The Why of the PaRaDiSe Mystery School ™ is:

TO END my suffering by clearing the confusion induced by the "God" label, whose abstraction keeps me lonely as I run from the Mystery, and angry as I won't see the Truth that I am creating IT all!

The How of the PaRaDiSe Mystery School ™ is:

TO OWN my projections by using *Golden XPR* as a scrying mirror, at once shocking and sobering, and see that the places in the decoding where I go in limbo exactly **Reflect** where my shame-based **Secrets** are at work.

The What of the PaRaDiSe Mystery School ™ is:

TO WILL with a Power that cannot be corrupted; TO KEEP SILENCE as both the practice and **Practicality** of self-mastery; TO DARE wielding energy to solve problems, TO HAVE the wisdom to know the **Difference** moment to moment.

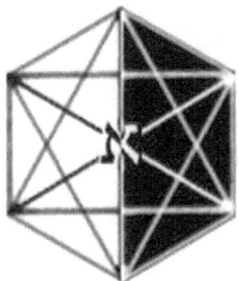

To apply to the PaRaDiSe Mystery School, visit https://www.goldenxpr. com/mystery-school-application/ or click on the image above.

List of Publications

> "I cannot teach anybody anything. I can only make them think."
> *Socrates*

TCO—the Series | here (https://thecodeofopposites.com)

1. Golden XPR
2. Golden XPR Distilled
3. Opening to the heART of XPR
4. The Genesis Pattern - book 1
5. The Genesis Pattern - book 2
6. This Year: EZ to Digest
7. Tweet tweeT
8. The LOVE Code
9. Sooo... I CAIN'T and *you're* ABEL?!
10. The Creation Tool
11. The Expire Tarot Advanced
12. Victim of my GENESis
13. The WHYS Bite
14. The ThREE of Sapphires
15. The 7x7 Count
16. PaRaDiSe Circle
17. TABU: The Anarchist Book of Understanding
18. The GR-Code
19. This Year in Jerusalem
20. Welcome to the PaRaDiSe Mystery School
21. The Sapphire Book
22. Mercury REDROgrade

The French Quarter | here (https://www.goldenxpr.com/francais/)

© 2022 emPowering NOW Press. www.emPoweringNOW.com

Epilogue

"When death comes, it does not ask your permission; it comes and takes you, it destroys you on the spot." *Krishnamurti*

I ONLY SAW the need for an epilogue when it revealed itself to be the next "write" thing. It is also a death of sorts, as this is the place where the meaning of the book's title merges with its sense. Indeed, may this epilogue give birth to the Word and allow for a heartfelt understanding of *The Code of Opposites*. And, yes! After trying to convince others that I had gotten it (and thus clearly doubting that I did), feeling the simplicity of grace filled my heart with humility. I learned from Cain's lineage, a being who was possessed by his ego and became murderous out of totally believing that he was unlovable. I learned until I could rest in peace. This Shabbat "rest" is at once a delight, a deliverance, and a relief! So yes, while I could hear our mother Eve saying "I've gotten me a man from YEWE" (*Genesis 4:1*), it didn't change the fact that my desire for a functional male side was still frustrated, and "THE decision," yet to be made. Will I step back from the pursuit, so that LOVE could come in to occupy the emptiness?

My Only Prayer

"Hail Mary, full of grace, the LORD is with thee; blessed art thou among women and blessed is the fruit of thy womb, Jesus. Holy Mary, Mother of God, pray for us sinners, now and at the hour of our death."

I had one prayer: health. I badly wanted to heal my mind whose insane games were creating havoc in my world. For me to have a discerning heart, I needed something that would go to the root of the universal pain story – a panacea. My prayer must have come from an unknown depth as I soon heard: "decode the soul of the Hebrew Bible (the QKabbalah) and you'll have an initiatory path to the integrity you seek. Thereon, embodying the Law of LOVE will be straightforward, as you will feel and sense that the sole objective of the law is the well-being of the soul and the body."

But how could decoding the Word – even if it were the Word that was "God" and with "God" –heal the mind and grant the wisdom I sought? This was especially puzzling when aware that languages introduce a separation from what is felt. If I could really know a tree beyond the label, I would know "God." Knowledge wouldn't be split from the knower anymore: I would sense it in my bones! Would savoring the codes as I would a rich dessert give me the nourishment of truth I crave and satiate the hunger for Love? I longed to stop burning myself with the fire-power of my words – to stop the lies. Surely, this was how to witness a daily increase in self-esteem and escort the "I am not enough" belief out!

To this end, *TCO—Book 1* speaks of SIX alchemical steps that interrelate with and grow out of each other. These codes were meant to reveal the very real way by which S/Hebrew qualifies as the tongue of Nature. No language has come so close to speaking in paradox, for us to actually feel the all-pervading realities that beckon us now, and be the sensorial energy beings that we are. The second of these four steps –

namely code Free Will – was not fully felt. Said differently, "the author" (me, myself and I) had yet to let go of her controlling and "free-willing" ways to allow for the unknown. When I could accept that my lack of peace signaled that there was something I didn't understand (or did not surrender), code Free Will was gracious enough to withdraw so that code Recognition could exist. Finding within the Love, approval and *recognition* I craved is and was a revelation!

Code Recognition is the code by which to disassociate from being identified to the ego and follow the heart's dictates. It ordains the seemingly impossible death of Cain – the part of me who was "possessed" by jealousy. Surely, when I know who I am, I yearn no more! As for this evolution of consciousness and acquisition of Power, I rejoice in the knowing that I am not the doer. I don't write. "IT" writes me. I was soon to realize that it was not only code Free Will that was yet to be felt, but the whole SIX steps that led to detach from being "Cain-possessed!"

One last thing as a way of introduction of an epilogue that dreamt to really be conclusive... I have seen time and again how TCO effects a *Tiqqun* (an "editing") in real time – of the text and of my lies (same). It was the beautiful Ba'al Shem Tov who stated that the letters of Torah rearrange themselves in different sequences to create a heaven and an earth that fits the evolution of one's environment; that is, of one's consciousness. Similarly, the Word of TCO is alive: it grows with the chilD to make it a Leader. So yes, dearest Cain, there is a time for every purpose under heaven; "a time to kill, and a time to heal; a time to break down, and a time to build up." *Ecclesiastes 3:3*

Feeling is healing. And Cain's hatred is certainly on the hit parade list of the feelings I have been taught to resist, deny and repress, next to shame, anger, loneliness... On the other hand, feeling awe at seeing the true awesomeness of the codes is inspiring. It gives me the courage and the permission to no longer resist the shame, the hatred, the rage and to feel them all, at last, so that they'd transition into peace. My story is your story. There is a place where you and I are able to wait until the path is clear. There is a time when to not compulsively give in to a false sense of obligation that robs us from speaking an honest "yes" and an honest "no" – that robs us from the Now. As for being the proverbial Word made flesh, this is a wonder, truly... There may, after all, be some truth to the claim that the Bible would hold the most crucial series of utterances ever expressed on Earth. After all, religion has been mandated to open the gate of the good, and thereby allow anyone who sincerely desires it to stop judging... and start loving!

When the people-signs speak...

"God is at home, it's we who have gone out for a walk." *Meister Eckhart*

All ancient traditions allude to a great **Power** that lives in everyone and everything, a Power by which to transcend any challenge. Through this Power, I can connect with the cosmic forces of creation in ways that defy the imagination. Will I ever have the Power to stop telling the pain story – when I saw myself as a slave to a hostile world? How long before I can detach from the clutch of the ego?

It is as if a global event wiped out some of my memory and left a gap in the knowledge of my own **Power**. Whereas I was born in the home of the haves, I took a walk and found myself being among the have-nots. The lost data explains how I feel separate from "you," from Love and from the cosmos. Once separate, it is easy for me to get discouraged and lose my **patience**. Where do I find the lost symbol by which to interface with the cosmic forces, heal my bodies, and contribute to abort the greatest tragedies that humankind is now facing?

Once upon a time, the people-signs (that is, symbols who had a life of their own) wondered how to restore the memory of the Self to the part of me who forgot that I was infused with divine Power. First, they had to convey patience, as patience with my conditions is peace of mind. Moreover, they also needed to transmit the sense that sustaining the kind of peace that passes understanding does not come from getting what I want. Instead, it is the result of renouncing the possession of what I desire. Such letting go takes patience. It also takes the willingness to inquire on whether what I want also serves the good of all. I can then make the **decision** to place my **attention** in that direction, and have the **recognition** of what it will take.

The more understanding, the greater my patience quota, until I come to witness the **transmutation** of hatred into Love, big LOVE. The hatred, shall you wonder, came from constructing a story of unrequited Love and rendering it impregnable by surrounding it with layers upon layers of massive **negativity**. When such hatred is metamorphosed, it shifts the quality of my patience to where I begin to stop counting time: no attachment to an outcome – a total **pleasure**. And it is in this blissful experience, between time and no time, mind and no mind, death and no death, that I come into the knowledge of opposites, a.k.a. serpent-Power. I am now ready to **connect** mind and body and body and soul, in an alchemy which completes in being still and knowing that I am LOVE. Ah, I am the people-sign – the Word that was with "God" and in "Good." I once was a lost symbol, and now, I'm found!

These keywords will be decoded using the letters in the image below to transmit the following Powers of the Children of *Elohim*: **Patience → Attention → Decision → Recognition → Transmutation → Negativity → Pleasure → Connection → the LOVE that has no opposite.**

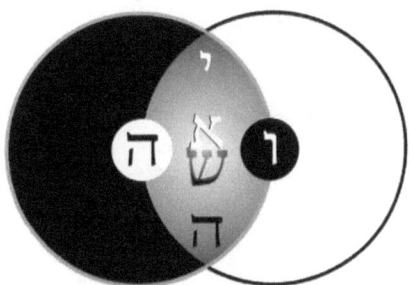

The Children of *Elohim*

On the Precedence of Patience

"The two most powerful warriors are patience and time." *Leo Tolstoy*

If I could just wait, I would see that life takes care of itself. Patience is how to overcome the fear of falling and failing. It is also how to let go of my attachment to an outcome. When I am patient, there is no time: I am absorbed by the Now and free of past and future. Under the spell of patience, I am at once the pain taking me over, the passion prompting it, and the compassion embracing it.

For now, I want enlightenment with a passion, but under one condition; when I cross the finish line into the infinite, I want my ego to stay intact so that I could get the love, approval and recognition I deserve. Since I don't understand and won't feel what it means to be as water and adopt a path of least resistance, I don't know that detachment is to be dispossessed by the illusion of separation. Detachment is the call that Cain must answer to be free of his calling as Cain – the one "possessed" by jealousy. Only then will he experience real change, as he will know Love. Love resembles the fisherman's hook. Unless the fish is caught on the hook, I cannot reel in the fish. If I am the fisherman, I also am the fish. Once I bite the hook, I may twist and turn. But when I can let myself be caught, I know the strongest of bonds with the Mystery, a Mystery which honored me by crossing over to merge with me. Like fishing, Love can't be hurried.

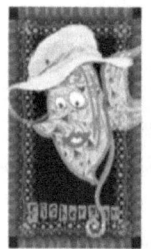

COMPATIENCE

Might you be too attached to an outcome to enjoy the princess?

MEM

The Fisherman Hat as the rendition of *Golden XPR* of the 12th Tarot known as the Hanged Man, a TARO inscribed by the 13th TORA letter Mem for "pairs of water."

This writing vows to inspire me to resist nothing by evoking the Power of the Logos to provoke the reverberation of what cannot be said. The intimacy of this transformation is felt via sentience or that which understands what understanding is. Patience now recognizes itself as patience. Whereas lovers cannot make their orgasm happen, they can adopt a path of least resistance to be overtaken by Love. Whereas the poet in me cannot write the poem, I can adopt a path of least resistance to witness the birthing of the Word. Whereas the patient in me cannot make healing happen, I can adopt a path of least resistance for the gift of healing to be received. Of my own will, I can't make any quickening happen, but I can freely adopt a path of least resistance to be overcome by what I am Powerless to attain. I recognize the mutuality that is Love when what I am powerless to attain attains me.

Code Patience - YE / EY

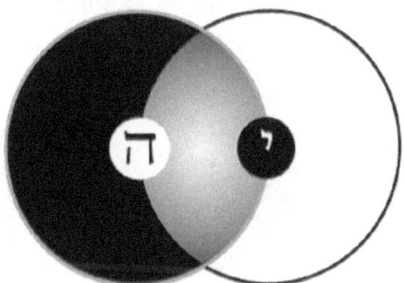

Imagine a language so pure and so sacred that it can reconcile opposites in one pair of letters...

Right: Hebrew letter Yod (י) → I, J, Y in Roman script
Left: Hebrew letter Heh (ה) → E in Roman script

TCO opened with the "NAME OF POWER" *Yah* (YE | יה) transmitted here as the Power of patience. I saw how Yod (Y) symbolizes the male seed, and Heh (E), the female womb. Having a psychic womb gives me the compassion to feel and embrace the darkest hatred. *Yah* always was a Love story. It became a hopeless pursuit when I attached to the HELLusion of separation.

This Heh (E | ה) womb contains the Yod (Y | י) seed that impregnates my creativity. When I feel that I am not missing anything or anyone, I am enough and can wait for the intuitive hit of inspiration. Patience is how to be successful, since patience comes with perseverance. There is no compulsive misuse of Power, as my male and female sides are balanced. I feel whole and "PAIRfect." How would I not, since I embody the Sacred Marriage inscribed by *Yah* via pair Yod Heh? Yod Heh is the S/Hebrew equivalent of the Sanskrit mantra *Om Mani Padme Hum* ("the Jewel is in the Lotus"). This is when I literally have what "s/he" is having! There is no frustrated desire for "the man," as I am also *HaYod* (EY | הי) "the male seed." However, the twin sense of fulfillment and freedom is thwarted as soon as I make the choice – albeit, unconsciously – to identify to the body. I have no more patience since I am possessed by my ego. Surely, the labelling man/woman is the first typology. Before that, I was just being and had no need of becoming.

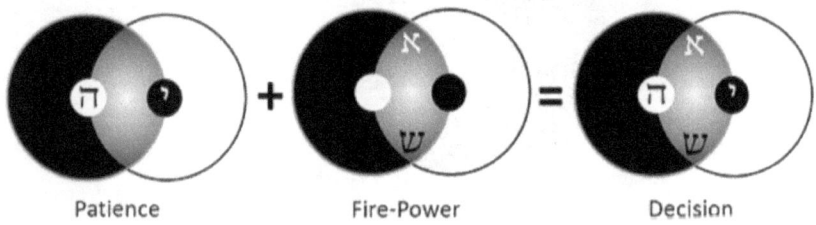

Patience   Fire-Power   Decision

When I can't relate to being "PAIRfect" **Patience** as *Yah* (יה), I don't have the *Esh* (אש) **Power** to choose peace. Therefore, my **decisions** can only be ungrounded.

In THE END was a Beginning...

"Once you make a decision, the universe conspires to make it happen." *Ralph Waldo Emerson*

Epilogue

There is a new book in the making that will unfold the Power of decision and its AS / YE code as pictured above. Will this book be called "A Lucifer Pill" or rather "The LOVE that Has No Opposite?" Michael and I rather liked the second option. Plus, it works "PAIRfectly" with *TCO —the Series* by moving us beyond opposites. And for now, dear reader, we ask for your patience. Or shall I say, for now, dear M&M, we ask for your patience… The fire-Power of these radical codes that are central to decision-making is yet to come, in its warmth, its strength and its brilliance.

LOL, one more thing needs to be shared before the epilogue of this epilogue: the transformation of code Free Will on the cover of *TCO— Book 1*. This code happened to be the answer to the prayer for health that began this work. To fulfill it, we must transcend our need for love, approval and recognition. Only then can the experience of "no yearning" be sustained! Therefore, and without any further ado, here is code Recognition, formerly code "Free Will."

Code Recognition - AB / BA

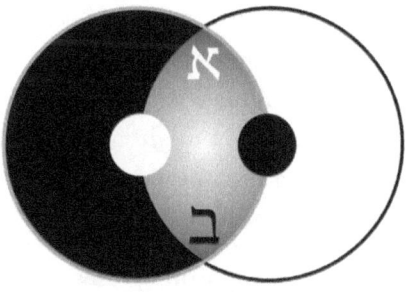

Imagine a language so pure and so sacred that it can reconcile opposites in just one pair of letters…

Top: Hebrew letter Aleph (א) → A in Roman script
Bottom: Hebrew letter Beth (ב) → B in Roman script

Here is how S/Hebrew inscribes code "Recognition" in just 2 words:

- From top to bottom: I read *Ab* (אב) for "father, alphabet."
- From bottom to top, I read *Ba* (בא) for "enter."

The Decoding: AB is "father, alphabet." **BA** is "enter." I intuitively know what to do. My **"father"** (the heart) clearly spells it out for me. But I don't want to hear it, see it or read it! While I like the idea of pursuing the mystical union, I'm still attached to the same condition: when time comes to cross over and **enter** "God's" House, I want to keep my ego. It is therefore my fear of death that keeps me from abiding in the sanctuary of my inner Self. What if, instead of being reluctant to obey (from Latin *ob* "toward" + *audire* "hearing"), I would listen to father **AlphaBet**? Instead of wasting my resources as a prodigal son, I would then fall and rise through 22 letters that decrypt archetypal stages in my evolution. I would then end up being risen when joining bottom Beth to top Aleph, thereby literally going to *Ab* the "Father." Father represents the heart – the very discerning heart I prayed for!

The S/Hebrew alphabet is my map, a map so thorough that it traces a grid that covers all archetypal expressions of pain. For now, I am in the mind, the darkest and densest forest there is. I am just one decision away: will I choose to come to the end of suffering? Until I can **recognize** what is in my way – and how I pretend to take care of others rather than doing the next "write" thing, I will not be able to answer with a clear YES to doing due diligence. I might as well look forward to lying to myself again. Indeed, I am the one who keeps the dissatisfaction in place by blaming others for my failures ("they made me!").

Recognizing where my responsibility lies is how to begin the process of transmutation and come to the LOVE that has no opposite.

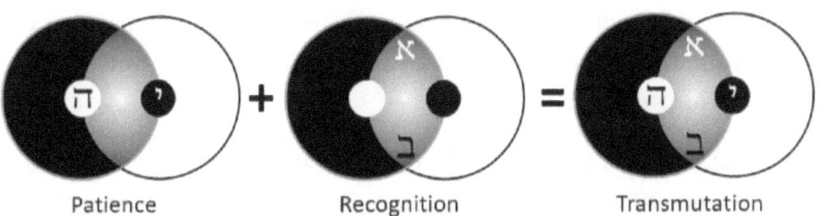

When I start in the "PAIRfection" of *Yah* (יה) "GOD/dess," I have enough **patience** to **recognize** what *Ab* (אב) the "father, alphabet" says. **Transmutation** is well on its way.

The Epilogue of an Epilogue

"Epilogues are for Tolstoy." *E. M. Forster*

I like Tolstoy. And I am SO happy this is THE END. Thank you for everything; I have no complaints whatsoever! I surprisingly experience more and more of the proverbial peace that passes understanding. **Understand. Choose peace. emPower the NOW.**

Here is what I tell myself: sickness or poverty, hunger or thirst, whatever "God" sends me or does not send me, what is granted or withheld, that is the partnering which is "Ulti-Mate." I even stretch the word "poverty" into the higher sense of emptiness: I am poor or empty when I desire nothing, will nothing, know nothing, and have nothing. FREEDOM!

More still, to emPower the NOW, I must be free of all the understanding that lives in me. Yep, after having inquired on my motivations to do harm, I can now live without a why as I am present to consistently doing the next "write" thing. For when I stand under the infinity of God, nothing else lives in me; I am empty of my own self: "I desire" nothing. "I will" nothing. I am as free from my own knowledge as I was when I was not – unborn. I will then stand idle as I let "God" do Her,

His, Its work. Such emptiness resonates with the following formula, which shift the place of understanding from cause to consequence: **Decide. Do. UnderStand.**

To decide, I welcome the double negative and even triple negative of Sanskrit *neti neti* and S/Hebrew *Ayin Ayin Ayin* as the veils of nullification of the ego. The negatives are there for me to begin feeling what is *not* creating as I immerse myself in worldly desires until nothing but humility remains. In turn, the exacerbated negation augurs the end of loneliness by allowing me to take back my projections from all creations and all creatures, in time and in eternity. Having let go of the outcome, I can now fully enjoy my action since what I do is total, unencumbered by ambivalent desires.

Yod (י)	Vav (ו) / Heh (ה)	Heh (ה)
"I will" nothing	"I know" / "I have" nothing	"I desire" nothing
Do	Decide	UnderStand

The XPR Formula of Inquiry:
Understand. Choose peace. emPower the NOW.

The XPR Formula of Surrender:
Decide. Do. UnderStand.

Epilogue

THROUGH PURE DEVOTION, THE SOUL IS NATURALLY UPLIFTED TO understand that which understands "God." It is the courage by which "I know" nothing and "have" nothing: I am *Dalut* ("poor, empty"), wide open to *Gimul* ("God's generous giving"). It is how to transcend my *Gad* (Gimel Dalet) "destiny" of *Dag* (Dalet Gimel) "fish" or fisher of my humanity.

Right: Gimel; Left: Dalet – when (my) Giving/Receiving knows such reciprocity that the story of unrequited love finally drops.

Henceforth, I have NO complaints whatsoever, as I recognize the most PAIRfect *Neged* (נגד) or "opposite" that the LOVE God gave me. In my case, my *Neged* came in the form of Michael Wolf as my "Ulti-Mate" nemesis. What's in a name, hum mm? It is clear that it was the plan for the wolf to end up making friend with the lamb. LOL; this lamb didn't even have to lose a rib over it... Thank you, dear friend, truly!

In THE END was the beginning, when I decide and rest while working.

THE END

www.ingramcontent.com/pod-product-compliance
Lightning Source LLC
Chambersburg PA
CBHW031359290426
44110CB00011B/210